Guide to ICSID Arbitration

KLUWER LAW INTERNATIONAL

Guide to ICSID Arbitration

Second edition

Lucy Reed
Jan Paulsson
Nigel Blackaby

Wolters Kluwer
Law & Business

AUSTIN   BOSTON   CHICAGO   NEW YORK   THE NETHERLANDS

Published by Kluwer Law International,
P.O. Box 316, 2400 AH Alphen aan den Rijn, The Netherlands
sales@kluwerlaw.com
http://www.kluwerlaw.com

Sold and distributed in North, Central and South America by
Aspen Publishers, Inc.
7201 McKinney Circle
Frederick, MD 21704
USA

Sold and distributed in all other countries by
Turpin Distribution Services Ltd.
Stratton Business Park
Pegasus Drive, Biggleswade
Bedfordshire SG18 8TQ
United Kingdom

© 2011 Kluwer Law International
ISBN 978-90-411-3401-1

Printed in the United Kingdom

Table of contents

Acknowledgements

We acknowledged in the first edition of this Guide that it is a far greater challenge to write a short book than a long one, with the challenge being magnified when the goal is to explain a complex field to newcomers rather than to analyze nuances for fellow experienced practitioners. Here we acknowledge that the major challenge in drafting the second edition was to cover the scores of new ICSID awards and decisions in investment treaty arbitrations without overwhelming our intended readers.

We could not have met this new challenge without the help of many of our valued colleagues in the Freshfields Bruckhaus Deringer international arbitration group. Greatest thanks go to our senior associate Jeffery Commission, who oversaw the painstaking task of collecting, reviewing and culling new ICSID jurisprudence, and who also prepared the extremely helpful tables of cases in Annex 10. We also thank our New York associates Katie Duglin, Katie Palms, Lindsay Gastrell, Patrick Childress and Jonathan Davis.

Foreword

by Meg Kinnear, ICSID Secretary-General

The last two decades have seen unprecedented growth in cross-border investment flows, the number of concluded investment treaties regulating those flows, and the number of international investment arbitrations. ICSID has been privileged to host the majority of these arbitrations and to play a leadership role in this field.

What may be less evident is the extent to which international investment arbitration has become an increasingly specialized and procedurally innovative endeavour. One need only consider recent cases and commentary on subjects as varied as arbitrator conflict of interest, the scope of provisional measures, the role of non-disputing third parties, or the standard of review for awards, to demonstrate the complexity of this field.

At the same time, the number and diversity of stakeholders involved in international investment arbitration has expanded. For example, 25% of the new cases at ICSID in fiscal year 2010 were initiated by investors from developing economies, more than in any prior year. An analogous trend emerged with respect to the identity of respondents, where the 27 newly registered ICSID cases named 24 different States from every region of the world.

Given this environment, the second edition of this guide is an especially welcome complement to the several excellent sources of information about the ICSID Convention and ICSID arbitration practice that are currently available. It provides a thorough yet succinct roadmap for parties and counsel navigating an ICSID arbitration, whether as novice or experienced litigants. The authors have shared their considerable expertise and knowledge of this field in a user-friendly, accessible and practical manner. In so doing, they have enhanced the ability of all stakeholders to put their best case forward in future arbitrations.

Meg Kinnear
Washington, D.C.
October 2010

Preface to the second edition

An impediment to foreign investment in many developing countries has been the investors' perception that, in the event of disputes with the host State, they would find themselves without an effective legal remedy. Investors cannot realistically rely on their own governments to raise their claims promptly and vigorously under traditional avenues of diplomatic protection. If investors proceed alone in the local courts against the host State, they often fear discrimination.

To help resolve this quandary, the World Bank conceived a unique forum for arbitrating investment disputes. Since its entry into force in 1966, the International Convention on the Settlement of Investment Disputes between States and Nationals of Other States (the **ICSID Convention** or the **Convention**) has offered Contracting States and eligible foreign investors the opportunity to bring their investment disputes to neutral arbitration tribunals constituted on an *ad hoc* basis. The tribunals are administered by the World Bank Group's International Centre for Settlement of Investment Disputes (**ICSID** or the **Centre**) in Washington, DC. They function independently of local courts and local procedural law. Most important, ICSID awards – unlike any other international arbitration awards – are immune from any form of national court review, and yet are enforceable in the courts of the more than 144 Contracting States as if they were national court judgments.

Nonetheless, because arbitration arising *directly* under the ICSID Convention is limited to cases in which foreign investors and States have explicitly provided for ICSID arbitration in an investment contract to which the relevant State (or a specifically designated subdivision of the State) is required to be a party, ICSID arbitration was little used for the first 20 years of its existence. There were isolated cases that did provide valuable guidance for investors and States and attracted scholarly interest, but ICSID arbitration remained rather esoteric.

The situation changed dramatically beginning in the mid-1990s as a consequence of the proliferation of bilateral treaties for the promotion and protection of investment, known as bilateral investment treaties (**BITs**) (as well as multilateral treaties, most notably the North American Free Trade Agreement and the Energy Charter Treaty), providing for ICSID arbitration of foreign investment disputes. Broadly speaking, each State party to a BIT pledges to provide investors from the other State with certain minimum substantive protections, including the right to fair and equitable treatment and the right to be compensated fairly for expropriation, and agrees that such investors may commence ICSID arbitration (or another agreed form of international arbitration) directly against it to obtain redress for violations of the substantive protections of the BIT. Between 1990 and 2008, the number of BITs increased from about 385 to 2,676. By 2002, almost 75 percent of the cases registered with ICSID were investment treaty arbitrations.

This dramatic legal development, which we predicted in 1995, involves the emergence of non-contractual arbitration – or "arbitration without privity" (see Chapter 3) – out of investment treaties. Today, any company considering a new investment in a foreign country and any financing entity playing a role in the investment must be aware of ICSID and of the growing matrix of BITs providing access to ICSID. At the project negotiation and documentation stage, as well as at possible junctures for restructuring, counsel for investors, financiers and government entities must be attuned to possible rights and responsibilities under the ICSID Convention and under available treaties. In sum, advisers to all sides must be at least familiar with the ICSID arbitration regime long before actual disputes develop.

Similarly, when a dispute arises in connection with an existing foreign investment, counsel for the investor must consider all of the potentially applicable BITs to identify the substantive rights and arbitral mechanisms that may be envisaged under them. This must be done promptly and effectively. Parties commencing litigation or pursuing other arbitration remedies may unknowingly waive the essential right of access to ICSID.

This fundamental change in the legal context of international investment flows inspired the first edition of this Guide in 2004. The wave of ICSID awards and decisions since 2004, as well as significant amendments to ICSID rules and practices, have provided the impetus for this second edition in 2010.

Scope of this Guide

We intend this Guide to be true to its purposefully modest title. It is designed to give international investors and their in-house counsel, as well as government legal advisers, an elemental understanding of the ICSID arbitration system and how it may (and may not) be used. For those desiring more detailed and analytical treatment of the ICSID regime, we have included a Selected Bibliography in Annex 9.

We start with a general introduction to the ICSID regime and the comparative merits of ICSID arbitration (Chapter 1). We then explain:

- the contours of an ICSID contractual arbitration and how to draft an effective ICSID arbitration clause (Chapter 2);

- the growth in bilateral investment treaties and other investment treaties providing for ICSID arbitration and the basics of ICSID treaty arbitration (Chapter 3);

- the ICSID rules and how the ICSID arbitration process works in practice (Chapter 4);

- the unique "self-contained" ICSID regime of post-award review, in particular, the annulment process (Chapter 5); and

- the recognition, enforcement and execution of ICSID awards in national courts (Chapter 6).

The ICSID Convention, the many sets of ICSID rules (most recently amended in 2006) and the ICSID case docket are readily available on the ICSID website at www.worldbank.org/icsid. For ease of reference, we have annexed the basic ICSID materials most useful for practitioners, as well as illustrative treaty materials, the Selected Bibliography previously mentioned, and charts of all ICSID awards and decisions on various issues as of January 2010:

- the ICSID Convention (Annex 1);

- the ICSID Institution Rules (Annex 2);

- the ICSID Arbitration Rules (Annex 3);

- the ICSID Additional Facility Rules and the Arbitration (Additional Facility) Rules (Annex 4);

- as an example, the UK Model BIT (Annex 5);

- as an example, the US-Argentina BIT (Annex 6);

- Chapter 11 of the North American Free Trade Agreement (Annex 7);

- Part III and Part V of the Energy Charter Treaty (Annex 8);

- a Selected Bibliography (Annex 9); and

- tables of ICSID awards and decisions on substantive, procedural and other issues (Annex 10).

A primer like this could not possibly be a complete instruction manual for conducting a case. ICSID arbitrations typically raise complex issues of public international law, including state responsibility and jurisdiction, as well as their interplay with local law. The disputes frequently arise in long-term major projects with multiple private and public players, so that the factual and contractual context also tends to be complex. To assume responsibility for such cases calls for experience and learning that cannot be distilled in an introductory guide such as this. Our goal here is much more circumscribed – to familiarize prospective or first-time users with the ICSID regime.

Although we have, of necessity, added significantly more description of ICSID awards and decisions in investor-state arbitration cases in Chapter 3 in this edition, we repeat the emphatic disclaimer from the first edition that critical analysis of ICSID case law is beyond the scope of this Guide. ICSID jurisprudence on issues of jurisdiction, merits and damages, as well as annulment of awards, continues to grow rapidly. In this brief book, our discussion of cases is illustrative rather than analytical.

Finally, this Guide assumes basic familiarity with the principles and practice of international commercial arbitration. ICSID arbitration has many distinct procedural and jurisdictional features, but the process as such bears many similarities to international commercial arbitration – as one would expect considering the predominance of economic issues. For those unversed in the basics or wishing a refresher, we recommend *The Freshfields Guide to Arbitration Clauses in International Contracts* (Kluwer Law International, 3rd edition, 2010) and *Redfern and Hunter on International Arbitration* (Oxford University Press, 5th edition, 2009).

Chapter 1

Introduction to ICSID

The International Centre for Settlement of Investment Disputes was established under the 1965 ICSID Convention, which came into force in October 1966 (Annex 1). Executed in Washington, DC, the ICSID Convention is also known as the Washington Convention. As of January 2010, 144 States had both signed and ratified the ICSID Convention (*Contracting States*).[1] Notable exceptions include Russia, Brazil, Canada (signed but not ratified) and Mexico. A list of the Contracting States is available on the ICSID website.

History of the ICSID Convention

The International Bank for Reconstruction and Development, more commonly known as the World Bank, sponsored the Convention. As described by Professor Sir Elihu Lauterpacht in his Foreword to the second edition of Christoph Schreuer's detailed commentary on the ICSID Convention,[2] Aron Broches, then General Counsel of the World Bank, conceived the idea for the Convention in

---

1   Since the publication of the first edition of this Guide in 2004, the Convention has entered into force in six additional States (the Republic of Yemen (2004), the Kingdom of Cambodia (2005), the Syrian Arab Republic (2006), the Republic of Serbia (2007), the Republic of Kosovo (2009) and the Republic of Haiti (2009)). Two States, the Plurinational State of Bolivia (2007) and the Republic of Ecuador (2009), have notified their withdrawal from the Convention.

2   C. Schreuer et al., *The ICSID Convention: A Commentary*, 2d ed. (Cambridge: Cambridge University Press, 2009), ix-x.

1961 in the wake of earlier efforts by the Organization for European Economic Co-operation (now the Organization for Economic Cooperation and Development, or **OECD**) to create a framework for the protection of international investment. The OECD exercise (which led to the OECD Draft Convention on the Protection of Foreign Property) revealed intractable controversy as to the proper level of compensation for expropriation of foreign investments. Broches and others recognized that it would be more productive to strive for multilateral agreement on a *process* for independent resolution of individual investment disputes rather than on actual substantive standards.

Broches conceived and pursued a *sui generis* strategy for negotiation of the necessary international convention. First, he convened consultative conferences of legal experts in Addis Ababa, Santiago de Chile, Geneva and Bangkok to discuss a preliminary draft. On the basis of the reports of these conferences,[3] the World Bank staff prepared a first official draft of the Convention, met with the Legal Committee of the Executive Directors of the World Bank, and then submitted the final draft to the Executive Directors for approval.

In March 1965, the Executive Directors approved the text of the ICSID Convention, issued an important companion Report,[4] and directed the President of the World Bank to circulate the Convention and Report to all member States. The mandatory minimum 20 States quickly ratified the Convention, and it entered into force on 14 October 1966. Industrialized and developing countries alike have signed on as Contracting States over the years, resulting in the remarkably high membership of 144 States (as of January 2010).

---

3   The detailed reports of the 1963 and 1964 regional conferences are compiled in *History of the ICSID Convention: Documents Concerning the Origin and Formulation of the Convention on the Settlement of Investment Disputes between States and Nationals of Other States*, vols. I–IV (Washington, DC: ICSID, 1970).

4   "Report of the Executive Directors on the Convention on the Settlement of Investment Disputes between States and Nationals of Other States 1965", *ICSID Reports* 1 (1993): 23-33.

Goals of the ICSID Convention

Given the now considerable body of ICSID jurisprudence, resulting from the proliferation of bilateral investment treaties and international agreements with investment provisions,[5] and the continued interest of arbitration practitioners in the ICSID dispute resolution process as a forensic art, it is easy to forget that the primary purpose of the ICSID Convention is to promote foreign investment. The Report of the Executive Directors on the Convention emphasizes the aim of promoting global economic development through private international investment. The theme of partnership and interdependence between industrialized and developing countries, protected by a regime of truly independent dispute resolution, is highlighted in the Report:

"9.   In submitting the attached Convention to governments, the Executive Directors are prompted by the desire to strengthen the partnership between countries in the cause of economic development. The creation of an institution designed to facilitate the settlement of disputes between States and foreign investors can be a major step toward promoting an atmosphere of mutual confidence and thus stimulating a larger flow of private international capital into those countries which wish to attract it.

10. The Executive Directors recognize that investment disputes are as a rule settled through administrative, judicial or arbitral procedures available under the laws of the country in which the investment concerned is made. However, experience shows that disputes may arise which the parties wish to settle by other methods; and investment agreements entered into in recent years show that both States and investors frequently consider that it is in their mutual interest to agree to resort to international methods of settlement.

---

5   International agreements with investment provisions include free trade agreements (such as the North American Free Trade Agreement (the **NAFTA**, *see* Annex 7) and the Dominican Republic–Central America–United States Free Trade Agreement) and sector-specific agreements (such as the Energy Charter Treaty (the **ECT**, *see* Annex 8)).

11. The present Convention would offer international methods of settlement designed to take account of the special characteristics of the dispute covered, as well as of the parties to whom it would apply. It would provide facilities for conciliation and arbitration by specially qualified persons of independent judgment carried out according to rules known and accepted in advance by the parties concerned. In particular, it would ensure that once a government or investor had given consent to conciliation or arbitration under the auspices of the Centre, such consent could not be unilaterally withdrawn.

12. The Executive Directors believe that private capital will continue to flow to countries offering a favorable climate for attractive and sound investments, even if such countries did not become parties to the Convention or, having joined, did not make use of the facilities of the Centre. On the other hand, adherence to the Convention by a country would provide additional inducement and stimulate a large flow of private international investment into its territories, which is the primary purpose of the Convention.

13. While the broad objective of the Convention is to encourage a larger flow of private international investment, the provisions of the Convention maintain a careful balance between the interests of investors and those of host States. Moreover, the Convention permits the institution of proceedings by host States as well as by investors and the Executive Directors have constantly had in mind that the provisions of the Convention should be equally adapted to the requirements of both cases."[6]

In sum, the Executive Directors of the World Bank underscored the importance of the balance inherent in the Convention: the basic goal of the ICSID system is to promote much-needed international investment by offering a neutral dispute resolution forum both to investors that are (rightly or wrongly) wary

---

6   "Report of the Executive Directors", *supra* note 4, at 25.

of nationalistic decisions by local courts and to host States that are (rightly or wrongly) wary of self-interested actions by foreign investors.

The Preamble of the Convention itself underlines this economic goal, and the operational objective of establishing an effective regime for neutral resolution of investment disputes that is attractive to States and investors alike:

"The Contracting States

Considering the need for international cooperation for economic development, and the role of private international investment therein;

Bearing in mind the possibility that from time to time disputes may arise in connection with such investment between Contracting States and nationals of other Contracting States;

Recognizing that while such disputes would usually be subject to national legal processes, international methods of settlement may be appropriate in certain cases;

Attaching particular importance to the availability of facilities for international conciliation or arbitration to which Contracting States and nationals of other Contracting States may submit such disputes if they so desire;

Desiring to establish such facilities under the auspices of the International Bank for Reconstruction and Development;

Recognizing that mutual consent by the parties to submit such disputes to conciliation or to arbitration through such facilities constitutes a binding agreement which requires in particular that due consideration be given to any recommendation of conciliators, and that any arbitral award be complied with; and

Declaring that no Contracting State shall by the mere fact of its ratification, acceptance or approval of this Convention and without its consent be deemed to be under any obligation to submit any particular dispute to conciliation or arbitration,

Have agreed as follows:" (emphasis in original).

The Convention then proceeds to its ten chapters and 75 articles, with aspirational language giving way to detailed legal procedures. As explained by Ibrahim Shihata, who served as the Secretary-General of ICSID from 1983 to 2000, the goal of the Convention in creating ICSID was "to provide a forum for conflict resolution in a framework which carefully balances the interests and requirements of all the parties involved, and attempts in particular to 'depoliticize' the settlement of investment disputes".[7]

The view from here

How has ICSID measured up against the goals set out in the Preamble and expressed by the Executive Directors in 1965? If this question were posed in the 1970s or 1980s, the answer would have to be qualified. There were few ICSID cases then and scant evidence that ICSID clauses were prevalent in international investment contracts.

The answer today is very different. On average, 27 cases have been registered annually with ICSID in recent years, with a peak of 37 cases in 2007.

This increase is due in large part to the proliferation of BITs and other international agreements with investment protection provisions, which contain dispute resolution provisions offering ICSID arbitration in the event of disputes. At the end of 2008, the total number of BITs worldwide reached a record 2,676, with the total number of other international agreements with investment provisions having reached 273.[8] Similarly, global foreign direct investment flows reached a historic record of US$1.9 trillion in 2007, before falling an estimated 15 percent in 2008 in the face of the global financial crisis.[9] The fact that many, if not most, BITs and international investment agreements include the option of ICSID dispute resolution perhaps confirms the connection between increased

---

7   I. Shihata, "Toward a Greater Depoliticization of Investment Disputes: The Roles of ICSID and MIGA", *ICSID Review – FILJ* 1 (1986): 4.

8   UNCTAD, "Recent Developments in International Investment Agreements (2008–June 2009)", *IIA Monitor* No. 3 (2009), <www.unctad.org/en/docs/webdiaeia20098_en.pdf>.

9   UNCTAD, "Assessing the Impact of the Current Financial and Economic Crisis on Global FDI Flows", <www.unctad.org/en/docs/diaeia20093_en.pdf>, 2009.

foreign investment and the availability of a neutral dispute resolution process, as envisioned by the drafters of the ICSID Convention some 40 years ago.

The first investment treaty case, *Asian Agricultural Products Ltd. (AAPL) v. Sri Lanka,*[10] was registered in 1987 (23 non-investment treaty cases had been registered at ICSID prior to *AAPL*). The flow of investment treaty cases has increased remarkably since then. As of January 2010, ICSID had registered 305 cases: 271 ICSID Convention arbitration cases, six ICSID Convention conciliation cases and 28 ICSID Additional Facility arbitration cases. These cases involve State parties from South America (30 percent), Eastern Europe and Central Asia (22 percent), Sub-Saharan Africa (16 percent), the Middle East and North Africa (10 percent), South and East Asia and the Pacific (8 percent), Central America and the Caribbean (7 percent), North America (6 percent) and Western Europe (1 percent).[11] The considerable majority of the ICSID Convention arbitration cases and ICSID Additional Facility arbitration cases (73 percent of all registered ICSID cases) are investment treaty cases, initiated under a BIT or other international investment agreement.[12] When compared to the broader universe of known investment treaty cases, ICSID continues to be the leading international arbitral institution for investment treaty arbitration: the 225 registered ICSID investment treaty cases represent 63 percent of the 357 known investment treaty disputes as of January 2010.[13]

As ICSID remains squarely in the international spotlight for investor-State arbitration, the obvious question is not whether but how the outcome of the many pending investment treaty cases will affect foreign investment (and ICSID itself). A developing jurisprudence is a given: investor-State arbitrations – which typically involve a political element – are less likely to settle than commercial arbitrations, and so a significant proportion of them lead to awards on the merits, available publicly.

---

10 *Asian Agricultural Products Ltd. (AAPL) v. Republic of Sri Lanka*, ICSID Case No. ARB/87/3.
11 ICSID, "The ICSID Caseload – Statistics", 2010-1: 7-8, 11, <icsid.worldbank.org/ICSID/ Index.jsp>.
12 *Id.* at 10.
13 UNCTAD, "Latest Developments in Investor-State Dispute Settlement", *IIA Issues Note* No. 1 (2010), <www.unctad.org/en/docs/webdiaeia20103_en.pdf>.

As of January 2010, ICSID investment treaty tribunals had rendered more than 200 publicly available decisions, awards and orders, including: (a) 76 awards on the merits; (b) 60 decisions on jurisdiction; (c) 26 decisions or orders on provisional measures; (d) ten decisions on annulment; (e) 13 decisions on whether or not to stay enforcement of an award; and (f) numerous other decisions and orders on a range of other procedural issues, including arbitrator and counsel challenges, the participation of non-disputing parties, ancillary claims and confidentiality issues. As to the outcomes of these decisions, it is telling that statistical studies by empiricist scholars on decisions and awards rendered by ICSID and other investment treaty tribunals indicate fairly even successes for investors and States.[14] The reasoning of these tribunals has generated a considerable number of treatises, monographs and articles on international investment law by both academics and practitioners. This developing jurisprudence on key jurisdictional and substantive issues is discussed in Chapter 3, and a Selected Bibliography is included in Annex 9.

In this context, it is worth revisiting Professor Lauterpacht's observations (again in the Foreword to the second edition of Professor Schreuer's commentary) about the many achievements of the ICSID Convention that are now taken for granted:

> "At the time the Convention was concluded, some of its most important features represented significant new developments, though in the light of subsequent advances in international law they now appear almost commonplace. For the first time a system was instituted under which non-State entities – corporations or individuals – could sue States directly; in which State immunity was much restricted; under which international law could be applied directly to the relationship between the investor and the host State; in which the operation of the local

---

14 *See, e.g.,* S. Franck, "Empirically Evaluating Claims About Investment Treaty Arbitration", *North Carolina Law Review* 86 (2007): 1; L. Ahee & R. Walck, "Investment Arbitration Update As Of December 31, 2007", *Transnational Dispute Management* 6, no. 1 (March 2009); L. Ahee & R. Walck, "Investment Arbitration Update As Of December 31, 2008", *Transnational Dispute Management* 6, no. 1 (March 2009); L. Ahee & R. Walck, "ICSID Arbitration in 2009", *Transnational Dispute Management* 7, no. 1 (2010).

remedies rule was excluded; and in which the tribunal's award would be directly enforceable within the territories of the States parties."[15]

ICSID: the institution

ICSID is one of the five international organizations that make up the World Bank Group. It is located at the World Bank headquarters in Washington, DC. The Centre itself does not conduct arbitration proceedings, but administers their initiation and functioning.

ICSID comprises an Administrative Council and a Secretariat. The former is the governing body. It meets in conjunction with the World Bank annual meeting, and is chaired ex officio by the President of the World Bank. It consists of one representative of each Contracting State, usually a finance minister or his or her deputy.

A Secretary-General and a Deputy Secretary-General, who are elected by the Administrative Council, head the Secretariat. Although the Secretary-General had traditionally been the general counsel of the World Bank, the two positions were formally separated in 2008. The Secretariat provides institutional support for arbitration by, among other things, maintaining the list of members of the Panel of Conciliators and Arbitrators, screening and registering arbitration requests, assisting in the constitution of arbitral tribunals and their operations, administering the funds required to cover the costs of the proceedings, adopting rules and regulations for the conduct of arbitrations, and drafting model arbitration clauses for investment agreements.

The Secretariat staff includes experienced and multi-lingual counsel, who are generally available for consultations with parties who may require clarification as to matters of procedure. The Secretary-General appoints one of them as the Secretary for each tribunal. The Secretary maintains the file, serves as the official conduit for the transmission of written submissions and evidence, makes the necessary practical arrangements for hearings, keeps minutes of hearings, ensures

---

15 Schreuer, *The ICSID Convention, supra* note 2, at ix.

that adequate funds to cover the costs of the arbitration are in hand, prepares drafts of procedural orders, and generally assists the arbitrators.

The ICSID staff performs substantial professional work beyond case administration, primarily with respect to publication of information and scholarship. The Centre publishes, among other things: (a) the *ICSID Review – Foreign Investment Law Journal*, a highly regarded journal containing articles, case reports, excerpts of the legal reasoning of unpublished decisions, and book reviews pertinent to investment law and international business transactions (biannually by subscription); (b) *News from ICSID*, a biannual bulletin (being discontinued); (c) *ICSID Basic Documents*, a bound booklet of the Convention and key rules (as amended); (d) the *ICSID Annual Report*; (e) the *ICSID Caseload – Statistics*, a biannual report profiling the ICSID caseload; and (f) a variety of bibliographies and compilations of BITs and investment laws. The majority of these resources are available on the ICSID website, which was substantially redesigned in November 2007 and began including extensive procedural details about ongoing ICSID cases in April 2008. The Centre also organizes conferences, and senior Secretariat attorneys make significant spoken and written contributions in the field of investment law.

As noted, the ICSID Secretariat is housed at the World Bank headquarters in Washington, DC. The World Bank provides the Centre with office space, general facilities such as hearing rooms and conference space, and administrative services. Pursuant to Convention Article 17, the World Bank funds the administrative budget of ICSID.[16] The practical effect is that Contracting States cannot delay proceedings, either in general or in specific cases, by failing to pay separate charges for ICSID membership. Both State and private parties to individual arbitrations pay only modest usage fees, in addition to the expenses of the tribunal constituted to deal with their case.

---

16 Article 17 of the Convention provides in full: "If the expenditure of the Centre cannot be met out of charges for the use of its facilities, or out of other receipts, the excess shall be borne by Contracting States which are members of the Bank in proportion to their respective subscriptions to the capital stock of the Bank, and by Contracting States which are not members of the Bank in accordance with rules adopted by the Administrative Council." The Bank and ICSID entered into a Memorandum of Administrative Arrangements on 13 February 1967, under which the Bank pays ICSID staff salaries and administrative expenses.

ICSID: the rules and regulations

ICSID has several sets of rules and regulations, designed to serve distinct purposes. All may be found on the ICSID website. The main rules and regulations include:

- The Administrative and Financial Regulations, which govern meetings of the Administrative Council and regulate the Centre's administration of conciliation and arbitration proceedings;

- The Institution Rules (Annex 2), which regulate the initiation of ICSID conciliation and arbitration proceedings;

- The Arbitration Rules (Annex 3), which set out procedures for the conduct of the various phases of arbitration proceedings, including the constitution of the tribunal, the written and oral presentations by the parties of their respective cases, and the preparation of the arbitral award; and

- The Conciliation Rules, which govern the conduct of conciliation proceedings.

In April 2006, following consultations among the ICSID Secretariat, Contracting State representatives, arbitration experts and civil society groups, significant amendments were made to the ICSID Rules and Regulations.[17] The amendments to ICSID Arbitration Rules 6, 32, 37, 39, 41 and 48, which came into effect on 10 April 2006, introduced a preliminary procedure concerning provisional measures, fast track procedures for dismissal of claims "manifestly without legal merit", access of non-disputing parties to proceedings, and increased disclosure requirements for arbitrators.[18] We discuss these amendments, and the other

---

17 ICSID Secretariat, "Possible Improvements of the Framework for ICSID Arbitration", <icsid. worldbank.org/ICSID/FrontServlet?requestType=ICSIDPublicationsRH&actionVal=Vie wAnnouncePDF&AnnouncementType=archive&AnnounceNo=14_1.pdf>, 22 October 2004; ICSID Secretariat, "Suggested Changes to the ICSID Rules and Regulations", <icsid. worldbank.org/ICSID/FrontServlet?requestType=ICSIDPublicationsRH&actionVal=Vie wAnnouncePDF&AnnouncementType=archive&AnnounceNo=22_1.pdf>, 12 May 2005.

18 The 2006 amendments to the ICSID Arbitration Rules were also made to the corresponding provisions of the Additional Facility Arbitration Rules, except for the amendment to Rule

rules and regulations most relevant to ICSID arbitration in practice, in detail in Chapter 4.

As provided for in Article 44 of the ICSID Convention, unless otherwise agreed by the parties to a dispute, an ICSID arbitration is conducted pursuant to the Arbitration Rules in effect on the date on which the parties consented to arbitration. Accordingly, the 2006 amended rules apply only to disputes where consent occurred on or after 10 April 2006. The prior version of the ICSID Arbitration Rules, effective 1 January 2003, is available on the ICSID website. (Experienced ICSID practitioners keep copies of the current and prior publications of *ICSID Basic Documents* close to hand for easy access to all potentially applicable Rules.)

In September 2009, ICSID informally adopted a new two-tier appointment process for the instances when the Centre is requested to nominate an arbitrator pursuant to Article 38 of the Convention. The new appointment process, similar to practices of other arbitral institutions, is based on the consent of the parties. It involves the Centre first circulating a list of three candidates (not necessarily from the Panel of Arbitrators) to both parties on a yes/no check-off ballot, to be returned by each party directly to the Centre; if there is agreement, ICSID proceeds to appoint from this list rather than using the Article 38 procedure. The new appointment process seeks to meet challenges ICSID has faced in appointing qualified arbitrators who are experienced, available and not conflicted, from the Panel of Arbitrators. This new process and the Article 38 process are explained in detail in Chapter 4.

Arbitration under the ICSID Convention

Essential criteria

In order for ICSID arbitration to be invoked, three criteria must first be fulfilled (each criterion is examined in detail elsewhere in this Guide):

---

39 on provisional measures.

- First, the parties must have *consented* to their dispute being submitted to ICSID arbitration. Consent must be given in writing. It may encompass either an existing dispute or a defined class of future disputes.

- Second, the dispute must be *between a Contracting State and a national of another Contracting State*. Contracting States may authorize constituent subdivisions or agencies to become parties to ICSID proceedings.

- Third, the dispute must be a *legal dispute arising directly out of an investment*. The term "investment" is not defined in the Convention, but has generally been given a broad interpretation by ICSID tribunals.

Contractual versus non-contractual ICSID arbitration

ICSID arbitration traditionally arose out of investor-State contracts containing express reference to ICSID for dispute resolution, provided that both the host State and the investor's home State were parties to the ICSID Convention and certain other jurisdictional limitations were met. As of January 2010, only 22 percent of the arbitrations registered with ICSID were brought under an arbitration clause in an investor-State contract.[19] We address contractual ICSID arbitration, and the relevant jurisdictional limitations, in Chapter 2.

As explained above, ICSID also accepts arbitrations that arise from State consent to ICSID arbitration contained in: (a) the host State's national investment laws; (b) a BIT between the host State and the investor's home State; or (c) a multilateral investment treaty (**MIT**) or free trade agreement between countries that include the host State and the investor's home State. Claimants are able to initiate ICSID arbitration on the basis of more than one source of consent, such as a combination of BITs or MITs and national investment laws. As of January 2010, 73 percent of the arbitrations registered with ICSID were brought under a BIT or other international investment agreement, and 5 percent under an investment law of the host State.[20] Non-contractual ICSID arbitration,

---

19 "The ICSID Caseload", *supra* note 11, at 10.
20 *Id.*

which differs in many significant respects from contractual ICSID arbitration, is examined in Chapter 3.

Why choose ICSID? Particular features of ICSID arbitration

Counsel to any corporation making a foreign investment in an ICSID Contracting State should always carefully evaluate the inclusion of an ICSID arbitration clause in its contract with the host State. Likewise, when a dispute has arisen under an investment treaty, counsel should carefully consider using the ICSID arbitration option. However, ICSID arbitration is not the best option in every situation. There may well be considerations militating in favor of other dispute resolution options, for example, *ad hoc* arbitration under the United Nations Commission on International Trade Law (**UNCITRAL**) Arbitration Rules, or arbitration under institutional rules other than those of ICSID. We address some of the main advantages of ICSID arbitration below.

Neutral and self-contained system

In typical international commercial arbitration, the parties select the place (or seat) of arbitration. In the absence of such selection, the relevant arbitration rules will provide a mechanism for determining the seat. The seat of arbitration, in turn, determines the procedural law for the conduct of the arbitration. The local courts of the seat of arbitration may, depending on the local law, have the opportunity to intervene to designate the arbitral tribunal, grant interim measures, or rule on applications to set aside awards.

By contrast, as detailed in Chapter 5, the ICSID Convention provides that the arbitration law of the place (or seat) of arbitration, wherever it may be, has no impact whatsoever on the proceedings. The ICSID process is entirely self-contained and hence delocalized. The Centre oversees the appointment of arbitrators to the tribunal, the tribunal handles provisional measures, and an ICSID-appointed *ad hoc* committee conducts annulment proceedings. ICSID awards are final and binding on the parties. They are not subject to any appeal or review by national courts, but only to the limited remedies provided in the

Convention itself: rectification, interpretation, revision and annulment (as discussed in Chapter 5).

Furthermore, as set out in Chapter 6, under the Convention, monetary obligations arising from ICSID awards must be recognized and enforced in all Contracting States as if they were final judgments of the local courts. This is a distinctive feature of ICSID arbitration, as other international arbitration regimes leave enforcement to domestic laws or other applicable treaties such as the 1958 Convention on the Recognition and Enforcement of Foreign Arbitral Awards (the *New York Convention*) and the Inter-American Convention on International Commercial Arbitration (the *Panama Convention*). These domestic laws and treaties typically provide for a minimum standard of review of arbitral awards in setting-aside proceedings, and provide limited grounds for refusal to recognize and enforce arbitral awards, including uncertain public policy grounds.

Increasing transparency

Most international arbitral proceedings are private, and some degree of confidentiality may be preserved (although attempts to define the nature of the confidentiality obligation and its exceptions have defeated drafters of legislation and many sets of arbitration rules).[21] As in other international arbitrations, ICSID hearings generally are private and submissions are confidential. However, as a result of the 2006 amendments to ICSID Arbitration Rules 32(2) and 37(2), it is possible for ICSID tribunals to allow non-disputing parties to observe oral hearings (unless either party objects) and file written submissions. As of January 2010, non-disputing parties (including various non-governmental organizations and the European Commission) had filed written observations in five registered ICSID cases.[22]

---

21 J. Paulsson & N. Rawding, "The Trouble with Confidentiality", *Arbitration International* 11 (1995): 303-320.

22 *Biwater Gauff (Tanzania) Ltd. v. United Republic of Tanzania*, ICSID Case No. ARB/05/22; *Aguas Argentinas S.A., Suez, Sociedad General de Aguas de Barcelona, S.A. and Vivendi Universal, S.A. v. Argentine Republic*, ICSID Case No. ARB/03/19; *AES Summit Generation Limited and AES-Tisza Erömü Kft. v. Republic of Hungary*, ICSID Case No. ARB/07/22; *Electrabel S.A.*

In contrast to other arbitration mechanisms, the Registers maintained by the ICSID Secretariat (under Administrative and Financial Regulations 22 and 23) – which are available on both the ICSID website and in the ICSID Annual Reports – ensure that the existence, current status and ultimate disposition of ICSID arbitrations are matters of public record. Article 48 of the Convention allows ICSID to publish awards itself only when both parties consent, but parties frequently publish unilaterally and, as a result of the 2006 amendments, ICSID must include excerpts of the legal reasoning of ICSID tribunals in its publications.[23] The Secretariat actively seeks consent of the parties to publish the awards and decisions and in practice, most ICSID awards are published and readily available.

This comparative transparency may have one strategically important side effect. Because many States want to be considered investment-friendly, the prospect of a host State being named – publicly – in an ICSID arbitration may provide investors with more leverage in early negotiations with the host State than the threat of international arbitral proceedings conducted under other rules.

Clear and reasonable cost schedules

Like most major international arbitral institutions, ICSID provides a transparent cost structure and keeps its administrative fees relatively low. ICSID is unusual, however, in including a fixed rate for the remuneration of conciliators, arbitrators and *ad hoc* annulment committee members. The fixed rate for conciliators, arbitrators and *ad hoc* annulment committee members alike, per day, is US$3,000, in addition to certain allowances and reimbursement of expenses.[24] These

---

v. Republic of Hungary, ICSID Case No. ARB/07/19; *Ioan Micula, Viorel Micula and others v. Romania*, ICSID Case No. ARB/05/20.

23   ICSID Arbitration Rule 48(4), as amended, provides: "The Centre shall not publish the award without the consent of the parties. The Centre shall, however, promptly include in its publications excerpts of the legal reasoning of the Tribunal."

24   ICSID, "Schedule of Fees", <icsid.worldbank.org/ICSID/FrontServlet?requestType=IC SIDDocRH&actionVal=ShowDocument&ScheduledFees=True&language=English>, 1 January 2008; ICSID, "Memorandum on the Fees and Expenses of ICSID Arbitrators", <icsid. worldbank.org/ICSID/FrontServlet?requestType=ICSIDDocRH&actionVal=Memorand um>, 6 July 2005. This schedule is subject to change and so should be checked periodically.

fees remain modest when compared with those typically charged by leading arbitration professionals in their other work. The parties in individual cases may agree to different rates for the arbitrators.

The "World Bank factor"

It remains true that most ICSID awards have been either successfully settled or voluntarily executed by the parties, although recent unpaid awards against the Argentine Republic are challenging this trend. This success (other than Argentina) may be due to ICSID being an organ of the World Bank, and the perception that failure to respect an ICSID award would have indirect political consequences in terms of credibility with the World Bank.[25] Whether the World Bank actively promotes respect for ICSID awards is open to question. ICSID claims no special clout and is obviously unlikely to browbeat the very States that constitute its governing Administrative Council. Nevertheless, it is difficult to imagine a World Bank lawyer seriously recommending the use of ICSID clauses in documentation for projects in a country whose government has notoriously ignored an ICSID award.

Additional services provided by ICSID

The Additional Facility

In the face of demand, the World Bank created the ICSID Additional Facility in 1978 to extend the availability of ICSID arbitration to certain types of

---

25 *See, e.g.,* "World Bank Operational Manual", BP 7.40(1), <web.worldbank.org/WBSITE/ EXTERNAL/PROJECTS/EXTPOLICIES/EXTOPMANUAL/0,,contentMDK:2006464 1~menuPK:64701637~pagePK:64709096~piPK:64709108~theSitePK:502184,00.html> ("When a dispute over default, expropriation, or governmental breach of contract comes to the attention of a Bank staff member, the staff member informs the country director (CD) and the Legal Vice Presidency (LEG). In consultation with LEG, the CD recommends a Bank position to the Regional vice president (RVP). If, on this basis, the RVP decides not to make any new loans to the member country or with the guarantee of the country, the RVP informs the relevant managing director and the Vice President and General Counsel.") (internal citations omitted).

proceedings between States and foreign nationals that fall outside the scope of the ICSID Convention. The Additional Facility is not a separate institution or even a physically separate part of ICSID. The same Secretariat serves both.

Arbitrations conducted under the Additional Facility include proceedings where either the State party or the home State of the foreign investor is not a member of ICSID. This possibility is particularly important in the context of cases brought under Chapter 11 of the NAFTA, because the United States is an ICSID Contracting State but Canada and Mexico are not. Although ordinary ICSID arbitration under the ICSID Convention is thus not an option between NAFTA States, Additional Facility arbitration is available, on the one hand, between US investors and Canada or Mexico and, on the other hand, between Canadian or Mexican investors and the United States. (In disputes between Canadian investors and Mexico or between Mexican investors and Canada, only UNCITRAL arbitration is available.) Article 26 of the ECT also provides for Additional Facility arbitration among other dispute resolution methods.

Under Article 4(3) of the Rules Governing the Additional Facility for the Administration of Proceedings by the Secretariat of the International Centre for Settlement of Investment Disputes (**Additional Facility Rules**) (Annex 4), the Secretary-General of ICSID may approve agreements to use the Additional Facility to resolve disputes even if they do not arise directly out of an investment, but only if he or she is satisfied that "the underlying transaction has features which distinguish it from an ordinary commercial transaction". This reflects the policy that ICSID is not to be used for commercial disputes of the type routinely handled by other international or national arbitration institutions.

The provisions of the ICSID Convention do not apply to Additional Facility proceedings (although many of the guiding principles are similar). Instead, arbitrations administered under the Additional Facility are subject to: (a) the Additional Facility Rules; (b) the Administrative and Financial Rules (Additional Facility); and (c) the Arbitration (Additional Facility) Rules (**Additional Facility Arbitration Rules**) (Annex 4).

Most important to potential users, these distinctions mean that the ICSID Convention's special self-contained provisions on recognition and enforcement of awards are not applicable to Additional Facility arbitrations, which have a seat of arbitration whose courts will exercise supervisory jurisdiction. Additional Facility awards thus may be equated with ordinary international commercial arbitration awards such as those rendered under the ICC, LCIA, ICDR (American Arbitration Association) and UNCITRAL arbitration rules. This explains why Article 19 of the Additional Facility Arbitration Rules provides that arbitral proceedings under the Additional Facility may be held only in countries that are parties to the New York Convention; otherwise the awards would be unduly vulnerable at the enforcement stage.

Potential users must also be aware that access to Additional Facility arbitration is subject to the Secretary-General's specific consent. According to Article 4 of the Additional Facility Rules, any agreement providing for arbitration proceedings under the auspices of the Additional Facility, whether in respect of existing or future disputes, requires the approval of the Secretary-General. As a practical matter, therefore, it is advisable for the parties to submit the relevant draft agreement to the Secretary-General for approval before the agreement is signed or enters into effect. If the dispute does not "arise directly out of an investment", it is at this stage that the Secretariat may examine whether the transaction nevertheless has "features that distinguish it from an ordinary commercial transaction" under Article 4(3) of the Additional Facility Rules.

The Additional Facility is being used increasingly in disputes between States and nationals of other States that fall outside the scope of the ICSID Convention under the NAFTA, the ECT and various BITs. As of January 2010, 28 arbitration cases had been registered by ICSID under the Additional Facility Rules, 21 of which were registered during the last ten years.[26] Of these 28 Additional Facility cases, 19 involve disputes where the State party was not a member of ICSID when the dispute arose (Canada, the Kyrgyz Republic, the Republic of Poland, the Republic of South Africa, Mexico and the Republic of Ukraine) while nine involve disputes where the home State of the foreign investor was not a member of ICSID (Canada and the Republic of Poland).

---

26 "The ICSID Caseload", *supra* note 11, at 8.

ICSID Secretariat administrative support in non-ICSID cases

Public and private parties occasionally seek the assistance of the Centre in con-nection with arbitrations conducted under rules other than those of ICSID, by having the Secretary-General appoint one or more arbitrators in the event the parties fail to do so, or having the Secretary-General decide proposals for the disqualification of an arbitrator.[27] The Centre has provided such administrative services in 67 non-ICSID cases since 2000, 61 of which were conducted under the UNCITRAL Arbitration Rules.[28] The Centre has also administered six non-ICSID cases, including the *Southern Bluefin Tuna* case (*Australia and New Zealand v. Japan*), an expert determination proceeding under the 1960 Indus Waters Treaty involving India and Pakistan, and an arbitration under the 2006 Canada–US Softwood Lumber Agreement.[29]

The Secretary-General is not obliged to act as appointing authority and does not always agree to do so. Consequently, parties wishing to utilize this service should obtain the Secretary-General's consent in advance. In practice, parties should submit the appointment provision in draft form to the Secretariat, together with a copy of the relevant arbitration agreement containing the provision. The appointment provision may be succinct, as illustrated by ICSID Model Clause 22:

> "Any dispute, controversy or claim arising out of or relating to this contract, or the breach, termination or invalidity thereof, shall be settled by arbitration in accordance with the UNCITRAL Arbitration Rules as at present in force. The appointing authority shall be the Secretary-General of the International Centre for Settlement of Investment Disputes. [The number of arbitrators shall be [*one*]/[*three*]. The place of arbitration shall be [*name of town or country*]. The languages to be used in the arbitral proceedings shall be [*name of language(s)*].]"

---

27 *Id.* at 9; *see, e.g., Grand River Enterprises Six Nations, Ltd., et al. v. United States of America*, UNCITRAL, Decision on the Challenge to Arbitrator (28 November 2007); *Vito G. Gallo v. Canada*, UNCITRAL, Decision on the Challenge to Mr. J. Christopher Thomas, QC (14 October 2009).

28 "The ICSID Caseload", *supra* note 11, at 9.

29 *Id.*

Alternative dispute resolution

Alternative dispute resolution processes, although rarely used in the ICSID framework, may be valuable in resolution of investor-State disputes. This particularly may be the case where an investor and the host State want to preserve an investment project notwithstanding the advent of a dispute.

Chapter III (Articles 28 to 35) of the ICSID Convention provides for conciliation as an institutionalized means of resolving investment disputes in a non-binding fashion. Either a Contracting State or a national of a Contracting State may institute conciliation by filing a request with the Secretary-General. As with arbitration, consent to conciliation by both parties is necessary. One or three persons comprise the Conciliation Commission, with the Secretary-General making appointments as necessary.

The heart of the ICSID conciliation process is not fundamentally different than other types of third party-assisted settlement, as illustrated by Convention Articles 34 and 35:

Article 34

"(1) It shall be the duty of the [Conciliation] Commission to clarify the issues in dispute between the parties and to endeavour to bring about agreement between them upon mutually acceptable terms. To that end, the Commission may at any stage of the proceedings and from time to time recommend terms of settlement to the parties. The parties shall cooperate in good faith with the Commission in order to enable the Commission to carry out its functions, and shall give their most serious consideration to its recommendations.

(2) If the parties reach agreement, the Commission shall draw up a report noting the issues in dispute and recording that the parties have reached agreement. If, at any stage of the proceedings, it appears to the Commission that there is no likelihood of agreement between the parties, it shall close the proceedings and shall draw up a report noting the submission of the dispute and recording the failure of the parties to reach agreement. If one party fails to appear or participate in the

proceedings, the Commission shall close the proceedings and shall draw up a report noting that party's failure to appear or participate."

Article 35

"Except as the parties to the dispute shall otherwise agree, neither party to a conciliation proceeding shall be entitled in any other proceeding, whether before arbitrators or in a court of law or otherwise, to invoke or rely on any views expressed or statements or admissions or offers of settlement made by the other party in the conciliation proceedings, or the report or any recommendations made by the Commission."

ICSID has reported only six conciliation cases (two involving the same pair of parties). The parties in two cases settled before a conciliation commission was constituted;[30] the parties in another case settled with the assistance of a conciliation commission;[31] and reports were issued by conciliation commissions in three cases where it remains unknown if settlements were reached.[32] In light of the limited use of ICSID conciliation services, we will not deal with the topic further in this Guide.

---

30 *SEDITEX Engineering Beratungsgesellschaft für die Textilindustrie m.b.H. v. Democratic Republic of Madagascar*, ICSID Case No. CONC/82/1; *TG World Petroleum Limited v. Republic of Niger*, ICSID Case No. CONC/03/1.

31 *Tesoro Petroleum Corp. v. Trinidad and Tobago*, ICSID Case No. CONC/83/1. *See* Lester Nurick & Stephen J. Schnably, "The First ICSID Conciliation: Tesoro Petroleum Corporation v. Trinidad and Tobago", *ICSID Review – FILJ* 1 (1986): 340.

32 *Togo Electricité v. Republic of Togo*, ICSID Case No. CONC/05/1; *Shareholders of SESAM v. Central African Republic*, ICSID Case No. CONC/07/1; *SEDITEX Engineering Beratungs-gesellschaft für die Textilindustrie m.b.H. v. Madagascar*, ICSID Case No. CONC/94/1.

Chapter 2

Contractual ICSID arbitration and drafting an effective ICSID arbitration agreement

If one were striving for brevity and nothing else, one might devise this ICSID clause for an investment contract:

> "The parties hereto consent to submit to the International Centre for Settlement of Investment Disputes any dispute relating to or arising out of this Agreement for settlement by arbitration pursuant to the Convention on the Settlement of Investment Disputes between States and Nationals of Other States."

Given the inherent complexity of contractual ICSID arbitration, however, the Centre has published no such succinct multipurpose model clause. The Centre has instead developed 22 highly sophisticated clauses for various uses (the *Model Clauses*), along with explanatory notes for each. The Model Clauses are tailored to different types of disputes and different circumstances, such as: (a) consent in anticipation of subsequent ratification of the ICSID Convention by a non-Contracting State; (b) contracts signed by government agencies or subdivisions; (c) deemed nationality of the investor; (d) preservation of the rights of the investor after compensation (including by insurers); and (e) exhaustion of local remedies. The Model Clauses are updated periodically on the ICSID website.

Parties to investment contracts are well-advised to consider the Model Clauses when negotiating and drafting an ICSID arbitration agreement. Given that the Convention strictly circumscribes ICSID jurisdiction, however, it would be negligent simply to cut and paste from the Model Clauses. An ICSID arbitration clause must be adapted to the particular parties, the particular investment contract, and the particular investment disputes most likely to arise. Investors and governments alike should insist upon specialist advice before drafting or agreeing to an ICSID arbitration clause. Failure to do so has on too many occasions led to unintended consequences and frustration.

This chapter describes traditional ICSID contractual arbitration under the Convention, especially the requirements of ICSID jurisdiction and other considerations relevant to drafting an effective ICSID arbitration agreement. As the jurisprudence on ICSID jurisdictional requirements is now principally developed through investment treaty decisions and awards, we will introduce these requirements briefly in this chapter and discuss them in greater detail in Chapter 3.

The scope of ICSID jurisdiction over investor-state disputes

Article 25 of the Convention defines the scope of ICSID jurisdiction. In the opening paragraph of that Article, the Contracting States agree:

"(1) The jurisdiction of the Centre shall extend to any legal dispute arising directly out of an investment, between a Contracting State (or any constituent subdivision or agency of a Contracting State designated to the Centre by that State) and a national of another Contracting State, which the parties to the dispute consent in writing to submit to the Centre. When the parties have given their consent, no party may withdraw its consent unilaterally."

Thus, in order for an investment dispute between an investor and a host State to be eligible for ICSID arbitration: (a) the dispute must be a legal dispute and arise out of an investment; (b) the dispute must involve, on the one hand, either a Contracting State or one of its subdivisions or agencies specifically designated to ICSID and, on the other hand, a national of another Contracting State; and (c) all parties to the dispute must consent in writing to have the investment dispute submitted to ICSID.

These jurisdictional requirements are mandatory. Before concluding their ICSID arbitration clause, parties to an investment contract therefore must ensure that these criteria are met or will have been met if and when a dispute arises between them. The parties may not waive these jurisdictional criteria by contractual stipulation. If the jurisdictional requirements are not met, the Centre must and will refuse to administer a dispute, even if the parties have contractually designated ICSID.

What constitutes an "investment dispute"?

The requirement of an investment

The ICSID Convention does not offer a specific definition of the term "investment". This was a deliberate decision by the drafters, who recognized that, given the pivotal role of consent, a definition of the term could prove unhelpfully restrictive.[33] To quote the Report of the Executive Directors on the Convention:

> "No attempt was made to define the term 'investment' given the essential requirements of consent by the parties, and the mechanism through which Contracting States can make known in advance, if they so desire, the classes of disputes which they would or would not consider submitting to the Centre (Article 25(4))."[34]

Instead the drafters preferred to leave it to the parties to agree upon what constitutes an investment under particular circumstances. Specific examples of projects and transactions that have been held by ICSID tribunals to qualify as investments under Article 25 range from infrastructure projects to the issuing of promissory notes. Tribunals have found "disputes arising directly out of an investment" to include disputes over capital contributions and other equity

---

33 "Report of the Executive Directors", *supra* note 4, at 28; *see also* A. Broches, "The Convention on the Settlement of Investment Disputes between States and Nationals of Other States of 1965: Explanatory Notes and Survey of its Application", in ed. A.J. van den Berg, *Yearbook Commercial Arbitration*, vol. XVIII (The Hague: Kluwer Law International, 1993), 642.

34 "Report of the Executive Directors", *supra* note 4, at 28; *see also* Broches, "The Convention on the Settlement of Investment Disputes", *supra* note 33, at 642.

investments in companies and joint ventures, as well as non-equity direct investments via service contracts, transfer of technology, natural resource concession agreements, and projects for the construction and operation of production and service facilities in the host State.[35]

The requirement of a legal dispute

As with the term "investment", the ICSID Convention does not define the phrase "legal dispute". ICSID tribunals have generally used the phrase to refer either to disputes regarding the existence or scope of a legal right or obligation, or to disputes regarding the nature or extent of the reparation to be made for the breach of a legal obligation.

As the parties obviously cannot anticipate all disputes that might arise in their relationship, particularly in the course of a long-term investment project, they should not attempt to include a "laundry list" of potential legal disputes in the arbitration clause. One of the legal disagreements they fail to predict or mention may well be the one that arises.

Who is considered a *"national of a Contracting State"*?

Article 25(2) of the ICSID Convention provides a specific definition of a "national of a Contracting State", as follows:

"(a) any natural person who had the nationality of a Contracting State other than the State party to the dispute on the date on which the parties consented to submit such dispute to conciliation or arbitration as well as on the date on which the request was registered pursuant to paragraph (3) of Article 28 or paragraph (3) of Article 36, but does not include any person who on either date also had the nationality of the Contracting State party to the dispute; and

(b) any juridical person which had the nationality of a Contracting State other than the State party to the dispute on the date on which the

---

35 *See* the detailed discussion in Chapter 3 on the divergent approaches taken by ICSID tribunals in their interpretations of the concept of investment within the meaning of Article 25(1).

parties consented to submit such dispute to conciliation or arbitration and any juridical person which had the nationality of the Contracting State party to the dispute on that date and which, because of foreign control, the parties have agreed should be treated as a national of another Contracting State for the purposes of this Convention."

Natural persons

The key issue for natural persons is their country of citizenship. The ICSID Convention permits a person to invoke ICSID arbitration only if he or she was a citizen of a Contracting State from the date a legal dispute arose over that investment. Thus, a French investor may consent to ICSID arbitration with respect to an investment made in the United States. However, if the French investor were to move to the United States and take US citizenship before a legal dispute arose, ICSID jurisdiction would fail. Similarly, a natural person who is a dual national of the State party to the legal dispute is ineligible for ICSID arbitration, and this ineligibility cannot be waived by the State party. Thus, in the above hypothetical, if the French investor retained his French citizenship and adopted dual US-French citizenship, he or she would also lose the right to commence an ICSID arbitration against the government of the United States – even if the United States agreed to consider him or her only a French citizen for ICSID purposes.

Juridical persons

To qualify as an investor for ICSID jurisdiction purposes, a juridical person must, in general, have the nationality of a Contracting State other than the host State on the date of consent to ICSID arbitration. This is quite straightforward in many investment scenarios.

The ICSID Convention, however, also anticipates the realities of modern investment project structures. Even when the juridical person does not have the requisite nationality on the date of consent, the Centre has jurisdiction if the parties have agreed that "because of foreign control" that juridical person "should be treated as a national of another Contracting State for the purposes of [the] Convention" (Convention Article 25(2)(b)). Essentially, this means that a corporation incorporated under the laws of the host State, such as a special purpose project company, will be considered a national of another Contracting State if the parties agree that, because such corporation is controlled by a natural or juridical person that has the requisite status as a national of another Contracting State, it should be treated that way. To give a concrete example, if a Dutch company were to incorporate a wholly-owned (or otherwise controlled) Czech company to construct a highway project under an investment contract with the government of the Czech Republic, the affiliate could be treated as a Dutch company for purposes of ICSID jurisdiction.

Again, the ICSID Convention does not define the terms "nationality" or "foreign control". The drafters desired to provide parties with the maximum flexibility.[36] The issues in play are well illustrated by the facts of five prominent cases addressing the question of foreign control.

- In *Amco Asia v. Indonesia*, the claimant, a United States corporation, formed a special purpose Indonesian company, PT Amco, to carry out the contemplated investment. Amco did so by applying to the Indonesian Foreign Investment Board for permission to incorporate PT Amco as an Indonesian company to build and manage a hotel in Indonesia. In the ensuing ICSID arbitration, Indonesia objected that PT Amco could not be treated as a US national because, even though it was controlled by a US corporation, the parties had not explicitly agreed to treat PT Amco (an Indonesian corporation) as a national of another State. The tribunal found that by accepting the application to incorporate PT Amco, which expressly stated that PT Amco was a "foreign business", Indonesia had agreed that PT Amco could be treated as a US company for ICSID purposes.[37]

---

36 Broches, "The Convention on the Settlement of Investment Disputes", *supra* note 33; *see also* P. Szasz, "A Practical Guide to the Convention on the Settlement of Investment Disputes", *Cornell International Law Journal* 1 (1968): 20 ("The Convention does not specify what constitutes 'control' for this purpose (i.e., must there be a majority of foreign shareholders), and thus it would be difficult to challenge later such a stipulation agreed to by the Contracting State concerned, regardless of the objective situation").

37 *Amco Asia Corporation and others v. Republic of Indonesia*, ICSID Case No. ARB/81/1, Decision on Jurisdiction (25 September 1983), *ICSID Reports* 1 (1993): 389.

- In *SOABI v. Senegal,* the claimant was a Senegalese company owned by a Panamanian joint stock corporation that was, in turn, owned by Belgian nationals. At the time the investment contract was signed, Panama was not an ICSID Contracting State but Belgium was. The relevant arbitration clause provided: "The undersigned expressly agree that arbitration shall be subject to the rules set out in the Convention for the Settlement of Disputes between States and the Nationals of Other States, produced by the 'International Bank of Reconstruction and Development' ('IBRD'). To this end, *the Government agrees that the requirements of nationality set out in Article 25 of the IBRD Convention shall be deemed to be fulfilled.*" (emphasis added). The tribunal upheld its jurisdiction over the dispute by interpreting the arbitration clause to mean that the parties had agreed to treat the Senegalese company as a Belgian national for ICSID purposes, and such interpretation would fulfill the nationality requirement of the ICSID Convention.[38]

- In *LETCO v. Liberia,* the claimant, a Liberian company controlled by French nationals, signed a concession agreement with the Liberian government. There was no explicit agreement among the parties as to the nationality of LETCO for the purposes of ICSID arbitration. The tribunal nevertheless held that it had jurisdiction over the dispute. The tribunal found, among other things, that a Contracting State, in signing an investment agreement containing an ICSID arbitration clause with a foreign controlled juridical person and knowing that it could be subject to ICSID jurisdiction only if it has agreed to treat that juridical person as a national of another Contracting State, should be deemed to have agreed to such treatment by having agreed to the ICSID arbitration clause. The tribunal concluded that this was especially the case when the Contracting

---

38 *Société Ouest Africaine de Bétons Industriels (SOABI) v. State of Senegal,* ICSID Case No. ARB/82/1, Decision on Jurisdiction (1 August 1984), *ICSID Reports* 2 (1994): 175; *see also Société Ouest Africaine de Bétons Industriels (SOABI) v. State of Senegal,* ICSID Case No. ARB/82/1, Award (25 February 1988), *ICSID Reports* 2 (1994): 272.

State's laws required the foreign investor to establish itself locally as a juridical person in order to carry out the investment.[39]

- In *Vacuum Salt v. Ghana*, the claimant was a Ghanaian company. Ghanaian nationals owned 80 percent of the Vacuum Salt shares and a Greek national owned the remaining 20 percent. The Greek national also sat on the board of directors of the company and served as the company's technical advisor. There was no agreement among the parties as to the nationality of Vacuum Salt. The tribunal held that it did not have jurisdiction over the dispute because the Greek individual's role in the company did not meet any objective criterion of foreign control and hence Vacuum Salt could not be treated as a Greek national for ICSID purposes.[40]

- Finally, in *Autopista v. Venezuela*, a national of a non-Contracting State, Mexico, was the 99 percent shareholder of Autopista Concesionada de Venezuela, C.A. (**Aucoven**), a Venezuelan company, at the time the contract was signed. The relevant concession contract provided for *ad hoc* arbitration in Venezuela. The parties also agreed in the contract, however, that in the event Aucoven's majority shareholder (then Mexican) should come to be a national of a Contracting State, they instead would arbitrate under the ICSID Convention. In the event, the Mexican shareholder transferred 75 percent of its shares in Aucoven to a corporate affiliate in the United States, with the permission of Venezuela. Venezuela challenged jurisdiction on the ground that Aucoven continued to be controlled by the Mexican holding company that owned 100 percent of the stock of the US affiliate that, in turn, controlled Aucoven. The tribunal upheld its jurisdiction over the dispute. The tribunal relied heavily on the fact that the parties themselves, as seen, had specifically agreed to look to the ownership of a majority of Aucoven's shares, rather than to the entity exercising ultimate effective control over Aucoven, to determine foreign

---

39 *Liberian Eastern Timber Corporation (LETCO) v. Republic of Liberia*, ICSID Case No. ARB/83/2, Award (31 March 1986), *ICSID Reports* 2 (1994): 346.

40 *Vacuum Salt Products Ltd. v. Republic of Ghana*, ICSID Case No. ARB/92/1, Award (16 February 1994), *ICSID Reports* 4 (1997): 329.

control of Aucoven by a national of another Contracting State for purposes of Convention Article 25(2)(b).[41]

The key issue for all five tribunals was the parties' agreement at the time the investment contract was signed. Potential investors should carefully consider this issue and strive to record the parties' agreement as to nationality explicitly in their arbitration clause. It may be advisable for the parties either: (a) to stipulate in the contract that the investor is a national of a Contracting State other than the host State; or (b) to agree that, although the investor is a national of the host State, it is controlled by nationals of another Contracting State and so shall be treated as a national of that other State for purposes of establishing ICSID jurisdiction. These strategies are acceptable to ICSID, as illustrated by its specific Model Clauses 6 and 7:

Clause 6 (Stipulation of Nationality of Investor)

"It is hereby stipulated by the parties that the Investor is a national of [*name of another Contracting State*]."

Clause 7 (Agreement that a Juridical Person is Under Foreign Control)

"It is hereby agreed that, although the Investor is a national of the Host State, it is controlled by nationals of [*name(s) of other Contracting State(s)*] and shall be treated as a national of [that]/[those] State[s] for the purposes of the Convention."

As the *Aucoven* case clearly demonstrates, parties may record an enforceable ICSID arbitration agreement even when, for a variety of reasons, ICSID is only prospectively a viable option. This topic is discussed further below in connection with ICSID's recognition that consent to ICSID arbitration may be conditional.

---

41 *Autopista Concesionada de Venezuela, C.A. v. Bolivarian Republic of Venezuela*, ICSID Case No. ARB/00/5, Decision on Jurisdiction (27 September 2001), *ICSID Review – FILJ* 16 (2001): 469.

When is a contract with a "Contracting State"?

In many cases, the question of whether an investor is contracting with a State that is a signatory to the ICSID Convention is easy to answer. When the investor is negotiating directly with the State or one of its ministries, the only issue is whether or not the State has ratified the Convention. This may be ascertained by referring to the list posted on the ICSID website or, in case of doubt, by contacting the ICSID Secretariat directly.

The more complicated question under Article 25 is whether a particular government subdivision (i.e., a territorial entity below the level of the State itself) or agency of a Contracting State qualifies as a party under the ICSID Convention. A subdivision or agency of a Contracting State may itself be party to an ICSID dispute if two special requirements are both fulfilled: (a) the host State has designated the subdivision or agency to the Centre under Convention Article 25(1) as capable of being a party to an ICSID arbitration; and (b) the host State has specifically approved the consent given by the subdivision or agency, or waived this approval right, under Article 25(3).

Under Article 25(1), host States may make such designations for all future disputes involving the subdivision or agency, for specific investment projects involving the subdivision or agency, or for a specific dispute once that dispute has arisen. The Contracting State must communicate the designation to the Centre no later than the filing of the relevant request for arbitration. Under Article 25(3), the host State may notify ICSID that it waives the requirement of specific approval in certain categories of transactions, thereby allowing subdivisions or agencies to consent to ICSID jurisdiction on their own with respect to those categories. In all events, the claimant should include detailed information on the Contracting State's approval of the relevant subdivision's or agency's consent in the request for arbitration.

The importance of designation and consent by the host State is illustrated in *Cable Television v. St. Kitts and Nevis*. The investor entered into an agreement containing an ICSID arbitration clause with the Nevis Island Administration (**NIA**), a subdivision of the Federation of St. Kitts and Nevis (the **Federation**). The Federation had neither designated NIA as a subdivision capable of being a party to an ICSID arbitration nor approved NIA's consent to ICSID arbitration.

The tribunal found that it did not have jurisdiction over NIA despite the ICSID arbitration clause in the investment agreement. The tribunal also rejected the investor's attempts to substitute the Federation itself as a party to the ICSID proceeding.[42]

In contrast, in instances where agencies or subdivisions are so designated by host States, tribunals have confirmed jurisdiction, for example in two cases involving agencies designated by the Republic of Ecuador: Petroecuador and Consejo Nacional de Electricidad.[43] In *Repsol v. Petroecuador*, an award (unpublished) on the merits was rendered in 2004, meaning that the tribunal must have found jurisdiction; in *Noble Energy v. Ecuador and Consejo Nacional de Electricidad*, a settlement agreement was reached after the tribunal confirmed its jurisdiction.[44] In another case, Tanzania designated Tanzania Electric as a state agency shortly before the filing of the request for arbitration by Tanzania Electric as claimant, ultimately leading to an award.[45]

A number of Contracting States, including Australia, the Republic of Guinea, the Republic of Kenya, the Republic of Madagascar, the Federal Republic of Nigeria, the Republic of Peru, the Republic of Portugal, the Republic of the Sudan, the Republic of Turkey and the United Kingdom, have designated specific subdivisions and agencies under Article 25 of the ICSID Convention. Such subdivisions and agencies include domestic states of a federation, as in the case of Australia, and public sector enterprises, such as State-owned or State-controlled mining, shipping and energy companies (for example, the Nigerian National Petroleum Corporation, and Perupetro S.A. of the Republic of Peru).

---

42 *Cable Television of Nevis, Ltd. and Cable Television of Nevis Holdings, Ltd. v. Federation of St. Kitts and Nevis*, ICSID Case No. ARB/95/2, Award (13 January 1997), *ICSID Reports* 5 (2002): 108.

43 Although no longer a Contracting State to the ICSID Convention, the Republic of Ecuador made two designations under Article 25: Corporación Estatal Petrolera Ecuatoriana (later known as Petroecuador) in 1988, and Consejo Nacional de Electricidad in 2002.

44 *Repsol YPF Ecuador S.A. v. Empresa Estatal Petróleos del Ecuador (Petroecuador)*, ICSID Case No. ARB/01/10; *Noble Energy Inc. and MachalaPower Cía. Ltda. v. Republic of Ecuador and Consejo Nacional de Electricidad*, ICSID Case No. ARB/05/12, Decision on Jurisdiction (5 March 2008).

45 *Tanzania Electric Supply Company Limited v. Independent Power Tanzania Limited*, ICSID Case No. ARB/98/8, Award (12 July 2001).

A small number of Contracting States have waived the need to approve consents by subdivisions and agencies, generally by declaring that domestic states or other such subdivisions in federally constituted countries are competent to give autonomous consent to ICSID arbitration.

When negotiating a contract with a subdivision or agency of a Contracting State, an investor wishing to ensure access to ICSID should ensure that these requirements are met in the arbitration clause. The clause should identify: (a) the precise name of the relevant subdivision or agency; (b) the details of its ICSID designation by the Contracting State; and (c) the instrument in which the Contracting State has authorized the subdivision or agency to consent to ICSID arbitration, or notified the Centre that it is unnecessary. The potential complexities of this situation – but also the roadmap to a drafting solution – are illustrated in ICSID Model Clause 5:

> "The [*name of constituent subdivision or agency*] is [a constituent subdivision]/[an agency] of the Host State, which has been designated to the Centre by the Government of that State in accordance with Article 25(1) of the Convention. In accordance with Article 25(3) of the Convention, the Host State [hereby gives its approval to this consent agreement]*/ [has given its approval to this consent agreement in *citation of instrument in which approval is expressed*]/[has notified the Centre that no approval of [this type of consent agreement]/[of consent agreements by *the name of constituent subdivision or agency* is required]].
>
> [*This alternative can only be used if the government is also a party to the agreement.]"

In the case of a long-term investment project, during the course of which the name of the designated subdivision or agency changes (or where the same functions are transferred to a new entity with the same attributes), the notification should still bind. It would, however, be prudent for the investor to add the following language to ICSID Model Clause 5: "The Host State hereby confirms that its notification binds all successors or assigns of the [*constituent subdivision or agency*]."

It is crucial for investors to be aware that a host State's designation of a subdivision or agency as eligible for ICSID arbitration, and its approval of the subdivision's or agency's consent to ICSID jurisdiction, do not represent consent to ICSID jurisdiction by the host State itself. Even if the host State has participated in the events leading to the investment dispute, or has in some way involved itself with the investment, an investor would need independent consent from the host State (perhaps via an investment treaty) to bring a claim against it before an ICSID tribunal.

What constitutes consent to ICSID jurisdiction?

Under Article 25 of the ICSID Convention, the parties' consent to submit a dispute to ICSID arbitration is a threshold requirement to establish an ICSID tribunal's jurisdiction over the matter. The Executive Directors of the World Bank, in their 1965 Report on the ICSID Convention, stated emphatically: "Consent of the parties is the cornerstone of the jurisdiction of the Centre."[46]

Consent is the explicit expression of acceptance of ICSID arbitration. The investor generally consents to arbitrate disputes that may arise with respect to a specific investment, while the host State may consent to arbitration either specifically or generically, i.e., anticipated *classes* of disputes. In contractual ICSID arbitrations, the State consents in a direct written agreement with the investor or in a letter (as addressed in this chapter); in arbitrations "without privity", in comparison, the State consents in its national laws, BITs or other international investment agreements (as addressed in Chapter 3). As is made clear in the Preamble to the ICSID Convention (see Chapter 1), ratification of the ICSID Convention alone does not constitute consent.

The form of consent

The only requirement of form is that consent must be in writing. Consent may otherwise take many forms.

---

46 "Report of the Executive Directors", *supra* note 4, at 28.

Consent may be given in advance with respect to a defined class of future disputes or with respect to an existing dispute. ICSID has Model Clauses for both situations:

Clause 1 (Consent in Respect of Future Disputes)

"The [Government]/[*name of constituent subdivision or agency*] of [*name of Contracting State*] (hereinafter the 'Host State') and [*name of investor*] (hereinafter the 'Investor') hereby consent to submit to the International Centre for Settlement of Investment Disputes (hereinafter the 'Centre') any dispute arising out of or relating to this agreement for settlement by [conciliation]/[arbitration]/ [conciliation followed, if the dispute remains unresolved within *time limit* of the communication of the report of the Conciliation Commission to the parties, by arbitration] pursuant to the Convention on the Settlement of Investment Disputes between States and Nationals of Other States (hereinafter the 'Convention')."

[Footnote omitted]

Clause 2 (Consent in Respect of Existing Disputes)

"The [Government]/[*name of constituent subdivision or agency*] of [*name of Contracting State*] (hereinafter the 'Host State') and [*name of investor*] (hereinafter the 'Investor') hereby consent to submit to the International Centre for Settlement of Investment Disputes (hereinafter the 'Centre') for settlement by [conciliation]/[arbitration]/[conciliation followed, if the dispute remains unresolved within *time limit* of the communication of the report of the Conciliation Commission to the parties, by arbitration] pursuant to the Convention on the Settlement of Investment Disputes between States and Nationals of Other States, the following dispute arising out of the investment described below: ..."

Consent may be encompassed in a single instrument, i.e., an arbitration clause included in the parties' investment contract or in a separate arbitration agreement, or recorded in separate instruments, i.e., by an exchange of correspondence. Although the issue apparently has not yet been tested specifically in the ICSID context, consent in the form of an electronic mail exchange (provided receipt is demonstrated or uncontested) presumably meets the writing requirement of Article 25.

Authority and capacity to consent should be ascertained whenever consent to ICSID arbitration is expressed. Special issues arise in connection with State action. It is not uncommon for national laws to subject the validity of the government's undertakings to arbitrate to particular legal requirements, such as parliamentary approval or assent by a specific ministry or the attorney-general's office. Some national laws flatly prohibit States from entering into arbitration commitments, whether generally or in certain sectors. Every party should examine the validity of the other party's consent as part of its due diligence, for example, by demanding certification letters, legal opinions and other appropriate evidence before a dispute arises, to avoid unnecessary jurisdictional challenges.

The scope of consent

Host States and investors may restrict the scope of their agreement to arbitrate disputes before ICSID by stipulating that only certain categories of dispute may be subject to ICSID jurisdiction.[47] In practice, however, broad consent clauses are thought preferable to avoid jurisdictional challenges.

The ambit of agreements to arbitrate may also be limited under Article 25(4) of the ICSID Convention:

> "Any Contracting State may, at the time of ratification, acceptance or approval of this Convention or at any time thereafter, notify the Centre of the class or classes of disputes which it would or would not consider submitting to the jurisdiction of the Centre. The Secretary-General shall forthwith transmit such notification to all Contracting States. Such notification shall not constitute the consent required by paragraph (1)."

The People's Republic of China, the Republic of Guatemala, Jamaica, the Independent State of Papua New Guinea, the Kingdom of Saudi Arabia and the Republic of Turkey have given such notifications. The notifications cover, for example, submission of disputes – or not – with respect to: (a) compensation

---

47   Model Clause 4.

resulting from expropriation or nationalization; (b) investments relating to minerals, oil or other natural resources; and (c) compensation from the State for damages due to armed conflict or civil disturbances. During contract negotiations, investors should determine whether the host State has made any potentially applicable notifications, either by checking the ICSID website or by contacting the Secretariat directly.

Consent is irrevocable

Once valid consent to ICSID arbitration is given, it may not be withdrawn. This prohibition against changing course by withdrawing consent reflects the importance of consent as the cornerstone of the ICSID regime.

Nor, once valid consent has been given, may host States use notifications of excepted disputes under Convention Article 25(4) to withdraw consent indirectly. Three cases involving Jamaica, all registered simultaneously and heard by the same ICSID tribunal, have confirmed that valid consent by the host State is irrevocable notwithstanding Article 25(4).[48] In each case, the Jamaican government and the investor had entered into agreements concerning bauxite mining, each containing a "no further tax" clause and a dispute resolution clause providing for ICSID jurisdiction. Jamaica subsequently notified ICSID that it would not submit to ICSID jurisdiction for legal disputes "arising directly out of an investment relating to minerals or other natural resources". Shortly thereafter, Jamaica enacted legislation that provided for an additional tax to be paid on all bauxite extracted in Jamaica. The tribunal held, in each case, that Jamaica's notification to ICSID under Article 25(4) could not withdraw the consent given in the prior agreements. The notification could operate only prospectively "by

---

48 *Kaiser Bauxite Company v. Jamaica*, ICSID Case No. ARB/74/3, Decision on Jurisdiction and Competence (6 July 1975), *ICSID Reports* 1 (1993): 296; *Alcoa Minerals of Jamaica, Inc. v. Jamaica*, ICSID Case No. ARB/74/2, Decision on Jurisdiction and Competence (6 July 1975) in ed. P. Sanders, *Yearbook Commercial Arbitration*, vol. IV (The Hague: Kluwer Law International, 1979), 206; *Reynolds Jamaica Mines Limited and Reynolds Metals Company v. Jamaica*, ICSID Case No. ARB/74/4 (unpublished).

way of information to [ICSID] and potential future investors in undertakings concerning minerals and other natural resources of Jamaica".[49]

Consent generally is exclusive

The general rule is that, in addition to being irrevocable, consent to ICSID arbitration creates an exclusive forum. This general rule applies unless it has been otherwise agreed, or unless the State has required exhaustion of local remedies as a condition of its consent. Under Article 26 of the ICSID Convention:

> "Consent of the parties to arbitration under this Convention shall, unless otherwise stated, be deemed consent to such arbitration to the exclusion of any other remedy. A Contracting State may require the exhaustion of local administrative or judicial remedies as a condition of its consent to arbitration under this Convention."

In light of this provision, careful drafting is necessary. If parties designate options in addition to ICSID arbitration in their investment agreement, they may face complications relating to overlap, precedence and res judicata. As for an exhaustion of local remedies requirement, ICSID Model Clause 13 suggests how an effective clause might be constructed:

> "Before either party hereto institutes an arbitration proceeding under the Convention with respect to a particular dispute, that party must have taken all steps necessary to exhaust the [following] [administrative] [and] [judicial] remedies available under the laws of the Host State with respect to that dispute [*list of required remedies*], unless the other party hereto waives that requirement in writing."

Conditional consent

Consent to ICSID jurisdiction may be valid even if conditional. This enables parties that do not qualify for access to ICSID nonetheless to agree that their investment disputes will be submitted to ICSID if future events bring their

---

49   *Kaiser Bauxite v. Jamaica* (Decision on Jurisdiction and Competence), *supra* note 48, at 304.

relations within the ambit of ICSID jurisdiction. This is a somewhat complex concept, best illustrated by an actual case.

The very first ICSID arbitration, *Holiday Inns v. Morocco*, affirmed the validity of conditional consent to ICSID arbitration.[50] In that case, the tribunal held that Morocco had validly agreed to ICSID jurisdiction in connection with a contract it had entered into with a Swiss corporation even though, on the date the contract was signed, the company had not yet been incorporated and, once created, was a national of a State that had not yet ratified the ICSID Convention.[51] In particular, the tribunal held that:

"[T]he Convention allows parties to subordinate the entry into force of an arbitration clause to the subsequent fulfilment of certain conditions, such as the adherence of the States concerned to the Convention, or the incorporation of the company envisaged by the agreement. On this assumption, it is the date when the conditions are definitely satisfied, as regards one of the Parties involved, which constitutes in the sense of the Convention the date of consent by that [p]arty."[52]

Similar facts arose in the *Aucoven* case described above. At the time the parties signed their investment contract, a national of a non-Contracting State (Mexico) owned 99 percent of the Venezuelan project company (Aucoven). The parties, however, agreed that if a national of a Contracting State came to be majority shareholder of Aucoven, any dispute under their contract could be arbitrated under the auspices of ICSID. A US entity (the United States being an ICSID Contracting State) did in fact become the majority shareholder, and the tribunal accepted jurisdiction on the basis of this conditional arrangement.

---

50 *Holiday Inns S.A. and others v. Morocco*, ICSID Case No. ARB/72/1 (unpublished).

51 P. Lalive, "The First 'World Bank' Arbitration (*Holiday Inns v. Morocco*) – Some Legal Problems", *ICSID Reports* 1 (1993): 645. The *Holiday Inns* case has not been published, but extracts appear in Professor Lalive's article.

52 *Id.* at 667-668.

Transfer of consent to successors in interest

Over the life of an investment, an investor may have commercial reasons to want to transfer to another entity all or some of its rights and obligations under the relevant investment agreement, including any right to ICSID arbitration. If the successor entity is not a party to the original consent agreement between investor and host State (which is the likely situation), the transfer could provide the host State with grounds to challenge ICSID jurisdiction (for lack of valid consent) in the event of a dispute. Cautious investors should consider the possibility of successors in interest when negotiating an ICSID arbitration clause. Although there is no ICSID Model Clause addressing consent and successors in interest, Georges Delaume has offered the following possible solution:

> "It is hereby agreed that the consent to the jurisdiction of the Centre shall equally bind any assignee ... to the extent that the Centre can assume jurisdiction over a dispute between such assignee and the other party, and that neither party to this Agreement shall, without the written consent of the other, transfer its interest in this Agreement to an assignee with respect to whom the Centre could not exercise such jurisdiction."[53]

Absent a contractual clause giving successors in interest access to ICSID arbitration, the investor might seek separate consent from the host State. In *Amco Asia v. Indonesia,* noted above, the Indonesian government challenged ICSID jurisdiction on the ground that its consent to arbitration did not extend to a successor in interest to Amco. Amco's original application to the Indonesian Foreign Investment Board, on the basis of which the Indonesian government authorized the incorporation of PT Amco, included consent to ICSID arbitration, but it did not explicitly provide for successors in interest. Subsequently, when Indonesia granted permission to Amco to transfer some of its shares in PT Amco to a successor entity, it did so with no mention of ICSID arbitration. Yet the tribunal held that Indonesia's approval of the share transfer itself constituted agreement that the successor in interest to Amco would acquire all rights attached

---

53 G. Delaume, "ICSID Arbitration: Practical Considerations", *Journal of International Arbitration* 1 (1984): 115, note 49.

to those shares, including the right to ICSID arbitration, because the right to ICSID arbitration was not expressly excluded by Indonesia in the approval.[54]

More recently, in *Noble Energy v. Ecuador and Consejo Nacional de Electricidad*, an ICSID tribunal held that a host State's consent to ICSID arbitration in an investment agreement that expressly extended its terms to "any Person acquiring the status of Investor" and "successors, assigns and designees" established jurisdiction. The agreement was executed between the Republic of Ecuador and the Samedan Oil Corporation, a wholly owned subsidiary of Noble Energy that was later merged into it. In its decision on jurisdiction, the tribunal confirmed that Noble Energy succeeded to all the rights and obligations of the Samedan Oil Corporation, noting that "[w]hen a parent absorbs its subsidiary and thus becomes formally the investor in the latter's place, there's no real change in the 'investor' from the State's perspective".[55]

With or without a contractual clause concerning transfer of rights of access to ICSID arbitration, any successor in interest must satisfy the underlying nationality requirements of the Convention for an ICSID tribunal to have jurisdiction of a dispute. In *Holiday Inns v. Morocco*, the original agreement containing consent to ICSID arbitration did in fact generally provide for successors and assigns, but did not specifically address the rights of any successors and assigns to seek ICSID arbitration. Holiday Inns subsequently assigned the agreement to four Moroccan subsidiaries. Holiday Inns, the four Moroccan subsidiaries and others commenced an ICSID arbitration against the Moroccan government under the contract. On a challenge made by Morocco, the tribunal dismissed the case with respect to the Moroccan subsidiaries for lack of jurisdiction. The tribunal held that, as Moroccan investors in a claim against the government of Morocco, the four Moroccan successors in interest did not meet the nationality requirements of the ICSID Convention.[56] The parties had not agreed to treat the four Moroccan subsidiaries as "nationals of another Contracting State" under ICSID Convention Article 25(2)(b). The drafting lesson to be remembered is that investors should

---

54 *Amco Asia v. Indonesia* (Decision on Jurisdiction), *supra* note 37, at 403.
55 *Noble Energy v. Ecuador* (Decision on Jurisdiction), *supra* note 44, at para. 107.
56 Lalive, *supra* note 51.

consider nationality, as well as the need to deal with succession in interest, in any investment contract containing an ICSID clause.

Practical checklist on jurisdiction

The best practical checklist for ensuring ICSID jurisdiction in contractual ICSID cases under Convention Article 25 is the text of Rule 2(1) of the ICSID Institution Rules. Rule 2(1), which sets out the minimum requirements for a request for ICSID arbitration, merits full quotation:

"The request shall:

(a) designate precisely each party to the dispute and state the address of each;

(b) state, if one of the parties is a constituent subdivision or agency of a Contracting State, that it has been designated to the Centre by that State pursuant to Article 25(1) of the Convention;

(c) indicate the date of consent and the instruments in which it is recorded, including, if one party is a constituent subdivision or agency of a Contracting State, similar data on the approval of such consent by that State unless it had notified the Centre that no such approval is required;

(d) indicate with respect to the party that is a national of a Contracting State:

(i) its nationality on the date of consent; and

(ii) if the party is a natural person:

(A) his nationality on the date of the request; and

(B) that he did not have the nationality of the Contracting State party to the dispute either on the date of consent or on the date of the request; or

(iii) if the party is a juridical person which on the date of consent had the nationality of the Contracting State party to the dispute, the agreement of the parties that it should be treated as a national of another Contracting State for the purposes of the Convention;

(e) contain information concerning the issues in dispute indicating that there is, between the parties, a legal dispute arising directly out of an investment; and

(f) state, if the requesting party is a juridical person, that it has taken all necessary internal actions to authorize the request."

What is necessary for a valid ICSID arbitration clause?

As set out at the opening of this chapter, the simplest possible effective ICSID arbitration clause would be something like the following:

"The parties hereto consent to submit to the International Centre for Settlement of Investment Disputes any dispute relating to or arising out of this Agreement for settlement by arbitration pursuant to the Convention on the Settlement of Investment Disputes between States and Nationals of Other States."

Well-advised parties, however, tailor their clauses and build upon the ICSID Model Clauses. As illustrated by the various samples quoted throughout this chapter, the Model Clauses provide guidance on drafting for recurring situations and cover important optional provisions for the arbitration clause.

The drafters of any international arbitration clause always face several key decisions during negotiations, such as selection of the number of arbitrators. Some of these decisions require special consideration in the ICSID context. At the same time, however, some decisions that are difficult in the context of international commercial arbitration clause drafting – for example, selection of venue and applicable law – are of only minor concern in ICSID clauses. We examine below, from an ICSID clause drafting perspective, certain particularly important issues: (a) method of constituting the tribunal; (b) applicable law; (c) place of arbitration; (d) language(s) of the arbitration; (e) a negotiation or "cooling off" period; (f) provisional measures; and (g) waiver of sovereign immunity. Several of these topics are also covered from a procedural perspective in Chapter 4.

Method of constituting the tribunal

The ICSID Convention gives the parties wide latitude to decide how to select their arbitral tribunal. The main relevant article, Article 37(2)(a) of the Convention, provides that an arbitral tribunal "shall consist of a sole arbitrator or any uneven number of arbitrators appointed as the parties shall agree", leaving the parties free to stipulate the number of arbitrators.

ICSID tribunals are almost always comprised of three members rather than a sole arbitrator. (There has never been a five-member tribunal.) It may be that parties prefer the security of having the case evaluated from several perspectives rather than putting their fate in the hands of one person, even if – unusually – they could agree on a sole arbitrator.

Indeed, when the parties have expressed no preference as to number, the Convention's default rule, contained in Article 37(2)(b), requires that the tribunal consist of three arbitrators:

> "Where the parties do not agree upon the number of arbitrators and the method of their appointment, the Tribunal shall consist of three arbitrators, one arbitrator appointed by each party and the third, who shall be the president of the Tribunal, appointed by agreement of the parties."

If, as is often the case, the parties cannot agree on a president, Convention Article 38 provides that the Chairman of the Administrative Council is to make the appointment after consultation with both parties. As explained in Chapter 4, ICSID informally adopted a new appointment process in September 2009 for the instances when the Centre is requested to nominate an arbitrator pursuant to Article 38. The parties may, but only occasionally do, stipulate that the Centre appoint all three arbitrators.

Applicable law

There are potentially four separate questions of applicable law in an ICSID arbitration: (a) what law governs the validity of the arbitration agreement? (b) what law governs the arbitration proceedings themselves? (c) what law applies to the substance of the dispute? and (d) in the event of a conflict regarding the substantive law, under what law is the conflict to be resolved? As compared to the challenges these questions pose in other arbitrations, the ICSID Convention answers all of these questions, should the parties be unable – as is often the case in investor-State contracts – to agree upon the applicable law in their arbitration agreement.[57]

First, as discussed above, Convention Articles 25 and 26 and the express terms of the parties' agreement govern the validity of an ICSID arbitration agreement. There is no need for the parties to select a law governing the validity of that agreement – it is governed by the Convention and therefore by international law.

Second, Article 44 of the Convention deals with applicable procedural law. It provides that the proceedings are to be conducted in accordance with the procedural provisions of the Convention (which are found in Articles 41 to 49) "and, except as the parties otherwise agree, in accordance with the Arbitration Rules in effect on the date on which the parties consented to arbitration". The parties cannot select a national procedural law or other international arbitration procedural rules to govern their ICSID arbitration, and should not attempt to do so. Nor should the parties try to alter the ICSID procedural regime, as there are mandatory provisions in the ICSID Convention and the various sets of ICSID rules. Parties should not invent procedural variations or "improvements" on the ICSID procedural framework unless they are wholly confident that they fall within the domain of acceptable *complements* to the ICSID conditions.

Third, by contrast and as in any major international agreement, the parties should strive to select one body of national law as the applicable substantive law and set it out plainly in a separate clause in the agreement. This is an important element of certainty in the resolution of legal disputes that may arise. Yet, it is often extremely difficult – if not impossible – for the host State to agree to designate the investor's home State law or for the investor to designate the host State's law. Other options (none of them free from difficulty) are to agree on the national law of a third State or on rules or principles of international law (in various permutations), or to remain silent.

---

57   *See* Model Clause 10.

Fourth, anticipating these difficulties, Article 42(1) of the ICSID Convention provides a default choice of law rule and conflicts guideline:

"The Tribunal shall decide a dispute in accordance with such rules of law as may be agreed by the parties. In the absence of such agreement, the Tribunal shall apply the law of the Contracting State party to the dispute (including its rules on the conflict of laws) and such rules of international law as may be applicable."

Despite its apparent simplicity, Article 42(1) probably has generated more debate than any other provision of the ICSID Convention. In extremely simplified and practical terms, Article 42(1) generally – but not without exception or controversy – has been interpreted to mean that, in the absence of party agreement on choice of substantive law, the tribunal should accord supremacy to international law in the event of any inconsistency with the host State's domestic law. As the tribunal in the *Santa Elena v. Costa Rica* case explained, "[t]o the extent that there may be any inconsistency between the two bodies of law, the rules of public international law must prevail".[58] According to the tribunal in *Amco Asia v. Indonesia*, "where there are applicable host-state laws, they must be checked against international laws, which will prevail in case of conflict. Thus international law is fully applicable and to classify its role as 'only' 'supplemental and corrective' seems a distinction without a difference."[59]

Additional Facility arbitration differs from ICSID Convention arbitration as to applicable law. Article 54 of the Additional Facility Arbitration Rules directs the tribunal to apply the substantive law selected by the parties or to decide the dispute *ex aequo et bono* if the parties have so decided.

---

58 *Compañía del Desarrollo de Santa Elena, S.A. v. Republic of Costa Rica*, ICSID Case No. ARB/96/1, Award (17 February 2000), *ICSID Review – FILJ* 15 (2000): 191; *see also Klöckner Industrie-Anlagen GmbH and others v. United Republic of Cameroon and Société Camerounaise des Engrais, S.A.*, ICSID Case No. ARB/81/2, Decision on Annulment (3 May 1985), *ICSID Reports* 2 (1994): 122 (international law prevails over the host State's law "should the State's law not conform on all points to the principles of international law").

59 *Amco Asia Corporation and others v. Republic of Indonesia*, ICSID Case No. ARB/81/1, Award in Resubmitted Case (31 May 1990), *ICSID Reports* 1 (1993): 580.

The seat of arbitration

Pursuant to Article 62 of the ICSID Convention, arbitration proceedings are to be held at the seat of the Centre in Washington, DC, unless the parties otherwise agree. Under Article 63(a), the parties may agree to conduct proceedings instead at the seat of the Permanent Court of Arbitration in The Hague or at the seat of another institution with which the Centre has entered into cooperation agreements. The Centre has such agreements for venues in Bahrain, Cairo, Cologne, Kuala Lumpur, Lagos, Melbourne, Singapore and Sydney.[60] Subject to approval by the tribunal after consultation with the ICSID Secretary-General, Article 63(b) also allows the parties to agree that hearings be held elsewhere.

A shift of physical location from Washington, DC to another venue has no legal effect on the arbitration proceedings. As explained above, the Convention insulates ICSID proceedings from the application of national procedural law. If the parties designate a seat of arbitration other than Washington, DC, they need only consider practical matters such as comparative cost, efficiency and convenience.

In practice, roughly half of ICSID arbitration proceedings are conducted in Washington, DC (at ICSID's headquarters) and half in Paris (at the European office of the World Bank). ICSID has also held hearings in several other cities, including London, Frankfurt, Geneva, The Hague, Singapore, Buenos Aires, Quito, Tegucigalpa and New York. Parties are increasingly conducting hearings by telephone or videoconference, an option encouraged by ICSID to reduce the time and cost of proceedings and accommodate the schedules of participants. In addition, ICSID now offers web-casting of hearings at the request of parties.

The language(s) of the arbitration

ICSID's official languages are English, French and Spanish. Rule 22(1) of the Arbitration Rules stipulates that the parties may agree on one or two languages for the proceedings. If the parties select a language that is not an

---

60   See A. Parra, "The Role of the ICSID Secretariat in the Administration of Arbitration Proceedings under the ICSID Convention", *ICSID Review – FILJ* 13 (1998): 93.

official language of the Centre, the tribunal must give its specific approval following consultation with the Secretary-General. If the parties do not agree on the language or languages for the proceedings, each may select one of the three official ICSID languages.

As in international arbitration in general, it is best for the parties to select the applicable language(s) in the arbitration agreement. The drafters of the arbitration clause may be able to identify the decisive factors for choosing a language or languages for the proceedings, looking, for example, to the choice of the applicable substantive law and the language of the contract, the language of other principal documents, the mother tongue of likely fact and expert witnesses, and the availability of suitable arbitrators and/or counsel with the necessary language skills.

Selecting two languages inevitably entails complications and expense. In addition to the substantially greater costs of translation and interpretation, the risk of misunderstandings and other problems caused by inexact translation or interpretation of legal concepts increases significantly in bilingual proceedings.

Nevertheless bilingual ICSID proceedings are conducted with some regularity. One method to limit translation costs is for the parties to agree to submit documents only in their original language, with each party translating only the documents upon which it intends to rely. In such a procedure, the parties also translate all memorials, witness statements and expert reports, and use interpretation services at the hearings. Of course, if the arbitrators and counsel are bilingual, the proceedings may be conducted in both languages without translation or interpretation.

Pre-arbitration negotiation period

ICSID arbitration clauses sometimes include a mandatory negotiation or "cooling off" period of between 30 and 90 days, during which time a party may not commence arbitration. Such contractually-mandated negotiation opportunities are aimed at forcing the parties to focus on the advantages of settlement in the initial stages of the dispute, rather than on the tactical advantages possibly gained by the early commencement of an arbitration. It may be particularly important for a host State to have the opportunity to investigate and settle a dispute with an investor without the attendant publicity of an ICSID arbitration. Mandatory negotiation or cooling off clauses in BITs and other international investment agreements (and the related jurisprudence) are discussed in Chapter 3.

Provisional measures

Pursuant to Article 47 of the ICSID Convention and Rule 39(5) of the Arbitration Rules, the parties may seek conservatory or provisional measures (for example, recommendations to attach assets or preserve evidence) only from the ICSID tribunal, and not from national courts, unless they agree otherwise (see Chapter 4). This unusual default restriction, which applies both before and after the tribunal is constituted, is a reflection of the intent that the ICSID system be self-contained.

Parties to ICSID contractual arbitration, however, are free to agree to possible resort to alternative or additional remedies[61] and application to local courts to secure attachment of assets or other provisional measures. Drafters have the choice of preserving this option either before or after the tribunal is constituted, as reflected in ICSID Model Clause 14:

> "Without prejudice to the power of the Arbitral Tribunal to recommend provisional measures, either party hereto may request any judicial or other authority to order any provisional or conservatory measure, including attachment, prior to the institution of the arbitration proceeding, or during the proceeding, for the preservation of its rights and interests."

This generally is a desirable component of an ICSID arbitration clause, and is particularly important to permit (without question) an application to a local court for relief prior to the often lengthy period required to constitute an ICSID tribunal.

ICSID has taken steps to ameliorate the impact of the delay in constitution of the tribunal on effective provisional measures under the Rule 39 default. As a result of the 2006 amendments to Arbitration Rule 39(5), parties may

---

61   Model Clause 12.

now submit requests for provisional measures from the tribunal prior to its constitution, which allows the request to be fully briefed by the parties and ready for consideration by the tribunal as soon as it is constituted.

Sovereign immunity waiver

Under Article 25 of the ICSID Convention, consent to arbitration on the part of the host State constitutes an irrevocable waiver of immunity from suit (i.e., arbitration). Bound by its consent, the host State is barred from raising any plea of immunity that would frustrate arbitration proceedings under the ICSID Convention, from the time the case is commenced by the investor until the tribunal's issuance of the award.

Once the award is issued, however, the Convention does not alter or supersede the applicable national law of sovereign immunity from enforcement and execution of the award against the State. In other words, the host State's consent to arbitrate, although a waiver of immunity from suit, does not necessarily amount to a waiver of immunity from execution.

It is therefore imperative that foreign investors attempt to obtain from the host State an express waiver of sovereign immunity from enforcement and execution in the arbitration agreement. ICSID Model Clause 15 provides possible language:

> "The Host State hereby waives any right of sovereign immunity as to it and its property in respect of the enforcement and execution of any award rendered by an Arbitral Tribunal constituted pursuant to this agreement."

Without such a waiver – unlikely if not impossible once an investment dispute has arisen – an investor obtaining an award against a host State may be far from certain of achieving practical satisfaction in the event there is no voluntary compliance. We address this important topic further in Chapter 6.

Chapter 3

ICSID investment treaty arbitration

National investment laws and international treaties make it possible for private investors to initiate ICSID arbitration against host States even when there is no contractual agreement between them. In 2010, ICSID reported that 78 percent of the 305 arbitration cases registered by the end of 2009 had been brought under an instrument other than an arbitration clause between investor and host State.[62]

This "arbitration without privity" is possible because Article 25 of the ICSID Convention, which defines the scope of ICSID's jurisdiction, requires only that the parties "consent in writing" to the jurisdiction of the Centre – it does not prescribe how they must do so. So long as the parties' consent is mutual and expressed in writing, it suffices to establish ICSID jurisdiction. The Centre has accepted jurisdiction over arbitrations that arise from consent to ICSID arbitration expressed in the host State's national investment legislation, in a BIT between the host State and the investor's home State, and in a MIT among countries that include the host State and the investor's home State.

In contract-based ICSID arbitration (as in private international commercial arbitration), the parties generally give their consent simultaneously, in an arbitration clause contained in their investment contract or in a separate submission agreement. In non-contractual arbitration, the parties express their consent in two steps. First, the consent of the host State to submit to ICSID jurisdiction is contained in its national legislation or in a BIT or MIT. Second, the investor consents either by writing to the host State at any time (for example, in a simple

---

62 "The ICSID Caseload", *supra* note 11, at 10.

letter or a notice of dispute) or by filing a request to arbitrate with ICSID. In this way, the parties' agreement to arbitrate is established.

National investment legislation claims

Consent by the host State

One basis for non-contractual ICSID arbitration is the national investment legislation of the host State, by which the State unilaterally consents to submit investment disputes to ICSID jurisdiction. The investor's consent to arbitrate may occur at any time while the national investment legislation is in force. The host State is thus at liberty to withdraw its consent to ICSID arbitration by amending or repealing the relevant investment law before the investor has communicated its consent (subject to, for example, estoppel arguments that may be raised by investors having relied on the State's consent in the meantime).

Investment protection laws contain consent to submit to ICSID arbitration in different terms. As a practical matter, therefore, each legislative act needs to be considered individually. Even slight distinctions are often significant and warrant close examination.

Some States consent to ICSID jurisdiction by expressly submitting to arbitration under either the ICSID Convention or the Additional Facility Arbitration Rules. References of this type are usually crafted in the alternative: they point to the ICSID Convention first but also allow investors to resort to the Additional Facility Arbitration Rules if they are nationals of non-Contracting States. To cite one example, the Ivory Coast's 1996 Investment Code, in establishing the avenue of ICSID arbitration to resolve investment disputes, refers to "the competence of [ICSID] or of the Supplementary Mechanism [Additional Facility], as the case may be, required by the instruments governing them".[63]

In comparison, a State may make a commitment to submit to ICSID jurisdiction by reference only to the Convention. For example, the relevant section of the 1993 Law on Foreign Investment of the Republic of Albania provides:

---

63 Republic of Côte d'Ivoire, Office of the Prime Minister (CEPICI), *The Investment Code*, Law No. 95-620 of 3 August 1996, <www.panapress.com/cepici/law1.asp>, Art. 24.

"If a foreign investment dispute arises between a foreign investor and the Republic of Albania and it cannot be settled amicably, then the foreign investor may choose to submit the dispute for resolution to a competent court or administrative tribunal of the Republic of Albania in accordance with its laws. In addition, if the dispute arises out of or relates to expropriation, compensation for expropriation, or discrimination and also for the transfers in accordance with Article 7, then the foreign investor may submit the dispute for resolution and the *Republic of Albania hereby consents to the submission thereof, to the International Centre for Settlement of Investment Disputes ('Centre') established by the Convention on the Settlement of Investment Disputes between States and Nationals of Other States,* done at Washington, March 18, 1965 ('ICSID Convention')." (emphasis added).[64]

No tribunal apparently has yet had the occasion to decide whether consent to ICSID jurisdiction articulated in laws such as this covers only arbitration under the Convention, or also includes, in a case where the foreign investor is from a non-Contracting State, arbitration under the Additional Facility Rules.

As a further alternative, a State may consent to ICSID arbitration as one among several dispute resolution methods including, for example, procedures contemplated in applicable BITs or arbitration under relevant investment contracts. As an example, Egypt's Law No. 43 of 1974 Concerning the Investment of Arab and Foreign Funds and the Free Zone provided in Article 8 that investment disputes may be settled by treaty or *ad hoc* arbitration or in another manner agreed by the parties:

"Investment disputes in respect of the implementation of the provisions of this Law shall be settled in a manner to be agreed upon with the investor, or within the framework of the agreements in force between the Arab Republic of Egypt and the investor's home country, or within the framework of the Convention for the Settlement of Investment Disputes between the State and the nationals of other countries to

---

64 Quoted in *Tradex Hellas S.A. v. Republic of Albania,* ICSID Case No. ARB/94/2, Decision on Jurisdiction (24 December 1996), *ICSID Reports* 5 (2002): 47, 54-55.

which Egypt has adhered by virtue of Law No. 90 of 1971, where such Convention applies.

Disputes may be settled through arbitration. An Arbitration Board shall be constituted, comprising a member on behalf of each disputing party and a third member acting as chairman to be jointly named by the same two members."[65]

The tribunal in *SPP v. Egypt*, after a detailed linguistic and legal analysis, interpreted this text as providing a hierarchal structure such that a specific agreement between the parties would take precedence, followed by any applicable BIT, and then by the ICSID Convention.

Full consent to ICSID arbitration should be distinguished from those references to ICSID contained in national investment legislation that require the host State to take further steps as part of consent. Some laws, for example, stipulate that the State's offer to submit to ICSID arbitration will be effective only if and when the government enters into a further agreement with the investor or issues an investment license explicitly referring to ICSID for the resolution of disputes. Such a condition precedent to consent by the State obviously must be satisfied before the investor may pursue ICSID remedies.

Consent by the investor

The investor may consent to ICSID arbitration for purposes of the State's investment legislation in different ways.

First, the investor may consent by way of a written communication to the State or a formal agreement with the State referring to the relevant national legislation. The investor may also resort to any other method provided for in the legislation itself, such as the filing of a license application with the relevant designated State authorities. In *SPP v. Egypt*, the tribunal found that the investor had perfected its consent to ICSID jurisdiction when, a year before initiating arbitration, it had written to the Egyptian ministry of tourism a letter stating:

---

65   Quoted in *Southern Pacific Properties (Middle East) Ltd. and Southern Pacific Properties Ltd. (Hong Kong) v. Arab Republic of Egypt*, ICSID Case No. ARB/84/3, Decision on Jurisdiction (27 November 1985), *ICSID Reports* 3 (1995): 131, para. 71.

"we hereby notify you that we accept [...] the uncontestable jurisdiction of [ICSID] [...] which is open to us as a result of Law No. 43 of 1974, Article 8 of which provides that investment disputes may be settled by ICSID arbitration".[66]

Second, if the investor has not consented in writing to arbitrate before it files its request for ICSID arbitration, it will be deemed to have done so under the Convention by virtue of the filing itself. In *Tradex v. Albania*, the tribunal found that a State's unilateral consent to ICSID arbitration "become[s] effective at the latest if and when the foreign investor files its claim with ICSID making use of the respective national law".[67]

Although the necessary agreement to arbitrate may be perfected in the request to arbitrate, well-advised investors express their consent as early as possible because, until they do, the State may be in a position to withdraw its consent by amending or repealing its national investment legislation. An investor should make its acceptance of ICSID jurisdiction unequivocal, and should comply with any conditions for acceptance such as time limits or other formalities required by the investment legislation.

Bilateral investment treaty claims

The first BIT is generally acknowledged as the one entered into in 1959 between Germany and Pakistan. BITs and other international agreements with investment arbitration provisions have proliferated since then. The number of BITs worldwide rose from about 385 at the end of the 1980s to nearly 2,700 as of 2008, with other international agreements containing investment arbitration provisions totaling 273.

The number of ICSID arbitrations under BITs has also risen dramatically in recent years. The first ever BIT arbitration under the ICSID regime was filed in 1987 in *AAPL v. Sri Lanka*. In that case, the Hong Kong shareholder of a Sri Lankan shrimp farm filed a claim against Sri Lanka under the United Kingdom–Sri Lanka BIT for damage caused by Sri Lankan security forces

---

66 *Id.* at para. 50.
67 *Tradex v. Albania* (Decision on Jurisdiction), *supra* note 64, at 63.

during a military operation against installations reported to be used by Tamil rebels. The *AAPL* tribunal rendered its award in 1990 requiring Sri Lanka to pay compensation for failing to afford "full protection and security" to AAPL's investment under the BIT.[68] Since then, BIT arbitrations have transformed the volume and nature of ICSID cases. As of January 2010, ICSID had registered 305 cases, the majority of which (73 percent) were instituted on the basis of the consent of the State included in BITs or MITs.

The basic nature of a BIT

As well as the direct dispute resolution methods for private investors and States that are the subject of this Guide, BITs establish comprehensive protections under international law. To illustrate the nature and scope of BITs, Annex 6 contains the full text of the "Treaty between the United States of America and the Argentine Republic Concerning the Reciprocal Encouragement and Protection of Investment", signed in 1991 and ratified in 1994 (and the basis of many ICSID cases and awards). Like most BITs, the US–Argentina treaty is not long – it consists of 14 articles and fewer than 12 pages.

Many States have developed model or prototype BITs, which reflect their negotiating goals and hence form the basis for negotiations of new treaties. The United States developed its first prototype BIT in 1983. The 1983 Model has since gone through several iterations, the latest being the 2004 Model (which itself is currently under review). As an example, a copy of the Model United Kingdom BIT is included in Annex 5.

The overarching goals of BITs typically appear in the introductory language. The preamble to the US–Argentina treaty is illustrative:

"The United States of America and the Argentine Republic, hereinafter referred to as the Parties;

Desiring to promote greater economic cooperation between them, with respect to investment by nationals and companies of one Party in the territory of the other Party;

---

68 *Asian Agricultural Products Ltd. (AAPL) v. Republic of Sri Lanka*, ICSID Case No. ARB/87/3, Award (27 June 1990), *ICSID Reports* 4 (1997): 245.

Recognizing that agreement upon the treatment to be accorded such investment will stimulate the flow of private capital and the economic development of the Parties;

Agreeing that fair and equitable treatment of investment is desirable in order to maintain a stable framework for investment and maximum effective use of economic resources;

Recognizing that the development of economic and business ties can contribute to the well-being of workers in both Parties and promote respect for internationally recognized worker rights; and

Having resolved to conclude a Treaty concerning the encouragement and reciprocal protection of investment;

Have agreed as follows:"

The preamble in the Model UK BIT is more succinct:

"The Government of the United Kingdom of Great Britain and Northern Ireland and the Government of _____;

Desiring to create favourable conditions for greater investment by nationals and companies of one State in the territory of the other State;

Recognising that the encouragement and reciprocal protection under international agreement of such investments will be conducive to the stimulation of individual business initiative and will increase prosperity in both States;

Have agreed as follows:"

In general, a BIT affords a qualifying investor certain protections in respect of its investment in a State with which its own State of nationality or domicile has concluded a BIT. If a host State breaches the substantive protections contained in a BIT in a manner that adversely affects the investor, the investor (subject to any stipulated requirement to exhaust local court remedies) typically may commence proceedings directly against that State. Most BITs open the way to ICSID arbitration in the event of such a dispute between investor and host State.

BITs are the product of negotiation between two sovereign States, and so the scope and content of BITs vary considerably. The variations reflect the States' different investment policies and bargaining positions. Regardless of models and prototypes, no State can expect that all the BITs it signs will be identical. It is therefore necessary, in the event of (and before) an investment dispute, to study the exact terms of any applicable BITs with great care.

Most treaties nevertheless do contain recurring provisions, dealing with such matters as: (a) scope of application of the BIT; (b) the definition of a qualifying investment; (c) the applicable law; (d) the substantive investment treaty protections; and (e) access to arbitration and other forms of dispute resolution. We discuss these provisions below by reference to various BITs, selected as examples of host State/investor State relationships – but which contain, nonetheless, several significant substantive and procedural differences (far beyond the scope of discussion in this Guide).

Establishing the existence of a BIT

The first step in determining whether an investor may enjoy investment treaty protection is to identify whether there is an applicable BIT in force between the host State and the investor's State. The ICSID website contains a list of BITs, but it is not necessarily current.[69] The United Nations Conference on Trade and Development (**UNCTAD**) also publishes a list of BITs and maintains a searchable online database of international investment agreements.[70] Other investment arbitration databases also include BITs and MITs, although the scope and coverage of such databases are not comprehensive.[71] Where there

---

69 The bilateral investment treaty list can be found on the ICSID website at <www.worldbank. org/icsid/treaties/treaties.htm>. As of January 2010, it was current to 2007. ICSID also publishes a loose-leaf collection of investment treaties which covers the period 1959-2007.

70 UNCTAD, "Bilateral Investment Treaties 1959-1999" (New York: United Nations, 2000), <www.unctad.org/Templates/WebFlyer.asp?intItemID=3138&lang=1>. As of September 2010, the UNCTAD searchable database of investment instruments online was stated to be current as of May 2010. UNCTAD, "Investment Instruments Online: Bilateral Investment Treaties", <www.unctadxi.org/templates/DocSearch_____779.aspx>, 10 May 2010.

71 For example, the <kluwerarbitration.com> and <investmentclaims.com> websites provide access to the text of a number of BITs.

is any doubt, the most reliable means of verifying the existence of a BIT is to contact the relevant ministry of foreign affairs or embassy.

Who is entitled to rely upon the BIT?

Where there is a potentially applicable BIT, the next issue is whether it entitles a particular investor to protection as a national of a State party.

Most BITs draw a distinction between two categories of investing entities potentially able to enjoy the protection of the treaty: (a) individuals or natural persons; and (b) companies and other juridical entities. As to the first, most BITs define "individuals" and their nationality by reference to the parties' domestic laws on citizenship. As to the second, many BITs determine the nationality of a company by reference to the domestic law concept of incorporation or constitution, according to which a company is deemed to take its identity from the State in which it is incorporated regardless of where it actually carries on its economic activities. For example, the US–Argentina BIT (Annex 6) defines a company as "any kind of corporation, company, association, state enterprise, or other organization, *legally constituted under the laws and regulations* of a Party or a political subdivision thereof whether or not organized for pecuniary gain, and whether privately or governmentally owned". (emphasis added).

Other BITs use the concept of the seat of company management, according to which the actual place of management of the company determines nationality; this is general German BIT practice. In still other BITs, including most of the recent Swiss treaties, the critical concept is control, according to which the nationality of the company is based on the nationality of the dominant shareholders of the company.

Most BITs may be relied upon either by: (a) the entity that makes the investment directly or indirectly; or (b) where the direct investor is a host State entity such as a locally-incorporated investment vehicle, by a foreign individual or company that directly or indirectly controls that entity. For example, the US–Kazakhstan BIT states that "'investment' means every kind of investment in the territory of one Party *owned or controlled directly or indirectly* by nationals or companies of the other Party". (emphasis added).[72] In other words, the obligation frequently imposed by host States on a foreign investor to incorporate a local entity as a special purpose vehicle for the investment does not prevent the controlling foreign investor from relying on the treaty.

Some BITs expressly protect investing entities, wherever located, that are directly or indirectly controlled by investors of a State party to the treaty.[73] Control, under international law, is a flexible and broad concept that may refer not only to the rights of majority shareholders but also to other "reasonable" criteria such as management responsibility, voting rights and nationality of board members. The ICSID tribunal in *Vacuum Salt v. Ghana*, while finding that a 20 percent Greek shareholder could not be considered as exercising control over a local company so as to be able to confer Greek nationality on the company, stated that acting or "being materially influenced in a truly managerial rather than technical or supervisory vein" or being "in a position to steer, through either positive or negative action, the fortunes" of the company would suffice to demonstrate control.[74]

A related question is whether a national of one State party that owns a minority (or other non-controlling) shareholding interest in a corporation that is a national of the host State may bring a claim – independent of the corporation – against the host State.[75] The tribunal in *CMS v. Argentina*, after canvassing relevant sources of international law, answered this question in the affirmative.[76] In that case, the government of Argentina – ultimately unsuccessfully – challenged the jurisdiction of the tribunal on a variety of grounds, most of which focused on CMS

---

72 Treaty Between the United States of America and the Republic of Kazakhstan Concerning the Reciprocal Encouragement and Protection of Investment, <tcc.export.gov/Trade_Agreements/All_Trade_Agreements/exp_005571.asp>, 12 January 1994, Art. I(1)(a).

73 *See, e.g.*, Agreement on Encouragement and Reciprocal Protection of Investments Between the Kingdom of the Netherlands and the Argentine Republic, <www.unctad.org/sections/dite/iia/docs/bits/netherlands_argentina.pdf>, 1 October 1994, Art. 1(b)(iii).

74 *Vacuum Salt Products v. Ghana* (Award), *supra* note 40, at para. 53.

75 *See also* the discussion of Convention Article 25(2)(b) in Chapter 2.

76 *CMS Gas Transmission Company v. Republic of Argentina*, ICSID Case No. ARB/01/8, Decision of the Tribunal on Objections to Jurisdiction (17 July 2003), *ICSID Reports* 7 (2005). Freshfields was counsel to the claimant.

Gas Transmission's status as a minority shareholder in an Argentine corporation (Transportadora de Gas del Norte or **TGN**) that held a government license for gas transportation. The applicable treaty in that case, the US–Argentina BIT, defines investment to mean "every kind of investment in the territory of one Party owned or controlled directly or indirectly by nationals or companies of the other Party".[77] In its decision, the tribunal first described the trend in general international law to recognize the independence of shareholders:

> "The Tribunal therefore finds no bar in current international law to the concept of allowing claims by shareholders independently from those of the corporation concerned, not even if those shareholders are minority or non-controlling shareholders. Although it is true, as argued by the Republic of Argentina, that this is mostly the result of *lex specialis* and specific treaty arrangements that have so allowed, the fact is that *lex specialis* in this respect is so prevalent that it can now be considered the general rule, certainly in respect of foreign investments and international claims and increasingly in respect of other matters."[78]

The tribunal went on to find, after detailed review, that "there is no bar to the exercise of jurisdiction in light of the 1965 Convention and its interpretation as reflected in its drafting history, the opinion of distinguished legal writers and the jurisprudence of ICSID tribunals".[79] The tribunal also found that CMS Gas Transmission's minority shareholding interest was an investment under the US–Argentina BIT (see the discussion immediately below) even though CMS Gas Transmission was not a party to TGN's license with the government:

> "[T]he Tribunal concludes that jurisdiction can be established under the terms of the specific provisions of the BIT. Whether the protected investor is in addition a party to a concession agreement or a license agreement with the host State is immaterial for the purpose of finding

---

77   *Id.* at para. 57.

78   *Id.* at para. 48.

79   *Id.* at para. 56. The tribunal relied heavily on *Lanco International, Inc. v. Argentine Republic*, ICSID Case No. ARB/97/6, Preliminary Decision: Jurisdiction of the Arbitral Tribunal (8 December 1998), *ICSID Reports* 5 (2002): 367.

jurisdiction under those treaty provisions, since there is a direct right of action of shareholders. It follows that the Claimant has *jus standi* before this Tribunal under international law, the 1965 Convention and the Argentina–United States Bilateral Investment Treaty."[80]

In *Siemens v. Argentina*, Argentina filed similar jurisdictional objections, including an objection asserting that the applicable BIT in that case, the Germany–Argentina BIT, required a direct relationship between the investor and the investment.[81] Unlike in *CMS*, in *Siemens*, the investor's ownership of shares in a local Argentine company was not direct but effectuated through a corporate affiliate, and the applicable BIT contained no explicit reference to direct or indirect investment. The tribunal nonetheless dismissed Argentina's objection, noting that the BIT did not require "that there be no interposed companies between the investment and the ultimate owner of the company".[82] ICSID tribunals in other cases have similarly held that the ownership of shares, direct or indirect, constitutes an investment under the Convention.[83]

It is imperative for international investors – just as they routinely structure and restructure their investments to take advantage of available tax and other benefits – to consider structuring investments in ways that enable them to benefit

---

80   *CMS v. Argentina* (Decision of the Tribunal on Objections to Jurisdiction), *supra* note 76, at para. 65.

81   *Siemens A.G. v. Argentine Republic*, ICSID Case No. ARB/02/8, Decision on Jurisdiction (3 August 2004).

82   *Id.* at para. 137.

83   *See, e.g., Azurix Corp. v. Argentine Republic*, ICSID Case No. ARB/01/12, Decision on Jurisdiction (8 December 2003); *Enron Corporation and Ponderosa Assets L.P. v. Argentine Republic*, ICSID Case No. ARB/01/3, Decision on Jurisdiction (14 January 2004); *LG&E Energy Corp. and others v. Argentine Republic*, ICSID Case No. ARB/02/1, Decision of the Arbitral Tribunal on Objections to Jurisdiction (30 April 2004); *Sempra Energy International v. Argentine Republic*, ICSID Case No. ARB/02/16, Decision on Objections to Jurisdiction (11 May 2005); *Camuzzi International S.A. v. Argentine Republic*, ICSID Case No. ARB/03/2, Decision on Objections to Jurisdiction (11 May 2005); *Gas Natural SDG, S.A. v. Argentine Republic*, ICSID Case No. ARB/03/10, Decision of the Tribunal on Preliminary Questions on Jurisdiction (17 June 2005); *El Paso Energy International Company v. Argentine Republic*, ICSID Case No. ARB/03/15, Decision on Jurisdiction (27 April 2006); *Ioannis Kardassopoulos v. Georgia*, ICSID Case No. ARB/05/18, Decision on Jurisdiction (6 July 2007).

from BIT protections. As stated by the *Aguas del Tunari v. Bolivia* tribunal, "it is not uncommon practice, and – absent a particular limitation – not illegal to locate one's operations in a jurisdiction perceived to provide a beneficial regulatory and legal environment".[84] Investors and their counsel should be familiar with the substantive protections and dispute resolution methods offered by the BITs entered into by various host jurisdictions. Specifically, along with other factors, an investor should consider selecting the nationality of its investing company or companies to take advantage of the most favorable regimes from among perhaps many potentially applicable BITs.

What constitutes an "investment"?

For a qualifying investor to rely on the substantive protections and procedural safeguards of a BIT, it must have made an investment protected by the treaty.

Most BITs define the term "investment" in a broad, open-ended way that ensures a high degree of flexibility in application. Definitions, for example from the UK–Russia or US–Argentina BITs, often include general language referring to "every kind of asset"[85] or "every kind of investment in the territory".[86] Treaty definitions often provide specific and non-exhaustive examples, such as:

(a) "movable and immovable property" (UK–Russia BIT); "tangible and intangible property" (US–Argentina BIT);

(b) "shares in, and stock, bonds and debentures of, and any other form of participation in a company or business enterprise" (UK–Russia BIT); "company or shares of stock or other interests in a company or interests in the assets thereof" (US–Argentina BIT);

---

84 *Aguas del Tunari S.A. v. Republic of Bolivia*, ICSID Case No. ARB/02/3, Decision on Respondent's Objections to Jurisdiction (21 October 2005), at para. 330.

85 *See, e.g.*, Agreement Between the Government of the United Kingdom of Great Britain and Northern Ireland and the Government of the Union of Soviet Socialist Republics for the Promotion and Reciprocal Protection of Investments, <www.unctad.org/sections/dite/iia/docs/bits/uk_ussr.pdf>, 3 July 1991, Art. 1(a).

86 *See, e.g.*, Treaty Between the United States of America and the Argentine Republic Concerning the Reciprocal Encouragement and Protection of Investment, <www.unctad.org/sections/dite/iia/docs/bits/argentina_us.pdf>, 20 October 1994, Art. I(1)(a) (Annex 6).

(c) "claims to money, and claims to performance under contract having a financial value" (UK–Russia BIT); "a claim to money or a claim to performance having economic value and directly related to an investment" (US–Argentina BIT); and

(d) "intellectual property" (US–Argentina BIT); "intellectual property rights, technical processes, know-how and any other benefit or advantage attached to a business" (UK–Russia BIT).

Some BITs explicitly apply only to investments made after the conclusion of the treaty. Most are broader in scope in terms of time. For example, Article 1(a) of the UK–Turkmenistan BIT states that "the term 'investment' includes all investments, whether made before or after the date of entry into force of this Agreement".[87]

Many BITs explicitly exclude from coverage investments in certain industries or other sectors. For example, the 1992 US Model BIT is drafted to reserve the right of the US to make exceptions to the "national treatment" protection (see below) in sectors such as banking, insurance, ownership of real property, use of land and natural resources, and mining on the public domain. It is also drafted to reserve the right to make exceptions to "most favored nation" treatment (see below) in the following sectors: ownership of real property, mining on the public domain, maritime services and maritime-related services, and primary dealership in US government securities. These exceptions accordingly have been introduced in a number of individual BITs, for example in the US–Kazakhstan BIT.

In some BITs the term "investment" is explicitly linked to specified criteria. For example, the Sweden–Argentina BIT provides that "the term 'investment' shall comprise every kind of asset, invested by an investor of one Contracting Party in the territory of the other Contracting Party, *provided that the investment*

---

87 Agreement Between the Government of the United Kingdom of Great Britain and Northern Ireland and the Government of Turkmenistan for the Promotion and Protection of Investments, <www.unctad.org/sections/dite/iia/docs/bits/uk_turkmenistan.pdf>, 9 February 1995, Art. 1(a).

has been made in accordance with the laws and regulations of the other Contracting Party". (emphasis added).[88]

BIT provisions of this kind have been the subject of a number of ICSID decisions and awards, with differing results. In *Gruslin v. Malaysia*, the tribunal held that Malaysia had not consented to ICSID arbitration with the claimant under the criteria set out in the Belgium–Malaysia BIT, which provided for protection of "approved projects" only.[89] The investment in question, an investment by Gruslin in shares listed on the Malaysian stock market, was found not to be of the type that could be considered an "approved project". In *Inceysa v. El Salvador*, which involved a similar approval provision in the El Salvador–Spain BIT, the tribunal held that it lacked jurisdiction on the basis of the need for the investment to be made lawfully in accordance with Spanish law, finding that "Inceysa's investment was made in a manner that was clearly illegal".[90] In *Plama v. Bulgaria*, which concerned a treaty that did not explicitly require conformity of an investment with local law, the tribunal held that such a requirement of legality nevertheless was implicit.[91] Several other ICSID tribunals have evaluated but rejected jurisdictional arguments that investments were not established in accordance with local law.[92]

---

88 Agreement Between the Government of the Kingdom of Sweden and the Government of the Republic of Argentina on the Promotion and Reciprocal Protection of Investments, <www. unctad.org/sections/dite/iia/docs/bits/argentina_sweden.pdf>, 28 September 1992, Art. 1(1).

89 *Phillipe Gruslin v. Malaysia,* ICSID Case No. ARB/99/3, Award (27 November 2000), *ICSID Reports* 5 (2002): 483-512. Freshfields was counsel to the respondent.

90 *Inceysa Vallisoletana S.L. v. Republic of El Salvador,* ICSID Case No. ARB/03/26, Award (2 August 2006); *see also Fraport AG Frankfurt Airport Services Worldwide v. Republic of the Philippines,* ICSID Case No. ARB/03/25, Award (16 August 2007).

91 *Plama Consortium Limited v. Bulgaria,* ICSID Case No. ARB/03/24, Award (27 August 2008); *see also Phoenix Action, Ltd. v. Czech Republic,* ICSID Case No. ARB/06/5, Award (15 April 2009).

92 *See, e.g., Salini Costruttori S.p.A. and Italstrade S.p.A. v. Kingdom of Morocco,* ICSID Case No. ARB/00/4, Decision on Jurisdiction (23 July 2001); *Tokios Tokelés v. Ukraine,* ICSID Case No. ARB/02/18, Decision on Jurisdiction (29 April 2004); *Bayindir Insaat Turizm Ticaret Ve Sanayi A.Ş. v. Islamic Republic of Pakistan,* ICSID Case No. ARB/03/29, Decision on Jurisdiction (14 November 2005); *Kardassopoulos v. Georgia* (Decision on Jurisdiction),

In early ICSID decisions and awards in BIT cases, jurisdictional objections challenging the existence of an investment were rare, and tribunals appeared to have little difficulty determining whether or not an investment existed for purposes of Convention Article 25(1). In *Fedax v. Venezuela*, for example, the tribunal held that promissory notes issued by Venezuela and acquired by the claimant from the original holder in the secondary market, through endorsement, constituted an investment under the Netherlands–Venezuela BIT.[93] The tribunal extensively analyzed the notion of investment under BITs and MITs and refused to limit it to the classic forms of direct investment as argued by Venezuela, i.e., "the laying out of money or property in business ventures, so that it may produce a revenue or income".[94]

A shift occurred with the decision on jurisdiction in *Salini v. Morocco* in 2001.[95] Morocco argued that the construction contract in question did not constitute an investment under the Morocco–Italy BIT or under the Convention. The tribunal stated that Article 25(1) criteria "would be easier to define if there were awards denying the Centre's jurisdiction on the basis of the transaction giving rise to the dispute", but that "the awards at hand only very rarely turned on the notion of investment".[96] The tribunal listed the characteristics or features of an investment – since occasionally referred to as the "*Salini* test" – as involving: (a) a contribution; (b) a certain duration; (c) an element of risk; and (d) a contribution to the host State's economic development. The tribunal held that the construction contract in question had these characteristics and hence constituted an investment under both the BIT and Convention Article 25.[97]

In the years following *Salini*, ICSID tribunals have adopted two basic approaches to the notion of investment under Convention Article 25(1) and

---

supra note 83; *Desert Line Projects LLC v. Republic of Yemen*, ICSID Case No. ARB/05/17, Award (6 February 2008).

93 *Fedax N.V. v. Republic of Venezuela*, ICSID Case No. ARB/96/3, Decision of the Tribunal on Objections to Jurisdiction (11 July 1997).

94 *Id.* at para. 19.

95 *Salini v. Morocco* (Decision on Jurisdiction), *supra* note 92.

96 *Id.* at para. 52.

97 *Id.*

applicable BITs.[98] The first approach presumes that there is a notion of "investment" under the ICSID Convention, which can be understood and illustrated through a number of characteristics. As explained by ICSID tribunals, this is not a strict test, and these criteria "are but benchmarks or yardsticks to help a tribunal in assessing the existence of an investment",[99] that "must be considered as mere examples".[100]

The second approach, in contrast, considers such criteria as necessary elements that must be satisfied cumulatively. ICSID tribunals following the second approach do not, however, agree on the exact criteria. Some tribunals have adopted three[101] or all four of the characteristics of the *Salini* test.[102] Others have added criteria to

---

98 *See* E. Gaillard, "Identify or Define? Reflections on the Evolution of the Concept of Investment in ICSID Practice", in *International Investment Law for the 21st Century*, eds. C. Binder et al. (Oxford: Oxford University Press, 2009), 403.

99 *RSM Production Corporation v. Grenada*, ICSID Case No. ARB/05/14, Award (13 March 2009), para. 241. Freshfields is counsel to the respondent.

100 *M.C.I. Power Group L.C. and New Turbine, Inc. v. Republic of Ecuador*, ICSID Case No. ARB/03/6, Award (31 July 2007), para. 165. *See also Biwater Gauff (Tanzania) Ltd. v. United Republic of Tanzania*, ICSID Case No. ARB/05/22, Award (24 July 2008); *Malaysian Historical Salvors, Sdn, Bhd v. Government of Malaysia*, ICSID Case No. ARB/05/10, Decision on the Application for Annulment (16 April 2009); *Pantechniki S.A. Contractors & Engineers v. Republic of Albania*, ICSID Case No. ARB/07/21, Award (30 July 2009).

101 *Consortium Groupement L.E.S.I.- DIPENTA v. Popular Democratic Republic of Algeria*, ICSID Case No. ARB/03/08, Award (10 January 2005); *Bayindir v. Pakistan* (Decision on Jurisdiction), *supra* note 92; *Víctor Pey Casado and President Allende Foundation v. Republic of Chile*, ICSID Case No. ARB/98/2, Award (8 May 2008); *see also* Z. Douglas, *The International Law of Investment Claims* (Cambridge: Cambridge University Press, 2009).

102 *Salini v. Morocco* (Decision on Jurisdiction), *supra* note 92; *Jan de Nul N.V. and Dredging International N.V. v. Arab Republic of Egypt*, ICSID Case No. ARB/04/13, Decision on Jurisdiction (16 June 2006); *Saipem S.p.A. v. People's Republic of Bangladesh*, ICSID Case No. ARB/05/07, Decision on Jurisdiction and Recommendation on Provisional Measures (21 March 2007); *Kardassopoulos v. Georgia* (Decision on Jurisdiction), *supra* note 83.

be fulfilled, such as a regularity of profit and return,[103] and investment of assets in good faith and in accordance with the laws of the host State.[104]

As of January 2010, ICSID tribunals had declined jurisdiction in five cases on the ground that the investment requirements of the Convention and applicable BIT or foreign investment law were not satisfied.[105] All are illustrative of the possible jurisdictional parameters of an "investment". In *Mihaly International v. Sri Lanka*, the tribunal held that expenses incurred by the claimant following execution of a letter of intent with Sri Lanka to construct a proposed power project, including substantial sums spent in planning the financial and economic modeling necessary for the negotiation and (unsuccessful) finalization of a contract, were not an investment under the applicable BIT.[106] Similarly, the tribunal in *Zhinvali v. Georgia* held that pre-development expenses incurred in negotiations relating to a hydroelectric power plant project did not qualify as an investment under the Georgian Investment Law or under Article 25(1) of the Convention.[107] In *Joy Mining v. Egypt*, the tribunal held that bank guarantees related to a phosphate mining project were "simply a contingent liability" and that "[t]o conclude that a contingent liability is an asset under Article 1(a) of the Treaty and hence a protected investment, would really go far beyond the concept

---

103 *Joy Mining Machinery Ltd. v. Arab Republic of Egypt*, ICSID Case No. ARB/03/11, Award on Jurisdiction (6 August 2004); *Helnan International Hotels A/S v. Arab Republic of Egypt*, ICSID Case No. ARB/05/19, Decision of the Tribunal on Objection to Jurisdiction (17 October 2006).

104 *Phoenix Action v. Czech Republic* (Award), *supra* note 91.

105 *Mihaly International Corporation v. Democratic Socialist Republic of Sri Lanka*, ICSID Case No. ARB/00/2, Award (15 March 2002); *Zhinvali Development Ltd. v. Republic of Georgia*, ICSID Case No. ARB/00/1, Award (24 January 2003), *ICSID Reports* 10 (2006): 3; *Joy Mining v. Egypt* (Award on Jurisdiction), *supra* note 103; *Patrick Mitchell v. Democratic Republic of the Congo*, ICSID Case No. ARB/99/7, Decision on the Application for Annulment of the Award (1 November 2006) (although the original tribunal held that it had jurisdiction, the award (unpublished) was subsequently annulled); *Malaysian Historical Salvors, Sdn, Bhd v. Malaysia*, ICSID Case No. ARB/05/10, Award on Jurisdiction (17 May 2007) (subsequently annulled).

106 *Mihaly v. Sri Lanka* (Award), *supra* note 105.

107 *Zhinvali v. Georgia* (Award), *supra* note 105.

of investment, even if broadly defined, as this and other treaties normally do".[108] The decisions rendered in the other two cases, *Mitchell v. DRC*[109] and *MHS v. Malaysia*,[110] are discussed in Chapter 5 (on annulment).

In two instances, the ICSID Secretary-General has refused to register requests for arbitration because the disputes in question were manifestly outside the jurisdiction of the Centre as not involving investments.[111]

The choice of law applicable to BIT claims

Certain bilateral investment treaties require application of some combination of the law of the relevant Contracting State, the provisions of the treaty and other agreements, general principles of international law and/or such rules of law as the parties may have agreed.

Most BITs, however, do not explicitly refer to the law that tribunals must apply in arbitrating disputes between investors and the host State. As noted above in Chapter 2, Article 42(1) of the ICSID Convention provides that, where the parties have not agreed upon applicable law, the tribunal should apply "the law of the Contracting State party to the dispute (including its rules on the conflict of laws) and such rules of international law as may be applicable". In practice, tribunals in BIT arbitrations generally apply the substantive provisions of the relevant treaty itself and other sources of international law, with "host State law rules also having a role" on certain questions by virtue of BIT provisions, such as whether or not a covered investment was made in accordance with local law

---

108 *Joy Mining v. Egypt* (Award on Jurisdiction), *supra* note 103, at para. 45.

109 *Mitchell v. DRC* (Decision on the Application for Annulment of the Award), *supra* note 105.

110 *MHS v. Malaysia* (Award on Jurisdiction), *supra* note 105; *MHS v. Malaysia* (Decision on the Application for Annulment), *supra* note 100.

111 In 1985, the ICSID Secretary-General refused to register a case on the basis that the alleged dispute related to a mere commercial sale and thus could not be considered as arising out of an investment. ICSID, "1985 Annual Report", at 6. In 1999, the Secretary-General refused registration of a request for arbitration arising out of a supply contract for the sale of goods. I.F.I. Shihata & A. Parra, "The Experience of the International Centre for Settlement of Investment Disputes", *ICSID Review – FILJ* 14 (1999): 308.

or the calculation of compensation for expropriation in accordance with the law of the expropriating state.[112]

The ICSID tribunals in the *Maffezini* and *Vivendi I* cases, which involved BITs containing applicable law clauses referencing national law, looked only to the treaties and to international law.[113] In the words of the *ad hoc* annulment committee in the *Vivendi I* case:

"[I]n respect of a claim based upon a substantive provision of that BIT ... the inquiry which the ICSID tribunal is required to undertake is one governed by the ICSID Convention, by the BIT and by applicable international law. Such an inquiry is neither in principle determined, nor precluded, by any issue of municipal law."[114]

Referring to the *Maffezini* and *Vivendi I cases*, among others, Professor Prosper Weil wrote in 2000:

"[These] cases are noteworthy illustrations of the trend – which can only grow stronger – toward ICSID arbitration governed by international law by virtue of the fact that the BIT implicitly or explicitly provides that disputes must be settled not only on the basis of the provisions of the treaty itself, but also, and more generally, on the basis of the principles and rules of international law."[115]

---

112 A. Parra, "Applicable Law in Investor-State Arbitration", in *Contemporary Issues in International Arbitration and Mediation*, ed. A.W. Rovine (Leiden: Martinus Nijhoff Publishers, 2008), 3.

113 *Emilio Agustín Maffezini v. Kingdom of Spain*, ICSID Case No. ARB/97/7, Decision of the Tribunal on Objections to Jurisdiction (25 January 2000); *Compañía de Aguas del Aconquija S.A. and Compagnie Générale des Eaux v. Argentine Republic*, ICSID Case No. ARB/97/3, Award (21 November 2000) (*Vivendi I (Award)*). *See also American Manufacturing & Trading, Inc. v. Republic of Zaire*, ICSID Case No. ARB/93/1, Award (21 February 1997); *Wena Hotels Ltd. v. Arab Republic of Egypt*, ICSID Case No. ARB/98/4, Decision on the Application by the Arab Republic of Egypt for the Annulment of the Arbitral Award dated December 8, 2000 (5 February 2002).

114 *Compañía de Aguas del Aconquija S.A. and Compagnie Générale des Eaux v. Argentine Republic*, ICSID Case No. ARB/97/3, Decision on Annulment (3 July 2002) (*Vivendi I (Decision on Annulment)*), para. 102.

115 P. Weil, "The State, the Foreign Investor, and International Law: The No Longer Stormy Relationship of a Ménage à Trois", *ICSID Review – FILJ* 15 (2000): 401, 412.

Given that it is the BITs that grant foreign investors direct access to arbitration to claim the substantive protections of the treaty itself, it follows that the substantive standards of the relevant treaty are *lex specialis* and a primary source of applicable law. And, as BITs are international law instruments, it also follows that international law is applicable by virtue of the Vienna Convention on the Law of Treaties, which provides that treaties are "governed by international law" and must be interpreted in light of "any relevant rules of international law applicable".[116] Article 3 of the International Law Commission's Articles on State Responsibility provides:

> "The characterization of an act of a State as internationally wrongful is governed by international law. Such characterization is not affected by the characterization of the same act as lawful by internal law."[117]

A third view is that domestic law has a broader role to play in cases, as propounded by the *CMS v. Argentina* tribunal:

> "[A] more pragmatic and less doctrinaire approach has emerged allowing for the application of both domestic law and international law if the specific facts of the dispute so justifies. It is no longer the case of one prevailing over the other and excluding it altogether. Rather, both sources have a role to play."[118]

There is no doctrine of precedent in international law. However, given the more than 200 publicly available ICSID decisions and awards rendered in investment treaty cases (as of January 2010), it is not surprising that ICSID tribunals routinely refer to prior decisions and awards.[119] ICSID tribunals also refer to international

---

116 Vienna Convention on the Law of Treaties, UNTS 1155 (27 January 1980), Arts. 2(1)(a) and 31(3)(c).

117 International Law Commission, "Articles on Responsibility of States for Internationally Wrongful Acts" (12 December 2001), Art. 3.

118 *CMS Gas Transmission Company v. Argentine Republic,* ICSID Case No. ARB/01/18, Award (12 May 2005), para. 116; *see also MTD Equity Sdn. Bhd. and MTD Chile S.A. v. Republic of Chile,* ICSID Case No. ARB/01/7, Decision on Annulment (21 March 2007), para. 72.

119 *See, e.g., Bayindir Insaat Turizm Ticaret Ve Sanayi A.Ş. v. Islamic Republic of Pakistan,* ICSID Case No. ARB/03/29, Award (27 August 2009), para. 76 ("The Tribunal is not bound by

73

case law, including the extensive jurisprudence of the Iran–United States Claims Tribunal, on disputes relating to illegal expropriation and nationalization, other takings and measures affecting property rights, as well as breach of contract.

What substantive rights do BITs afford investors?

Although they vary considerably in precise scope and content, BITs in general grant investors common categories of protections for their investments, many of which are derived from principles of customary international law on the protection of alien property. A detailed discussion is beyond the scope of this Guide, but we introduce the main principles below by reference to key features. (Lists of the ICSID cases in which each of these protections has been at issue are set forth in Tables I and II.A–G in Annex 10.)

Fair and equitable treatment

Nearly all BITs require host States to accord "fair and equitable treatment" to investors of the other State party. For example, the Argentina–Netherlands BIT provides:

> "Each Contracting Party shall ensure fair and equitable treatment to investments of investors of the other Contracting Party and shall not impair, by unreasonable or discriminatory measures, the operation, management, maintenance, use, enjoyment or disposal thereof by those investors."[120]

---

previous decisions of ICSID tribunals, but will certainly carefully consider such decisions whenever appropriate"); J. Paulsson, "International Arbitration and the Generation of Legal Norms: Treaty Arbitration and International Law", *ICCA Congress Series No. 13, International Arbitration 2006: Back to Basics* (The Hague: Kluwer Law International, 2007); J. Commission, "Precedent in Investment Treaty Arbitration – A Citation Analysis of a Developing Jurisprudence", *Journal of International Arbitration* 24(2) (2007): 129; J. Paulsson, "The Role of Precedent in Investment Arbitration", in *Arbitration Under International Investment Agreements*, ed. K. Yannaca-Small (Oxford: Oxford University Press, 2010), 699.

120 Argentina–Netherlands BIT, *supra* note 73, at Art. 3(1).

The notion of fair and equitable treatment cannot readily be reduced to a precise statement of an exact legal obligation. Rather, the principle leaves considerable room for judgment and appreciation to tribunals charged with reviewing the "fairness" and "equity" of the host State's actions in light of all the circumstances of the case and without necessarily embarking upon deliberations on the requirements of either municipal or international law.[121]

As of January 2010, fair and equitable treatment claims had been advanced in 50 decided ICSID cases. In just over half of the cases (26 out of 50), ICSID tribunals upheld fair and equitable claims brought by claimants.[122] Also of interest, in non-ICSID investment treaty cases (for which there is no public registry), there were at least 12 cases (as of January 2010) where tribunals have upheld fair and equitable treatment claims[123] and at least six where tribunals

---

121 *See, e.g.*, K. Yannaca-Small, "Fair and Equitable Treatment Standard", in *Arbitration Under International Investment Agreements, supra* note 119, 385; I. Tudor, *The Fair and Equitable Treatment Standard in International Foreign Investment Law* (Oxford: Oxford University Press, 2008); C. Schreuer, "Fair and Equitable Treatment in Arbitral Practice", *Journal of World Investment & Trade* 6 (2005); R. Dolzer, "Fair and Equitable Treatment: A Key Standard in Investment Treaties", *International Lawyer* 39 (2005): 87; S. Vasciannie, "The Fair and Equitable Treatment Standard in International Investment Law and Practice", *British Yearbook of International Law* 70 (1999): 99, 163; F.A. Mann, "British Treaties for the Promotion and Protection of Investments", *British Yearbook of International Law* 52 (1981): 241, 244 (an arbitral tribunal must "decide whether in all the circumstances the conduct in issue is fair and equitable or unfair and inequitable").

122 *See* Table II.A in Annex 10.

123 *S.D. Myers, Inc. v. Government of Canada*, UNCITRAL, First Partial Award (13 November 2000); *Pope & Talbot Inc. v. Government of Canada*, UNCITRAL, Award on the Merits of Phase 2 (10 April 2001); *CME Czech Republic B.V. v. Czech Republic*, UNCITRAL, Partial Award (13 September 2001); *Occidental Exploration and Production Company v. Republic of Ecuador*, LCIA Case No. UN3467, Final Award (1 July 2004); *Petrobart Ltd. v. Kyrgyz Republic*, SCC Case No. 126/2003, Award (29 March 2005); *Eureko B.V. v. Republic of Poland*, Partial Award (19 August 2005); *Iurii Bogdanov and others v. Republic of Moldova*, SCC, Award (22 September 2005); *Saluka Investments B.V. (The Netherlands) v. The Czech Republic*, UNCITRAL, Partial Award (17 March 2006); *Eastern Sugar B.V. v. Czech Republic*, SCC Case No. 088/2004, Partial Award (27 March 2007); *BG Group plc v. Republic of Argentina*, UNCITRAL, Final Award (24 December 2007); *National Grid plc v. Argentine Republic*, UNCITRAL, Award (3 November 2008); *Walter Bau A.G. v. Kingdom of Thailand*, UNCITRAL, Award (1 July 2009).

denied such claims (also as of January 2010).[124]

Of necessity, the parameters of the fair and equitable treatment standard have been elaborated in the context of particular fact situations in many ICSID and non-ICSID decisions and awards. The tribunal in *Lemire v. Ukraine* summarized the standard as requiring "an action or omission by the State which violates a certain threshold of propriety, causing harm to the investor, and with a causal link between action or omission and harm".[125] In the words of that tribunal, this threshold of propriety is to be defined on a case-by-case basis, against the background of factors such as:

"– whether the State has failed to offer a stable and predictable legal framework;

– whether the State made specific representations to the investor;

– whether due process has been denied to the investor;

– whether there is an absence of transparency in the legal procedure or in the actions of the State;

– whether there has been harassment, coercion, abuse of power or other bad faith conduct by the host State; [and]

– whether any of the actions of the State can be labeled as arbitrary, discriminatory or inconsistent".[126]

---

124 *Ronald S. Lauder v. Czech Republic*, UNCITRAL, Final Award (3 September 2001); *GAMI Investments Inc. v. Government of the United Mexican States*, UNCITRAL, Final Award (15 November 2004); *Methanex Corporation v. United States of America*, UNCITRAL, Final Award of the Tribunal on Jurisdiction and Merits (3 August 2005); *International Thunderbird Gaming Corporation v. United Mexican States*, UNCITRAL, Arbitral Award (26 January 2006); *United Parcel Service of America Inc. v. Government of Canada*, UNCITRAL, Award on the Merits (24 May 2007); *Glamis Gold, Ltd. v. United States of America*, UNCITRAL, Award (8 June 2009).

125 *Joseph Charles Lemire v. Ukraine*, ICSID Case No. ARB/06/18, Decision on Jurisdiction and Liability (14 January 2010), para. 284. Jan Paulsson acted as arbitrator in the case.

126 *Id.*

Equally, however, according to the *Lemire v. Ukraine* tribunal, tribunals should not perform this exercise in the abstract and only in consideration of the investor's rights. Tribunals should also consider the following countervailing factors:

"– the State's sovereign right to pass legislation and to adopt decisions for the protection of its public interests, especially if they do not provoke a disproportionate impact on foreign investors;

– the legitimate expectations of the investor, at the time he made his investment;

– the investor's duty to perform an investigation before effecting the investment; [and]

– the investor's conduct in the host country".[127]

The evaluation of these various factors can be illustrated (not exhaustively) by reference to a few well-known cases:

– In *Metalclad v. Mexico*, the tribunal held that Mexico violated the fair and equitable standard by failing to ensure a transparent and predictable framework for the investor's landfill project;[128]

– In *CME v. Czech Republic*, the tribunal held that the Czech Republic had breached the fair and equitable treatment standard by failing to provide a predictable framework for the claimant's investment in a television services company, contrary to the claimant's legitimate expectations and reliance on the State's earlier commitments;[129]

---

127 *Id.* at para. 285.

128 *Metalclad Corporation v. United Mexican States*, ICSID Case No. ARB (AF)/97/1, Award (30 August 2000); *see also United Mexican States v. Metalclad Corporation*, Supreme Court of British Columbia (2001 BCSC 664) (partially setting aside the award).

129 *CME v. Czech Republic* (Partial Award), *supra* note 123, at para. 611. (Note, however, that a different tribunal in a related arbitration found, after examining the same facts, that the State had not breached the fair and equitable treatment standard even though it too held that under the fair and equitable treatment standard a State is required to maintain a predictable

- In *Tecmed v. Mexico,* the tribunal held that Mexico breached the fair and equitable treatment standard in the Spain–Mexico BIT by failing to renew an investor's permit for a landfill site and engaging in a course of conduct prejudicial to the investor;[130]

- In *Saluka v. Czech Republic,* the tribunal held that the Czech Republic breached the fair and equitable treatment standard of the Netherlands–Czech Republic BIT in according differential treatment to domestically owned banks without a reasonable justification and acting with a lack of even-handedness, consistency and transparency;[131] and

- In *LG&E v. Argentina,* the tribunal found that Argentina breached the fair and equitable treatment provision in the US–Argentina BIT in dismantling the legal framework that attracted the claimant's investment in Argentina's gas-distribution market.[132]

In sum, the contours of the fair and equitable treatment standard vary from case to case, as it remains "a concept that depends on the interpretation of specific facts for its content".[133] The fair and equitable treatment standard has acquired much prominence in investment arbitrations because, in the words of the tribunal in *PSEG v. Republic of Turkey,* "it clearly does allow for justice to be done in the absence of the more traditional breaches of international law standards".[134]

---

investment framework. *Lauder v. Czech Republic* (Final Award), *supra* note 124, at paras. 289-304).

130 *Técnicas Medioambientales Tecmed, S.A. v. The United Mexican States,* ICSID Case No. ARB (AF)/00/2, Award (29 May 2003).

131 *Saluka v. Czech Republic* (Partial Award), *supra* note 123. Freshfields was counsel to the claimant.

132 *LG&E Energy Corp. and others v. Argentine Republic,* ICSID Case No. ARB/02/1, Decision on Liability (3 October 2006).

133 *Biwater Gauff v. Tanzania* (Award), *supra* note 100, at para. 593 (quoting P. Mulchinski, *Multinational Enterprises and The Law* (Oxford: Oxford University Press, 1995)). Freshfields was counsel to the respondent.

134 *PSEG Global Inc. and Konya Ilgin Elektrik Üretim ve Ticaret Limited Sirketi v. Republic of Turkey,* ICSID Case No. ARB/02/5, Award (19 January 2007), para. 239.

Full protection and security

As with "fair and equitable treatment", it is difficult to give an exact meaning to the concept of "full protection and security" in the abstract. Indeed, these two concepts are often linked, as for example in Article 2(2) of the Model UK BIT (Annex 5):

> "Investments of nationals or companies of each Contracting Party shall at all times be accorded fair and equitable treatment and shall enjoy full protection and security in the territory of the other Contracting Party."

As of January 2010, full protection and security claims had been advanced in 36 decided ICSID cases. In 30 percent of these cases (11 out of 36), the tribunals upheld full protection and security claims in favor of claimants.[135]

In three cases, ICSID tribunals found breaches of the full protection and security obligation in situations where the host State failed to take reasonably expected protective measures to prevent the physical destruction of the investor's property, in particular, measures that fell within the normal exercise of governmental functions.[136] For example, in *AAPL v. Sri Lanka*, mentioned above as the first ICSID BIT award, Sri Lankan security forces destroyed the investor's shrimp farm and killed more than 20 of its employees in efforts to try to curb Tamil insurgents. Applying a standard of due diligence, the tribunal held that Sri Lanka had violated its obligation of full protection and security by not taking all possible measures to prevent the killings and destruction of investment property.[137]

Although this standard historically has been discussed in situations of physical protection for real and tangible property, some tribunals have extended its coverage to other circumstances such as legal security.[138] In *Azurix v. Argentina*, for example, the tribunal noted that full protection and security is not just a matter of physical security, as "the stability afforded by a secure investment environment is

---

135 *See* Table II.B in Annex 10.
136 *AAPL v. Sri Lanka* (Award), *supra* note 68; *American Manufacturing & Trading v. Zaire* (Award), *supra* note 113; *Wena Hotels Ltd. v. Arab Republic of Egypt*, ICSID Case No. ARB/98/4, Award (8 December 2000).
137 *See AAPL v. Sri Lanka* (Award), *supra* note 68.
138 *See* Table II.B in Annex 10.

as important from an investor's point of view" and "when the terms 'protection and security' are qualified by 'full' and no other adjective or explanation, they extend, in their ordinary meaning, the content of this standard beyond physical security".[139] In *Siemens v. Argentina*, the tribunal explained that: "[a]s a general matter and based on the definition of investment, which includes tangible and intangible assets, the Tribunal considers that the obligation to provide full protection and security is wider than 'physical' protection and security".[140] In *Biwater v. Tanzania*, the tribunal stated that "[i]t would in the Arbitral Tribunal's view be unduly artificial to confine the notion of 'full security' only to one aspect of security, particularly in the light of the use of this term in a BIT, directed at the protection of commercial and financial investments".[141] In contrast, several ICSID[142] and non-ICSID tribunals[143] have held that the full protection and security standard has a more limited scope and "is not meant to cover just any kind of impairment of an investor's investment, but to protect more specifically the physical integrity of an investment against interference by use of force".[144]

No arbitrary or discriminatory measures impairing the investment

Treaties usually impose a legal obligation on the host State not to impair the management or operation of the investment by "arbitrary or discriminatory measures" (sometimes referred to as the "non-impairment standard"). For example, the Sweden–Estonia Treaty provides:

---

139 *Azurix Corp. v. Argentine Republic*, ICSID Case No. ARB/01/12, Award (14 July 2006), para. 408; *see also Compañía de Aguas del Aconquija S.A. and Vivendi Universal v. Argentine Republic*, ICSID Case No. ARB/97/3, Award (20 August 2007) (***Vivendi II (Award)***).

140 *Siemens A.G. v. Argentine Republic*, ICSID Case No. ARB/02/8, Award (6 February 2007), para. 303.

141 *Biwater Gauff v. Tanzania* (Award), *supra* note 100, at para. 729; *see also National Grid v. Argentina* (Award), *supra* note 123.

142 *PSEG Global v. Turkey* (Award), *supra* note 134; *Rumeli Telekom A.S. and Telsim Mobil Telekomikasyon Hizmetleri A.S. v. Republic of Kazakhstan*, ICSID Case No. ARB/05/16, Award (29 July 2008).

143 *Saluka v. Czech Republic* (Partial Award), *supra* note 123; *BG Group v. Argentina* (Final Award), *supra* note 123; *Eastern Sugar v. Czech Republic* (Partial Award), *supra* note 123.

144 *Saluka v. Czech Republic* (Partial Award), *supra* note 123, at para. 484.

"Each Contracting Party [...] shall not impair the management, maintenance, use, enjoyment or disposal [of the investments by investors of the other Contracting Party] as well as the acquisition of goods and services and the sale of their production, through unreasonable or discriminatory measures."[145]

Again, the notion of what constitutes "arbitrary" or "discriminatory" measures is not defined in the treaties. Tribunals often look to the test of arbitrariness the International Court of Justice formulated in the context of investment protection in the well-known *ELSI* case. The Chamber of the Court explained:

"Arbitrariness is not so much something opposed to a rule of law, as something opposed to the rule of law. [...] It is a wilful disregard of due process of law, an act which shocks, or at least surprises, a sense of juridical propriety."[146]

As for discrimination, in general a measure is discriminatory if it results in treatment of an investor different than that accorded to other investors in a similar or comparable situation.[147]

As might be expected, whether a measure is arbitrary, discriminatory or unreasonable is a question of fact, to be determined in light of the circumstances of each case. As of January 2010, non-impairment claims had been brought in 21 ICSID cases resulting in awards on the merits. Claims for an alleged breach of the non-impairment standard were successful in 23 percent of the cases (5 out of 21).[148]

---

145 Agreement Between the Government of the Kingdom of Sweden and the Government of the Republic of Estonia on the Promotion and Reciprocal Protection of Investments, <www. unctad.org/sections/dite/iia/docs/bits/sweeden_estonia.pdf>, 31 March 1992, Art. 2(2).

146 *Case Concerning Elettronica Sicula S.p.A. (ELSI) (United States v. Italy)*, Judgment (20 July 1989), 1989 *ICJ Reports* 15, para. 128.

147 *Antoine Goetz and others v. Republic of Burundi*, ICSID Case No. ARB/95/3, Award (10 February 1999).

148 *Azurix v. Argentina* (Award), *supra* note 139; *LG&E v. Argentina* (Decision on Liability), *supra* note 132; *Siemens v. Argentina* (Award), *supra* note 140; *Biwater Gauff v. Tanzania* (Award), *supra* note 100; *Waguih Elie George Siag and Clorinda Vecchi v. Arab Republic of Egypt*, ICSID Case No. ARB/05/15, Award (June 1, 2009).

In one such case, *Siag v. Egypt*, the claimants invested in two Egyptian corporations, Touristic Investments and Hotels Management Company (**SIAG**) and Siag Taba Company (**Siag**), for the purpose of developing an oceanfront tourist resort in the Gulf of Aqaba on the Red Sea.[149] After the claimants acquired oceanfront land from the Egyptian ministry of tourism, Egypt took a number of measures that the tribunal found to be unreasonable, including: (a) expropriating claimants' investment in May 1996 on the ground that SIAG did not meet its construction deadlines, which had not yet arrived; (b) seizing control of claimants' investment in June 1996 on the basis of a ministerial resolution that claimants had already sought to enjoin; (c) retaking claimants' investment in August 1996 even though the ministerial resolution had been enjoined by the Cairo Administrative Court; and (d) failing to comply with several court orders invalidating the ministerial resolution. The tribunal held that Egypt breached the arbitrary and discriminatory article of the Italy–Egypt BIT, noting that any one of Egypt's abovementioned actions "would constitute unreasonable behaviour; viewed *in toto* the matter is beyond question".[150]

National and "most favored nation" treatment

Investment treaties typically describe the protections required for the investment in relation to treatment accorded other investments, in two general categories. Under the "national treatment" standard, the host State must treat foreign investments no less favorably than investments of its own nationals and companies. Under the "most favored nation" (**MFN**) standard, the host State may not treat one foreigner's investment less favorably than that of an investor from another foreign country. The two standards, which are usually combined, are illustrated in the MFN clause (Article 2(1)) of the US–Argentina BIT (Annex 6):

> "1. Each Party shall permit and treat investment, and activities associated therewith, on a basis no less favorable than that accorded in like situations to investment or associated activities of its own nationals or companies, or of nationals or companies of any third country, whichever

---

149 *Siag v. Egypt* (Award), *supra* note 148.
150 *Id.* at para. 459.

is the more favorable, subject to the right of each Party to make or maintain exceptions falling within one of the sectors or matters listed in the Protocol to this Treaty. Each Party agrees to notify the other Party before or on the date of entry into force of this Treaty of all such laws and regulations of which it is aware concerning the sectors or matters listed in the Protocol. Moreover, each Party agrees to notify the other of any future exception with respect to the sectors or matters listed in the Protocol, and to limit such exceptions to a minimum. Any future exception by either Party shall not apply to investment existing in that sector or matter at the time the exception becomes effective. The treatment accorded pursuant to any exceptions shall, unless specified otherwise in the Protocol, be not less favorable than that accorded in like situations to investments and associated activities of nationals or companies of any third country."

Article 7 of the Model UK BIT (Annex 5) reflects the preference of the UK, among other countries, to except from the treaty protections of national treatment and MFN treatment any benefits under a "customs union or similar international agreement" and under "any international agreement or arrangement relating wholly or mainly to taxation or any domestic legislation relating wholly or mainly to taxation".

As of January 2010, claimants had advanced national treatment claims in ten decided ICSID cases.[151] National treatment claims were upheld in four cases, all of which were NAFTA arbitrations under the ICSID Additional Facility Arbitration Rules.[152]

---

151 *See* Table II.D in Annex 10.

152 *Marvin Roy Feldman Karpa v. United Mexican States,* ICSID Case No. ARB(AF)/99/1, Award (16 December 2002); *Archer Daniels Midland Company and Tate & Lyle Ingredients Americas, Inc. v. United Mexican States,* ICSID Case No. ARB(AF)/04/5, Award (21 November 2007); *Corn Products International, Inc. v. United Mexican States,* ICSID Case No. ARB(AF)/04/1, Decision on Responsibility (15 January 2008); *Cargill, Inc. v. United Mexican States,* ICSID Case No. ARB(AF)05/2, Award (18 September 2009). In one other NAFTA case, *S.D. Myers Inc. v. Canada,* a non-ICSID tribunal held that the Government of Canada breached its national

ICSID tribunals have looked to practice under NAFTA Article 1102 when faced with national treatment claims under BITs.[153] The text of Article 1102, the NAFTA national treatment provision, requires that an investor, or an investment of an investor, be accorded "(1) treatment that is (2) 'no less favorable' than that accorded to a domestic investor or investment (3) 'in like circumstances' with the covered investor or investment".[154] Article 1102 encompasses both *de jure* discrimination (measures that on their face treat entities differently) and *de facto* discrimination (measures that are neutral on their face but result in differential treatment).

By way of example, in *Feldman v. Mexico*, Feldman, an individual US national, claimed that Mexico's application of certain tax laws to the export of tobacco products violated Mexico's obligations under the NAFTA.[155] Feldman alleged that Mexico breached its obligations under Article 1102 in discriminating against his company by refusing to rebate excise taxes on cigarettes the company exported. The tribunal held that his company was "treated in a less favorable manner than domestically owned resellers/exporters of cigarettes",[156] resulting in *de facto* discrimination inconsistent with Mexico's obligations under Article 1102.

Most favored nation treatment is a relative standard, and so by definition its scope varies according to the circumstances of each case. Foreign investors traditionally relied on the MFN clause in the context of substantive rights.[157] For example, if the host State provides tax concessions to Italian investors in

---

treatment obligations in Article 1102 in respect of measures banning the commercial export of PCB waste for disposal. *S.D. Myers v. Canada* (First Partial Award), *supra* note 123.

153 *See, e.g., Bayindir v. Pakistan* (Award), *supra* note 119; *Champion Trading Company and Ameritrade International, Inc. v. Arab Republic of Egypt*, ICSID Case No. ARB/02/9, Award (October 27, 2006); A. Bjorklund, "The National Treatment Obligation", in *Arbitration Under International Investment Agreements, supra* note 119, at 411, 416 (observing that "NAFTA Chapter 11 awards have played a leading role in developing the national treatment jurisprudence").

154 M. Kinnear, A. Bjorklund & J. Hannaford, *Investment Disputes Under NAFTA: An Annotated Guide to NAFTA Chapter 11* (The Netherlands: Kluwer Law International, 2009), 20-1102.

155 *Feldman v. Mexico* (Award), *supra* note 152.

156 *Id.* at para. 173.

157 *See, e.g., MTD Equity Sdn. Bhd. and MTD Chile S.A. v. Republic of Chile*, ICSID Case No. ARB/01/7, Award (25 May 2004); *Bayindir v. Pakistan* (Award), *supra* note 119.

the oil industry but not to UK investors, a UK investor could rely on an MFN clause in an applicable BIT to claim the same treatment or compensation for loss suffered as a result of being denied the same treatment.

The question of MFN treatment beyond substantive rights has arisen recently in numerous ICSID cases, particularly with respect to jurisdiction.[158] As of January 2010, no fewer than 11 ICSID tribunals had considered the question, with differing results depending on the particular terms of the treaty and the nature of the MFN treatment sought.[159]

Maffezini v. Spain was the first ICSID treaty case to consider the question of MFN treatment for procedural rights, specifically concerning the dispute resolution mechanism between host States and investors.[160] In *Maffezini*, an Argentine investor filed an ICSID claim against Spain, although he had not previously submitted the dispute to the Spanish courts as required by the Argentina–Spain BIT. Maffezini argued, however, that he could by-pass this precondition to ICSID arbitration by invoking the MFN clause of the Argentina–Spain BIT to claim an equally favorable benefit under Spain's BIT with Chile, which does not require investors to seek prior recourse in local courts. The ICSID tribunal agreed, holding that, on the basis of the MFN clause in the Argentina–Spain treaty, the Argentine investor could rely on the less stringent procedural provisions of the Chile–Spain BIT.

Since *Maffezini*, tribunals in five ICSID cases have held similarly that an MFN clause can extend to dispute resolution provisions, specifically to avoid the requirement of submission of a dispute to local courts during an 18-month waiting period.[161] As explained by the tribunal in *Gas Natural v. Argentina*,

---

158 *See, e.g.*, A. Cohen Smutny & L. Steven, "The MFN Clause: What are its Limits?", in *Arbitration Under International Investment Agreements, supra* note 119, at 351.

159 *See* Table II.D in Annex 10.

160 *Maffezini v. Spain* (Decision of the Tribunal on Objections to Jurisdiction), *supra* note 113.

161 *Siemens v. Argentina* (Decision on Jurisdiction), *supra* note 81; *Camuzzi v. Argentina* (Decision on Objections to Jurisdiction), *supra* note 83; *Gas Natural v. Argentina* (Decision of the Tribunal on Preliminary Questions on Jurisdiction), *supra* note 83; *Suez, Sociedad General de Aguas de Barcelona S.A., and InterAguas Servicios Integrales del Agua S.A. v. Argentine Republic*, ICSID Case No. ARB/03/17, Decision on Jurisdiction (16 May 2006) (**Suez I (Decision on Jurisdiction)**); *Suez, Sociedad General de Aguas de Barcelona, S.A. and Vivendi Universal,*

"[u]nless it appears clearly that the state parties to a BIT or the parties to a particular investment agreement settled on a different method for resolution of disputes that may arise, most-favored-nation provisions in BITs should be understood to be applicable to dispute settlement".[162] In contrast, in one other case, an ICSID tribunal refused to allow a claimant to use an MFN clause to avoid such an 18-month waiting period.[163]

In five other cases, which did not involve waiting periods, ICSID tribunals have refused to allow claimants to use MFN clauses to obtain the benefits of dispute resolution provisions in other BITs. In those cases, the tribunals were faced with attempts by claimants to use MFN clauses to enlarge subject-matter jurisdiction, to modify the dispute resolution mechanism, and to expand the scope of temporal jurisdiction.[164] In specific, these included attempts by claimants: (a) to substitute ICSID arbitration for *ad hoc* arbitration limited to the amount of compensation arising from an expropriation;[165] (b) to expand the scope of permitted ICSID claims beyond expropriation claims;[166] (c) to substitute ICSID arbitration for local court litigation for contractual disputes;[167] (d) to circumvent

---

S.A. v. Argentine Republic, ICSID Case No. ARB/03/19, Decision on Jurisdiction (3 August 2006) (***Suez II (Decision on Jurisdiction)***). *See also National Grid plc v. Argentine Republic*, UNCITRAL, Decision on Jurisdiction (20 June 2006).

162 *Gas Natural v. Argentina* (Decision of the Tribunal on Preliminary Questions on Jurisdiction), *supra* note 83, at para. 49. Freshfields was counsel to the claimant.

163 *Wintershall Aktiengesellschaft v. Argentine Republic*, ICSID Case No. ARB/04/14, Award (8 December 2008).

164 Non-ICSID tribunals faced with attempts by claimants to invoke MFN clauses in similar circumstances have, with one exception, refused to extend MFN clauses to dispute resolution provisions. *See, e.g., Berschader v. Russian Federation*, SCC Case No. 080/2004, Award (21 April 2006); *RosInvestCo UK Ltd. v. Russian Federation*, SCC Case No. Arb. V079/2005, Award on Jurisdiction (October 2007); *Renta 4 S.V.S.A et al. v. Russian Federation*, SCC No. 24/2007, Award on Preliminary Objections (20 March 2009); *Austrian Airlines v. Slovak Republic*, UNCITRAL, Final Award (20 October 2009).

165 *Plama Consortium Limited v. Bulgaria*, ICSID Case No. ARB/03/24, Decision on Jurisdiction (8 February 2005).

166 *Telenor Mobile Communications A.S. v. Republic of Hungary*, ICSID Case No. ARB/04/15, Award (13 September 2006).

167 *Salini Costruttori S.p.A. and Italstrade S.p.A. v. Jordan*, ICSID Case No. ARB/02/13, Decision on Jurisdiction (9 November 2004).

requirements that claims be based only on events after entry into force of the treaty and be filed within three years;[168] and (e) to override a requirement limiting ICSID arbitration to expropriation disputes, leaving other disputes subject to the State parties' agreement.[169]

Against this background, a foreign investor considering a claim under a BIT containing an MFN clause should systematically review other treaties concluded by the relevant host State not only for more beneficial substantive protections but also for more possibly beneficial dispute resolution procedures. This is particularly the case for any foreign investor facing potential jurisdictional hurdles under the BIT (or BITs) underlying its claim. Equally, legal advisers to States must be familiar with the variations in the MFN landscape created by the States' universe of investment treaties.

Free transfer of funds related to investments

Many treaties provide that the host State must "permit all transfers related to an investment to be made freely and without delay into and out of its territory".[170] Foreign investors are entitled to compensation if they are affected by currency control regulations or other acts of the host State that effectively freeze investor funds maintained in the host State.

Free transfer provisions are usually broad in scope and are not restricted to certain types of funds, but instead cover any amounts derived from or associated with an investment. These would include profits, dividends, interest, capital gains, royalty payments, management, technical assistance or other fees, and returns in kind. Some BITs reserve the possibility for the host State to restrict transfers of funds during periods of limited foreign exchange availability, or due to balance of payments problems.

As of January 2010, free transfer of funds claims had been advanced in seven ICSID cases, resulting in four awards on the merits – all against the investors on

---

168 *Tecmed v. Mexico* (Award), *supra* note 130.

169 *Tza Yap Shum v. Republic of Peru,* ICSID Case No. ARB/07/6, Decision on Jurisdiction and Competence (19 June 2009).

170 *See, e.g.,* US–Argentina BIT, *supra* note 86 and Annex 6, Art. V(1).

the free transfer of funds claims.[171] For instance, in *Biwater Gauff v. Tanzania*, Biwater Gauff claimed that Tanzania breached its obligation under the relevant BIT provision (Article 6) by preventing the "unrestricted transfer" of its investment and returns. The tribunal found that Article 6 was "not a guarantee that investors will have funds to transfer" but that "if investors have funds, they will be able to transfer them, subject to the conditions stated in Article 6".[172]

No expropriation without compensation

A core protection offered by BITs is the host State's obligation to compensate foreign investors – promptly, adequately and effectively – in the event of expropriation. Indeed, foreign investors regularly claim under expropriation provisions in ICSID investment treaty and national investment law arbitrations, almost always in cases of alleged regulatory or indirect expropriation.

The notion of expropriation is expansive in nature. It is a well-accepted principle of public international law that expropriation may result from either: (a) a direct and deliberate formal act of taking, such as an outright nationalization; or (b) an indirect taking (for example, cancellation of a license) that substantially deprives the investor of the use or enjoyment of its investment, even if the legal and beneficial title of the asset remains with the investor. An expropriation may be immediate. An expropriation may be "creeping" or "constructive", unfolding through one or a series of acts, the cumulative effect of which is loss of the economic value of their investment. Government measures may amount to expropriation regardless of their form and purpose. Government measures such as tax increases, environmental regulations or customs restrictions may, in certain circumstances, amount to an expropriation.

International law does not prohibit expropriation as such. Rather, it requires that expropriation be for a public purpose and be non-discriminatory, and that the State pay fair compensation to the investors. The provisions setting out the

---

171 *Genin and others v. Estonia,* ICSID Case No. ARB/99/2, Award (25 June 2001); *Metalpar S.A. and Buen Aire S.A. v. Argentine Republic,* ICSID Case No. ARB/03/5, Award (6 June 2008); *Biwater Gauff v. Tanzania* (Award), *supra* note 100; *Continental Casualty Company v. Argentina,* ICSID Case No. ARB/03/9, Award (5 September 2008). *See* Table II.E in Annex 10.

172 *Biwater Gauff v. Tanzania* (Award), *supra* note 100, at para. 735.

acceptable parameters for expropriation vary from BIT to BIT. The expropriation clause in the US–Argentina BIT (Annex 6, Article 4) is comparatively detailed:

"1. Investments shall not be expropriated or nationalized either directly or indirectly through measures tantamount to expropriation or nationalization ('expropriation') except for a public purpose; in a non-discriminatory manner; upon payment of prompt, adequate and effective compensation; and in accordance with due process of law and the general principles of treatment provided for in Article II (2). Compensation shall be equivalent to the fair market value of the expropriated investment immediately before the expropriatory action was taken or became known, whichever is earlier; be paid without delay; include interest at a commercially reasonable rate from the date of expropriation; be fully realizable; and be freely transferable at the prevailing market rate of exchange on the date of expropriation.

2. A national or company of either Party that asserts that all or part of its investment has been expropriated shall have a right to prompt review by the appropriate judicial or administrative authorities of the other Party to determine whether any such expropriation has occurred and, if so, whether such expropriation, and any compensation therefore, conforms to the provisions of this Treaty and the principles of international law.

3. Nationals or companies of either Party whose investments suffer losses in the territory of the other Party owing to war or other armed conflict, revolution, state of national emergency, insurrection, civil disturbance or other similar events shall be accorded treatment by such other Party no less favorable than that accorded to its own nationals or companies or to nationals or companies of any third country, whichever is the more favorable treatment, as regards any measures it adopts in relation to such losses."

Focusing on examples of compensation standards, Article 5(1) of the UK–Russia BIT requires that compensation amount to "the real value of the investment expropriated immediately before the expropriation or before the impending expropriation became public knowledge, whichever is the earlier [to be paid] within two months of the date of expropriation, after which interest at a normal commercial rate shall accrue until the date of payment".[173] The US–Kazakhstan BIT speaks, at Article III(1), of "compensation [...] equivalent to the fair market value of the expropriated investment" with similar provisions as to interest, although without a grace period for payment.[174]

These substantive BIT protections against uncompensated expropriation are not new. They reflect customary international law on the protection of what historically was referred to as alien property, including those standards set out in treaties of friendship, commerce and navigation of an earlier vintage. What is new in BITs is the opportunity for private investors to proceed directly – without espousal of their claims as a matter of "diplomatic protection" by their home governments – against the expropriating State in an international forum such as ICSID to seek compensation.

As of January 2010, expropriation claims had been advanced in 53 decided ICSID investment treaty cases. Tribunals upheld expropriation claims in 28 percent of these cases (15 out of 53), as listed in Table II.F in Annex 10.[175] Although it is beyond the scope of this Guide to canvas the 53 awards, examples of awards involving direct and indirect expropriation claims follow.

---

173 UK–Russia BIT, *supra* note 85.

174 US–Kazakhstan BIT, *supra* note 72.

175 As of January 2010, in non-ICSID investment treaty cases, there were at least three cases where tribunals upheld expropriation claims. See *Swembalt AB, Sweden v. Latvia*, UNCITRAL, Award (23 October 2000); *CME v. Czech Republic* (Partial Award), *supra* note 123; *Eureko v. Poland* (Partial Award), *supra* note 123. There are at least 14 cases where non-ICSID tribunals denied expropriation claims (as of January 2010). See *S.D. Myers v. Canada* (First Partial Award), *supra* note 123; *Lauder v. Czech Republic* (Final Award), *supra* note 124; *GAMI Investments v. Mexico* (Final Award), *supra* note 124; *Petrobart v. Kyrgyz Republic* (Award), *supra* note 123; *Methanex v. United States* (Award), *supra* note 124; *Bogdanov v. Moldova* (Award), *supra* note 123; *International Thunderbird v. Mexico* (Arbitral Award), *supra* note 124; *EnCana Corporation v. Republic of Ecuador*, LCIA Case No. UN3481, UNCITRAL, Award (3 February 2006); *Glamis Gold v. United States* (Award), *supra* note 124; *Saluka v. Czech Republic* (Partial Award), *supra* note 123; *Eastern Sugar v. Czech Republic* (Partial Award), *supra* note 123; *BG Group v. Argentina*, (Final Award), *supra* note 123; *National Grid v. Argentina* (Award), *supra* note 123; *Walter Bau v. Thailand* (Award), *supra* note 123.

In *Funnekoter v. Zimbabwe,* one of the few ICSID cases to date involving a direct expropriation, Dutch nationals lost their investments in large commercial farms in Zimbabwe under a government land acquisition program and by actual invasions.[176] A later amendment to the Zimbabwe constitution formalized the expropriation of the claimants' farms. The claimants received no compensation. The ICSID tribunal held that Zimbabwe expropriated the claimants' property in violation of the Netherlands–Zimbabwe BIT by failing to pay just compensation.[177]

ADC v. Hungary is an example of an award involving the far more common claims of indirect expropriation.[178] The dispute concerned Hungary's alleged unlawful expropriation of ADC's investment in the Budapest–Ferihegy International Airport, Hungary's principal airport for domestic and international flights. Following a public tender process, ADC was awarded contracts to renovate an existing terminal, construct a new terminal, and participate in the operation of both terminals. Several years into the project, the government transformed the legal and regulatory regime applicable to the airport through various legislative amendments and a ministerial decree. ADC was instructed to vacate its offices and informed that its contracts were voided, after which ADC could no longer operate the terminals or collect revenues. The tribunal held that the expropriation of ADC's interest was unlawful because the taking was not in the public interest, did not comply with due process, was discriminatory, and was not accompanied by just compensation.[179]

As indicated by the *ADC* case, commentators have identified a number of key principles applied by ICSID tribunals in assessing whether or not an indirect expropriation has occurred. For example:

> "First, the form of the measure is not determinative nor is the intent of the state. Second, the claimant must establish that the measure in

---

176 *Bernardus Henricus Funnekotter and others v. Republic of Zimbabwe,* ICSID Case No. ARB/05/6, Award (22 April 2009).

177 *Id.* at para. 107.

178 *ADC Affiliate Limited and ADC & ADMC Management Limited v. Republic of Hungary,* ICSID Case No. ARB/03/16, Award (2 October 2006).

179 *Id.* at para. 476.

question results in a substantial deprivation. Third, the character of the government measures in question must be taken into account in determining whether a police powers exception applies. Fourth, the investment-backed legitimate expectations of the investor are relevant in assessing whether there has been an indirect expropriation. Finally, the indirect expropriation analysis is context and fact specific."[180]

In the majority of the 53 expropriation claims advanced to date in ICSID BIT cases, claimants alleged both indirect expropriation and violation of the fair and equitable treatment standard. In such cases, any line separating the breach of the fair and equitable treatment standard from an indirect expropriation is oftentimes thin. The reluctance of many ICSID tribunals to find States liable for expropriation by indirect measures has contributed to the growing prominence of the fair and equitable treatment standard, which is often the claim that investors succeed with in lieu of indirect expropriation.[181]

Observance of specific undertakings

Treaties often also contain provisions obligating the host State to observe, or guarantee the observance of, specific undertakings towards investors. An example of such a clause appears in Article 2(2) of the Model UK BIT (Annex 5):

"Each Contracting Party shall observe any obligation it may have entered into with regard to investments of nationals or companies of the other Contracting Party."

Such clauses are sometimes referred to as "umbrella clauses", the idea being that they are meant to cover all government commitments with respect to investments flowing between the two States.

---

180 A. Newcombe & L. Paradell, *Law and Practice of Investment Treaties: Standards of Treatment* (The Netherlands: Kluwer Law International, 2009), 341.

181 L. Reed & D. Bray, "Fair and Equitable Treatment: Fairly and Equitably Applied in Lieu of Unlawful Indirect Expropriation?", in *Contemporary Issues in International Arbitration and Mediation*, ed. A.W. Rovine (Leiden: Martinus Nijhoff Publishers, 2008), 13. *See* Table I in Annex 10.

Umbrella clauses are the focus of much discussion in ICSID decisions and awards. An immediate challenge is the relationship between such an umbrella clause and any relevant investor-State contract.[182]

The ICSID tribunal in *SGS v. Pakistan* was the first to rule on the legal effect of such a clause in a jurisdictional context, in 2003.[183] SGS brought a claim against Pakistan for alleged breaches of both a contract for customs-related pre-shipment inspection services and the Switzerland–Pakistan BIT. Pakistan challenged the tribunal's jurisdiction of SGS's claims for breach of the services contract on the ground, among others, that such claims were subject exclusively to the (non-ICSID) arbitration clause in the contract. In response (again on one among many grounds), SGS relied on Article 11 of the BIT, which provided:

"Either Contracting Party shall constantly guarantee the observance of the commitments it has entered into with respect to the investments of the investors of the other Contracting Party."

SGS argued that Article 11 was a "clause that takes breaches of contract under municipal law and elevates them immediately to the level of a breach of an international treaty",[184] thereby automatically giving the tribunal jurisdiction under the BIT of all of SGS's claims for breach of the services contract.

Applying the governing rules of treaty interpretation, and thus examining the language of Article 11 with regard to the object and purpose of the BIT, the tribunal rejected SGS's characterization of Article 11. The tribunal based its Article 11 decision in part on burden of proof:

"Considering the widely accepted principle with which we started, namely, that under general international law, a violation of a contract entered into by a State with an investor of another State, is not, by itself, a violation of international law, and considering further that the legal consequences

---

182 *See, e.g.*, ed. I. Shihata, *The World Bank in a Changing World: Selected Essays and Lectures* (The Netherlands: Martinus Nijhoff, 1995).

183 *SGS Société Générale de Surveillance S.A. v. Islamic Republic of Pakistan*, ICSID Case No. ARB/01/13, Decision of the Tribunal on Objections to Jurisdiction (6 August 2003). Freshfields was counsel to the respondent.

184 *Id.* at para. 163.

that the Claimant would have us attribute to Article 11 of the BIT are so far-reaching in scope, and so automatic and unqualified and sweeping in their operation, so burdensome in their potential impact upon a Contracting Party, we believe that clear and convincing evidence must be adduced by the Claimant. Clear and convincing evidence of what? Clear and convincing evidence that such was indeed the shared intent of the Contracting Parties to the Swiss–Pakistan Investment Protection Treaty in incorporating Article 11 in the BIT. We do not find such evidence in the text itself of Article 11. We have not been pointed to any other evidence of the putative common intent of the Contracting Parties by the Claimant."[185]

The tribunal noted that SGS's reading of Article 11 would tend to make substantive BIT standards (such as those for expropriation and fair and equitable treatment) superfluous, because an investor would not have to prove a violation of those standards if any simple contract breach met the jurisdictional hurdle for a treaty claim.

Shortly after the *SGS v. Pakistan* decision, in a case involving the same investor and similar operations in the Philippines, another ICSID tribunal took a different approach. In *SGS v. Philippines*, the umbrella clause in the Switzerland–Philippines BIT at issue provided:

"Each Contracting Party shall observe any obligation it has assumed with regard to specific investments in its territory by investors of the other Contracting Party."

Unlike in *SGS v. Pakistan*, the tribunal held that it had jurisdiction under the umbrella clause.[186] However, the tribunal also found that the scope of the obligations in the SGS–Philippines services contract remained subject to the governing law of the contract, and that the BIT could not override the exclusive jurisdiction clause in the contract directing the parties to the Philippine courts to resolve contractual claims.

---

185 *Id.* at para. 167.
186 *SGS Société Générale de Surveillance SA v. Republic of the Philippines*, ICSID Case No. ARB/02/6, Decision of the Tribunal on Objections to Jurisdiction (29 January 2004).

Since the decisions in *SGS v. Pakistan* and *SGS v. Philippines* (and as of January 2010), ICSID tribunals have rendered 28 decisions and awards on umbrella clauses: 17 awards on the merits, ten decisions on jurisdiction, and one annulment decision.[187] In six of the 17 merits awards, claims for an alleged breach of an umbrella clause were successful.[188] However, in one of those cases the umbrella clause holding was subsequently annulled,[189] and in two others the underlying awards were annulled on other grounds.[190]

The umbrella clause decisions have been categorized into four schools of thought or camps by one noted commentator, a framework that was adopted by the *Toto Costruzioni v. Lebanon* tribunal:[191]

> "The first camp adopts an extremely narrow interpretation of umbrella clauses, holding that they are operative only where it is possible to discern a shared intent of the parties that any breach of contract is a breach of the BIT.[192] The second camp seeks to limit umbrella clauses to breaches of contract committed by the host state in the exercise of

---

187 *See* Table II.G in Annex 10.

188 *Fedax N.V. v. Republic of Venezuela*, ICSID Case No. ARB/96/3, Award (9 March 1998); *CMS v. Argentina* (Award), *supra* note 118; *LG&E v. Argentina* (Decision on Liability), *supra* note 132; *Enron Corporation and Ponderosa Assets L.P. v. Argentine Republic*, ICSID Case No. ARB/01/3, Award (22 May 2007); *Sempra Energy International v. Argentine Republic*, ICSID Case No. ARB/02/16, Award (28 September 2007); *Duke Energy Electroquil Partners & Electroquil S.A. v. Republic of Ecuador*, ICSID Case No. ARB/04/19, Award (18 August 2008).

189 *CMS Gas Transmission Company v. Argentine Republic*, ICSID Case No. ARB/01/8, Decision of the *ad hoc* Committee on the Application for Annulment of the Argentine Republic (25 September 2007).

190 *Sempra Energy International v. Argentine Republic*, ICSID Case No. ARB/02/16, Decision on the Argentine Republic's Application for Annulment of the Award (29 June 2010); *Enron Creditors Recovery Corporation and Ponderosa Assets, L.P. v. Argentine Republic*, ICSID Case No. ARB/01/3, Decision on the Application for Annulment of the Argentine Republic (30 July 2010).

191 J. Crawford, "Treaty and Contract in Investment Arbitration", *Arbitration International* 24 (2008): 351-374; *see also Toto Costruzioni Generali S.P.A. v. Republic of Lebanon*, ICSID Case No. ARB/07/12, Decision on Jurisdiction (11 September 2009).

192 *See, e.g., SGS v. Pakistan* (Decision of the Tribunal on Objections to Jurisdiction), *supra* note 183; *Joy Mining v. Egypt* (Award on Jurisdiction), *supra* note 103.

sovereign authority.[193] A third view goes to the other extreme: the effect of umbrella clauses is to internationalise investment contracts, thereby transforming contractual claims into treaty claims directly subject to treaty rules.[194]

Finally there is the view that [...] an umbrella clause is operative and may form the basis for a substantive treaty claim, but that it does not convert a contractual claim into a treaty claim. On the one hand it provides, or at least may provide, a basis for a treaty claim even if the BIT in question contains no generic claims clause;[195] on the other hand, the umbrella clause does not change the proper law of the contract or its legal incidents, including its provisions for dispute settlement."[196]

In light of this divergence of approaches, and in the words of one ICSID tribunal in 2009, "there is no *jurisprudence constante* on the effect of umbrella clauses" and "each particular clause falls to be interpreted and applied according to its precise wording and the context in which it is included in a BIT".[197]

Enforcement of rights under a BIT

In addition to substantive protections, BITs set out a variety of dispute resolution procedures and conditions. Investors and their counsel must review these sections of the applicable BIT or BITs thoroughly and early.

---

193 *Pan American Energy LLC and BP Argentina Exploration Co. v. Argentine Republic*, ICSID Case No. ARB/03/13, Decision on Preliminary Objections (27 July 2006); *El Paso v. Argentina* (Decision on Jurisdiction), *supra* note 83.

194 *Fedax v. Venezuela* (Decision of the Tribunal on Objections to Jurisdiction), *supra* note 93; *Fedax v. Venezuela* (Award), *supra* note 188; *Eureko v. Poland* (Partial Award), *supra* note 123; *Noble Ventures, Inc. v. Romania*, ICSID Case No. ARB/01/11, Award (12 October 2005).

195 *SGS v. Philippines* (Decision of the Tribunal on Objections to Jurisdiction), *supra* note 186; *CMS v. Argentina* (Decision of the *Ad Hoc* Committee on the Application for Annulment of the Argentine Republic), *supra* note 189.

196 Crawford, *supra* note 191, at 366-367 (citations in original).

197 *Bureau Veritas, Inspection, Valuation, Assessment and Control, BIVAC B.V. v. Republic of Paraguay*, ICSID Case No. ARB/07/9, Decision of the Tribunal on Objections to Jurisdiction (29 May 2009), para. 141. Freshfields is counsel to the claimant.

Cooling off period

BITs typically include a negotiation or "cooling off" period before a claim may be brought. The period is usually three or six months from the date the dispute arises or is notified by the investor to the host State. For example, Article 8(1) of the Model UK BIT (Annex 5) provides:

> "Disputes between a national or company of one Contracting Party and the other Contracting Party concerning an obligation of the latter under this Agreement in relation to an investment of the former which have not been amicably settled shall, after a period of three months from written notification of a claim, be submitted to international arbitration if the national or company concerned so wishes."

The practical purpose of the cooling off period is to facilitate settlement out of the public eye before positions become entrenched. This objective theoretically assumes particular importance for a State wanting to protect a pro-investment reputation.

Either as a treaty requirement or as a matter of practice, the investor typically starts the negotiation period by sending a letter – commonly referred to as a "trigger letter" – to the most senior central authorities of the host State (such as the head of state and the minister in charge of foreign investment) notifying them of the existence of a dispute under the relevant BIT.[198] (Notification to a subdivision of a State, such as a provincial governor, may not be sufficient, even if the underlying investment agreement is with the province.) The trigger letter typically provides a basic summary of the background and nature of the dispute and then requests negotiations. If negotiations do not ensue, the invitation may be repeated periodically. Upon expiry of the negotiation period without settlement, the investor is free to institute the arbitration.

The practice of ICSID tribunals in applying such negotiation clauses has been mixed. Most have held that waiting periods, when properly construed, are

---

198 Some BITs require investors to submit a written notification of dispute (e.g., the Model UK BIT, Annex 5). Others do not (e.g., the US–Argentina BIT, Annex 6).

"procedural and directory in nature, rather than jurisdictional and mandatory".[199] Among the factors examined are whether the parties have actually commenced consultations and, if not, whether the host State has indicated a willingness to negotiate. As explained by the tribunal in *Biwater Gauff v. Tanzania*, non-compliance with a cooling off period does not preclude the tribunal from proceeding; if it did, it "would have curious effects", including "forcing the claimant to do nothing until six months have elapsed, even where further negotiations are obviously futile, or settlement obviously impossible for any reason" and "forcing the claimant to recommence an arbitration started too soon".[200]

Other ICSID tribunals have taken the opposite tack.[201] The Belgium–Burundi BIT at issue in *Goetz v. Burundi* required written notification in the event of a dispute and a three-month waiting period following such written notification.[202] Although Goetz had properly notified Burundi of his claim relating to the legality and the legal consequences of the withdrawal of a free zone certificate issued by Burundi, he had not properly notified the government of his claim for reimbursement of taxes, duties and convertible shares. The tribunal held that, consequently, these reimbursement claims could not be decided. Similarly, in *Western NIS Enterprise Fund v. Ukraine*, the tribunal stressed the importance of

---

199 *Biwater Gauff v. Tanzania* (Award), *supra* note 100, at para. 343; *see also SGS v. Pakistan* (Decision of the Tribunal on Objections to Jurisdiction), *supra* note 183; *Ethyl Corporation v. Government of Canada*, UNCITRAL, Award on Jurisdiction (24 June 1998); *Occidental Petroleum Corporation and Occidental Exploration and Production Company v. Republic of Ecuador*, ICSID Case No. ARB/06/11, Decision on Jurisdiction (9 September 2008); *Bayindir v. Pakistan* (Decision on Jurisdiction), *supra* note 92; *Consortium Groupement L.E.S.I.- DIPENTA v. Algeria* (Award), *supra* note 101; *TSA Spectrum de Argentina S.A. v. Argentine Republic*, ICSID Case No. ARB/05/5, Award (19 December 2008).

200 *Biwater Gauff v. Tanzania* (Award), *supra* note 100, at para. 343.

201 In *Enron v. Argentina* (Decision on Jurisdiction), *supra* note 83, the tribunal, while holding that the six-month waiting period was satisfied in the circumstances, noted in *obiter dicta* that "the conclusion reached is not because the six-month negotiation period could be a procedural and not a jurisdictional requirement as has been argued by the Claimants and affirmed by other tribunals. Such requirement is in the view of the Tribunal very much a jurisdictional one. A failure to comply with that requirement would result in a determination of lack of jurisdiction." *Id.* at para. 88 (citations omitted).

202 *Goetz and others v. Burundi* (Award), *supra* note 147.

the six-month waiting period requirement in the US–Ukraine BIT, stating that "[p]roper notice is an important element of the State's consent to arbitration, as it allows the State, acting through its competent organs, to examine and possibly resolve the dispute by negotiations".[203]

Prior reference to local courts

Some BITs also require the investor to present disputes to the courts of the host State before proceeding to arbitration. If those courts do not issue a decision within a specified period of time, the investor is then entitled to resort to arbitration. For example, the Argentina–Netherlands BIT requires submission of disputes to local courts with a waiting period of 18 months before arbitration may be commenced, as well as a three-month negotiation period:

"1) Disputes between one Contracting Party and an investor of the other Contracting Party regarding issues covered by this agreement shall, if possible, be settled amicably.

2) If such disputes cannot be settled according to the provisions of paragraph (1) of this article within a period of three months from the date on which either party to the dispute requested amicable settlement, either party may submit the dispute to the administrative or judicial organs of the Contracting Party in the territory of which the investment has been made.

3) If within a period of eighteen months from submissions of the dispute to the competent organs mentioned in paragraph (2) above, these organs have not given a final decision or if the decision of the aforementioned organs has been given but the parties are still in dispute, then the investor concerned may resort to international arbitration or conciliation. Each Contracting Party hereby consents to the submission

---

203 *Western NIS Enterprise Fund v. Ukraine*, ICSID Case No. ARB/04/2, Order (16 March 2006). The tribunal nonetheless allowed the claimant 30 days to give proper notice. Jan Paulsson acted as arbitrator in the case.

of a dispute referred to in paragraph (1) of this Article to international arbitration."[204]

As discussed above in connection with *Maffezini*, investors may use MFN clauses to bypass such local court requirements.[205]

"Fork in the road" provisions

Generally speaking, the dispute resolution mechanisms in BITs present the parties, or sometimes the investor alone, with a series of options ranging from pursuing the claim in the local courts of the host State, to ICSID arbitration, to another form of international arbitration. Some BITs restrict the investor's freedom of choice, with what is known as a "fork in the road" provision. This is a stipulation that if the investor chooses to submit a dispute to the host State courts or to any other agreed dispute resolution procedure (for example, to ICC arbitration under the dispute resolution clause in the relevant investment contract), the investor forever loses the right to submit the same claims to the international arbitration procedure in the BIT. An illustration of a fork in the road provision is Article VI(2) and (3) of the US–Kazakhstan BIT:

> "2. In the event of an [investor/State] investment dispute, the parties to the dispute should initially seek a resolution through consultation and negotiation. If the dispute cannot be settled amicably, the national or company concerned may choose to submit the dispute for resolution: (a) to the courts or administrative tribunals of the Party that is a Party to the dispute; or (b) in accordance with any applicable, previously agreed dispute-settlement procedures; or (c) in accordance with the terms of paragraph 3 [below].

---

204 Argentina–Netherlands BIT, *supra* note 73, at Art. 10.

205 *See, e.g., Maffezini v. Spain* (Decision of the Tribunal on Objections to Jurisdiction), *supra* note 113; *Siemens v. Argentina* (Decision on Jurisdiction), *supra* note 81; *Gas Natural v. Argentina* (Decision of the Tribunal on Preliminary Questions on Jurisdiction), *supra* note 83; *Suez I* (Decision on Jurisdiction), *supra* note 161; *Suez II* (Decision on Jurisdiction), *supra* note 161. *But see Wintershall v. Argentina* (Award), *supra* note 163.

3.(a) *Provided that the national or company concerned has not submitted the dispute for resolution under paragraph 2(a) or (b) [above]* and that six months have elapsed from the date on which the dispute arose, the national or company concerned may choose to consent in writing to the submission of the dispute for settlement by binding arbitration:

(i) to the International Centre for the Settlement of Investment Disputes ('Centre') established by the [Convention], provided that the Party is a Party to such Convention; or

(ii) to the Additional Facility of the Centre, if the Centre is not available; or

(iii) in accordance with the Arbitration Rules of [UNCITRAL]; or

(iv) to any other arbitration institution, or in accordance with any other arbitration rules, as may be mutually agreed between the parties to the dispute." (emphasis added).[206]

In interpreting fork in the road provisions, and borrowing the words of the tribunal in *Toto Construzioni v. Lebanon*, a tribunal "has to consider whether the same claim is 'on a different road,' i.e., that a claim with the same object, parties and cause of action, is already brought before a different judicial forum", before precluding a claim.[207] ICSID tribunals constituted under treaties have generally distinguished contractual claims from treaty claims, and rejected fork in the road jurisdictional objections to treaty claims.[208] This was not the case in *Pantechniki*

---

206 US–Kazakhstan BIT, *supra* note 72, at Art. VI.

207 *Toto Costruzioni v. Lebanon* (Decision on Jurisdiction), *supra* note 191, at para. 211.

208 *See, e.g., Olguín v. Paraguay,* ICSID Case No. ARB/98/5, Decision on Jurisdiction (8 August 2000), *ICSID Reports* 6 (2004): 156; *Vivendi I* (Award), *supra* note 113; *Genin v. Estonia* (Award), *supra* note 171; *Middle East Cement Shipping and Handling Co. S.A. v. Arab Republic of Egypt,* ICSID Case No. ARB/99/6, Award (12 April 2002); *Vivendi I* (Decision on Annulment), *supra* note 114; *Azurix v. Argentina* (Decision on Jurisdiction), *supra* note 83; *CMS v. Argentina* (Decision of the Tribunal on Objections to Jurisdiction), *supra* note 76; *Champion Trading Company, Ameritrade International, Inc., James T. Wahba, John B. Wahba, Timothy T. Wahba v. Arab Republic of Egypt,* ICSID Case No. ARB/02/9, Decision on Jurisdiction (21 October 2003); *Enron v. Argentina* (Decision on Jurisdiction), *supra* note 83; *LG&E v.*

v. Albania, however, where the tribunal held that a fork in the road provision in the Albania–Greece BIT was triggered when the investor pursued a court action in Albania that had the same fundamental basis as its treaty claim.[209]

The lesson is that an investor must very carefully evaluate any inclination to proceed with claims before a domestic tribunal if the possibility of ICSID arbitration under a BIT also exists. The risk of not doing so is that the investor inadvertently – and irrevocably – will take the wrong fork in the road.

The Vivendi I "essential basis of claim" test

Fork in the road and local court issues may be particularly complex in cases where an investor is pursuing both contract breach claims and treaty breach claims in the same proceeding. This is illustrated in the landmark *Vivendi I* ICSID arbitration, in which the first award was annulled in part.[210] (Vivendi proceeded to a second ICSID arbitration, *Vivendi II*, followed by a second annulment proceeding.)[211] The case arose from a dispute under a concession contract entered into by a French company and its Argentine affiliate, on the one hand, and Tucumán, a province of Argentina, on the other, for the operation of the Tucumán water and sewage system. Although the concession contract provided that the parties would submit disputes to the local administrative courts, the claimants instead filed claims against Argentina under the France–Argentina BIT, seeking damages for breaches of the concession contract that they alleged amounted to breach of the BIT.

Argentina (Decision of the Arbitral Tribunal on Objections to Jurisdiction), *supra* note 83; *Pan American v. Argentina* (Decision on Preliminary Objections), *supra* note 193; *Desert Line v. Yemen* (Award), *supra* note 92; *Toto Costruzioni v. Lebanon* (Decision on Jurisdiction), *supra* note 191.

209 *Pantechniki v. Albania* (Award), *supra* note 100. Jan Paulsson acted as sole arbitrator in the case.

210 *Vivendi I* (Award), *supra* note 113; *Vivendi I* (Decision on Annulment), *supra* note 114.

211 *Vivendi II* (Award), *supra* note 139; *Compañiá de Aguas del Aconquija S.A. and Vivendi Universal v. Argentine Republic*, ICSID Case No. ARB/97/3, Decision on the Argentine Republic's Request for Annulment of the Award Rendered on 20 August 2007 (10 August 2010) (**Vivendi II (Decision on Annulment)**).

The first tribunal found that it had jurisdiction, but refused to consider the treaty breach claims on grounds that those claims were inextricably linked with questions of interpretation of the concession contract, which were reserved for the Argentine administrative courts under the dispute resolution clause of that contract. The *ad hoc* committee convened for the first annulment proceeding set aside this part of the *Vivendi I* award. The *ad hoc* committee found that, among other things, the tribunal exceeded its authority by refusing to rule on the merits of the treaty claims over which it had found jurisdiction, even if there was an overlap between the contract and treaty claims. The *ad hoc* committee emphasized the legal distinction between the two categories of claims:

> "95. As to the relation between breach of contract and breach of treaty in the present case, it must be stressed that Articles 3 [fair and equitable treatment] and 5 [expropriation] of the BIT do not relate directly to breach of a municipal contact. Rather they set an independent standard. A state may breach a treaty without breaching a contract, and *vice versa*, and this is certainly true of these provisions of the BIT. The point is made clear in Article 3 of the ILC Articles, which is entitled 'Characterization of an act of a State as internationally wrongful':
>
>> The characterization of an act of a State as internationally wrongful is governed by international law. Such characterization is not affected by the characterization of the same act as lawful by internal law.
>
> 96. In accordance with this general principle (which is undoubtedly declaratory of general international law), whether there has been a breach of the BIT and whether there has been a breach of contract are different questions. Each of these claims will be determined by reference to its own proper or applicable law – in the case of the BIT, by international law; in the case of the Concession Contract, by the proper law of the contract, in other words, the law of Tucumán."[212]

The *Vivendi I ad hoc* committee proceeded to develop an "essential basis of the claim" or "fundamental basis of the claim" test:

---

212 *Vivendi I* (Decision on Annulment), *supra* note 114, at paras. 95-96.

"98. In a case where the essential basis of a claim brought before an international tribunal is a breach of contract, the tribunal will give effect to any valid choice of forum clause in the contract. [Footnote omitted]

...

101. On the other hand, where 'the fundamental basis of the claim' is a treaty laying down an independent standard by which the conduct of the parties is to be judged, the existence of an exclusive jurisdiction clause in a contract between the claimant and the respondent state or one of its subdivisions cannot operate as a bar to the application of the treaty standard. [Footnotes omitted] At most, it might be relevant – as municipal law will often be relevant – in assessing whether there has been a breach of the treaty."[213]

In subsequent decisions, numerous ICSID tribunals have followed and applied the *Vivendi I* "essential basis of the claim" test.[214]

Common arbitral mechanisms

The choice of dispute resolution mechanisms in BITs typically includes more than one type of international arbitration, alongside local court litigation and any contractually agreed dispute settlement procedures. The most frequently designated international arbitration institution by far is ICSID. *Ad hoc* arbitration under the UNCITRAL Arbitration Rules is increasingly selected by investors. ICSID will administer UNCITRAL arbitrations at the request of the parties. There are also occasional options to refer disputes to commercial arbitration institutions such as the ICC or the Stockholm Chamber of Commerce.

---

213 *Id.* at paras. 98, 101.

214 *See, e.g., SGS v. Pakistan* (Decision of the Tribunal on Objections to Jurisdiction), *supra* note 183; *Impregilo S.p.A v. Islamic Republic of Pakistan*, ICSID Case No. ARB/03/3, Decision on Jurisdiction (22 April 2005); *Bayindir v. Pakistan* (Decision on Jurisdiction), *supra* note 92; *BIVAC v. Paraguay* (Decision of the Tribunal on Objections to Jurisdiction), *supra* note 197; *Toto Costruzioni v. Lebanon* (Decision on Jurisdiction), *supra* note 191.

The US–Argentina and UK–Turkmenistan BITs provide two examples of sets of choices for dispute resolution mechanisms. The US–Argentina BIT (Annex 6) provides that, after the negotiation period, an investor may choose to submit a dispute to the ICSID Centre if it is available, or the Additional Facility of ICSID; to arbitration in accordance with the UNCITRAL Rules; or to any other arbitration institution or in accordance with any other arbitration rules agreed between the parties to the dispute. The UK–Turkmenistan BIT provides that the investor and the host State "may agree to refer the dispute" to ICSID or the Additional Facility of ICSID; the ICC; or an international arbitrator or *ad hoc* tribunal to be appointed by a special agreement or established under the UNCITRAL Rules.[215]

Duration of bilateral investment treaties

Investors obviously need to be attentive to the duration of BIT protections. The typical duration of a BIT is ten years, with the term automatically extended unless and until one party terminates the treaty with notice. In light of the long-term nature of major foreign investment projects, a critical extra protection is a lengthy extension of treaty coverage for investments made before treaty termination. The Model UK BIT (Annex 5, Article 14) envisions a sunset period of 20 years:

> "This Agreement shall remain in force for a period of ten years. Thereafter it shall continue in force until the expiration of twelve months from the date on which either Contracting Party shall have given written notice of termination to the other. Provided that in respect of investments made whilst the Agreement is in force, its provisions shall continue in effect with respect to such investments for a period of twenty years after the date of termination and without prejudice to the application thereafter of the rules of general international law."

The US–Argentina BIT (Annex 6, Article 14) provides for ten years of post-termination protection:

---

215 UK–Turkmenistan BIT, *supra* note 87, at Art. 8.

"2. Either Party may, by giving one year's written notice to the other Party, terminate this Treaty at the end of the initial ten year period or at any time thereafter.

3. With respect to investments made or acquired prior to the date of termination of this Treaty and to which this Treaty otherwise applies, the provisions of all of the other Articles of this Treaty shall thereafter continue to be effective for a further period of ten years from such date of termination."

The recent vintage of most BITs – the real boom having started less than 15 years ago – means that there is little experience with expiry and termination of BITs. To date only Ecuador and Venezuela have denounced BITs.[216]

Multilateral investment treaty claims

The "investment chapters" of multilateral economic cooperation treaties and free trade agreements contain substantive protections and investor-State arbitration procedures similar to those in BITs. Among these are Chapter 11 of the NAFTA (Annex 7) and Part III and Article 26 of the ECT (Annex 8), both described below. Others include the 1987 ASEAN Agreement for the Promotion and Protection of Investments, the 1994 Colonia and Buenos Aires Investment Protocols of Mercosur, Chapter 17 of the 1990 Group of Three Agreements and, most recently, the Dominican Republic–Central America–United States Free Trade Agreement.

---

216 In 2008, Ecuador denounced nine of its 25 BITs (mainly with Latin American countries) and Venezuela denounced one BIT (with The Netherlands). BITs have also been denounced recently by other States in different circumstances, such as intra-EU BITs as part of the accession process to the EU. *See* UNCTAD, "Recent Developments (2008–June 2009)", *supra* note 8; UNCTAD, "Recent Developments in International Investment Agreements (2007–June 2008)", *IIA Monitor* No. 2 (2008), < www.unctad.org/en/docs/webdiaeia20081_en.pdf>.

NAFTA arbitration

In 1992, Canada, Mexico and the United States concluded the NAFTA establishing the North American Free Trade Area. The NAFTA, which came into force on 1 January 1994, removes trade barriers and is intended to promote economic cooperation between the three participating States and increase investment opportunities in their territories. The investment chapter of the NAFTA, Chapter 11, implements these objectives by identifying the standards for treatment of investors and establishing a dispute resolution mechanism for arbitration of investor-State disputes.

The Chapter 11 dispute resolution mechanism may be invoked by any investor of a NAFTA State that has invested in the territory of another NAFTA State and allegedly incurred loss or damage as a result of measures adopted or maintained by the host State. To provide the basis for a claim, the measures in question must have been in breach of the substantive obligations contained in Chapter 11. The full text of Chapter 11, which includes both substantive investment protections (Section A) and dispute resolution mechanisms (Section B), is set out in Annex 7.

The jurisprudence developing from NAFTA Chapter 11 tribunals affects the interests of more than Canada, Mexico, the United States and their respective investors. This is because many of the provisions of Chapter 11 are similar to the most common substantive and procedural BIT provisions. As of January 2010, 14 NAFTA cases had been initiated under the ICSID Additional Facility Rules, including one against Canada,[217] three against the United States,[218] and ten against Mexico.[219] Of the total 21 ICSID and non-ICSID NAFTA cases

---

217 *Mobil Investments Canada Inc. and Murphy Oil Corporation v. Canada,* ICSID Case No. ARB(AF)/07/4.

218 *Loewen Group, Inc. and Raymond L. Loewen v. United States of America,* ICSID Case No. ARB(AF)/98/3; *Mondev International Ltd. v. United States of America,* ICSID Case No. ARB(AF)/99/2; *ADF Group Inc. v. United States of America,* ICSID Case No. ARB(AF)/00/1.

219 *Metalclad Corporation v. United Mexican States,* ICSID Case No. ARB(AF)/97/1; *Robert Azinian and others v. United Mexican States,* ICSID Case No. ARB(AF)/97/2; *Waste Management, Inc. v. United Mexican States,* ICSID Case No. ARB(AF)/98/2; *Marvin Roy Feldman Karpa v. United Mexican States,* ICSID Case No. ARB(AF)/99/1; *Waste Management, Inc. v. United Mexican States,* ICSID Case No. ARB(AF)/00/3; *Fireman's Fund Insurance Company v. United*

resulting in awards on the merits (as of January 2010), one third (7 out of 21) resulted in awards in favor of investors.[220] Although a full account of Chapter 11 and NAFTA jurisprudence is beyond the parameters of this Guide, we set out certain key points below.[221]

Procedural framework

Articles 1118 to 1120 of NAFTA Chapter 11 authorize an investor to initiate arbitration against a host State for the alleged breach of one of the investment protections contained in the NAFTA after the passage of: (a) a negotiation period of six months, which runs from the date of the events giving rise to the claim; and (b) 90 days' written notice of the intent to submit a claim. A claim is allowed only within three years from the date on which the investor knew or should have known of the alleged treaty breach and resulting damage (Article 1113(2)).

A special feature of NAFTA Chapter 11 is that, under Article 1121(1), an investor must waive its rights "to initiate or continue before any administrative tribunal or court under the law of any Party, or other dispute settlement procedures, any proceedings with respect to the measure of the disputing Party" alleged to be a NAFTA breach (other than certain applications for non-monetary interim relief). The operation of this waiver requirement is illustrated in the well-known *Waste Management v. Mexico* case. In 1998, Waste Management, a US company, filed a claim against Mexico alleging various breaches of NAFTA Chapter 11.

Mexican States, ICSID Case No. ARB(AF)/02/1; *Corn Products International, Inc. v. United Mexican States*, ICSID Case No. ARB(AF)/04/1; *Archer Daniels Midland Company and Tate & Lyle Ingredients Americas, Inc. v. United Mexican States*, ICSID Case No. ARB(AF)/04/5; *Bayview Irrigation District and others v. United Mexican States*, ICSID Case No. ARB(AF)/05/1; *Cargill, Inc. v. United Mexican States*, ICSID Case No. ARB(AF)05/2.

220 *S.D. Myers v. Canada* (First Partial Award), *supra* note 123; *Pope & Talbot v. Canada* (Award on the Merits of Phase 2), *supra* note 123; *Metalclad v. Mexico* (Award), *supra* note 128; *Feldman v. Mexico* (Award), *supra* note 152; *Corn Products v. Mexico* (Decision on Responsibility), *supra* note 152; *Archer Daniels v. Mexico* (Award), *supra* note 152; *Cargill v. Mexico* (Award), *supra* note 152.

221 For a comprehensive review of NAFTA Chapter 11 arbitration, *see* M. Kinnear, A. Bjorklund & J. Hannaford, *supra* note 154.

The ICSID Additional Facility tribunal constituted to hear the case declined jurisdiction on the ground that Waste Management, in pursuing remedies in Mexico while also taking part in the NAFTA Chapter 11 proceedings, had failed to waive its rights to initiate or continue non-NAFTA legal actions relating to the measures adopted.[222] The case, therefore, was dismissed. Waste Management then resubmitted its claim in 2000, having concluded or discontinued all claims in Mexican courts that involved breaches also alleged to be breaches of Chapter 11. The *Waste Management II* tribunal ruled that the dismissal of the earlier claim for lack of a proper waiver did not preclude Waste Management from resubmitting the same case, provided that it subsequently had made a proper waiver.[223] In its final award, the *Waste Management II* tribunal held that Mexico did not breach NAFTA Articles 1105 or 1110.[224]

Under Article 1120 of NAFTA Chapter 11, the investor has the option of bringing its arbitration claim under the ICSID Convention, the ICSID Additional Facility Rules or the UNCITRAL Rules. Subject to the specific mandatory provisions of the NAFTA, the procedural rules chosen by the investor govern the arbitration.

Although NAFTA Chapter 11 includes ICSID arbitration as one of the options open to an aggrieved investor, the ICSID Convention proper remains of limited relevance to NAFTA claims. As of 2010, the only NAFTA State to have ratified the ICSID Convention was the United States. Consequently, unless and until Canada and/or Mexico becomes a party to the ICSID Convention, the Centre may not administer NAFTA arbitrations under the ICSID Convention. Instead, the Centre administers arbitrations involving the US and either Mexico or Canada under the Additional Facility Rules. UNCITRAL arbitration is also available for NAFTA disputes, with the Secretary-General of ICSID available to assist as appointing authority (Article 1124).

---

222 *Waste Management, Inc. v. United Mexican States,* ICSID Case No. ARB/98/2, Award (2 June 2000), *ICSID Reports* 5 (2002): 443.

223 *Waste Management, Inc. v. United Mexican States,* ICSID Case No. ARB(AF)/00/3, Decision of the Tribunal (26 June 2002).

224 *Waste Management, Inc. v. United Mexican States,* ICSID Case No. ARB(AF)/00/3, Award (30 April 2004).

Except where the parties agree otherwise, a NAFTA tribunal is comprised of three arbitrators, one appointed by each party and the third, the "presiding arbitrator", by agreement between the parties (Article 1123). Unless there is an agreement to the contrary, the Secretary-General of ICSID is the appointing authority in the event of default by a party in making its appointment or the parties' failure to agree upon the presiding arbitrator of the tribunal (Article 1124).

NAFTA Article 1131(1) addresses applicable law:

> "A Tribunal established under this Section shall decide the issues in dispute in accordance with this Article and applicable rules of international law."

This reflects a different approach than that found in the ICSID Convention. As compared to Article 42 of the ICSID Convention, NAFTA Article 1131(1) makes no provision for application of the law of the NAFTA State party to the arbitration.

The NAFTA contains consolidation avenues not available in the ICSID Convention or in BIT arbitration provisions. Where several claims arise from the same measures taken by a NAFTA State, Article 1126 allows a disputing party, whether the NAFTA State or the investor, to request the Secretary-General of ICSID to establish a special three-member tribunal pursuant to the UNCITRAL Rules to hear a request to consolidate the claims. In the event the special tribunal determines that the claims "have a question of law or fact in common" and that the "interests of fair and efficient resolution of the claims" favor consolidation, the special tribunal may either assume jurisdiction over all or part of the claims, or assume jurisdiction over one or more of the claims to assist in the resolution of the others. The special tribunal may also order that the proceedings of a previously established Chapter 11 tribunal be stayed.

These consolidation provisions of NAFTA Chapter 11 are designed to avoid inconsistent results in cases arising from the same State measures and similar facts. However, parties inclined to try to take advantage of consolidation must be aware that the consolidation process is complex, brings with it the mandatory application of the UNCITRAL Rules, and involves special provisions governing constitution of the tribunal.

A NAFTA Chapter 11 tribunal may order interim measures, including orders to preserve evidence in the possession or control of a party or to protect the tribunal's jurisdiction, but cannot "order attachment or enjoin the application of the measure alleged to constitute a breach" of Chapter 11 (Article 1134). As an exception to the strict waiver of alternative remedies in Article 1121(1), the NAFTA also provides for the right to request provisional measures including "injunctive, declaratory or other extraordinary relief, not involving the payment of damages" before the competent domestic courts.

Article 1135 explicitly circumscribes the final relief a NAFTA tribunal may award: monetary damages plus applicable interest, or restitution of property. In respect of the latter, the award must provide that the State may choose to pay monetary damages and applicable interest in lieu of restitution of property. Article 1135(3) specifically prohibits any award of punitive damages. In terms of remedies, therefore, NAFTA Chapter 11 leaves only the issue of costs to the arbitration rules chosen by the investor.

NAFTA awards are binding as "between the disputing parties and in respect of the particular case" (Article 1136(1)). NAFTA Chapter 11 does not deal with the questions of review of awards or recourse against awards; this crucial matter is left to the rules selected by the investor. Therefore, unless and until Mexico and/or Canada ratify the ICSID Convention and NAFTA arbitrations are conducted under the ICSID Arbitration Rules (with their special annulment procedures, as discussed in Chapter 5), NAFTA awards will remain open to review by the national courts at the place of arbitration. To cite a leading example, an application for judicial review of the *Metalclad* award was made in Vancouver, the place of arbitration, on several grounds including alleged violation of "public policy". The Canadian court set aside the award in part and suggested that the matter be remitted to the NAFTA tribunal if the parties were unable to agree on the issues at stake.[225]

The NAFTA has mandatory and automatic waiting periods for enforcement of awards (Article 1136(3)). In the (still theoretical) case of a final NAFTA award made under the ICSID Convention, a disputing party may not seek

---

225 *United Mexican States v. Metalclad Corporation* (Supreme Court of British Columbia), *supra* note 128.

enforcement until either: (a) 120 days have elapsed from the date the award was rendered and no disputing party has requested revision or annulment of the award; or (b) any revision or annulment proceedings that were initiated have been completed. In the case of an award rendered under the ICSID Additional Facility Arbitration Rules or the UNCITRAL Rules, the comparable waiting period is: (a) three months from the date the award was rendered provided no party has commenced proceedings to revise, set aside or annul the award; or (b) the date the relevant court dismissed or allowed an application to revise, set aside or annul the award absent a further appeal.

Given that the United States is the only NAFTA State to have ratified the ICSID Convention, NAFTA awards rendered under the auspices of ICSID do not benefit from the self-contained Convention enforcement regime and hence are not enforceable as if they were final court judgments of the country of enforcement (see Chapter 6). Instead, NAFTA awards must be enforced under the New York Convention. Indeed, under Article 1130 of the NAFTA, the tribunal is required to hold the arbitration in the territory of a State party to the New York Convention unless the parties agree otherwise – which they would be ill-advised to do, except in highly unusual circumstances.

NAFTA Article 1136(4) directs each State party to "provide for the enforcement of an award in its territory". If a NAFTA State fails to comply with a final award, the investor's home State may request the formation of a dispute resolution panel under NAFTA Chapter 20. The complaining NAFTA State may seek a determination from that panel that the responding State's failure to comply with the award is inconsistent with the NAFTA and a recommendation in favor of compliance.

Jurisdiction

Only an investor of a State party – Canada, Mexico or the United States – has the right to bring a claim under NAFTA Chapter 11. The term "investor" includes an "enterprise", which is broadly defined to include any corporation, trust or other association, whether privately or governmentally owned (Articles 201 and 1139).

NAFTA Article 1117 provides that an investor may submit to arbitration a claim against the host State on behalf of an enterprise constituted or organized under the host State's law, which the investor owns or controls directly or indirectly. In *S.D. Myers v. Canada*, the claimant was a US-based private company owned by an individual who also owned a company incorporated in Canada. The Canadian government argued that S.D. Myers lacked standing as an investor because it held no shares in the Canadian company and there was no joint venture agreement between the two companies. The tribunal found jurisdiction on the ground that the same individual effectively controlled the two entities.[226] In so doing, the tribunal refused to allow technical arguments regarding corporate structure to defeat the claim.

Subject to prior notification, a NAFTA State may deny the benefits of Chapter 11 to an enterprise of another NAFTA State if non-NAFTA State investors own or control the enterprise and the enterprise has no substantial business activities in the NAFTA State under the laws of which it is organized. The practical effect of this provision is to prevent non-NAFTA parties from creating a legal entity in one of the NAFTA States solely to benefit from the investment protections and dispute resolution mechanism of NAFTA Chapter 11.

The Chapter 11 definition of "investment" is also broad. It includes not only traditional concepts like enterprises, securities, and tangible and intangible property, but also interests under construction contracts, concessions or other "contracts where remuneration depends substantially on the production, revenues or profits of an enterprise" (Article 1139). Claims to money under simple sales contracts or trade credits are excluded.

An investor may bring a claim in relation to any "measure" – any law, regulation, procedure, requirement or practice, with no specific requirement that the measure have legal force – that is adopted or maintained by a State party and that causes damage to an investor or the enterprise of an investor. The measure must constitute a breach of one of the substantive obligations set out in NAFTA Chapter 11.

---

226 *S.D. Myers v. Canada* (First Partial Award), *supra* note 123.

Substantive obligations

Section A of NAFTA Chapter 11 establishes the following investment protection obligations: (a) national and MFN standards of treatment (Articles 1102 and 1103); (b) minimum standards of treatment, including fair and equitable treatment and full protection and security (Article 1105); (c) freedom from performance obligations (e.g., obligations to export, to favor domestic suppliers or to transfer technology) (Article 1106); (d) the right to control investments using senior managers of any nationality (Article 1107); (e) the right to repatriate without delay and in a freely usable currency all profits, fees or other proceeds resulting from investments (Article 1109); and (f) conditions of expropriation, notably non-discrimination and compensation at "fair market value of the expropriated investment immediately before the expropriation took place" (Article 1110).

In four Chapter 11 cases, NAFTA tribunals have found that the respondent State breached the fair and equitable treatment standard set out in Article 1105. The tribunals found that certain acts of public authorities – for example, the lack of a "transparent and predictable framework" and of an "orderly process and timely disposition" of the investor's permit applications, as well as threats, denial of reasonable demands and information requests requiring the investor to incur necessary expenses – violated the fair and equitable treatment standard and amounted to effective discrimination in favor of domestic entities.[227]

NAFTA Chapter 11 disputes, not surprisingly, have fueled the long-simmering legal debate as to whether the fair and equitable treatment standard is tantamount to the minimum standard required by customary international law or instead represents an independent concept affording greater protection. In the wake of the refusal of NAFTA tribunals to adopt a restrictive interpretation of the principle, the NAFTA States effectively sought to impose such an interpretation by issuing in 2001 a binding interpretative statement of NAFTA Article 1105 in the "Notes of Interpretation" of the NAFTA Free Trade Commission.[228] The

---

227 See S.D. Myers v. Canada (First Partial Award), supra note 123; Metalclad v. Mexico (Award), supra note 128; Pope & Talbot v. Canada (Award on the Merits of Phase 2), supra note 123; Cargill v. Mexico (Award), supra note 152.

228 NAFTA Free Trade Commission, "Notes of Interpretation of Certain Chapter 11 Provisions", <www.international.gc.ca/trade-agreements-accords-commerciaux/disp-diff/nafta-interpr.

statement provides that fair and equitable treatment does "not require treatment in addition to or beyond that which is required by the customary international law minimum standard of treatment of aliens".[229] This process of interpretation, and the interpretation itself, have provoked controversy. The *Pope & Talbot* tribunal had occasion to reevaluate its award on the merits, in which it had found Canada had violated the fair and equitable treatment standard, against the Notes of Interpretation. The tribunal, effectively, interpreted the Notes of Interpretation as not warranting a more restrictive interpretation of the NAFTA fair and equitable treatment standard than the tribunal had originally provided.[230]

As noted above in connection with BIT claims, NAFTA tribunals in five cases have found respondent States in violation of national treatment obligations under Article 1102.[231]

NAFTA tribunals have also found breaches of Article 1106, which prohibits member States from imposing performance requirements on investors from the NAFTA region, in two cases, *Archer Daniels v. Mexico*, and *Cargill v. Mexico*. In both cases, the performance requirement was use of cane sugar (instead of high fructose corn syrup) in order to qualify for a 20 percent tax exemption in Mexico. The tribunals held that the tax exemption discriminated against the high fructose corn syrup industry, in which claimants made their investments, and consequently was inconsistent with Article 1106.[232]

NAFTA tribunals have developed considerable jurisprudence on expropriation. Although expropriation claims have been advanced in numerous NAFTA cases,[233] only one tribunal – in *Metalclad v. Mexico* – so far has held that an

---

aspx?lang=en>, 3 July 2001.

229 *Id.* at para. 2(2).

230 *Pope & Talbot v. Canada* (Award on the Merits of Phase 2), *supra* note 123.

231 *S.D. Myers v. Canada* (First Partial Award), *supra* note 123; *Feldman v. Mexico* (Award), *supra* note 152; *Archer Daniels v. Mexico* (Award), *supra* note 152; *Corn Products International v. Mexico* (Decision on Responsibility), *supra* note 152; *Cargill v. Mexico* (Award), *supra* note 152.

232 *Archer Daniels v. Mexico* (Award), *supra* note 152; *Cargill v. Mexico* (Award), *supra* note 152.

233 *See, e.g., S.D. Myers v. Canada*, UNCITRAL; *Robert Azinian and others v. United Mexican States*, ICSID Case No. ARB(AF)/97/2; *Marvin Roy Feldman Karpa v. United Mexican States*, ICSID Case No. ARB(AF)/99/1; *Pope & Talbot, Inc. v. Government of Canada*, UNCITRAL; *Waste Management, Inc. v. United Mexican States*, ICSID Case No. ARB(AF)/00/3; *GAMI Investments,*

expropriation occurred.[234] The dispute in *Metalclad* arose out of actions taken by Mexico, through two local municipalities, to interfere in the development and operation of the US investor Metalclad's hazardous waste facility after Metalclad had received the necessary federal government permits for the waste facility. In its award, the tribunal defined the test of indirect or *de facto* expropriation under Chapter 11 as follows:

> "[E]xpropriation under NAFTA includes not only open, deliberate and acknowledged takings of property, such as outright seizure or formal or obligatory transfer of title in favour of the host State, but also covert or incidental interference with the use of property which has the effect of depriving the owner, in whole or in significant part, of the use or reasonably-to-be expected economic benefit of property even if not necessarily to the obvious benefit of the host State."[235]

The tribunal held that the measures taken by the Mexican municipalities amounted to an indirect expropriation of Metalclad's investment because they resulted in "the complete frustration of the operation of the [investment] and negate the possibility of any meaningful return on Metalclad's investment".[236]

The Energy Charter Treaty

In 1994, 49 States plus the European Communities signed the ECT (Annex 8).[237] The signatories include major energy producing or purchasing powers,

---

Inc. v. United Mexican States, UNCITRAL; *Methanex Corporation v. United States of America*, UNCITRAL; *Archer Daniels Midland Company and Tate & Lyle Ingredients Americas, Inc. v. United Mexican States*, ICSID Case No. ARB(AF)/04/5; *Corn Products International, Inc. v. United Mexican States*, ICSID Case No. ARB(AF)/04/1; *Loewen Group, Inc. and Raymond L. Loewen v. United States of America*, ICSID Case No. ARB(AF)/98/3; *Mondev International Ltd. v. United States of America*, ICSID Case No. ARB(AF)/99/2; *International Thunderbird Gaming Corp. v. United Mexican States*, UNCITRAL.

234 *Metalclad v. Mexico* (Award), *supra* note 128.

235 *Id.* at para. 103.

236 *Id.* at para. 113.

237 *Energy Charter Treaty*, opened for signature Dec. 17, 1994, 34 ILM 381 (1995).

including France, Germany, Italy, Japan, Kazakhstan, The Netherlands, Russia, Spain and the United Kingdom. The United States has declined to sign.

The ECT provides a comprehensive international legal framework for cross-border economic cooperation in the energy sector. The treaty's primary aim is to promote a climate of legal stability and predictability to attract investment and stimulate business activity in the energy sectors of member States. To this end, it includes wide-ranging provisions designed to open the energy sector, including: (a) non-discriminatory treatment of foreign investors; (b) free transit of energy products; (c) freedom of transfer of investment capital and returns; and (d) elimination of anti-competitive practices. Article 26 of the ECT grants foreign investors of State parties the right to bring legal proceedings against other State parties for breach of Part III of the Treaty, which contains the provisions relating to investment promotion and protection.

Jurisdiction

The definitions in Article 1 of the ECT are broad. "Investment" includes the familiar generic language seen in NAFTA and in many BITs and also, more broadly, "claims to money and claims to performance pursuant to a contract having an economic value and associated with an Investment". The definition includes "returns", defined as "the amounts derived from or associated with an Investment, irrespective of the form in which they are paid, including profits, dividends, interest, capital gains, royalty payments, management, technical assistance or other fees and payments in kind".

Procedural framework

As stated above, a foreign investor of one Contracting State may invoke Article 26 of the ECT in relation to any alleged breach by another (host) Contracting State of an obligation under Part III of the treaty. There is no requirement that the investor exhaust local remedies or, indeed, that the investor exhaust any other form of dispute resolution that may have been agreed upon with the host State. Article 26 does not apply to other disputes in which a foreign investor may be involved; for example, if a country fails to promote conditions for access of foreign investors to its capital markets, such investors may not bring claims under the ECT, because the relevant provision is not contained in Part III.

Following a three-month negotiation period, the foreign investor may choose to submit the dispute: (a) to the domestic courts or administrative tribunals of the host State; (b) to any previously agreed dispute resolution procedure, for example, under an arbitration clause in a contract; or (c) to international arbitration. If a foreign investor chooses international arbitration, it then has to make a further choice between ICSID (including the ICSID Additional Facility Arbitration Rules), the UNCITRAL Rules or the Stockholm Chamber of Commerce Rules. Factors affecting the choice include the amount in dispute, the legal issues raised, the nationalities of the parties, the arbitration venue thought desirable, and the effect of the choice of rules on the composition of the arbitral tribunal.

Where a local company is subject to foreign control, ECT Article 26(7) provides that a company having the nationality of a Contracting State party to the dispute and, before the dispute arises, having been under the control of investors of another Contracting State, is to be treated as a national of another Contracting State for the purposes of the ICSID Convention and the ICSID Additional Facility Rules. In a separate understanding adopted together with the ECT by Contracting States, control is defined as meaning "control in fact, determined after an examination of the actual circumstances in each situation".[238] Relevant factors to be considered include the investor's: "(a) financial interest, including equity interest, in the Investment; (b) ability to exercise substantial influence over the management and operation of the Investment; and (c) ability to exercise substantial influence over the selection of members of the board of directors or any other managing body".[239] Where there is any doubt, the burden of proof is on the investor to demonstrate control over the entity in question.

Under the ECT, each Contracting State is deemed to have given its unconditional consent to international arbitration under the treaty of a dispute under Part III, subject to two exceptions set forth in Article 26(3):

---

238 *Id.* at Understanding IV(3).
239 *Id.*

(a) certain Contracting States have declined to give their unconditional consent to international arbitration where the investor has previously submitted the dispute to another dispute resolution forum; and

(b) certain Contracting States have not given unconditional consent to international arbitration in respect of disputes relating to the obligations under an investment contract between a Contracting State and an investor or investment of another Contracting State.

Regardless of the type of arbitration or other dispute resolution mechanism chosen, Article 26 requires the dispute to be decided in accordance with the ECT itself and with applicable rules and principles of international law. The ECT limits remedies against a State to monetary damages. Therefore, ECT tribunals may not order specific performance, order restitution of property or "annul governmental acts".

As of January 2010, ICSID had registered 16 of the 24 cases instituted under the ECT: 14 ICSID Convention cases and two ICSID Additional Facility cases. Three of these 16 cases have resulted in settlements,[240] five have resulted in awards,[241] and eight remain pending.[242] The five awards merit brief mention.

---

240 *AES Summit Generation Limited v. Republic of Hungary*, ICSID Case No. ARB/01/4; *Alstom Power Italia SpA and Alstom SpA v. Republic of Mongolia*, ICSID Case No. ARB/04/10; *Barmek Holding A.S. v. Republic of Azerbaijan*, ICSID Case No. ARB/06/16.

241 *Plama Consortium Limited v. Republic of Bulgaria*, ICSID Case No. ARB/03/24; *Ioannis Kardassopoulos v. Georgia*, ICSID Case No. ARB/05/18; *Cementownia "Nowa Huta" S.A. v. Republic of Turkey*, ICSID Case No. ARB(AF)/06/2; *Azpetrol International Holdings B.V., Azpetrol Group B.V. and Azpetrol Oil Services Group B.V. v. Republic of Azerbaijan*, ICSID Case No. ARB/06/15; *Europe Cement Investment and Trade S.A. v. Republic of Turkey*, ICSID Case No. ARB(AF)/07/2. As to the eight ECT cases initiated under non-ICSID rules, three have resulted in final awards. *Nykomb Synergetics Technology Holding AB (Sweden) v. Latvia*, SCC Case No. 118/2001 (Award rendered on 16 December 2003); *Petrobart Ltd. (Gibraltar) v. Kyrgyz Republic*, SCC Case No. 126/2003 (Award rendered on 29 March 2005); *Limited Liability Company Amto (Latvia) v. Ukraine*, SCC Case No. 080/2005 (Award rendered on 26 March 2008).

242 *Hrvatska Elektroprivreda d.d. v. Republic of Slovenia*, ICSID Case No. ARB/05/24; *Libananco Holdings Co. Limited v. Republic of Turkey*, ICSID Case No. ARB/06/8; *Liman Caspian Oil BV and NCL Dutch Investment BV v. Republic of Kazakhstan*, ICSID Case No. ARB/07/14;

In the first ICSID-registered case under the ECT to result in an award, *Plama v. Bulgaria,* a Cypriot investor claimed that Bulgaria took adverse actions against its investment in a Bulgarian oil refinery. In its award, the tribunal decided that Plama's "investment was obtained by deceitful conduct that is in violation of Bulgarian law" and therefore Plama could not benefit from the substantive protections of the ECT.[243] The tribunal went on to hold that, even assuming Plama would have been entitled to ECT substantive protections, its claims on the merits would have failed because Bulgaria did not violate or breach its obligations.

In *Azpetrol v. Azerbaijan,* although the parties reached an "in principle settlement" of their dispute, complications ensued and the tribunal was asked to confirm that a binding settlement had in fact been reached through an exchange of emails between the parties' counsel.[244] Left to deal only with the question of whether a settlement had been reached, the tribunal held in its award that it did not have jurisdiction to hear the claims as there was no longer any "dispute" between the parties as required under Article 25(1) of the ICSID Convention and Article 26(1) of the ECT.[245]

The awards rendered in *Europe Cement v. Republic of Turkey*[246] and *Cementownia "Nowa Huta" v. Republic of Turkey*[247] concerned alleged ownership of two Turkish electricity companies, Çukurova Elektrik A.Ş. (*ÇEAŞ*) and Kepez Elektrik Türk A.Ş. (*Kepez*). In each case, the tribunal dismissed the claims for lack of jurisdiction because the claimants failed to prove that they owned shares in ÇEAŞ and Kepez. As explained by the tribunal in *Europe Cement,* "the

---

Electrabel S.A. v. Republic of Hungary, ICSID Case No. ARB/07/19; *AES Summit Generation Limited and AES-Tisza Erömü Kft. v. Republic of Hungary,* ICSID Case No. ARB/07/22; *Alapli Elektrik B.V. v. Republic of Turkey,* ICSID Case No. ARB/08/13; *Vattenfall AB, Vattenfall Europe AG, Vattenfall Europe Generation AG v. Federal Republic of Germany,* ICSID Case No. ARB/09/6; *EVN AG v. Former Yugoslav Republic of Macedonia,* ICSID Case No. ARB/09/10.

243 *Plama v. Bulgaria* (Award), *supra* note 91, at para. 143.

244 *Azpetrol International Holdings B.V., Azpetrol Group B.V. and Azpetrol Oil Services Group B.V. v. Republic of Azerbaijan,* ICSID Case No. ARB/06/15, Award (8 September 2009).

245 *Id.* at para. 105.

246 *Europe Cement Investment and Trade S.A. v. Republic of Turkey,* ICSID Case No. ARB(AF)/07/2, Award (13 August 2009). Freshfields was counsel to the respondent.

247 *Cementownia "Nowa Huta" S.A. v. Republic of Turkey,* ICSID Case No. ARB(AF)/06/2, Award (17 September 2009). Freshfields was counsel to the respondent.

claim to ownership of shares in CEAS and Kepez was based on documents that on examination appear to have been back-dated and thus fraudulent".[248] In *Cementownia "Nowa Huta"*, the tribunal granted declaratory relief holding that the claimant's case was "fraudulent and was brought in bad faith".[249] Further, as addressed in Chapter 4, the *Europe Cement* and *Cementownia "Nowa Huta"* tribunals effectively sanctioned the conduct of the claimants in the allocation of costs by requiring each claimant to pay 100 percent of the Republic of Turkey's legal fees and expenses as well as the Republic of Turkey's share of the arbitration costs.

The award rendered in the remaining ECT case registered with ICSID, *Ioannis Kardassopoulos v. Georgia,* remained unpublished as this Guide went to press in September 2010.[250]

---

248 *Europe Cement v. Turkey* (Award), *supra* note 246, at 180.
249 *Cementownia "Nowa Huta" v. Turkey* (Award), *supra* note 247, at para. 179.
250 *Ioannis Kardassopoulos v. Georgia*, ICSID Case No. ARB/05/18, Award (3 March 2010) (unpublished).

Chapter 4

ICSID arbitration procedure

In this chapter, we describe the basic process of arbitration under the auspices of ICSID, from the filing of the request to the issuance of the award.

The ICSID arbitral process is governed not only by the ICSID Convention itself, but also by the Rules of Procedure for the Institution of Conciliation and Arbitration Proceedings (the *Institution Rules*) (Annex 2); the Rules of Procedure for Arbitration Proceedings (the *Arbitration Rules*) (Annex 3); and the Administrative and Financial Regulations (the *Regulations*). The requirements of the Convention are few in number, but are for the most part mandatory. There is more flexibility with respect to the Rules and Regulations. The parties may modify provisions of the Arbitration Rules (not mandated by the Convention) by agreement, and depart from the Regulations to the extent expressly provided therein.

Arbitrations under the aegis of the ICSID Additional Facility are governed by the Additional Facility Rules and the Additional Facility Arbitration Rules (Annex 4). Most of the provisions that apply to Additional Facility arbitrations are identical or very similar to those that apply to ICSID Convention arbitrations. This chapter singles out only those Additional Facility Rules or Arbitration Rules that differ.

Substantial amendments to ICSID's rules and regulations took effect on 10 April 2006. Prior rules will still be relevant in certain arbitrations, however, because Article 44 of the Convention specifies that arbitration proceedings are governed by the rules in force at the time the parties consent to ICSID arbitration.[251] When ICSID arbitrations are based on bilateral investment treaties, the applicable Arbitration Rules are likely to be those in force when the investor consents to arbitration, usually when the investor files its request for arbitration with ICSID (see Chapter 3), but possibly earlier if such consent is contained in a separate letter.[252]

Commencing an ICSID arbitration

Initiating arbitration under the ICSID Convention

The Rules of Procedure for the Institution of Conciliation and Arbitration Proceedings, as the title suggests, govern the claimant's commencement of an ICSID arbitration (or conciliation) under the Convention.[253] ICSID also maintains a detailed list of submission requirements on its website.

Institution Rule 1 provides that a Contracting State or a national of a Contracting State wishing to institute an arbitration must send a written request to the Secretary-General at ICSID headquarters (together with five additional signed copies, under Institution Rule 4). An electronic copy of the request should also be submitted. The request must be in one of ICSID's official languages (English, French and Spanish), signed by the claimant or its duly authorized representative, and dated. The rule envisions that the parties to the dispute (State and investor) may in theory file a joint request, although this is unknown in practice.

Convention Article 59 and Regulation 16 require the claimant to pay a non-refundable "lodging fee" (filing fee), set at US$25,000 in the January 2008 Schedule of Fees. This represents a considerable increase from the US$7,000

---

251 The 1984 version of the Arbitration Rules is available at *ICSID Reports* 1 (1993): 157-179. The 2003 version of the Arbitration Rules is available at *ICSID Reports* 7 (2005): 525-546.
252 Institution Rule 2(3) provides that "'[d]ate of consent' means the date on which the parties to the dispute consented in writing" and "if both parties did not act on the same day, it means the date on which the second party acted".
253 The Institution Rules, like the other ICSID Rules, identify the two parties with the terms "requesting party" and "other party". This Guide uses the terms "claimant" and "respondent", which are more common in international arbitration.

filing fee for ICSID Convention arbitrations in the 2003 Schedule of Fees, thus raising the bar against nuisance actions.

The request for arbitration

Article 36(2) of the ICSID Convention requires the request for arbitration to "contain information concerning the issues in dispute, the identity of the parties and their consent to arbitration". Accordingly, Institution Rule 2(1) (which is set out as a jurisdiction checklist in Chapter 2, and is quoted again for convenience) provides:

"The request shall:

(a) designate precisely each party to the dispute and state the address of each;

(b) state, if one of the parties is a constituent subdivision or agency of a Contracting State, that it has been designated to the Centre by that State pursuant to Article 25(1) of the Convention;

(c) indicate the date of consent and the instruments in which it is recorded, including, if one party is a constituent subdivision or agency of a Contracting State, similar data on the approval of such consent by that State unless it had notified the Centre that no such approval is required;

(d) indicate with respect to the party that is a national of a Contracting State:

(i) its nationality on the date of consent; and

(ii) if the party is a natural person:

(A) his nationality on the date of the request; and

(B) that he did not have the nationality of the Contracting State party to the dispute either on the date of consent or on the date of the request; or

    (iii) if the party is a juridical person which on the date of consent had the nationality of the Contracting State party to the dispute, the agreement of the parties that it should be treated as a national of another Contracting State for the purposes of the Convention;

    (e) contain information concerning the issues in dispute indicating that there is, between the parties, a legal dispute arising directly out of an investment; and

    (f) state, if the requesting party is a juridical person, that it has taken all necessary internal actions to authorize the request."

Institution Rule 2(2) requires that the request be accompanied by documentation supporting the information called for under Rules 2(1)(c), 2(1)(d)(iii) and 2(1)(f) (above). Rule 2(1)(c), which deals with consent, and Rule 2(1)(d)(iii), which deals with nationality, are critical to ICSID jurisdiction and are discussed at length in Chapter 2. The purpose of Rule 2(1)(f), which requires juridical entities to affirm their authorization to commence arbitration, is to ensure that shareholders do not bring ICSID cases on behalf of a corporation without express authorization from the corporation.

Under Institution Rule 3, if the parties have previously agreed on the number of arbitrators and/or the method of their appointment (i.e., in their investment contract or in the applicable treaty), the claimant should so state in the request.

Experienced ICSID practitioners include a brief summary of the facts and the substantive breaches of the relevant treaty or investment contract in the request, because this may be the first substantive document to be studied by the respondent and, later, by the tribunal. Practitioners may consult the Secretariat about additional technical form and scope questions, which can facilitate registration.

The Convention does not set any time limitations for the filing of a request, but there may well be such limits in the parties' arbitration agreement or in the applicable legislation or treaty authorizing ICSID arbitration. As noted, such instruments typically mandate negotiation or "cooling off" periods before the parties may institute arbitration.

Registration historically was slow, with the average registration time being 83 days from the request filing date.[254] ICSID has, however, radically improved registration times – for the second half of 2009, the average time for registration was only 29 days.[255]

Acknowledgement and registration of the request

Under Institution Rule 5, the ICSID Secretary-General first sends an acknowledgment of receipt of the request to the claimant. Provided the claimant has paid the lodging fee, the Secretary-General also forwards a copy of the request and supporting documentation to the respondent.

The Secretary-General either registers the request or refuses it (Convention Article 36(3) and Institution Rule 6(1)). The Secretary-General may refuse to register the request only "if he finds, on the basis of the information contained in the request, that the dispute is manifestly outside the jurisdiction of the Centre" (Institution Rule 6(1)(b)). This threshold test is purposefully lenient, as the drafters of the Convention intended to prevent registration only of cases patently lacking a jurisdictional foundation.[256] This would be the case, for example, where one party is neither a Contracting State nor a national of a Contracting State, or where the claimant has provided no evidence of written consent to ICSID jurisdiction.

If there is any doubt whether the request meets ICSID jurisdictional requirements, or whether it is otherwise incomplete, it is common for the Secretariat to contact the claimant's representative and provide an opportunity to correct or supplement the request. Even if the Secretary-General refuses registration based on a technical deficiency, the claimant may subsequently file a new request based on the same claim once the deficiency is cured.

In practice, requests are seldom so deficient as to warrant refusal of registration. The Secretary-General's decision to register a request, of course, in no way

---

254 A. Sinclair, "ICSID arbitration: how long does it take?", *Global Arbitration Review* 4, no. 5 (2009).

255 Global Arbitration Review, "ICSID predicts steady case-numbers and falling case times", <www.globalarbitrationreview.com/news/article/19589/>, 9 December 2009.

256 "Report of the Executive Directors", *supra* note 4, at 27.

prejudges the ICSID tribunal's subsequent determination of its own competence and the Centre's jurisdiction.[257]

Institution Rule 6(2) establishes that an ICSID arbitration "shall be deemed to have been instituted on the date of the registration of the request". The registration date is important in several respects, for example, in measuring time limits for naming arbitrators (see below).

Under Institution Rules 6(1)(a) and 7, the Secretary-General sends a notice of registration to both parties on the registration date. The notice of registration, among other things, invites the parties to inform the Secretary-General of any agreement regarding the number and method of appointment of the arbitrators and directs the parties to proceed to constitute the tribunal as soon as possible. A claimant may unilaterally withdraw its request only up to the registration date; thereafter, the proceedings may be discontinued only with the respondent's consent (Institution Rule 8).

Initiating arbitration under the Additional Facility Rules

A party's access to the ICSID Additional Facility is conditional on the Secretary-General's specific approval. Under Article 2 of the Additional Facility Rules, the Additional Facility may administer three categories of proceedings:

"(a) conciliation and arbitration proceedings for the settlement of legal disputes arising directly out of an investment which are not within the jurisdiction of the Centre because either the State party to the dispute or the State whose national is a party to the dispute is not a Contracting State;

(b) conciliation and arbitration proceedings for the settlement of legal disputes which are not within the jurisdiction of the Centre because

---

257 Schreuer, *The ICSID Convention, supra* note 2, at 471; A. Parra, "The Institution of ICSID Arbitration Proceedings", *News from ICSID* 20, no. 2 (2003): 12; *see* Lalive, *supra* note 51, at 645-682 (finding that registration of the proceeding by the Secretary-General did not preclude a finding by the tribunal that the dispute lay outside the jurisdiction of the Centre); *see also American Manufacturing & Trading, Inc. v. Zaire* (Award), *supra* note 113, at para. 5.01 (noting the "extremely light control" conferred upon the Secretary-General by Convention Article 36(3)).

they do not arise directly out of an investment, provided that either the State party to the dispute or the State whose national is a party to the dispute is a Contracting State; and

(c) fact-finding proceedings."

Where one of the parties is neither a Contracting State nor a national of a Contracting State, the Secretary-General will approve access to the Additional Facility only if the parties have also conditionally consented to jurisdiction under the Convention in the event the non-Contracting State party does become a party to the Convention by the time arbitration proceedings are actually instituted (Article 4(2), Additional Facility Rules). Where the relevant dispute does not arise directly out of an investment, the Secretary-General's approval depends on whether "the underlying transaction has features which distinguish it from an ordinary commercial transaction" (Article 4(3), Additional Facility Rules). The Secretary-General's approval in this category may also be made conditional on the parties' undertaking to submit their dispute to arbitration under the Convention proper if the Secretary-General deems it "likely" that a tribunal will decide that the dispute does in fact arise directly out of an investment (Article 4(4), Additional Facility Rules).

Pursuant to Article 4 of the Additional Facility Arbitration Rules, the Secretary-General will register the request if he or she is satisfied that it "conforms in form and substance to the provisions of Article 3". Arguably, the words "form and substance" give the Secretary-General somewhat greater discretion here than with registration of requests for Convention arbitration. Article 3 requires that an Additional Facility request:

"(a) designate precisely each party to the dispute and state the address of each;

(b) set forth the relevant provisions embodying the agreement of the parties to refer the dispute to arbitration;

(c) indicate the date of approval by the Secretary-General pursuant to Article 4 of the Additional Facility Rules of the agreement of the parties providing for access to the Additional Facility;

(d) contain information concerning the issues in dispute and an indication of the amount involved, if any; and

(e) state, if the requesting party is a juridical person, that it has taken all necessary internal actions to authorize the request."

Under the January 2008 Schedule of Fees, the claimant is assessed US$25,000, which includes the fee for requesting approval for access to the Additional Facility and the fee for lodging the request itself. This represents a substantial increase from the US$7,000 Additional Facility filing fee in the 2003 Schedule of Fees, identical to the increase with respect to Convention cases.

Constitution of an ICSID Tribunal

Tribunals under the ICSID Convention

Articles 37 to 40 of the Convention and Arbitration Rules 1 to 6 deal with the constitution of arbitration tribunals. These provisions encourage the parties to establish the tribunal "as soon as possible" and "with all possible dispatch" after the Secretary-General has registered the request. In practice, the constitution of an ICSID tribunal usually takes more than three months, and in some cases has consumed far more time.

The Panel of Arbitrators

As envisioned in Article 12 of the Convention, ICSID maintains a Panel of Arbitrators. The Panel is not exclusive; the parties are not obliged to appoint arbitrators from this Panel.

Under Article 13 of the Convention, each Contracting State may designate four individuals – who need not be its nationals – to the Panel of Arbitrators. In addition, the Chairman of the Administrative Council may designate ten individuals to the Panel of Arbitrators, each of a different nationality. Each Panel designee serves for a renewable six-year term and is not remunerated unless and until appointed to a tribunal.

Not all Contracting States designate their full complement of four individuals to the Panel of Arbitrators, and many neglect to update their rosters even after the designated individuals have become inactive. Nor may it be said that all designees are experienced international arbitrators. As a consequence, ICSID has undertaken an effort to update and replenish the Panel of Arbitrators by contacting States that have not designated candidates to the Panel or have allowed appointments to lapse.[258]

Appointment of arbitrators by the parties

The Convention and the Arbitration Rules contain certain limitations on the parties' freedom to select their tribunal, both as to the number and as to the specific arbitrators. First, Article 37(2)(a) of the Convention provides that a tribunal "shall consist of a sole arbitrator or any uneven number of arbitrators". Second, pursuant to Article 39 of the Convention and Arbitration Rule 1(3), the tribunal may not consist of a majority of arbitrators with the same nationality as either party, unless the parties have appointed the arbitrators by agreement; with respect to a three-member tribunal, one party may not appoint a national of either State involved unless the other party agrees. Third, a person who previously acted as either a conciliator or an arbitrator in proceedings to settle the same dispute brought to arbitration may not be appointed to the tribunal (Arbitration Rule 1(4)).

If the parties have not previously agreed on the number of arbitrators or the method of their appointment, Arbitration Rule 2 establishes a procedure under which the parties exchange proposals regarding the constitution of the tribunal. The parties have 60 days from registration of the request in which to reach an agreement. This time limit may be, and often is, extended by agreement. If the parties cannot agree within the deadline on the parameters for constituting a tribunal, Arbitration Rule 3 provides that either party may invoke the default formula for a three-member panel set out in Article 37(2)(b) of the Convention: each party names one arbitrator and the two parties then agree on the third arbitrator, who becomes president of the tribunal. This default mechanism

---

258 "ICSID predicts steady case-numbers and falling case times", *supra* note 255.

prevents one party from frustrating the constitution process. If one party refuses to appoint its arbitrator or to cooperate in selecting the president, the Chairman of the Administrative Council takes action under Article 38 of the Convention (see below).

Under Arbitration Rule 5, the parties must notify the Secretary-General of the name and method of appointment of each arbitrator, and the Secretary-General then asks the appointee if he or she accepts the appointment. If the appointee does not accept the position within 15 days, the Secretary-General invites the relevant party to appoint another arbitrator. Until the date of the Secretary-General's notification that the tribunal has been constituted, each party may unilaterally replace its own appointee and the parties together, by agreement, may replace any arbitrator (Arbitration Rule 7).

Appointment of arbitrators by the Centre

If the parties fail to constitute the tribunal within 90 days of the registration of the request, or within such further time as agreed, either party may invoke Article 38 of the Convention and request the Centre's assistance.

In September 2009, ICSID informally adopted a new two-tier appointment process for appointments under Article 38 of the Convention. The Centre first circulates a list of three candidates – not necessarily from the Panel of Arbitrators – to both parties on a yes/no check-off ballot, to be returned by each party privately to the Centre. If there is agreement, ICSID appoints from this list rather than using the Article 38 procedure.[259]

If there is no agreement on a name from the first list, ICSID proceeds with the appointment process under Article 38 and Arbitration Rule 4(4). The Chairman of the Administrative Council appoints any remaining arbitrators from the Panel of Arbitrators, after consultation with both parties, using his or her "best efforts" to do so within 30 days. None of the arbitrators appointed by the Chairman of the Administrative Council from the Panel may be of the same nationality as either of the parties. This ICSID-driven procedure ensures

---

259 *Id.*

that an uncooperative party cannot prevent the constitution of the tribunal and thereby frustrate the arbitration process.

Notification of final constitution of an ICSID tribunal

Once all arbitrators have accepted their appointments, the Secretary-General sends a formal notice to the parties. The tribunal is then deemed constituted under Arbitration Rule 6, and the arbitration proceedings officially begin.

Tribunals under the Additional Facility Rules

Arbitrators for Additional Facility tribunals are selected in largely the same manner as arbitrators for ICSID tribunals (Articles 6 to 11, Additional Facility Arbitration Rules). One significant exception is that the Chairman of the Administrative Council, if called upon to name one or more Additional Facility arbitrators, need not appoint from the Panel of Arbitrators.

Arbitrator qualifications and challenges

Tribunals constituted under the ICSID Convention

Whether ICSID arbitrators are appointed by the parties or by the Chairman of the Administrative Council, and whether they are selected from the Panel of Arbitrators or otherwise, Articles 14(1) and 40(2) of the Convention mandate that all ICSID arbitrators "be persons of high moral character and recognized competence in the fields of law, commerce, industry or finance, who may be relied upon to exercise independent judgment". Article 14 specifies that "[c]ompetence in the field of law shall be of particular importance in the case of persons on the Panel of Arbitrators". In practice, most ICSID arbitrators are international lawyers.

As of the tribunal's first session, each ICSID arbitrator must have signed a declaration affirming his or her independence and agreement to respect the confidentiality of the proceedings (Arbitration Rule 6). ICSID amended Rule 6(2) in 2006 to require arbitrators to disclose not only their professional, business and other relationships with the parties, but also any other circumstances that might cause their reliability for independent judgment to be questioned by a party. The amendment makes disclosure an ongoing obligation throughout the arbitration.

Article 57 of the Convention sets a high bar for challenging an arbitrator (or a member of an *ad hoc* annulment committee (see Chapter 5)). The challenge application must establish that the arbitrator has exhibited "a manifest lack of the qualities" required by Article 14(1) of the Convention. A party must base a challenge on facts, rather than inference, proving the arbitrator's manifest lack of high moral character, manifest lack of recognized competence in his or her field, or manifest lack of ability to exercise independent judgment. As stated in the Decision on the Challenge to the President of the *ad hoc* Committee in *Vivendi I*:

> "[I]n cases where [...] the facts are established and no further inference of impropriety is sought to be derived from them, the question seems to us to be whether a real risk of lack of impartiality based upon those facts (and not on any mere speculation or inference) could reasonably be apprehended by either party."[260]

As of January 2010, parties had challenged arbitrators in 26 registered ICSID cases. Challenges tend to rest on three grounds: relationships with parties,[261] relationships with parties' counsel or law firms,[262] and/or involvement in

---

260 *Compañía de Aguas del Aconquija S.A. & Vivendi Universal v. Argentine Republic*, ICSID Case No. ARB/97/3, Decision on the Challenge to the President of the Committee (3 October 2001) (***Vivendi I (Decision on the Challenge to the President of the Committee)***), *ICSID Review – FILJ* 17 (2002): 180, at para. 25.

261 *See, e.g., Vivendi I* (Decision on the Challenge to the President of the Committee), *supra* note 260; *Suez, Sociedad General de Aguas de Barcelona S.A. and Vivendi Universal S.A. v. Argentine Republic*, ICSID Case No. ARB/03/19 and *Suez, Sociedad General de Aguas de Barcelona S.A. and InterAguas Servicios Integrales del Agua S.A. v. Argentine Republic*, ICSID Case No. ARB/03/17, Decision on a Second Proposal for the Disqualification of a Member of the Arbitral Tribunal (12 May 2008) (***Suez v. Argentina (Second Disqualification Decision)***); *EDF International S.A., SAUR International S.A. and León Participaciones Argentinas S.A. v. Argentine Republic*, ICSID Case No. ARB/03/23, Challenge Decision Regarding Professor Gabrielle Kaufmann-Kohler (25 June 2008).

262 *See, e.g., Amco Asia Corporation and others v. Republic of Indonesia*, ICSID Case No. ARB/81/1, Decision on the proposal to disqualify an arbitrator (24 June 1982) in M. Reisman et al.,

other arbitrations raising similar issues.[263] A list of ICSID arbitrator challenges, including details about the decisions, the identity of the arbitrator challenged, the decision-maker on the challenge, and the outcome of the challenge, is set out in Table III.C in Annex 10.

In principle, an arbitrator may also be removed under Convention Article 57 on grounds of ineligibility for appointment to the tribunal because of nationality and/or membership on the Panel of Arbitrators. This is rare in practice, given the detailed scrutiny undertaken by the parties and the Centre during the appointment process.[264]

Under Article 57 of the Convention, and specifically under Arbitration Rule 9, a party must file with the Secretary-General a reasoned proposal to disqualify an arbitrator "promptly, and in any event before the proceeding is declared closed". Pursuant to Arbitration Rule 27, failure to do so can result in a waiver of rights. Tribunals have held that delays of approximately eight months,[265] approximately

---

International Commercial Arbitration (New York: The Foundation Press, Inc., 1997), 624-631; *SGS Société Générale de Surveillance S.A. v. Islamic Republic of Pakistan*, ICSID Case No. ARB/01/13, Decision on Claimant's Proposal to Disqualify Arbitrator (19 December 2002), *ICSID Reports* 8 (2005): 398; *Azurix Corp. v. Argentine Republic*, ICSID Case No. ARB/01/12, Decision on the Application for Annulment of the Argentine Republic (1 September 2009).

263 See, e.g., *Suez, Sociedad General de Aguas de Barcelona S.A. and Vivendi Universal S.A. v. Argentine Republic*, ICSID Case No. ARB/03/19 and *Suez, Sociedad General de Aguas de Barcelona S.A. and InterAguas Servicios Integrales del Agua S.A. v. Argentine Republic*, ICSID Case No. ARB/03/17, Decision on the Proposal for the Disqualification of a Member of the Arbitral Tribunal (22 October 2007) (*Suez v. Argentina (First Disqualification Decision)*); *Electrabel S.A. v. Republic of Hungary*, ICSID Case No. ARB/07/19, Decision on the Proposal for the Disqualification of an Arbitrator (25 February 2008) (unpublished); *Saba Fakes v. Republic of Turkey*, ICSID Case No. ARB/07/20, Award (14 July 2010); *Participaciones Inversiones Portuarias S.A.R.L. v. Gabonese Republic*, ICSID Case No. ARB/08/17, Decision on the Proposal to Disqualify an Arbitrator (12 November 2009).

264 See *Eudoro A. Olguín v. Republic of Paraguay*, ICSID Case No. ARB/98/5, Decision on Jurisdiction (8 August 2000), *ICSID Reports* 6 (2004): 154.

265 *Azurix v. Argentina* (Decision on the Application for Annulment of the Argentine Republic), *supra* note 262.

six months,[266] 147 days,[267] and 53 days[268] in submitting disqualification proposals are unreasonable, and those delays have resulted in waiver.

A challenge to a single member of a tribunal must be "promptly" decided by the other members of the tribunal; if they cannot agree, the Chairman of the Administrative Council will use "best efforts" to make a decision on the application within 30 days.[269] It is also the Chairman of the Administrative Council who decides a challenge to a sole arbitrator or to a majority of the arbitrators on a multi-arbitrator tribunal, again within a "best efforts" 30-day time period.[270] The Chairman of the Administrative Council occasionally has requested another authority, such as the Secretary-General of the Permanent Court of Arbitration (*PCA*) in The Hague, to rule upon a challenge to an arbitrator in an ICSID case.[271]

The ICSID standard for arbitrator challenges is mandatory. However, limited modification by the parties to the procedure is not unknown. By way of example, the parties in *Perenco Ecuador Limited v. Republic of Ecuador and Empresa Estatal Petróleos del Ecuador* agreed in advance to submit arbitrator challenges to the Secretary-General of the PCA and articulated a less stringent standard for successful challenge.[272] The PCA ultimately affirmed the chal-

---

266 *CEMEX Caracas Investments B.V. and CEMEX Caracas II Investments B.V. v. Bolivarian Republic of Venezuela*, ICSID Case No. ARB/08/15, Decision on the Respondent's Proposal to Disqualify a Member of the Tribunal (6 November 2009).

267 *CDC Group plc v. Republic of Seychelles*, ICSID Case No. ARB/02/14, Decision of the Ad Hoc Committee on the Application for Annulment of the Republic of the Seychelles (29 June 2005).

268 *Suez v. Argentina* (First Disqualification Decision), *supra* note 263.

269 *See Generation Ukraine Inc. v. Ukraine*, ICSID Case No. ARB/00/9, Award (16 September 2003); *Siemens v. Argentina* (Award), *supra* note 140; *PIP v. Gabon* (Decision on the Proposal to Disqualify an Arbitrator), *supra* note 263.

270 *See Pey Casado v. Chile* (Award), *supra* note 101; *Sempra v. Argentina* (Award), *supra* note 188.

271 *See Generation Ukraine v. Ukraine* (Award), *supra* note 269; *Siemens v. Argentina* (Award), *supra* note 140; *Pey Casado v. Chile* (Award), *supra* note 101.

272 *Perenco Ecuador Ltd. v. Republic of Ecuador and Empresa Estatal Petróleos del Ecuador (Petroecuador)*, ICSID Case No. ARB/08/6, Decision on Challenge to Arbitrator (8 December 2009).

lenge and the challenged arbitrator notified ICSID of his resignation shortly thereafter.

The ICSID Convention does not allow truncated tribunals, meaning tribunals operating with less than a full complement of members. Under Article 56 of the Convention and Arbitration Rules 10 to 12, if a vacancy occurs on the tribunal due to the disqualification, death, incapacity or resignation of an arbitrator, the proceedings must be suspended until the vacancy is filled. The vacant position is usually filled by the same process used to appoint the original arbitrator. However, if the vacancy occurred because an arbitrator resigned without the consent of the tribunal (as theoretically could happen if an unscrupulous party-appointed arbitrator resigned for tactical purposes) or if the vacancy has not been filled within 45 days and the parties so request, the Chairman of the Administrative Council appoints a replacement from the Panel of Arbitrators. The proceedings then resume, with the possibility of any earlier hearing being repeated.

Additional Facility tribunals

The procedures and standards for appointment and challenge of arbitrators in ICSID Additional Facility proceedings are largely similar to those for arbitrators in Convention arbitrations. They must meet the same basic personal qualifications (Articles 8 and 15, Additional Facility Arbitration Rules) and make a similar declaration (Article 13, Additional Facility Arbitration Rules). Identical provisions also govern the procedures for filling vacancies on tribunals (Articles 16 to 18, Additional Facility Arbitration Rules), with the exception that the Chairman of the Administrative Council is not limited to the Panel of Arbitrators if he or she must appoint a replacement arbitrator.

Conduct of proceedings

Arbitration proceedings under the ICSID Convention

Articles 41 to 47 of the Convention and Arbitration Rules 13 to 38 regulate the conduct of ICSID proceedings from the constitution of the tribunal through issuance of the award.

The tribunal's first session(s) and basic procedure

The tribunal must hold its first session within 60 days of its official constitution, or within such other time period as is agreed by the parties (Arbitration Rule 13). The session takes place in person at ICSID headquarters in Washington, DC, unless the parties have agreed to an alternative location with the approval of the tribunal and Secretary-General. It is also possible for agreement to be reached to conduct the first session by conference call.

The first session typically includes the "preliminary procedural consultation" described in Arbitration Rule 20. Under that rule, the president of the tribunal is mandated to ascertain the parties' views on issues of procedure. Questions to be resolved include: (a) the number of arbitrators necessary for a quorum (Arbitration Rule 14 requires a majority unless the parties agree otherwise); (b) the language(s) of the proceedings; (c) the number, sequence and timing of written pleadings; (d) the number of copies of filings; (e) whether to dispense with either the oral or the written procedure; (f) the manner of apportioning the costs of the proceedings; and (g) the manner of keeping the record. In practice, the Secretariat circulates a standard form agenda and asks the parties to communicate any agreement on the agenda items. In this context, counsel on both sides of the dispute will consult in advance of the session. If counsel adopt a sensible approach this can materially narrow the issues for debate, which in turn can cause the parties to agree to a conference call rather than a physical meeting.

That being said, a physical first meeting has certain "subliminal" benefits. It is the parties' first opportunity to meet the tribunal and see how the arbitrators interact, and is often the first face-to-face meeting of the two sides and their counsel. Experienced arbitrators are aware that the tone for the entire proceeding may be set at the first session.

Arbitration Rule 21 envisions an additional pre-hearing conference to allow an exchange of information and a stipulation of uncontested facts among the parties, with a view to reaching an amicable settlement. In practice, given the logistical complexity and expense of convening arbitrators, parties and counsel from several countries, ICSID tribunals rarely hold this second pre-hearing session. A cost-effective alternative is to conduct subsequent procedural sessions, if not the first session, by conference call or video conference.

Consistent with the principle of (reasonable) party autonomy, ICSID tribunals may adopt the procedural sequence and schedule agreed by the parties, as long as the Convention and the Regulations are not contravened (Arbitration Rule 20). Although some procedural aspects may be agreed by the parties, it is usually the tribunal that establishes the various steps of the proceedings and their time limits and eventual extensions (Arbitration Rule 26). Under Arbitration Rule 29 and as described below, unless the parties agree otherwise, ICSID arbitration proceedings consist of both a written phase and an oral phase.

The parties may be represented by counsel or other agents (Arbitration Rule 18). In practice, advocates in ICSID arbitrations tend to be specialized counsel in international law firms, scholars of international law, and counsel within the attorney general's office (or equivalent) or ministries of justice and foreign affairs of State parties. The parties' representatives – like the Centre, the Secretariat and the arbitrators – enjoy immunity from legal process and other national restrictions.

Written procedure

As set out in Arbitration Rule 31, the main pleadings in the written phase of an ICSID arbitration typically include a "memorial" (the common name for an advocacy brief in international proceedings) filed by the claimant and a "countermemorial" filed by the respondent. If the tribunal so requests or if the parties so agree, the parties may also file a second round of memorials termed a "reply" for the claimant and a "rejoinder" for the respondent. The tribunal has discretion to order post-hearing memorials.

The claimant's memorial should contain a statement of relevant facts, a statement of law, and the claimant's submissions (i.e., pleas) and request for relief. The respondent's countermemorial, the claimant's reply, and the respondent's rejoinder each must contain a response to the facts in the prior pleading, any additional relevant facts, a response to the statement of law in the prior pleading, and the submitting party's submissions. In practice, the relevant contemporaneous documents, witness statements (for fact witnesses) and expert reports (for independent expert witnesses) on which each party relies are also filed with the pleadings, and form an important part of the record.

Convention Article 46 and Arbitration Rule 40 contemplate the filing of counterclaims, "incidental" claims and "additional" claims that arise directly out of the subject matter of the main dispute. The respondent must file any counterclaim no later than in its countermemorial. The claimant must assert any incidental or additional claims (together called "ancillary claims") no later than in its reply or, if a second round of memorials is not ordered, no later than in its memorial. Ancillary claims include, for example, claims for interest and costs, provided they are within the scope of the parties' consent to arbitration and otherwise meet the relevant ICSID jurisdictional requirements. The tribunal may authorize later filing of ancillary claims by either party for good cause. In practice, ICSID tribunals generally are liberal in allowing ancillary claims.

Unlike in many other forms of international arbitration, the parties do not transmit their filings directly to the arbitrators. Until the tribunal is constituted, the parties are required to deliver to the ICSID Secretariat the original signed version of each filing plus five copies. Thereafter, they must deliver to the Secretariat two copies more than the number of arbitrators on the panel (Arbitration Rule 23). Supporting documentation, witness statements and expert reports are ordinarily filed with the pleading to which they relate and, in any case, must be filed within the time limit for the relevant pleading (Arbitration Rule 24). Most ICSID tribunals now require electronic filing as well. In a number of recent cases, the tribunal and counsel have agreed to modify the rules to allow filing to take place electronically with only a single hard copy delivered to the Secretariat. Increasingly, parties are taking advantage of technological advances, for example, by submitting memorials on USB drives with hyperlinks to exhibits, witness statements and expert reports, for the convenience of the tribunal.

Parties may correct errors in the written record, with the permission of the other party or the tribunal, at any time until the award is rendered (Arbitration Rule 25). The Secretary to the tribunal (or opposing counsel) may take the initiative to point out technical mistakes (for example, missing or illegible exhibits, significant typographical errors) to a party representative to allow immediate correction and thus avoid confusion and complication.

As in other forms of international arbitration, the written submissions and accompanying contemporaneous documents in ICSID cases are generally the most influential part of the record for the arbitrators. ICSID tribunals put a high premium on well-organized, well-researched, clear and measured pleadings, and on reliable and straightforward witness statements and expert reports.

Written submissions by non-disputing parties

The 2006 amendments to Arbitration Rule 37(2) permit non-disputing parties to file submissions in an ICSID arbitration, provided certain conditions are met. Tribunals may permit non-disputing parties to file written observations after the tribunal consults with the parties and evaluates three factors: (a) whether an amicus submission would assist the tribunal by providing a fresh perspective; (b) whether an amicus submission would address a matter within the scope of the dispute; and (c) whether the non-disputing party has a significant interest in the proceeding.

As of January 2010, non-disputing parties had made submissions in five ICSID cases. These parties were various non-governmental organizations in *Biwater Gauff v. Tanzania* and *Aguas Argentinas, S.A., Suez, Sociedad General de Aguas de Barcelona, S.A. and Vivendi Universal, S.A. v. Argentina*; and the European Commission in *AES Summit Generation Ltd. and AES-Tisza Erömü Kft. v. Hungary, Electrabel S.A. v. Hungary* and *Micula and others v. Romania*. A list of the ICSID cases in which non-disputing parties have made applications is set out in Table III.A in Annex 10.

Oral procedure

The ICSID oral procedure, like the written procedure, is similar to that in other international arbitrations. There may be one or more hearings on jurisdiction, merits and quantum issues before the tribunal. Hearings are comparatively short, seldom longer than two weeks even for merits hearings in the most complex cases – hence the premium on excellence and persuasiveness in the written procedure.

Under Arbitration Rule 32, hearings are open only to the parties and their representatives, witnesses and experts, unless the tribunal and the parties agree otherwise. The 2006 amendments to Article 32 illustrate the balance between the traditional principle of privacy of proceedings and increasing demands for transparency – tribunals, at their discretion, may permit third parties and the public to attend hearings, unless either party objects.

Arbitration Rule 35 provides that witnesses and experts, who must preface their testimony with declarations of veracity, "shall be examined before the Tribunal by the parties under the control of its President" and may be questioned by the tribunal itself. In light of the control given to the president in Arbitration Rule 35, counsel cannot expect to conduct extensive direct examination or overly aggressive cross-examination. Although the tribunal has discretion to admit written rather than oral testimony and to arrange for oral examination other than before the tribunal itself (Arbitration Rule 36), this rarely happens.

Given short hearings and the importance of written witness statements and expert reports, the main purpose of presenting fact witnesses and experts at the hearing is to allow cross-examination by the opposing side and, most important, questions from the tribunal. A hearing is not an occasion to repeat the written submissions, but rather an opportunity to gauge – and respond to – the arbitrators' main concerns. Discernment and responsiveness in advocacy are critical.

Evidence, disclosure and discovery

Arbitration Rule 34 gives the tribunal discretion to decide on both the admissibility and probative value of evidence. A tribunal's approach will depend on several factors, not the least of which is the balance of civil and common lawyers on the panel. Formal rules of evidence, such as those developed under national procedural codes, do not apply.

Convention Article 43 provides for voluntary disclosure of evidence, subject to the parties' agreement otherwise. Arbitration Rule 33 provides for the transmission by each party of "precise information regarding the evidence which it intends to produce and that which it intends to request the Tribunal to call for, together with an indication of the points to which such evidence will be directed", within time limits fixed by the tribunal. Arbitration Rule 34 authorizes the tribunal to require the production of documents and the presentation of fact witnesses and experts, and to make site visits. As a matter of practice, parties annex copies of the contemporaneous documents on which they rely to their written submissions.

In sum, in ICSID arbitration any discovery of evidence beyond voluntary disclosure is firmly in the control of the tribunal. Parties to ICSID proceedings cannot expect extensive, US-style document discovery. Depositions are unheard of.

If a party fails to cooperate in the evidentiary process, Arbitration Rule 34(3) directs the ICSID tribunal to take "formal note" of such failure and any reasons given by the party. Although the Arbitration Rules do not contain any further explicit sanction, a party's uncooperative conduct, as in any international arbitration, may lead the tribunal to draw adverse inferences from that lack of cooperation and may affect the assessment of damages and allocation of costs. In *AGIP v. Congo*, for example, the government of Congo's failure to comply with a provisional measure ordering it to produce documentation was reflected in the tribunal's assessment of damages.[273] As in any arbitration proceeding, it is unwise for a party to flout the procedural decisions of the tribunal that is proceeding to decide the merits of its case.

Objections to jurisdiction

Article 41 of the ICSID Convention affirms that the tribunal "shall be the judge of its own competence", meaning that the tribunal itself is to decide questions regarding its jurisdiction. Given the rapid rise in the number of bilateral investment treaty arbitrations under the Convention, and their often unfamiliar jurisdictional foundations, respondent States almost routinely object to ICSID jurisdiction under the relevant treaty. Claimant investors should expect to invest substantial time and resources on jurisdictional issues, which may or may not be joined to the merits.

Under Arbitration Rule 41, a party raising jurisdictional objections must do so "as early as possible" in the proceedings, but in any event not later than in its countermemorial, unless the relevant facts were not known until later. Under the 2003 version of Arbitration Rule 41, proceedings on the merits are automatically suspended when a party submits jurisdictional objections, which it may do either

---

273 *AGIP S.p.A. v. The Government of the People's Republic of the Congo*, ICSID Case No. ARB/77/1, Award (30 November 1979), *ICSID Reports* 1 (1993): 306, 317-318.

separately (if such possibility is envisioned in the procedural order) or as part of its countermemorial. The 2006 amendments to Rule 41 give the tribunal discretion whether or not to suspend the proceedings on the merits. In either case, the tribunal must consider whether to join the jurisdictional objections to the merits or establish a separate jurisdictional phase, including a schedule for pleadings on the jurisdictional objections.

As a practical matter, when ICSID tribunals deal with jurisdictional objections as preliminary questions, this may add a year or more to the duration of an ICSID arbitration. Where the case is bifurcated in this way, if the tribunal finds that it lacks jurisdiction the case comes to an end; the tribunal issues an award dismissing the case for lack of jurisdiction, which is subject to the limited avenues of post-award proceedings available under the Convention (discussed at the end of this chapter and in Chapter 5). If, to the contrary, the tribunal finds that it has jurisdiction, it issues a reasoned decision on jurisdiction (rather than an award) and proceeds to calendar further proceedings on the merits and quantum. Such jurisdictional decisions are not defined as awards under the definition in Convention Article 48(3) and so are not subject to the post-award proceedings available under the Convention. They are, however, an integral part of the award, when issued, and may accordingly be challenged at that stage under the Convention.

Preliminary objections to claims

The 2006 amendments to the Arbitration Rules introduced an important new provision, Arbitration Rule 41(5), allowing a summary determination of whether a claim is "manifestly without legal merit".[274] Such a summary dismissal

---

274 Rule 41(5) provides as follows: "Unless the parties have agreed to another expedited procedure for making preliminary objections, a party may, no later than 30 days after the constitution of the Tribunal, and in any event before the first session of the Tribunal, file an objection that a claim is manifestly without legal merit. The party shall specify as precisely as possible the basis for the objection. The Tribunal, after giving the parties the opportunity to present their observations on the objection, shall, at its first session or promptly thereafter, notify the parties of its decision on the objection. The decision of the Tribunal shall be without prejudice to the right of a party to file an objection pursuant to paragraph (1) or to object, in the course of the proceeding, that a claim lacks legal merit."

must be requested by the respondent under Rule 41(5) within 30 days of the constitution of the tribunal. The tribunal, in turn, must make a decision at the first session or promptly thereafter, and must issue a final award dismissing the case if it finds the objection to be well-founded. To ensure procedural fairness with such a short timeline, Rule 41(5) requires that the challenge be as precise as possible and that both parties have the opportunity to present their observations, typically in writing.

As of January 2010, respondents had made applications under Rule 41(5) in three cases: *Trans-Global Petroleum v. Jordan;*[275] *Brandes Investment Partners v. Venezuela;*[276] and *Global Trading Resource Corp. v. Ukraine.* The outcomes differed, but the tribunals in both *Trans-Global* and *Brandes* agreed that the standard for an application under Rule 41(5) is set high and "requires the respondent to establish its objection clearly and obviously, with relative ease and dispatch".

In *Trans-Global,* the tribunal denied Jordan's Rule 41(5) application, but noted that the claimant had withdrawn one of its claims that was manifestly without legal merit.[277] The tribunal in *Brandes* denied Venezuela's Rule 41(5) application, finding that the application raised questions that "necessitate[d] the examination of complex legal and factual issues" and could not be resolved in summary proceedings.[278] The *Global Trading* application remained pending as of September 2010.

Provisional measures

Under Convention Article 47 and Arbitration Rule 39, a party may request at any point during the proceedings "that provisional measures for the preservation

---

275 *Trans-Global Petroleum, Inc. v. Hashemite Kingdom of Jordan,* ICSID Case No. ARB/07/25, Decision on the Respondent's Objection Under Rule 41(5) of the ICSID Arbitration Rules (12 May 2008), at para. 88.

276 *Brandes Investment Partners, LP v. Bolivarian Republic of Venezuela,* ICSID Case No. ARB/08/3, Decision on the Respondent's Objection Under Rule 41(5) of the ICSID Arbitration Rules (2 February 2009), para. 63.

277 *Trans-Global Petroleum v. Jordan* (Decision on the Respondent's Objection Under Rule 41(5) of the ICSID Arbitration Rules), *supra* note 275, paras. 120, 124.

278 *Brandes v. Venezuela* (Decision on the Respondent's Objection Under Rule 41(5) of the ICSID Arbitration Rules), *supra* note 276, at para. 71.

of its rights be *recommended* by the Tribunal". (emphasis added). Despite the apparent limitation in the use of the word "recommend" as compared to the word "order", many ICSID tribunals have determined that provisional measures decisions are binding on the parties.[279] A recommendation for provisional measures, however, does not constitute an award and is not subject to post-award proceedings under the Convention.

The request for provisional measures must describe the rights to be preserved, the measures requested and the circumstances. Although the tribunal may also recommend provisional measures on its own initiative, it cannot proceed before giving each party the opportunity to present observations (Arbitration Rules 39(3) and (4)). Arbitration Rule 39 was amended in 2006 to permit a party to file a request for provisional measures any time after the arbitration is initiated, even before the Tribunal is constituted. The Secretariat may administer the exchange of written submissions on the provisional measure in parallel with the constitution of the tribunal, thus expediting the earliest possible resolution. This is particularly important given the limitations imposed by the ICSID regime on accessing the courts for urgent relief.

ICSID tribunals do not readily recommend provisional measures. As of January 2010, parties had made requests for recommendation of provisional measures in 58 registered ICSID cases, resulting in recommendations in only some 16 cases. These 16 decisions involved provisional measures directing a party: (a) to preserve or produce documents;[280] (b) to discontinue parallel proceedings in local courts, or not to take steps that would exacerbate the dispute;[281] and

---

279 *Emilio Agustín Maffezini v. Kingdom of Spain,* ICSID Case No. ARB/97/7, Procedural Order No. 2 (28 October 1999), *ICSID Review–FILJ* 16 (2001): 212; *Víctor Pey Casado and President Allende Foundation v. Republic of Chile,* ICSID Case No. ARB/98/2, Decision on Provisional Measures (25 September 2001); *Occidental Petroleum Corporation and Occidental Exploration and Production Company v. Republic of Ecuador,* ICSID Case No. ARB/06/11, Decision on Provisional Measures (17 August 2007).

280 *See, e.g., AGIP v. Congo* (Award), *supra* note 273; *Biwater Gauff (Tanzania) Ltd. v. United Republic of Tanzania,* ICSID Case No. ARB/05/22, Procedural Order No. 1 (31 March 2006).

281 *See, e.g., Maritime International Nominees Establishment (MINE) v. Republic of Guinea,* ICSID Case No. ARB/84/4, Award (6 January 1988), *ICSID Reports* 4 (1997): 54-78; *see also Československá Obchodní Banka, A.S. v. Slovak Republic,* ICSID Case No. ARB/97/4,

(c) to maintain the confidentiality of the proceedings.[282] A list of the requests for provisional measures advanced in ICSID cases, including details about the measures requested and the outcomes, is set out in Table III.E in Annex 10.

As highlighted in Chapter 2, parties arbitrating under the Convention – whether pursuant to an investor-State contract, a BIT or a MIT – may not seek provisional measures from an authority other than the tribunal, i.e., from a national court, unless this is expressly provided for in the agreement or the relevant treaty (Arbitration Rule 39(6)). Investors anticipating the need for urgent interim measures from local courts in connection with particular projects must, in the absence of favorable legislation, negotiate for such rights in their investment contracts.

Default, discontinuance and settlement

The rules envision default and discontinuance, including discontinuance by reason of settlement. Default, not surprisingly, is rare. Discontinuance is common; as of January 2010, 34 percent of ICSID Convention and ICSID Additional Facility arbitrations ended in discontinuance.[283]

Article 45 of the Convention and Arbitration Rule 42 govern default. If a party fails to appear or to present its case at any stage of the proceedings, the tribunal may, at the request of the other party, render an award on the issues before it. Prior to ruling, the tribunal must notify the defaulting party of the other party's request to proceed and, unless satisfied that the defaulting party has no intention

---

Decision on Objections to Jurisdiction (24 May 1999); *Tokios Tokelés v. Ukraine*, ICSID Case No. ARB/02/18, Order No. 1, Claimant's Request for Provisional Measures (1 July 2003); *Perenco Ecuador Ltd. v. Republic of Ecuador and Empresa Estatal Petróleos del Ecuador (Petroecuador)*, ICSID Case No. ARB/08/6, Decision on Provisional Measures (8 May 2009); *Burlington Resources, Inc. and others v. Republic of Ecuador and Empresa Estatal Petróleos del Ecuador (Petroecuador)*, ICSID Case No. ARB/08/5, Procedural Order No. 1 on Burlington Oriente's Request for Provisional Measures (29 June 2009).

282 *See, e.g., World Duty Free Company Ltd. v. Republic of Kenya*, ICSID Case No. ARB/00/7, Award (4 October 2006); *Biwater Gauff (Tanzania) Ltd. v. United Republic of Tanzania*, ICSID Case No. ARB/05/22, Procedural Order No. 3 (29 September 2006).

283 "The ICSID Caseload", *supra* note 11, at 13.

to participate, grant a grace period. The defaulting party's failure to present its case is not deemed an admission of the other party's claims.

Default proceedings, as in any international arbitration, place a substantial and difficult burden on both the tribunal and the sole participating party. To illustrate, in the *LETCO v. Liberia* case, in which Liberia failed to appear or present its case, the tribunal emphasized in the award that it had submitted the claimant's assertions to careful scrutiny and had appointed an accounting firm to examine the claim for damages.[284]

ICSID arbitrations may be discontinued in three ways. First, either party may request a discontinuance, which the tribunal will grant if the other party does not object (Arbitration Rule 44). Second, the proceedings are deemed discontinued if the parties fail to act for six consecutive months or such other time period as agreed between them and approved by the tribunal (Arbitration Rule 45). Third, the parties may agree to settle their dispute and request the tribunal to record the terms of their settlement in the form of an award (Arbitration Rule 43). Such an award on agreed terms allows the parties to benefit from the ICSID enforcement regime (see Chapter 6).

Closure of the proceedings and deliberations

Assuming an ICSID arbitration proceeds through the jurisdiction, merits and quantum phases, the tribunal is to declare the proceedings closed "[w]hen the presentation of the case by the parties is completed" (Arbitration Rule 38(1)). Once the tribunal has closed the proceedings, it may "exceptionally" reopen them for new evidence or a "vital need for clarification on certain specific points" (Arbitration Rule 38(2)).

Closure of the proceedings triggers the 120-day period set in Arbitration Rule 46 for the tribunal's rendering of the award. Closure is meant to take place either at the end of the hearing on the merits and quantum or, if there are post-hearing memorials, as of the date those memorials are filed. An unfortunate practice has arisen of tribunals waiting to close proceedings until the award is drafted, which

---

284 *LETCO v. Liberia* (Award), *supra* note 39, at 343-380.

in some cases has taken as long as three years. This is an area where clarification is needed and can be expected.

Pursuant to Arbitration Rule 15, the tribunal must deliberate in private. All arbitrators must keep the deliberations secret. Any non-unanimous award or decision of the tribunal must be made by the majority, with abstention counting as a negative vote (Arbitration Rule 16).

Arbitral proceedings under the Additional Facility Rules

Arbitration proceedings under the ICSID Additional Facility Rules are conducted in substantially the same manner as those under the ICSID Convention, except for two notable differences (discussed below) concerning the place of the proceedings and provisional measures. The Additional Facility Arbitration Rules contain provisions similar to the Arbitration Rules regarding the conduct of the tribunal's early session(s) (Articles 21 to 35); written and oral procedures and evidentiary matters (Articles 36 to 44); challenges to the tribunal's competence (Article 45); and default (Article 48), settlement (Article 49) and discontinuance (Articles 49 to 51).

Unlike Convention arbitrations, which may take place anywhere without effect on the enforceability of the award, arbitrations under the Additional Facility Rules must be conducted in a country that is a party to the New York Convention (Article 19, Additional Facility Arbitration Rules). This rule is intended to facilitate enforcement of Additional Facility awards by ensuring that, even though such awards do not benefit from the automatic recognition and enforcement regime of the Convention, they may be readily recognized and enforced under the favorable scheme of the New York Convention (see Chapter 6). As long as this geographical requirement is satisfied, the tribunal may select any place for the arbitration, in consultation with the parties and the Secretariat of the Additional Facility (Article 20, Additional Facility Arbitration Rules).

The Additional Facility procedures for provisional measures also differ slightly from those applicable to ICSID Convention arbitrations. Both the Arbitration Rules and the Additional Facility Arbitration Rules allow parties to request provisional measures from the tribunal and authorize the tribunal to recommend provisional measures at its discretion. However, unlike ICSID Arbitration Rule 39(5) and in terms similar to those found in many international commercial arbitration rules, Article 46(4) of the Additional Facility Rules allow access to local courts to seek provisional measures without prejudicing the arbitration:

"The parties may apply to any competent judicial authority for interim or conservatory measures. By doing so they shall not be held to infringe the agreement to arbitrate or to affect the powers of the Tribunal."

Given this open avenue to national courts for provisional measures in Additional Facility arbitrations, the 2006 amendment to Arbitration Rule 39 – permitting a party to file a request for provisional measures before the tribunal is constituted – is not available in Additional Facility arbitration.

ICSID awards

ICSID Convention awards

Time limits

It is perhaps not surprising that ICSID arbitrations, which necessarily involve issues of State responsibility, proceed slowly. ICSID arbitrations have averaged approximately three and one-half years from the registration of the initial request to the issuance of the award.[285] Many take longer. As of January 2010, the longest recorded arbitration, *Pey Casado v. Chile*, had taken ten and one-half years. There is, however, some limited ground for optimism – in recent years, the average length has fallen to three years and two months.[286]

The arbitrators are not always to blame for the extended duration of an ICSID arbitration. It is the written and oral proceedings, not the drafting of the award, that typically take the most time. It is not unusual for the parties themselves to request multiple extensions of time for filings and hearings, and sometimes

---

285 Sinclair, *supra* note 254.
286 *Id.*

suspension of the proceedings to explore possibilities of settlement. This is, of course, not to be held against the ICSID regime when assessing its alacrity.

ICSID tribunals have a circumscribed period to draft and issue the award. Under Arbitration Rule 46, the award must be signed within 120 days of the closure of the proceedings, with the possibility of a 60-day extension. However, as noted above, the practice that has evolved of closing proceedings only when the award is almost ready for dispatch has rendered Arbitration Rule 46 something of a dead letter. Proceedings should be closed promptly upon termination of the final hearing or receipt of post-hearing memorials, to provide a degree of discipline in finalizing the award.

When the tribunal signs the award, the Secretary-General, in accordance with Article 49(1) of the ICSID Convention and Arbitration Rule 48, must promptly authenticate the original text of the award and dispatch a certified copy to each party. There is nothing like the well-known provision of the ICC Arbitration Rules for the ICSID Secretariat to scrutinize a draft award.

The award is deemed rendered on the date the Secretary-General dispatches the certified copies. It is the date of dispatch that triggers the time limits for post-award remedies (see Chapter 5).

The form of awards

The rules concerning the form of ICSID awards do not differ substantially from other international arbitration rules. Under Articles 48(2) and 48(3) of the ICSID Convention, an award must: (a) be in writing; (b) be signed by the members of the tribunal who support it; (c) deal with every question submitted to the tribunal; and (d) state the reasons upon which it is based. These provisions are mandatory.

ICSID Arbitration Rule 47 provides more detail:

"(1) The award shall be in writing and shall contain:

(a) a precise designation of each party;

(b) a statement that the Tribunal was established under the Convention, and a description of the method of its constitution;

(c) the name of each member of the Tribunal, and an identification of the appointing authority of each;

(d) the names of the agents, counsel and advocates of the parties;

(e) the dates and place of the sittings of the Tribunal;

(f) a summary of the proceeding;

(g) a statement of the facts as found by the Tribunal;

(h) the submissions of the parties;

(i) the decision of the Tribunal on every question submitted to it, together with the reasons upon which the decision is based; and

(j) any decision of the Tribunal regarding the cost of the proceeding.

(2) The award shall be signed by the members of the Tribunal who voted for it; the date of each signature shall be indicated.

(3) Any member of the Tribunal may attach his individual opinion to the award, whether he dissents from the majority or not, or a statement of his dissent."

The requirement that the award contain "the decision of the Tribunal on every question submitted to it" does not mean that the arbitrators must address every argument that may have been advanced by the parties in their pleadings, but that the tribunal must decide each and every claim submitted to it. The tribunal's failure to deal explicitly with a claim in the award may constitute a possible ground for annulment, as discussed in Chapter 5.

As noted, Article 48(1) of the ICSID Convention authorizes decisions by a majority vote. Article 48(4) allows arbitrators to attach individual opinions to the award, in the form of either a dissenting or concurring opinion. In ICSID practice, even with the increased treaty caseload, separate opinions are not common.

Supplementary decision and rectification

Under Article 49 of the ICSID Convention, either party may file with the Secretary-General, within 45 days of the date on which the award is rendered, a request that the tribunal decide an issue it omitted or that the tribunal "rectify" the award by correcting a "clerical, arithmetical or similar error". Rectification is meant to provide the parties opportunity to review the award and alert the tribunal to obvious mistakes; it is not a mechanism for reconsidering the merits.[287]

Publication

Article 48(5) of the ICSID Convention authorizes the Centre to publish an award or decision only with the consent of both parties. Parties themselves may – and almost invariably do – publish awards and decisions unilaterally. At this point, virtually all ICSID decisions and awards are available online, both on the ICSID website and on arbitration websites such as Investment Treaty Arbitration (<ita.law.uvic.ca>) and Investment Claims (<www.investmentclaims.com>).

The Secretariat is able to reveal certain information about ICSID cases under Regulations 22 and 23, including the identity of the parties, the date of the request, the membership and constitution of the tribunal, the subject matter of the dispute, significant procedural milestones, and the outcome of the proceedings. The information is published in the biannual ICSID News, in the ICSID Annual Reports, and on the ICSID website.

Under the 2006 amendments, Arbitration Rule 48(4) now requires the Centre promptly to include in its publications excerpts of the legal reasoning of tribunals. The obvious purpose is to increase transparency.

Additional Facility awards

Provisions in the Additional Facility Arbitration Rules dealing with the form of awards are similar to those in the Arbitration Rules.

---

287 See *Compañía de Aguas del Aconquija S.A. and Vivendi Universal S.A. v. Argentine Republic*, ICSID Case No. ARB/97/3, Decision of the ad hoc Committee on the Request for Supplementation and Rectification of its Decision Concerning Annulment of the Award (28 May 2003), para. 11.

Costs of ICSID arbitration

Parties to ICSID arbitrations are exposed to three main categories of costs: (a) the administrative costs of the Centre; (b) the fees and expenses of the arbitrators; and (c) the attorneys' fees and other expenses incurred by the parties themselves. The tribunal allocates responsibility for these costs as between the parties in the award, as discussed below and in Chapter 5.

Advances on costs

In addition to the non-refundable registration fee of US$25,000 due with the request for arbitration, the Regulations call for the parties to pay an administrative charge of US$20,000 (per the January 2008 Schedule of Fees) following the constitution of the tribunal and then make provisional advances to the Secretariat as requested to cover the costs of the proceedings for three to six month periods at a time (Regulation 14(3)(a)). Without prejudice to the ultimate allocation of costs in the award, the parties must advance the costs of arbitration equally unless the tribunal decides otherwise (Regulation 14(3)(d); Arbitration Rule 28(1)). In annulment proceedings, however, the party seeking annulment must deposit the entire advance on costs (Regulation 14(3)(e)).

Neither the Centre nor the arbitrators serve for free. Under Regulation 14(3)(d), if a party does not pay an advance in full within 30 days of a request for payment, the Secretary-General gives both parties the opportunity to make the payment. If neither party does so within 15 days, the Secretary-General may request the tribunal to suspend the proceedings. If such a suspension lasts for more than six months, the Secretary-General may move the tribunal to discontinue the proceedings. In practice, the Secretariat consults closely with the parties' representatives on all payment matters throughout the duration of the arbitration.

Level of costs

The conventional wisdom is that ICSID administrative and arbitrator costs are relatively low compared to those assessed in other international arbitration regimes. On the administrative side, this may be in part due to the World

Bank's commitment to subsidize ICSID, undertaken before the adoption of the Convention.[288] As for the arbitrators, the ICSID maximum daily rate (discussed below) is substantially below the rates that the leading arbitrators command under other rules.

The ICSID cost structure is not based on the amount in dispute (as is the case, for example, for the ICC), but rather on the administrative services actually provided by the Centre and the time actually devoted by the arbitrators in an arbitration (Regulation 14). Unless the parties agree otherwise – which sometimes happens – the arbitrators are compensated at a maximum daily rate. Pursuant to the January 2008 Schedule of Fees, arbitrators are entitled to US$3,000 per day (pro-rated as appropriate) for hearings, meetings, deliberations, study time and other work, as well as their reasonable direct expenses, a subsistence allowance and (business class) travel expenses. In addition to the lodging fee and initial administrative fees of US$25,000 and US$20,000, respectively (as of January 2008), the Centre charges for its actual disbursements for interpretation, court reporting and other services that it arranges in support of an arbitration.

In contrast, the parties' own costs in pursuing an ICSID arbitration are typically high. Given the frequent separate jurisdiction phase (as discussed above), the complexity of legal and factual issues that arise in the investor-State context, the number and length of written pleadings, and the use of fact witnesses and experts in hearings, legal fees mount quickly. The in-house opportunity costs of lawyers and principals (for example, executives, engineers and accountants), who must devote time and other resources to the case, are also extremely significant. The seemingly high costs of the parties must be viewed in perspective, however, as ICSID arbitrations often involve disputes in major long-term investments where the amount at stake dwarfs the arbitration expenses.

Interest

Whether a successful party is entitled to interest and, if so, how interest is to be calculated, are matters to be determined according to the applicable law. For the

---

288 As discussed in Chapter 1. *See also* Regulations 17 and 18; International Centre for the Settlement of Investment Disputes, "2009 Annual Report", (30 June 2009): 11 and Annex 6.

purpose of this Guide, it is sufficient to note that ICSID tribunals increasingly award compound interest.[289] One tribunal noted in 2008 that the "discretionary approach to the award of compound interest under international law may now represent a form of *'jurisprudence constante'* in ICSID awards".[290]

Award of costs

Pursuant to Article 61(2) of the Convention, unless the parties agree otherwise – which is rare – in the award the tribunal assesses and allocates the parties' arbitration expenses, the fees and expenses of the tribunal itself, and the Centre's administrative charges. Tribunals typically require each party to submit an accounting of its costs, including counsel fees and expenses incurred in producing documentary evidence, fact witnesses and experts. The detail in such cost submissions varies substantially.

ICSID tribunal decisions on the allocation of costs between the parties depend on the arbitrators' perception of the reasonableness with which the parties pursued their claims and defenses, the parties' general cooperativeness in achieving cost-effective results, and the novelty of the legal issues presented. Tribunals are especially likely to award costs to the prevailing party in the face of misconduct, fraudulent activity or abuse of process by the losing party.[291] A list of costs decisions is set out in Table III.D in Annex 10.

---

289 *See, e.g., Rumeli v. Kazakhstan* (Award), *supra* note 142; *Vivendi II* (Award), *supra* note 139; *Azurix v. Argentina* (Award), *supra* note 139; S. Ripinsky and K. Williams, *Damages in International Investment Law* (London: British Institute of International and Comparative Law, 2008), 379 ("arbitral awards show that there is a trend away from only awarding simple interest to generally awarding compound interest"); I. Marboe, *Calculation of Compensation and Damages in International Investment Law* (Oxford: Oxford University Press, 2009), 375 ("compound interest as opposed to simple interest appears to be predominantly accepted as appropriate in recent international investment arbitration").

290 *Continental Casualty v. Argentina, supra* note 171, at para. 312.

291 *Telenor v. Hungary* (Award), *supra* note 166; *ADC v. Hungary* (Award), *supra* note 178; *Plama v. Bulgaria* (Award), *supra* note 91; *Phoenix Action v. Czech Republic* (Award), *supra* note 91; *Siag v. Egypt* (Award), *supra* note 148; *Europe Cement v. Turkey* (Award), *supra* note 246; *Cementownia "Nowa Huta" v. Turkey* (Award), *supra* note 247.

In decisions on annulment, ICSID *ad hoc* committees generally have directed the parties to bear the tribunal and administrative costs in equal shares and to bear their own legal costs. There are exceptions. *Ad hoc* committees have ordered the losing party to pay all of the committee and administrative costs in five cases.[292] In two of the five cases, the *ad hoc* committees assessed against the losing party not only committee and administrative costs, but also a part of the prevailing party's costs of legal representation.[293] Details may be found in the list of annulment decisions in Table III.B and the list of costs decisions in Table III.D, both in Annex 10.

---

292 *CDC Group v. Seychelles* (Decision of the Ad Hoc Committee on the Application for Annulment), *supra* note 267; *Repsol YPF Ecuador, S.A. v. Empresa Estatal Petróleos del Ecuador (Petroecuador)*, ICSID Case No. ARB/01/10, Decision on the Application for Annulment (8 January 2007); *MHS v. Malaysia* (Decision on the Application for Annulment), *supra* note 100; *Azurix v. Argentina* (Decision on the Application for Annulment of the Argentine Republic), *supra* note 262; *M.C.I. Power Group L.C. and New Turbine, Inc. v. Republic of Ecuador*, ICSID Case No. ARB/03/6, Decision on Annulment (19 October 2009).

293 *CDC Group v. Seychelles* (Decision of the Ad Hoc Committee on the Application for Annulment), *supra* note 267; *Repsol v. Petroecuador* (Decision on the Application for Annulment), *supra* note 292.

Chapter 5

The ICSID review regime

The ICSID Convention provides three mechanisms to review final awards: interpretation, revision and annulment. (Decisions and other non-dispositive orders are not subject to formal review.) Article 53(1) precludes parties from challenging awards by appealing to national courts or resorting "to any other remedy except those provided for in this Convention". Under Article 26, the ICSID review regime is mandatory and exclusive – parties may not contract out of the regime by agreeing to subject their awards to any other form of review.

Convention Articles 50, 51 and 52 and Arbitration Rules 50 to 55 set out the detailed procedures for interpretation, revision and annulment, respectively. In accordance with Regulation 16 of the Administrative and Financial Regulations, each procedure requires the advance payment of a non-refundable fee, set in the January 2008 Schedule of Fees at US$10,000. Enforcement of the award may be stayed pending the outcome of these review procedures, under conditions discussed below.

Interpretation of the award

Article 50 of the ICSID Convention allows either party to apply to the Secretary-General for an "interpretation" of the award's scope or meaning. Interpretation does not encompass, directly or indirectly, a review or reconsideration of the merits of the award. Nor does interpretation compromise the finality of the award.

The Convention does not stipulate a deadline for a request for interpretation to be filed, but it does require that the application specify the points to be interpreted (Arbitration Rule 50(1)(c)(i)). The Secretary-General forwards the request to the tribunal that rendered the award; if the tribunal has been dissolved and cannot be reconstituted, the Secretary-General invites the parties to constitute a new tribunal (Arbitration Rule 51(2) and (3)).

As of January 2010, ICSID had received only two requests for interpretation in ICSID Convention cases: one resulted in a decision[294] and the other was discontinued.[295] In the one case resulting in a decision, *Wena Hotels v. Egypt*, Wena sought interpretation of a US$20 million award rendered against Egypt for expropriation and failure to accord fair and equitable treatment and full protection and security. Specifically, Wena sought interpretation of the tribunal's holding that Egypt's expropriation deprived Wena of its fundamental rights of ownership. The tribunal interpreted the holding to encompass total deprivation of Wena's rights as a result of Egypt's expropriation, but rejected Wena's application for a further interpretation insofar as it related to the consequences of the expropriation for Wena's legal relationships with third parties.

There have been three interpretation requests filed in ICSID Additional Facility cases, decisions in two of which were unpublished as of September 2010.[296] In the one available decision, *Feldman v. Mexico*, Mexico requested interpretation of an award holding it responsible for violating the NAFTA national treatment

---

294 *Wena Hotels Ltd. v. Arab Republic of Egypt*, ICSID Case No. ARB/98/4, Decision on the Application by Wena Hotels Ltd. for Interpretation of the Arbitral Award dated December 8, 2000 in the above matter (31 October 2005). Freshfields was counsel for the respondent.

295 *Tanzania Electric Supply Company Limited v. Independent Power Tanzania Limited*, ICSID Case No. ARB/98/8. Freshfields was counsel for the respondent.

296 *Marvin Roy Feldman Karpa v. United Mexican States*, ICSID Case No. ARB(AF)/99/1, Decision on Correction and Interpretation of the Award (13 June 2003); *Archer Daniels Midland Company and Tate & Lyle Ingredients Americas, Inc. v. United Mexican States*, ICSID Case No. ARB(AF)/04/5, Decision on the Requests for Supplementary Decision, Interpretation and Correction of the Award (10 July 2008) (unpublished); *Corn Products International, Inc. v. United Mexican States*, ICSID Case No. ARB(AF)/04/1, Decision on the Correction and Interpretation of the Award (23 March 2010) (unpublished). Article 55(1) of the Additional Facility Rules provides as follows: "Within 45 days after the date of the award either party, with notice to the other party, may request that the Secretary-General obtain from the Tribunal an interpretation of the award."

protections in relation to Feldman's investment in tobacco product exports.[297] Specifically, Mexico requested that the tribunal consider the application of NAFTA Article 2105 (disclosure of information by parties) in connection with the tribunal's holding on Feldman's national treatment claim. The tribunal found that Mexico's request did not raise a proper question of interpretation, as Mexico "never invoked NAFTA Article 2105 during the proceedings" and was therefore now "effectively … seeking a new decision".[298]

Revision of the award

Under Article 51 of the ICSID Convention, either party may request that an award be "revised", or amended, but only, under Article 51(1), "on the ground of discovery of some fact of such a nature as decisively to affect the award". The applicant must show that the fact is indeed new: "that when the award was rendered that fact was unknown to the Tribunal and to the applicant and that the applicant's ignorance of the fact was not due to negligence" (Article 51(1)). The application must specify the change sought in the award.

A party must file a revision request with the Secretary-General within 90 days after discovering the new fact and, in any event, within three years after the award was rendered (Article 51(2); Arbitration Rule 50(3)(a)). If possible, the Secretary-General forwards the application for revision to the original tribunal; otherwise, the Secretary-General arranges for the constitution of a new tribunal (Article 51(3); Arbitration Rule 51(2) and (3)).

As of January 2010, there had been three requests for revision. Two of them were resolved by agreement before the applications could be heard.[299]

---

297 *Feldman v. Mexico* (Decision on Correction and Interpretation of the Award), *supra* note 296.

298 *Id.* at paras. 10-11.

299 *American Manufacturing & Trading, Inc. v. Zaire*, ICSID Case No. ARB/93/1 (an application for revision was registered by ICSID on 29 January 1999, and the proceeding was discontinued on 26 July 2000 following settlement); *Siemens A.G. v. Argentine Republic*, ICSID Case No. ARB/02/8 (an application for revision was registered by ICSID on 9 July 2008, and the proceeding was discontinued on 9 September 2009 following settlement).

In the third, *Víctor Pey Casado and President Allende Foundation v. Chile*,[300] the claimants requested the upward revision of a US$10 million award rendered against Chile, an amount significantly less than the damages originally sought. In their request for revision, the claimants argued that a press release issued by a Chilean government agency concerning a high court decision in an unrelated dispute (like the ICSID dispute, arising out of an expropriation during the 1970s), would have had a decisive influence on the tribunal's determination. The tribunal rejected the claimants' revision request, holding that the newly adduced facts, even if previously unknown to the claimants, would not have had a decisive influence on the award.

Annulment of the award

The most significant remedy available under the ICSID Convention is the annulment of an award, in whole or in part, under Article 52. Unlike requests for the interpretation or revision of awards under Articles 50 and 51, which may be considered by the original tribunal that issued the award, applications for annulment must be submitted to a new three-member *ad hoc* committee constituted for that sole purpose.

ICSID annulment proceedings differ from typical judicial appeals in two key respects. First, a successful annulment application leads to the invalidation of the award (or parts of the award), and never to its revision or amendment. Unlike an appeals court, an *ad hoc* annulment committee may not issue a decision substituting its views on any aspect of the case for those of the original tribunal. The effect of annulment, instead, is to restore the blank page, leaving the parties only with the opportunity to arbitrate the same issues again before a new ICSID tribunal.

Second, in a related vein, an *ad hoc* committee lacks jurisdiction even to review the merits of the original award in any way. The annulment system is designed to safeguard the integrity, not the outcome, of ICSID arbitration proceedings.

---

300 *Víctor Pey Casado and President Allende Foundation v. Republic of Chile*, ICSID Case No. ARB/98/2, Decision on the Application for the Revision of the Award (18 November 2009).

Ad hoc committees have jurisdiction to review and annul awards only on the limited grounds described in Article 52(1):

"Either party may request annulment of the award by an application in writing addressed to the Secretary-General on one or more of the following grounds:

(a) that the Tribunal was not properly constituted;

(b) that the Tribunal has manifestly exceeded its powers;

(c) that there was corruption on the part of a member of the Tribunal;

(d) that there has been a serious departure from a fundamental rule of procedure; or

(e) that the award has failed to state the reasons on which it is based."

As of September 2010,[301] 40 annulment proceedings had been registered by ICSID, 11 of which remained pending as this Guide went to press.[302] The 29 concluded proceedings have resulted in 22 published decisions.[303] These decisions provide

---

301 As explained above, the cut-off date for most case statistics for this Guide is January 2010. However, in light of several significant annulment decisions rendered in the summer of 2010, we have extended the cut-off date for our discussion of annulment decisions to September 2010.

302 *Víctor Pey Casado and President Allende Foundation v. Republic of Chile*, ICSID Case No. ARB/98/2; *LG&E Energy Corp., LG&E Capital Corp. and LG&E International Inc. v. Argentine Republic*, ICSID Case No. ARB/02/1; *Ahmonseto, Inc. and others v. Arab Republic of Egypt*, ICSID Case No. ARB/02/15; *Continental Casualty Company v. Argentine Republic*, ICSID Case No. ARB/03/9; *Fraport AG Frankfurt Airport Services Worldwide v. Republic of the Philippines*, ICSID Case No. ARB/03/25; *Duke Energy International Peru Investments No. 1 Ltd. v. Republic of Peru*, ICSID Case No. ARB/03/28; *Sociedad Anónima Eduardo Vieira v. Republic of Chile*, ICSID Case No. ARB/04/7; *RSM Production Corporation v. Grenada*, ICSID Case No. ARB/05/14; *Ioannis Kardassopoulos v. Georgia*, ICSID Case No. ARB/05/18; *Ron Fuchs v. Georgia*, ICSID Case No. ARB/07/15; *ATA Construction, Industrial and Trading Company v. Hashemite Kingdom of Jordan*, ICSID Case No. ARB/08/2.

303 *See* Table III.B in Annex 10. The remaining seven proceedings did not result in published decisions: three proceedings were discontinued by agreement of the parties; one proceeding was discontinued for nonpayment of fees; one proceeding was discontinued for the parties' failure to act; and two decisions remain unpublished.

a significant gloss on Article 52. Each of the 22 published decisions discusses a combination of the three most frequently invoked Article 52(1) grounds for annulment: 52(1)(b), manifest excess of powers; 52(1)(d), serious departure from a fundamental rule of procedure; and 52(1)(e), failure to state reasons. Two annulment decisions also discuss the allegedly improper constitution of the tribunal as a ground for annulment under Article 52(1)(a).[304] ICSID *ad hoc* annulment committees have not, to date, considered the fifth possible ground for annulment, namely corruption of the tribunal under Article 52(1)(c).

Looking first at "manifest excess of powers" as a ground for annulment under Article 52(1)(b), *ad hoc* committees have found that tribunals manifestly exceeded their powers by clearly exceeding or failing to exercise the competence granted by the ICSID Convention.[305] A tribunal's failure to apply the applicable law has also been held to constitute a manifest excess of authority but only, it appears, when the tribunal failed to apply that law altogether, rather than to misapply it.[306] As stated by the *ad hoc* committee in *MINE*, "[d]isregard of the applicable rules of law must be distinguished from erroneous application of those rules which, even if manifestly unwarranted, furnishes no ground for annulment".[307]

To prevail under Article 52(1)(d) on a claim that there was "a serious departure from a fundamental rule of procedure", a party must satisfy both prongs of the test, namely that: (a) the rule from which the tribunal departed was fundamental; and (b) the departure was serious.[308] As explained by the *ad hoc* committee in *Vivendi I*, "[u]nder Article 52(1)(d), the emphasis is clearly on the term 'rule of procedure', that is, on the manner in which the Tribunal proceeded, not on

---

304 *Azurix v. Argentina* (Decision on the Application for Annulment of the Argentine Republic), *supra* note 262; *Vivendi II* (Decision on Annulment), *supra* note 211.

305 *Mitchell v. DRC* (Decision on the Application for Annulment of the Award), *supra* note 105; *MHS v. Malaysia* (Decision on the Application for Annulment), *supra* note 100.

306 *Klöckner v. Cameroon* (Decision on Annulment), *supra* note 58; *CMS v. Argentina* (Decision of the *ad hoc* Committee on the Application for Annulment of the Argentine Republic), *supra* note 189.

307 *Maritime International Nominees Establishment v. Republic of Guinea*, ICSID Case ARB/84/4, Decision on Annulment (22 December 1989), *ICSID Reports* 4 (1997): 87.

308 *Id.*

the content of its decision".[309] A rule of procedure is fundamental if it goes to the heart of the integrity of the arbitration proceedings, as do, for example, the principles of fairness, impartiality, equal treatment and respect for the right to be heard. A departure is serious if it is substantial and material, that is, if it "deprive[s] a party of the benefit or protection which the rule was intended to provide"[310] or causes a tribunal "to reach a result substantially different from what it would have awarded had such a rule been observed".[311]

An award "has failed to state the reasons on which it is based" for purposes of Article 52(1)(e) if the tribunal is silent as to its reasoning on particular findings or offers radically contradictory reasoning for particular decisions. Keeping in mind that an *ad hoc* committee lacks authority to review the merits of the original award, it is not surprising that faulty reasoning by a tribunal does not constitute a failure to state reasons justifying annulment. Nor is insufficient or inadequate reasoning likely to satisfy this requirement. *Ad hoc* committees have been disinclined to annul awards if they are able to reconstruct missing reasoning; as stated in the *MINE* annulment decision, the reasons "must enable the reader to follow the reasoning of the Tribunal on points of fact and law" and enable "one to follow how the tribunal proceeded from Point A. to Point B. and eventually to its conclusion".[312]

Improper constitution of a tribunal as a ground of annulment under Article 52(1)(a) is measured against the provisions of the ICSID Convention and the ICSID Arbitration Rules concerning constitution. For example, as stated by the *Azurix ad hoc* committee, annulment may be justified "under Article 52(1)(a) if a proposal for disqualification was made under Article 57, but was never decided under Article 58 before the award was given, or if a decision on a proposal for disqualification was purportedly taken by a person or body other than the person or body prescribed by Article 58".[313]

---

309 *Vivendi I* (Decision on Annulment), *supra* note 114, at para. 83.
310 *MINE v. Guinea* (Decision on Annulment), *supra* note 307, at 87.
311 *Wena Hotels v. Egypt* (Decision on the Application for Annulment), *supra* note 113, at 142.
312 *MINE v. Guinea* (Decision on Annulment), *supra* note 307, at 88; *Wena Hotels v. Egypt* (Decision on the Application for Annulment), *supra* note 113, at 145-146.
313 *Azurix v. Argentina* (Decision on the Application for Annulment of the Argentine Republic), *supra* note 262, at para. 282.

Annulment application procedure

A party must submit its application for annulment to the Secretary-General within 120 days after the award is rendered; in cases of alleged corruption, the request is due within 120 days after the corruption is discovered and, in any event, within three years after the award is rendered (Article 52(2); Arbitration Rule 50(3) (b)). The application must identify the Article 52 grounds on which it is based.

Upon receiving a request for annulment, the Chairman of the Administrative Council appoints three persons from the Panel of Arbitrators to constitute an *ad hoc* committee to decide the challenge. The criteria for appointment, in addition to the obvious restriction that the *ad hoc* committee members may not have sat on the original panel, are that: (a) each must be of a different nationality than all of the original arbitrators; and (b) none may be a national of either State affected by the dispute or have been designated to the Panel of Arbitrators by those States (Article 52(3)).

Again, under Convention Article 52(6), if the *ad hoc* committee annuls the award, there is no remand to the original tribunal. All a party can do is resubmit the dispute to a new tribunal.

Annulment decisions

As noted above, as of September 2010, 40 annulment applications had been filed with ICSID and 22 annulment decisions were available in the public realm. *Ad hoc* committees rejected 12 and granted ten of those 22 applications. A list of the ICSID cases in which annulment applications have been filed and decisions rendered, including details about the composition of the committee, the annulment grounds invoked and the outcomes, appears at Table III.B in Annex 10.

Commentators have described three generations (to date) of *ad hoc* annulment committee decisions.[314] The first generation, in the 1980s, attracted substantial attention. The *ad hoc* committees in the first two cases – *Klöckner v. Cameroon*

---

314 C. Schreuer, "Three Generations of ICSID Annulment Proceedings", in *IAI International Arbitration Series No. 1, Annulment of ICSID Awards*, eds. E. Gaillard and Y. Banifatemi (New York: Juris Publishing, Inc., 2004); *see also* I. Marboe, "ICSID Annulment Decisions: Three Generations Revisited", in *International Investment Law for the 21st Century, supra* note 98.

and *Amco Asia v. Indonesia* – annulled both awards under review. Each dispute was submitted to a new tribunal, leading to new awards and ultimately in each case to a second round of annulment proceedings from which the second awards emerged intact.

Klöckner v. Cameroon arose out of disputes over interlocking contracts for the supply and management of a fertilizer factory in Cameroon. Both the private investor (Klöckner) and the government of Cameroon raised claims in the arbitration, all of which the original tribunal rejected in 1983.[315] Klöckner applied for annulment, arguing that the tribunal had: (a) manifestly exceeded its power by failing to apply the applicable law and asserting jurisdiction over disputes arising out of a contract with a dispute resolution clause calling for ICC arbitration; (b) seriously departed from fundamental rules of procedure by failing to act impartially, failing to hold a true deliberation and committing other irregularities; and (c) failed to deal with all the questions submitted to it and to state adequately the reasons for deciding the questions it did address. In 1985, the *ad hoc* committee annulled the award in its entirety, on the basis that the tribunal had manifestly exceeded its powers by failing to apply the applicable law; the *ad hoc* committee found that the tribunal had postulated, but not actually demonstrated, the application of certain principles of French law.[316] The *ad hoc* committee also found that the tribunal had failed to explain certain of its rulings: "Despite many readings of the text, it is impossible to discern how and why the Tribunal could reach its decision on this point".[317]

In 1984, the tribunal in *Amco Asia v. Indonesia* awarded Amco US$3.2 million in damages for what it found to be the government of Indonesia's unlawful revocation of the investment authorization it had granted Amco for developing and managing a hotel in Indonesia.[318] Indonesia requested annulment of the award on the same three grounds invoked by Klöckner: (a) manifest excess of

---

315 *Klöckner Industrie-Anlagen GmbH and others v. United Republic of Cameroon and Société Camerounaise des Engrais*, ICSID Case No. ARB/81/2, Award (21 October 1983), *ICSID Reports* 2 (1994): 9.

316 *Klöckner v. Cameroon* (Decision on Annulment), *supra* note 58.

317 *Id.* at 148.

318 *Amco Asia Corporation and others v. Indonesia*, ICSID Case No. ARB/81/1, Award (20 November 1984), *ICSID Reports* 1 (1993): 413.

powers; (b) serious departure from fundamental procedural rules; and (c) failure to state reasons. The *ad hoc* committee ruled that the tribunal had correctly identified the proper law but failed actually to apply it. Having found that the tribunal had thus mistakenly held Indonesia's license revocation to be illegal, the *ad hoc* committee annulled the award of damages that hinged on that finding.[319]

The first *ad hoc* committees in *Klöckner* and *Amco Asia* were severely criticized.[320] Commentators argued that the committees had overstepped their mandates by examining the merits of the awards under consideration, thus effectively turning into an appeals process what the ICSID Convention's drafters had intended to be only a safety net against egregiously irregular awards.[321] Because the first two annulments seemed to presage a cycle of appellate-type proceedings, it was widely feared that the annulment process in practice would undercut the much-touted finality of ICSID awards and undermine investor confidence in ICSID arbitration.

However, the ICSID system soon appeared to have reestablished balance in the second generation of ICSID annulment decisions, as a result of the more measured holdings of *ad hoc* committees in *MINE*, *Klöckner II* and *Amco Asia II*. In 1989, the *MINE v. Guinea ad hoc* committee let stand the original tribunal's rulings on Guinea's liability, annulling only the tribunal's damages ruling for failure to state reasons. In *Klöckner II* in 1990 and *Amco Asia II* in 1992, the second *ad hoc* committees constituted in each case rejected the parties' respective annulment applications.[322] As stated by the *ad hoc* committee in *CDC*, "[s]ince those two Decisions, *Klöckner I* and *Amco Asia I*, ad hoc Committees consistently

---

319 *Amco Asia Corporation and others v. Indonesia,* ICSID Case No. ARB/81/1, Decision on the Application for Annulment (16 May 1986), *ICSID Reports* 1 (1993): 509.

320 *CDC Group v. Seychelles* (Decision of the Ad Hoc Committee on the Application for Annulment), *supra* note 267, at para. 35.

321 *See* Schreuer, *The ICSID Convention, supra* note 2, at 901, 912.

322 *Klöckner v. Cameroon,* Resubmitted Case: Decision on Annulment (17 May 1990) (*Klöckner II*), *ICSID Reports* 14 (2009): 101; *Amco v. Indonesia,* Resubmitted Case: Decision on Annulment (3 December 1992) (*Amco Asia II*), *ICSID Reports* 9 (2006): 9.

have taken a much more restrictive view of the role of the ad hoc Committee and the annulment process".[323]

After a quiet decade during which no annulment applications were filed, the winter of 2000-2001 witnessed the filing of three annulment applications within weeks of one another. The annulment proceedings in *Philippe Gruslin v. Malaysia* were quickly discontinued because the applicant (the claimant) failed to pay the requisite ICSID fees. Those in *Wena Hotels Ltd. v. Arab Republic of Egypt* and *Vivendi I* were completed, and marked the emergence of the third generation of ICSID annulment decisions.[324] The distinguishing factor of the third generation is that *Wena* and *Vivendi I* were brought under BITs, rather than under contractual ICSID arbitration clauses as in the *Klöckner–Amco–MINE* trilogy. This generation of annulments has raised a host of new issues pertaining to arbitrations under investment treaties.

In *Wena*, the government of Egypt sought the annulment of an award holding it responsible for the expropriation of a UK hotel management company. Egypt argued that the original tribunal had: (a) manifestly exceeded its authority by failing to apply the applicable law; (b) seriously departed from fundamental rules of procedure by, among other things, depriving Egypt of its right to be heard and inappropriately shifting the burden of proof; and (c) failed both to state reasons for certain of its findings and to address all questions put to it. The *ad hoc* committee rejected all grounds for annulment, including Egypt's claim that the tribunal had misconstrued Convention Article 42, the choice of law article in the Convention (see Chapter 4), when it applied the relevant UK–Egypt BIT and other international law without regard for Egyptian law. In particular, the *ad hoc* committee held that the tribunal had not manifestly exceeded its authority when it applied the substantive provisions of the BIT and supplemented the treaty with other international law, even though the parties had not expressly selected international law as the governing law.[325]

---

323 *CDC Group v. Seychelles* (Decision of the Ad Hoc Committee on the Application for Annulment), *supra* note 267, at para. 35.

324 Schreuer, *The ICSID Convention, supra* note 2.

325 *Wena Hotels v. Egypt* (Decision on the Application for Annulment), *supra* note 113.

In *Vivendi I*, the dispute arose out of a concession contract for the operation of the water and sewage system of the Tucumán province in Argentina. After the original tribunal dismissed the French investor's claim in its entirety,[326] the investor sought partial annulment of the award on grounds that the tribunal had: (a) manifestly exceeded its powers in failing to exercise jurisdiction over treaty claims it mistakenly construed as contractual claims; (b) seriously departed from a fundamental rule of procedure in not giving the investor the opportunity to present its case on a jurisdictional matter; and (c) failed to state the reasons upon which the award was based. The *Vivendi I ad hoc* committee partially annulled the award, finding, among other things, that the tribunal had exceeded its powers by finding that it had jurisdiction of the investor's treaty breach claims against the province of Tucumán but then refusing to consider, as its mandate required, the merits of those treaty claims because they overlapped with contract claims requiring (in the tribunal's view) consideration by local administrative tribunals.[327] Vivendi then proceeded to a second ICSID arbitration, *Vivendi II*, followed by a second annulment proceeding. As with the *Klöckner II* and *Amco Asia II* annulment decisions, the *ad hoc* committee in *Vivendi II* rejected the annulment application.[328] Like the annulment decision in *CMS v. Argentina* (described below), the *Vivendi II* decision includes discussion of certain issues in *obiter dicta*, including alleged conflicts of interest of a tribunal member and the role of the ICSID Secretariat in the arbitral process, that have led to critical commentary.

In the eight years since the *ad hoc* committee decisions in *Wena* and *Vivendi I* (until September 2010), annulment decisions had been rendered in 16 cases: one in 2005, two in 2006,[329] five in 2007, three in 2009, and five in 2010. In ten of the 16 cases, *ad hoc* committees rejected the applications for annulment.[330]

---

326 *Vivendi I* (Award), *supra* note 113.
327 *Vivendi I* (Decision on Annulment), *supra* note 114.
328 *Vivendi II* (Decision on Annulment), *supra* note 211.
329 The annulment decision in *Consortium RFCC v. Morocco*, rendered on 18 January 2006, remains unpublished.
330 *CDC Group plc v. Republic of Seychelles*, ICSID Case No. ARB/02/14; *Repsol YPF Ecuador S.A. v. Empresa Estatal Petróleos del Ecuador (Petroecuador)*, ICSID Case No. ARB/01/10; *MTD Equity Sdn. Bhd. & MTD Chile S.A. v. Republic of Chile*, ICSID Case No. ARB/01/7; *Hussein*

In the remaining six cases – *Mitchell v. DRC, CMS v. Argentina, MHS v. Malaysia, Helnan v. Egypt, Sempra v. Argentina* and *Enron v. Argentina* – the *ad hoc* committees accepted the annulment applications in whole or in part. Each of these six decisions is described below.

In *Mitchell v. DRC,* the DRC requested annulment of a US$750,000 award holding it responsible for the expropriation of the claimant's legal consulting firm operating in the DRC. The DRC sought annulment on the two grounds that the tribunal had: (a) manifestly exceeded its powers with regard to jurisdiction in respect of the definition of investment and with regard to the law applicable to the dispute; and (b) failed to state reasons for its subject matter jurisdiction with regard to the characterization of the disputed measures as expropriation, and the amount of damages.[331] The *ad hoc* committee annulled the award on the grounds of manifest excess of power and failure to state reasons in relation to acceptance of jurisdiction on the basis of an existing investment within the meaning of the ICSID Convention. Specifically, the *ad hoc* committee held that the tribunal was "incomplete and obscure as regards what it considers an investment" and went on to state that, for purposes of the ICSID Convention, an investment must contribute to the economic development of a host state.[332]

In *CMS v. Argentina,* Argentina sought annulment of what was the first award in the many treaty cases arising out of the Argentine financial crisis in the early 2000s. The *CMS* tribunal awarded CMS US$133 million, holding that Argentina breached the US–Argentina BIT by failing to accord CMS fair and equitable treatment and by failing under the treaty's umbrella clause to observe obligations it entered into with respect to CMS's investment. In its annulment application, Argentina alleged that the tribunal had: (a) manifestly exceeded its powers by exercising jurisdiction over claims by company shareholders for income lost by a company, by transforming the fair and equitable treatment and umbrella clauses

---

Nuaman Soufraki v. United Arab Emirates, ICSID Case No. ARB/02/7; Indústria Nacional de Alimentos, S.A. and Indalsa Perú, S.A. (formerly Empresas Lucchetti, S.A. and Lucchetti Perú, S.A.) v. Republic of Peru, ICSID Case No. ARB/03/4; Azurix Corp. v. Argentine Republic, ICSID Case No. ARB/01/12; M.C.I. Power Group L.C. and New Turbine, Inc. v. Ecuador, ICSID Case No. ARB/03/6.

331 Mitchell v. DRC (Decision on the Application for Annulment of the Award), supra note 105.
332 Id. at para. 40.

of the BIT into strict liability provisions, and by rejecting Argentina's defense of necessity under customary international law and the BIT; and (b) failed to state the reasons for its decision on jurisdiction, its findings on Argentina's necessity defense and its calculation of damages.[333] Although noting, in *obiter dicta*, that the award "contained manifest errors of law" and "suffered from lacunae and elisions", the Committee recognized its "narrow and limited mandate conferred by Article 52 of the ICSID Convention" and annulled only the holding relating to the umbrella clause.[334] This left the full monetary award intact.

In *MHS v. Malaysia*, a sole arbitrator declined jurisdiction on the ground that MHS, a marine salvage company based in the United Kingdom, did not make an investment in Malaysia within the ambit of the ICSID Convention.[335] MHS sought annulment on the ground that the tribunal had manifestly exceeded its powers by failing to exercise the jurisdiction with which it was endowed. The *ad hoc* committee, in a two-one decision, annulled the award, finding that the tribunal manifestly exceeded its powers because it: (a) failed to take account of and apply the definition of investment in the Malaysia–United Kingdom BIT, which was broad and encompassing; (b) improperly elevated the ICSID Convention Article 25(1) criteria to jurisdictional conditions, and interpreted the criterion of contribution to the economic development of the host State so as to exclude small contributions and contributions of a cultural and historical nature; and (c) reached conclusions not consonant with the Convention's *travaux préparatoires* in key respects.

In *Helnan v. Egypt*, the tribunal dismissed Helnan's claims that Egypt had breached the Denmark–Egypt BIT by taking actions that allegedly led to the termination of Helnan's management contract for a Cairo hotel. Helnan sought annulment of the award on the following grounds: (a) the award failed to state the reasons on which it is based; (b) the tribunal manifestly exceeded its powers; and (c) there was a serious departure from a fundamental rule of procedure. In its decision, the *ad hoc* committee annulled a portion of the award, finding that the

---

333 *CMS v. Argentina* (Decision of the *ad hoc* Committee on the Application for Annulment of the Argentine Republic), *supra* note 189.

334 *Id.* at 158.

335 *MHS v. Malaysia* (Decision on the Application for Annulment), *supra* note 100.

tribunal manifestly exceeded its powers by rejecting Helnan's fair and equitable treatment claim because Helnan had not sought recourse first in Egyptian courts. The *ad hoc* committee determined, however, that the annulled portion of the award was not essential to the tribunal's dismissal of Helnan's claims on the merits and upheld the operative part of the award.[336]

Pausing here, one can say that this third generation of ICSID annulment decisions has generally stayed true to the limited function of annulment,[337] recognizing that an *ad hoc* committee "cannot substitute its determination on the merits for that of the tribunal",[338] and that "annulment is not a remedy against an incorrect decision alone".[339] As stated by the *ad hoc* committees in *Azurix* and *MTD*, "[a] more interventionist approach by committees on the merits of disputes would risk a renewed cycle of tribunal and annulment proceedings of the kind observed in *Klöckner* and *Amco*".[340]

However, in the wake of two annulment decisions rendered in the summer of 2010, commentators are debating whether the *Klöckner* and *Amco* cycle is perhaps beginning anew. In *Sempra v. Argentina* and *Enron v. Argentina*, both arising out of the Argentine financial crisis, *ad hoc* committees annulled awards rendered in favor of the claimants.[341] The tribunals in both cases held that Argentina's actions following its financial crisis were unfair and inequitable and that Argentina failed under the umbrella clause to observe its obligations with respect to each claimant's investment, and denied Argentina's defenses based on necessity under

---

336 *Helnan International Hotels A/S v. Arab Republic of Egypt*, ICISD Case No. ARB/05/19, Decision of the *ad hoc* Committee (14 June 2010).

337 The *ad hoc* committee decision in *Mitchell* appears to be an outlier of unlikely influence. *See MHS v. Malaysia* (Decision on the Application for Annulment), *supra* note 100.

338 *MTD v. Chile* (Decision on Annulment), *supra* note 118, at para. 54.

339 *CDC Group plc v. Seychelles* (Decision of the Ad Hoc Committee on the Application for Annulment of the Republic of the Seychelles), *supra* note 267, at para. 35.

340 *Azurix Corp. v. Argentina* (Decision on the Application for Annulment of the Argentine Republic), *supra* note 262, at para. 42; *MTD v. Chile* (Decision on Annulment), *supra* note 118, at para. 54.

341 *Sempra v. Argentina* (Decision on the Argentine Republic's Application for Annulment of the Award), *supra* note 190 (US$128 million award annulled); *Enron v. Argentina* (Decision on the Application for Annulment of the Argentine Republic), *supra* note 190 (US$106 million award annulled).

customary international law and under Article XI of the US–Argentina BIT.[342] In *Sempra*, the award was annulled on the basis that the tribunal had manifestly exceeded its powers when it applied customary international law to Argentina's necessity defence but did not separately analyze Article XI of the BIT. The *ad hoc* committee held that the tribunal "made a fundamental error in identifying and applying the applicable law" by "its total failure to apply Article XI of the BIT".[343] In *Enron*, the *ad hoc* committee took issue with the tribunal's finding that the various requirements of the customary international law defense of necessity, as reflected in Article 25 of the ILC Articles on State Responsibility, were not satisfied. The committee held that, in its consideration of the Article 25 requirements, the tribunal had manifestly exceeded its powers and failed to state the reasons for its decision.[344]

It remains to be seen whether or not this more interventionist approach taken by the *Sempra* and *Enron* committees marks the beginning of a fourth generation of annulment decisions similar to the first generation, with a similar impact on users' assessment of the ICSID regime.

Developments in ICSID's selection of ad hoc committee members

In recent years, ICSID has made serial appointments to *ad hoc* committees from a small pool of highly experienced arbitrators, the goal being "to promote coherence in the application of the Convention and Rules by annulment committees".[345]

---

342 Article XI of the US–Argentina BIT (Annex 6) provides that: "This Treaty shall not preclude the application by either Party of measures necessary for the maintenance of public order, the fulfillment of its obligations with respect to the maintenance or restoration of international peace or security, or the Protection of its own essential security interests."

343 *Sempra v. Argentina* (Decision on the Argentine Republic's Application for Annulment of the Award), *supra* note 190, at paras. 208, 214.

344 *Enron v. Argentina* (Decision on the Application for Annulment of the Argentine Republic), *supra* note 190.

345 "Recent Developments at ICSID", *News From ICSID* 25, no. 2 (2008): 3; *see also*, K. Yannaca-Small, "Annulment of ICSID Awards: Limited Scope But is There Potential?", in *Arbitration Under International Investment Agreements*, *supra* note 119 (noting that "there is an effort undertaken by ICSID for a pool of arbitrators to be appointed almost exclusively in annulment proceedings").

As a result, the 20 *ad hoc* committees constituted by ICSID between January 2007 and September 2010 have been made up primarily of arbitrators serving on multiple committees. Out of a total of 60 *ad hoc* committee member positions, 15 arbitrators have held over three-quarters of the appointments (49 out of 60 positions, or 81 percent).[346]

Waiving the right to seek annulment

Parties wishing to avoid the uncertainty created by the prospect of ICSID annulment proceedings might consider waiving the right to annulment in the arbitration agreement. Although the validity of such waivers apparently has not been tested, some commentators contend that Convention Article 52 is not subject to modification by the parties and that such waivers could be challenged before an *ad hoc* committee.[347] In any event, investors and host States alike should be mindful that, given the Convention's exclusion of any recourse to external review, a waiver of their right to annulment (if effective) would foreclose the only remedy available to them to challenge a truly aberrant award.

Stay of enforcement pending review proceedings

Pending resolution of an application for interpretation, revision or annulment, the enforcement of an award may be stayed. Article 53(1) of the Convention provides, in relevant part:

> "Each party shall abide by and comply with the terms of the award except to the extent that enforcement shall have been stayed pursuant to the relevant provisions of this Convention."

---

346 These are, with the number of cases in parentheses: Peter Tomka (6), Dominique Hascher (5), Campbell McLachlan (5), Gavan Griffith (4), Stephen Schwebel (4), Cecil W.M. Abraham (3), Bola Ajibola (3), Piero Bernardini (3), Ahmed Sadek El-Kosheri (3), Christer Söderlund (3), Karl-Heinz Böckstiegel (2), Andreas Jacovides (2), Azzedine Kettani (2), Mohamed Shahabuddeen (2), and Eduardo Silva Romero (2).
347 *See* Schreuer, *The ICSID Convention, supra* note 2, at 918-920.

The effect of a stay, simply put, is to suspend the losing party's obligation "to abide by and comply with" the award. On the one hand, because this phrase has been construed to encompass both recognition and enforcement of the award, a stay neutralizes the practical effect of the award, including its authority as res judicata.[348] On the other hand, a stay does not affect the intrinsic legal validity of the award, at least not until the award has been interpreted, revised or annulled.

It is generally for the relevant tribunal or *ad hoc* committee to decide, in its discretion, whether to grant a stay (Convention Articles 50(2), 51(4) and 52(5)). A stay is automatic only if the moving party requests the stay at the time it files its application (Convention Articles 51(4) and 52(5)). If so, the Secretary-General may not refuse the request for the initial stay, and must notify the parties of the stay. This stay terminates automatically upon the constitution of the tribunal or *ad hoc* committee, unless the tribunal or *ad hoc* committee extends it, at a party's request, within 30 days (Arbitration Rule 54(2)). The practice is for tribunals and *ad hoc* committees to consider a further stay only on a request from a party and after hearing both sides.

The guiding principles for ordering a stay of an award, as they have evolved in ICSID practice, are similar to those that apply to requests for provisional measures. In determining whether to grant a stay, *ad hoc* committees have found it particularly relevant to consider whether: (a) enforcement of the award, if upheld, would be prompt; (b) the party requesting the stay was engaged in dilatory tactics; (c) the party requesting the stay offered security; and (d) proceeding with enforcement would likely cause irreparable injury to the award debtor because, for example, it would have difficulty recovering monies paid to the prevailing party under the award if the award were later annulled.[349] An *ad hoc* committee considering annulment may continue a stay unconditionally or on

---

348 A. Broches, "Awards Rendered Pursuant to the ICSID Convention: Binding Force, Finality, Recognition, Enforcement, Execution", *ICSID Review–FILJ* 2 (1987): 317.

349 *Amco v. Indonesia* (Decision on the Application for Annulment), *supra* note 319; *CDC Group plc v. Republic of Seychelles*, ICSID Case No. ARB/02/14, Decision on Whether or Not to Continue Stay and Order (14 July 2004).

condition that the party benefiting from the stay provide security. The practice of *ad hoc* committees on requiring security has varied.[350]

As of January 2010, there had been requests to stay enforcement of awards in 16 annulment proceedings, all of which involved monetary awards. In all 16 cases, the *ad hoc* committees continued the stays of enforcement.[351] *Ad hoc* committees granted stays of enforcement without conditions in seven of the cases. In the other nine cases, the committees conditioned the stay on provision of security, such as a letter of guarantee in the amount of the award plus interest,[352] the furnishing of a commitment letter (so far, in practice, of doubtful reliability),[353] or the placement of funds constituting a portion of the award into an escrow account.[354] In two of these annulment proceedings, the *ad hoc* committees terminated stays after respondents failed to post the security ordered.[355] A list of the annulment proceedings in which decisions have been rendered on requests for stays of enforcement is set out at Table III.F in Annex 10.

---

350 *See* M. Stevens, "The Power of ICSID Ad Hoc Committees to Order Security When Granting a Stay of Enforcement", in *Enforcement of Arbitral Awards Against Sovereigns*, ed. D. Bishop (New York: Juris Publishing, Inc., 2009).

351 *See* Table III.F in Annex 10.

352 *Id.* These were the *Amco Asia, Amco Asia* (resubmitted), *SPP, Wena Hotels, CDC* and *Repsol* cases.

353 *Id.* These were the *Vivendi II* and *Rumeli* cases.

354 *Id.* This was the *Sempra* case.

355 *Id.* These were the *Repsol* and *Sempra* cases.

Chapter 6

Recognition, enforcement and execution of ICSID awards

The effectiveness of international arbitration depends on the degree of finality of the award and the ease with which the award may be enforced by the prevailing party. The ICSID Convention provides for rigorous finality and seeks to establish optimal preconditions for the enforcement of awards in a manner that distinguishes ICSID from other international arbitral regimes.

As with other classes of disputes subject to judicial or arbitral jurisdiction, most ICSID cases settle. In the cases that do proceed to award, participants must understand what will happen if the losing party fails to comply with the award voluntarily and the prevailing party takes the award through phases known as "recognition", "enforcement" and "execution".

"Recognition" is the formal certification that an ICSID award is a final and binding disposition of contested claims. The primary purpose of recognition is to confirm the res judicata effect of an award – that is, to establish that the issues resolved in the award may not be reexamined in other court or arbitration proceedings. Recognition is, by definition, the first legal step in any contested post-award process. In those cases where the establishment of rights or the absence of obligation is all that is sought, it is also the only step.

The last possible step in a contested ICSID post-award process – "execution" – is the prevailing party's actual collection of monetary damages, or achievement of other relief granted in the award. Execution generally requires the assistance of local courts, which exercise their authority to cause awards to be satisfied by, for example, issuing judgments and ordering attachment of assets of the award debtor.

The middle step – "enforcement" – is less precise than the other two. In some legal systems, enforcement refers to the judicial practice of issuing "exequatur", or declaring in an order that an arbitration award is in fact enforceable. In other legal systems, "enforcement" loosely refers to an award creditor's legal right to execute its award – i.e., to collect monetary damages or benefit from other remedies granted – and is thus another way of referring to execution. In the context of ICSID arbitration, enforcement is generally indistinguishable from recognition. The two terms – recognition and enforcement – tend to be used in a single phrase that broadly refers to all steps leading up to, but stopping short of, actual execution of an award.

International arbitration awards may not be appealed like court judgments. Under most national systems, international arbitration awards cannot be reviewed on the merits at all, whether by a court or another arbitral tribunal. The national courts at the place of arbitration nevertheless retain power to set aside awards (at the instance of the losing party before the commencement of enforcement proceedings) or to refuse to enforce awards (in the course of enforcement proceedings commenced by the prevailing party), on grounds that vary somewhat according to national law but in most jurisdictions are extremely limited. Before the 1958 New York Convention came into force, national courts would generally recognize and enforce international arbitration awards (or refuse to do so) according to their domestic laws, including, for example, their particular understanding of comity.[356] Today, awards issued in the territory of any of the New York Convention's 144 State parties (as of January 2010) benefit from facilitated recognition and enforcement in the territory of any other State party. The New York Convention presumes the validity of international arbitration awards and mandates their enforcement, except on narrowly circumscribed procedural and public policy grounds.

A strength of the ICSID Convention is that it is even more favorable to recognition and enforcement of awards than the New York Convention. The ICSID Convention accepts no grounds whatsoever for national courts to refuse recognition and enforcement of ICSID tribunal awards. It requires, instead, that

---

356 The Geneva Protocol on Arbitration Clauses of 1923 and the Geneva Convention on the Execution of Foreign Awards of 1927, where they applied, had limited effect.

the national courts of Contracting States recognize and enforce monetary awards immediately, as if they were final judgments of the local courts themselves. The courts may not vacate ICSID awards, because they are a-national and subject to the ICSID treaty regime rather than to national law.

The parties may contest awards only out of court and under the limited review mechanism in the ICSID Convention: on restricted grounds, before a three-member *ad hoc* committee constituted under the Convention in the case of annulment, or before the original (or successor) tribunal in the case of interpretation or revision proceedings. Again, this self-contained and delocalized enforcement scheme shelters ICSID arbitration awards from the scrutiny of national courts, which play a role only when the award needs to be executed.

This chapter addresses recognition, enforcement and execution of ICSID awards. These processes apply only to awards rendered under the ICSID Convention, and not to awards issued under the ICSID Additional Facility Rules or the UNCITRAL Rules administered by ICSID (like those in NAFTA cases, for example). Awards in the latter categories are governed by the New York Convention, as implemented in Contracting State jurisdictions where they are issued or where their recognition and enforcement ultimately is sought.

The final and binding nature of ICSID awards

Article 53(1) of the ICSID Convention establishes the finality of ICSID awards:

"The award shall be binding on the parties and shall not be subject to any appeal or any other remedy except those provided for in this Convention."

This is straightforward. Provided any available review proceedings under the Convention are complete, Article 53(1) obliges the losing party – State or investor – to comply with the award immediately.

Two points related to Article 53(1) bear mention. First, an ICSID award binds only the parties to the dispute, not third parties. This point may raise difficult questions. There is, for example, no general rule to establish whether the State itself is bound when an ICSID tribunal issues an award against a subdivision or agency designated by the State to the Centre as a party.[357] It depends on the circumstances.

Second, not all ICSID decisions are awards, let alone final awards. Pursuant to Convention Article 48(3), an award is final if it disposes of all questions put to the tribunal. As discussed in Chapter 4, an award is definitively final if the tribunal holds that it lacks jurisdiction or resolves all substantive issues on the merits. An award that affirms jurisdiction, and thus allows the case to proceed to the merits, is not a final award (and is denominated a decision). In *SPP v. Egypt*, when the government of Egypt filed an application to annul the tribunal's decision affirming jurisdiction,[358] the Secretary-General refused to register the application on the ground that it was not an award under the Convention. Orders that recommend provisional measures and procedural decisions are not awards. Nor is an order discontinuing proceedings a final award, unless it leads to a settlement that is recorded in the form of an award under Convention Article 53(2).

Recognition and enforcement

Article 54(1) is the heart of the ICSID Convention's automatic recognition and enforcement mechanism. Unlike Article 53(1), which only concerns the parties to a dispute, Article 54(1) is addressed to all Contracting States:

> "Each Contracting State shall recognize an award rendered pursuant to this Convention as binding and enforce the pecuniary obligations imposed by that award within its territories as if it were a final judgment of a court in that State. A Contracting State with a federal constitution may enforce such an award in or through its federal courts and may provide that such courts shall treat the award as if it were a final judgment of the courts of a constituent state."

---

357 Broches, "Awards Rendered pursuant to the ICSID Convention", *supra* note 348.
358 *SPP v. Egypt* (Decision on Jurisdiction), *supra* note 65.

This text appears to contemplate three types of awards, as follows: (a) pecuniary awards; and (b) non-pecuniary awards, including (i) declarations of rights and obligations, and (ii) orders of specific performance.

Against the background of this categorization, the first proposition inherent in Article 54(1) is that all three types of award shall be recognized as binding. That suffices for the declaratory relief in category (b)(i) above, but more is required for the two others, i.e., to recover and apply funds to satisfy the award debt or to require that certain measures be taken, such as the restitution of seized property, the issuance of licenses or the restoration of shareholder rights to appoint managers. As to category (a), pecuniary awards, Convention Article 54(1) mandates enforcement of awards to make payment "as if" they were a "final judgment of a court" of the Contracting State. But as to the fate of category (b)(ii), awards ordering specific performance, the Convention is silent as to enforcement, thus apparently leaving the matter to be dealt with in light of other international instruments or national law.

Given this difference in treatment of monetary and non-monetary awards under the ICSID regime, claimants are well-advised to consider framing all their demands as monetary claims or, at very least, asking for alternative pecuniary forms of relief if their primary claims are for specific performance. For example, an investor could seek specific performance of a State's obligation to reinstate a license and also, as an alternative, liquidated damages for non-performance of that obligation under the governing law.

Under Convention Article 54(2), a party seeking recognition and enforcement of an ICSID award in the territory of a Contracting State must provide a certified copy of the award to the competent court or other authority designated by the State. It is also Article 54(2) that requires each Contracting State to notify the Secretary-General of the designation of such competent court or other authority. Some States, for example the United Kingdom, have taken the opportunity to include with these notifications detailed instructions for parties applying for the recognition, enforcement and execution of an ICSID award in their territory (i.e., requirements as to time limits, currencies and evidence that the award is not subject to annulment). Other Contracting States have provided little, if any, guidance. In all cases, as requirements vary from one Contracting State to another, a party with an ICSID award in its favor must seek the advice of local counsel before initiating recognition and enforcement proceedings.

Interpreting Articles 53 and 54

The obligation for the losing party to comply with awards under Article 53 is not contingent on the prevailing party's pursuit of enforcement efforts under Article 54, because Article 53 imposes an unambiguous autonomous obligation to pay outstanding awards.[359] Recently, however, Argentina has argued that Article 54 requires successful claimants first to obtain enforcement of ICSID awards against it in the Argentine courts.[360] *Ad hoc* committees have consistently disagreed with such a limited view of a State's obligations under Articles 53 and 54. For example, in *Continental Casualty Company v. Argentine Republic*, the *ad hoc* committee rejected "Argentina's position that in order for Continental to obtain payment of the Award, it would be necessary for Continental to follow the formalities applicable to enforcement in Argentina of final judgments of Argentine courts", adopting the position of previous *ad hoc* committees that "this position of Argentina is inconsistent with Argentina's obligation under Article 53 of the ICSID Convention to carry out without delay the provisions of the award without the need for enforcement action under Article 54 ...".[361] The *Continental Casualty* decision mirrors the findings of the *ad hoc* committees in the *Enron, Vivendi* and *Sempra* cases.[362]

---

359 *See, e.g.,* S. Alexandrov, "Enforcement of ICSID Awards: Articles 53 and 54 of the ICSID Convention", in *International Investment Law for the 21ˢᵗ Century, supra* note 98, 322.

360 L. Peterson, "Argentine Crisis Arbitration Awards Pile Up, But Investors Still Wait for a Payout", *Focus Europe*, 25 June 2009; "High Noon – A Round Table Over Unpaid ICSID Awards", *Global Arbitration Review* 3, no. 6 (2008).

361 *Continental Casualty Company v. Argentine Republic*, ICSID Case No. ARB/03/9, Decision on Argentina's Application for a Stay of Enforcement of the Award (23 October 2009), para. 12.

362 *See Enron Corporation and Ponderosa Assets, L.P. v. Argentine Republic*, ICSID Case No. ARB/01/3, Decision on the Argentine Republic's Request for a Continued Stay of Enforcement of the Award (Rule 54 of the ICSID Arbitration Rules) (7 October 2008), para. 101; *Enron Creditors Recovery Corp. (formerly Enron Corp.) and Ponderosa Assets, L.P. v. Argentine*

Execution of ICSID Awards

"Recognition and enforcement" versus "execution"

Although the ICSID Convention specifically insulates awards from review under national laws at the recognition and enforcement stage, it offers no such insulation when awards are to be executed against specific assets. The Convention, however supportive of foreign investment and investors, does not obligate a Contracting State to execute an ICSID award in circumstances where an equivalent final judgment of its own courts could not be executed. In such circumstances, national law on sovereign immunity from execution may prevail (subject to other international instruments).

Convention Article 54(3) stipulates that the execution of ICSID awards "shall be governed by the laws concerning the execution of judgments in force in the State in whose territories such execution is sought". Article 55 reiterates and emphasizes this:

> "Nothing in Article 54 shall be construed as derogating from the law in force in any Contracting State relating to immunity of that State or of any State from execution."

In other words, national courts in Contracting States must recognize and enforce awards according to the Convention, i.e., immediately and without review, but they may execute them according to their own national law.[363]

Republic, ICSID Case No. ARB/01/3, Decision on the Claimants' Second Request to Lift Provisional Stay of Enforcement of the Award (Rule 54 of the ICSID Arbitration Rules) (20 May 2009), paras. 23–29; *Compañía de Aguas del Aconquija S.A. and Vivendi Universal S.A. v. Argentine Republic*, ICSID Case No. ARB/97/3, Decision on the Argentine Republic's Request for a Continued Stay of Enforcement of the Award rendered on 20 August 2007 (Rule 54 of the ICSID Arbitration Rules) (4 November 2008), para. 45; *Sempra Energy International v. Argentine Republic*, ICSID Case No. ARB/02/16, Decision on the Argentine Republic's Request for a Continued Stay of Enforcement of the Award (Rule 54 of the ICSID Arbitration Rules) (5 March 2009), paras. 103-104.

363 *See, e.g.,* E. Baldwin, M. Kantor & M. Nolan, "Limits to Enforcement of ICSID Awards", *Journal of International Arbitration* 23, no. 1 (2006): 1.

Although in theory this distinction raises the spectre of complicated execution proceedings, parties generally comply voluntarily with ICSID awards, as they do with awards delivered under the auspices of other respected arbitration institutions. In practice, payment (in full or in part) is often the result of a post-award settlement. Of the 271 ICSID Convention arbitration cases registered through January 2010, only four have so far led to execution proceedings – albeit convoluted ones, as we describe below.[364]

The conventional wisdom (challenged by the recent conduct of Argentina) is that the system is largely self-enforcing because Contracting States presumably recognize that blocking the execution of awards against them would alienate the very investors they are trying to attract by ratifying the ICSID Convention. Although investment disputes do not proceed in a political vacuum, it is inconsistent for a State to sign investment contracts and bilateral investment treaties and enact pro-investment legislation and then flagrantly disregard the obligations they create. Award debtor States (theoretically) may also be wary of fallout within the World Bank community: their recalcitrance could alienate other Contracting States, which have undertaken to enforce ICSID awards on the understanding that all State parties to the Convention would do the same.

Sovereign immunity from execution

The laws on sovereign immunity vary greatly from one State to another. Under the law of the vast majority of countries, a waiver of sovereign immunity from suit – evidenced, as relevant here, by ratification of the ICSID Convention – does not imply a waiver of sovereign immunity from execution.[365] Some national laws shield States with absolute immunity from execution, whereas others allow execution against sovereign assets used for commercial purposes or against assets related to the obligation to be enforced. In addition, national laws extend

---

364 *See, e.g.*, A. Parra, "The Enforcement of ICSID Arbitral Awards", in *Enforcement of Arbitral Awards Against Sovereigns, supra* note 350, 131.

365 For an extended discussion of sovereign immunity and its impact on execution, *see* A. Bjorklund, "State Immunity and the Enforcement of Investor-State Arbitral Awards", in *International Investment Law for the 21st Century, supra* note 98, 302.

sovereign immunity to a greater or lesser degree to the State's constituent subdivisions and agencies.

As noted, as of January 2010, foreign investors with favorable ICSID awards had pursued execution proceedings in only four cases. All were procedurally complicated and raised issues regarding the immunity of sovereign assets used for commercial purposes. We briefly describe each in turn.

In *Benvenuti and Bonfant v. Congo*, Benvenuti applied to the Paris Tribunal de Grande Instance for an order enforcing its ICSID award. The court granted the enforcement order, but added that it could not be executed against assets of the Congo located in France without the court's prior authorization because those assets might be protected by sovereign immunity.[366] Benvenuti appealed the decision to the Paris Court of Appeal, which in 1981 struck out the qualifying language on the ground that it contradicted the ICSID Convention's simplified enforcement procedure and that the court had exceeded its authority by making a finding on the execution of the award when it had been asked only to enforce it.[367]

Execution efforts in *SOABI v. Senegal* led to similar results.[368] The Paris Tribunal de Grande Instance granted SOABI an order for the enforcement of its ICSID award against Senegal. The Paris Court of Appeal reversed the order and blocked execution of the award because it was not satisfied that SOABI would enforce the award only against assets specifically earmarked by Senegal for economic and commercial activities.[369] In 1991, the Court of Cassation then reversed the Court of Appeal, on the ground that the lower court's enforcement

---

366 *Benvenuti and Bonfant Srl. v. Government People's Republic of the Congo*, ICSID Case No. ARB/77/2, Decision of Tribunal de Grande Instance, Paris (13 January 1981), *ICSID Reports* 1 (1993): 368.

367 *Benvenuti & Bonfant Srl. v. Government People's Republic of the Congo*, ICSID Case No. ARB 77/2, Decision of Cour d'Appel, Paris (26 June 1981), *ICSID Reports* 1 (1993): 368.

368 *SOABI v. Senegal* (Award), *supra* note 38.

369 *Société Ouest Africaine de Bétons Industriels (SOABI) v. State of Senegal*, ICSID Case No. ARB/82/1, Decision of Cour d'Appel, Paris (5 December 1989), *ICSID Reports* 2 (1994): 337.

order in itself did not amount to an act of execution entitling Senegal to claim sovereign immunity.[370]

In *LETCO v. Liberia*, LETCO obtained an award of damages of approximately US$9 million (after rectification) for breach of forestry concessions.[371] The US District Court for the Southern District of New York (a federal court of first instance) granted an order for the recognition and enforcement of LETCO's award against Liberia.[372] Shortly thereafter, a writ of execution was issued in LETCO's favor attaching various registration fees and taxes owed to the government of Liberia. Liberia appealed the execution order, arguing that those fees and taxes were sovereign assets immune from execution under the US Foreign Sovereign Immunities Act (*FSIA*). The court agreed and quashed the execution order, but it also gave LETCO leave to seek execution against commercial assets of the government of Liberia, under the commercial exception to general immunity in the FSIA.[373] LETCO then obtained execution orders attaching bank accounts of the Embassy of Liberia in Washington, DC. The US District Court for the District of Columbia (again, a federal court of first instance) quashed those orders, finding that the accounts were immune from attachment under the FSIA even though they contained funds used for both public purposes and commercial activities. The court ruled that the use of certain embassy funds for commercial activities incidental to embassy operations did not deprive the entire bank accounts of the mantle of sovereign immunity.[374]

---

370 *Société Ouest Africaine de Bétons Industriels (SOABI) v. State of Senegal*, ICSID Case No. ARB/82/1, Decision of Cour de Cassation (11 June 1991), *ICSID Reports* 2 (1994): 341.

371 *Liberian Eastern Timber Corporation (LETCO) v. Republic of Liberia*, ICSID Case No. ARB/83/2, Decision on Rectification (14 May 1986), *ICSID Reports* 2 (1994): 380.

372 *Liberian Eastern Timber Corporation (LETCO) v. Republic of Liberia*, ICSID Case No. ARB/83/2, Decision of United States District Court, Southern District of New York (5 September 1986), *ICSID Reports* 2 (1994): 384.

373 *Liberian Eastern Timber Corporation (LETCO) v. Republic of Liberia*, ICSID Case No. ARB/83/2, Decision of United States District Court, Southern District of New York (12 December 1986), *ICSID Reports* 2 (1994): 384 (The Decision was affirmed on appeal on 19 May 1987 with no published opinion, 650 F.Supp. 73 (S.D.N.Y. 1986)).

374 *Liberian Eastern Timber Corporation (LETCO) v. Republic of Liberia*, ICSID Case No. ARB/83/2, Decision of United States District Court, District of Columbia (16 April 1987), *ICSID Reports* 2 (1994): 390, 659 F.Supp. 606 (D.D.C. 1987).

Finally, in *AIG v. Kazakhstan*, AIG sought enforcement and execution of an ICSID award related to land expropriated by the government of Kazakhstan.[375] AIG registered the award in England pursuant to the UK law implementing the ICSID Convention and obtained interim third party debt and charging orders against the assets of the National Bank of Kazakhstan (**NBK**) held by various London banks. NBK intervened in the attachment proceedings, seeking discharge of the orders based on sovereign immunity. The English High Court granted NBK's request, discharging the orders based on the 1978 UK State Immunity Act, which states that "[p]roperty of a State's central bank or monetary authority shall not be regarded ... as in use or intended for use for commercial purposes".[376] The High Court concluded that although NBK possessed the assets at issue, the "London assets were at all times the 'property' of the Republic of Kazakhstan ... [and] so are immune from the enforcement process of the United Kingdom courts".[377]

Given the possible complications illustrated by the *Benvenuti, SOABI, LETCO* and *AIG* execution efforts, investors should assess possible execution fora carefully before finalizing investments and certainly before they initiate collection proceedings on ICSID awards. An investor with a monetary award in hand should attempt to locate assets of the losing State and then obtain comparative law advice to identify jurisdictions that allow attachment of at least certain categories of sovereign assets.

An alternative at the investment stage, of course, is for the investor to request the relevant State expressly to waive any and all sovereign immunity from execution in the relevant investment contract. The practical – and political – reality is that States and State entities, although willing to waive their immunity from suit in contracts by agreeing to ICSID arbitration, are reluctant to take the next step and waive the immunity of State assets from attachment by foreign investors. Even when the relevant State or State entity (unusually) is prepared

---

375 *AIG Capital Partners, Inc. and CJSC Tema Real Estate Company v. Republic of Kazakhstan*, ICSID Case No. ARB/01/6, Decision of the High Court, Queens Bench Division (Commercial Court) (20 October 2005), *ICSID Reports* 11 (2007): 118.

376 State Immunity Act of 1978, § 14(4) (UK).

377 *AIG v. Kazakhstan* (Decision of the High Court), *supra* note 375, at para. 94.

to provide a waiver of execution immunity, the investor must also obtain advice confirming the validity of such a waiver under the sovereign immunity laws of possible enforcement jurisdictions.

Recourse for failure to recognize, enforce or execute ICSID awards

Investors have limited recourse against States that refuse to recognize, enforce and execute ICSID awards in the face of their Convention obligations. An investor cannot bring proceedings against the delinquent State in its own name, but must rely on its home State to institute proceedings on its behalf, perhaps before the International Court of Justice. Although Article 27 of the ICSID Convention expressly bars a Contracting State from espousing its nationals' claims directly against another State (an otherwise accepted expression of diplomatic protection under international law), Article 64 allows an investor's home State to do so for the specific purpose of enforcing a Convention obligation that the host State has failed to honor. This default procedure obviously requires the good offices of the investor's home government, which, depending on the political circumstances, may be reluctant to proceed. As of September 2010, no ICSID Contracting State had invoked rights under Article 64.

This is not surprising, given that the ICSID regime is remarkably favorable to the recognition and enforcement (and, to a lesser degree, execution) of awards. Even its most daunting features – the prospect of annulment proceedings under Article 52 and protracted execution efforts against sovereign assets – have prompted more theoretical debates among commentators than practical problems for investor and State parties.

Annex 1

Convention on the Settlement of Investment Disputes Between States and Nationals of Other States
(done in Washington, 18 March 1965)

PREAMBLE

The Contracting States

Considering the need for international cooperation for economic development, and the role of private international investment therein;

Bearing in mind the possibility that from time to time disputes may arise in connection with such investment between Contracting States and nationals of other Contracting States;

Recognizing that while such disputes would usually be subject to national legal processes, international methods of settlement may be appropriate in certain cases;

Attaching particular importance to the availability of facilities for international conciliation or arbitration to which Contracting States and nationals of other Contracting States may submit such disputes if they so desire;

Desiring to establish such facilities under the auspices of the International Bank for Reconstruction and Development;

Recognizing that mutual consent by the parties to submit such disputes to conciliation or to arbitration through such facilities constitutes a binding agreement which requires in particular that due consideration be given to any recommendation of conciliators, and that any arbitral award be complied with; and

Declaring that no Contracting State shall by the mere fact of its ratification, acceptance or approval of this Convention and without its consent be deemed to be under any obligation to submit any particular dispute to conciliation or arbitration,

Have agreed as follows:

CHAPTER I
International Centre for Settlement of Investment Disputes

Section 1
Establishment and Organization

Article 1

(1) There is hereby established the International Centre for Settlement of Investment Disputes (hereinafter called the Centre).

(2) The purpose of the Centre shall be to provide facilities for conciliation and arbitration of investment disputes between Contracting States and nationals of other Contracting States in accordance with the provisions of this Convention.

Article 2

The seat of the Centre shall be at the principal office of the International Bank for Reconstruction and Development (hereinafter called the Bank). The seat may be moved to another place by decision of the Administrative Council adopted by a majority of two-thirds of its members.

Article 3

The Centre shall have an Administrative Council and a Secretariat and shall maintain a Panel of Conciliators and a Panel of Arbitrators.

Section 2
The Administrative Council

Article 4

(1) The Administrative Council shall be composed of one representative of each Contracting State. An alternate may act as representative in case of his principal's absence from a meeting or inability to act.

(2) In the absence of a contrary designation, each governor and alternate governor of the Bank appointed by a Contracting State shall be *ex officio* its representative and its alternate respectively.

Article 5

The President of the Bank shall be *ex officio* Chairman of the Administrative Council (hereinafter called the Chairman) but shall have no vote. During his absence or inability to act and during any vacancy in the office of President of the Bank, the person for the time being acting as President shall act as Chairman of the Administrative Council.

Article 6

(1) Without prejudice to the powers and functions vested in it by other provisions of this Convention, the Administrative Council shall:

  (a) adopt the administrative and financial regulations of the Centre;

  (b) adopt the rules of procedure for the institution of conciliation and arbitration proceedings;

  (c) adopt the rules of procedure for conciliation and arbitration proceedings (hereinafter called the Conciliation Rules and the Arbitration Rules);

(d) approve arrangements with the Bank for the use of the Bank's administrative facilities and services;

(e) determine the conditions of service of the Secretary-General and of any Deputy Secretary-General;

(f) adopt the annual budget of revenues and expenditures of the Centre;

(g) approve the annual report on the operation of the Centre.

The decisions referred to in sub-paragraphs (a), (b), (c) and (f) above shall be adopted by a majority of two-thirds of the members of the Administrative Council.

(2) The Administrative Council may appoint such committees as it considers necessary.

(3) The Administrative Council shall also exercise such other powers and perform such other functions as it shall determine to be necessary for the implementation of the provisions of this Convention.

Article 7

(1) The Administrative Council shall hold an annual meeting and such other meetings as may be determined by the Council, or convened by the Chairman, or convened by the Secretary-General at the request of not less than five members of the Council.

(2) Each member of the Administrative Council shall have one vote and, except as otherwise herein provided, all matters before the Council shall be decided by a majority of the votes cast.

(3) A quorum for any meeting of the Administrative Council shall be a majority of its members.

(4) The Administrative Council may establish, by a majority of two-thirds of its members, a procedure whereby the Chairman may seek a vote of the Council without convening a meeting of the Council. The vote shall be considered valid

only if the majority of the members of the Council cast their votes within the time limit fixed by the said procedure.

Article 8

Members of the Administrative Council and the Chairman shall serve without remuneration from the Centre.

Section 3
The Secretariat

Article 9

The Secretariat shall consist of a Secretary-General, one or more Deputy Secretaries-General and staff.

Article 10

(1) The Secretary-General and any Deputy Secretary-General shall be elected by the Administrative Council by a majority of two-thirds of its members upon the nomination of the Chairman for a term of service not exceeding six years and shall be eligible for re-election. After consulting the members of the Administrative Council, the Chairman shall propose one or more candidates for each such office.

(2) The offices of Secretary-General and Deputy Secretary-General shall be incompatible with the exercise of any political function. Neither the Secretary-General nor any Deputy Secretary-General may hold any other employment or engage in any other occupation except with the approval of the Administrative Council.

(3) During the Secretary-General's absence or inability to act, and during any vacancy of the office of Secretary-General, the Deputy Secretary-General shall act as Secretary-General. If there shall be more than one Deputy Secretary-General, the Administrative Council shall determine in advance the order in which they shall act as Secretary-General.

Article 11

The Secretary-General shall be the legal representative and the principal officer of the Centre and shall be responsible for its administration, including the appointment of staff, in accordance with the provisions of this Convention and the rules adopted by the Administrative Council. He shall perform the function of registrar and shall have the power to authenticate arbitral awards rendered pursuant to this Convention, and to certify copies thereof.

Section 4
The Panels

Article 12

The Panel of Conciliators and the Panel of Arbitrators shall each consist of qualified persons, designated as hereinafter provided, who are willing to serve thereon.

Article 13

(1) Each Contracting State may designate to each Panel four persons who may but need not be its nationals.

(2) The Chairman may designate ten persons to each Panel. The persons so designated to a Panel shall each have a different nationality.

Article 14

(1) Persons designated to serve on the Panels shall be persons of high moral character and recognized competence in the fields of law, commerce, industry or finance, who may be relied upon to exercise independent judgment. Competence in the field of law shall be of particular importance in the case of persons on the Panel of Arbitrators.

(2) The Chairman, in designating persons to serve on the Panels, shall in addition pay due regard to the importance of assuring representation on the Panels of the principal legal systems of the world and of the main forms of economic activity.

Article 15

(1) Panel members shall serve for renewable periods of six years.

(2) In case of death or resignation of a member of a Panel, the authority which designated the member shall have the right to designate another person to serve for the remainder of that member's term.

(3) Panel members shall continue in office until their successors have been designated.

Article 16

(1) A person may serve on both Panels.

(2) If a person shall have been designated to serve on the same Panel by more than one Contracting State, or by one or more Contracting States and the Chairman, he shall be deemed to have been designated by the authority which first designated him or, if one such authority is the State of which he is a national, by that State.

(3) All designations shall be notified to the Secretary-General and shall take effect from the date on which the notification is received.

Section 5
Financing the Centre

Article 17

If the expenditure of the Centre cannot be met out of charges for the use of its facilities, or out of other receipts, the excess shall be borne by Contracting States which are members of the Bank in proportion to their respective subscriptions to the capital stock of the Bank, and by Contracting States which are not members of the Bank in accordance with rules adopted by the Administrative Council.

Section 6
Status, Immunities and Privileges

Article 18

The Centre shall have full international legal personality. The legal capacity of the Centre shall include the capacity:

(a) to contract;

(b) to acquire and dispose of movable and immovable property;

(c) to institute legal proceedings.

Article 19

To enable the Centre to fulfil its functions, it shall enjoy in the territories of each Contracting State the immunities and privileges set forth in this Section.

Article 20

The Centre, its property and assets shall enjoy immunity from all legal process, except when the Centre waives this immunity.

Article 21

The Chairman, the members of the Administrative Council, persons acting as conciliators or arbitrators or members of a Committee appointed pursuant to paragraph (3) of Article 52, and the officers and employees of the Secretariat

(a) shall enjoy immunity from legal process with respect to acts performed by them in the exercise of their functions, except when the Centre waives this immunity;

(b) not being local nationals, shall enjoy the same immunities from immigration restrictions, alien registration requirements and national service obligations, the same facilities as regards exchange restrictions and the same treatment in respect of travelling facilities as are accorded by Contracting States to the representatives, officials and employees of comparable rank of other Contracting States.

Article 22

The provisions of Article 21 shall apply to persons appearing in proceedings under this Convention as parties, agents, counsel, advocates, witnesses or experts; provided, however, that sub-paragraph (b) thereof shall apply only in connection with their travel to and from, and their stay at, the place where the proceedings are held.

Article 23

(1) The archives of the Centre shall be inviolable, wherever they may be.

(2) With regard to its official communications, the Centre shall be accorded by each Contracting State treatment not less favourable than that accorded to other international organizations.

Article 24

(1) The Centre, its assets, property and income, and its operations and transactions authorized by this Convention shall be exempt from all taxation and customs duties. The Centre shall also be exempt from liability for the collection or payment of any taxes or customs duties.

(2) Except in the case of local nationals, no tax shall be levied on or in respect of expense allowances paid by the Centre to the Chairman or members of the Administrative Council, or on or in respect of salaries, expense allowances or other emoluments paid by the Centre to officials or employees of the Secretariat.

(3) No tax shall be levied on or in respect of fees or expense allowances received by persons acting as conciliators, or arbitrators, or members of a Committee appointed pursuant to paragraph (3) of Article 52, in proceedings under this Convention, if the sole jurisdictional basis for such tax is the location of the Centre or the place where such proceedings are conducted or the place where such fees or allowances are paid.

CHAPTER II
Jurisdiction of the Centre

Article 25

(1) The jurisdiction of the Centre shall extend to any legal dispute arising directly out of an investment, between a Contracting State (or any constituent subdivision or agency of a Contracting State designated to the Centre by that State) and a national of another Contracting State, which the parties to the dispute consent in writing to submit to the Centre. When the parties have given their consent, no party may withdraw its consent unilaterally.

(2) "National of another Contracting State" means:

(a) any natural person who had the nationality of a Contracting State other than the State party to the dispute on the date on which the parties consented to submit such dispute to conciliation or arbitration as well as on the date on which the request was registered pursuant to paragraph (3) of Article 28 or paragraph (3) of Article 36, but does not include any person who on either date also had the nationality of the Contracting State party to the dispute; and

(b) any juridical person which had the nationality of a Contracting State other than the State party to the dispute on the date on which the parties consented to submit such dispute to conciliation or arbitration and any juridical person which had the nationality of the Contracting State party to the dispute on that date and which, because of foreign control, the parties have agreed should be treated as a national of another Contracting State for the purposes of this Convention.

(3) Consent by a constituent subdivision or agency of a Contracting State shall require the approval of that State unless that State notifies the Centre that no such approval is required.

(4) Any Contracting State may, at the time of ratification, acceptance or approval of this Convention or at any time thereafter, notify the Centre of the class or classes of disputes which it would or would not consider submitting to the

jurisdiction of the Centre. The Secretary-General shall forthwith transmit such notification to all Contracting States. Such notification shall not constitute the consent required by paragraph (1).

Article 26

Consent of the parties to arbitration under this Convention shall, unless otherwise stated, be deemed consent to such arbitration to the exclusion of any other remedy. A Contracting State may require the exhaustion of local administrative or judicial remedies as a condition of its consent to arbitration under this Convention.

Article 27

(1) No Contracting State shall give diplomatic protection, or bring an international claim, in respect of a dispute which one of its nationals and another Contracting State shall have consented to submit or shall have submitted to arbitration under this Convention, unless such other Contracting State shall have failed to abide by and comply with the award rendered in such dispute.

(2) Diplomatic protection, for the purposes of paragraph (1), shall not include informal diplomatic exchanges for the sole purpose of facilitating a settlement of the dispute.

CHAPTER III
Conciliation

Section 1
Request for Conciliation

Article 28

(1) Any Contracting State or any national of a Contracting State wishing to institute conciliation proceedings shall address a request to that effect in writing to the Secretary-General who shall send a copy of the request to the other party.

(2) The request shall contain information concerning the issues in dispute, the identity of the parties and their consent to conciliation in accordance with the rules of procedure for the institution of conciliation and arbitration proceedings.

(3) The Secretary-General shall register the request unless he finds, on the basis of the information contained in the request, that the dispute is manifestly outside the jurisdiction of the Centre. He shall forthwith notify the parties of registration or refusal to register.

Section 2
Constitution of the Conciliation Commission

Article 29

(1) The Conciliation Commission (hereinafter called the Commission) shall be constituted as soon as possible after registration of a request pursuant to Article 28.

(2)(a) The Commission shall consist of a sole conciliator or any uneven number of conciliators appointed as the parties shall agree.

(b) Where the parties do not agree upon the number of conciliators and the method of their appointment, the Commission shall consist of three conciliators, one conciliator appointed by each party and the third, who shall be the president of the Commission, appointed by agreement of the parties.

Article 30

If the Commission shall not have been constituted within 90 days after notice of registration of the request has been dispatched by the Secretary-General in accordance with paragraph (3) of Article 28, or such other period as the parties may agree, the Chairman shall, at the request of either party and after consulting both parties as far as possible, appoint the conciliator or conciliators not yet appointed.

Article 31

(1) Conciliators may be appointed from outside the Panel of Conciliators, except in the case of appointments by the Chairman pursuant to Article 30.

(2) Conciliators appointed from outside the Panel of Conciliators shall possess the qualities stated in paragraph (1) of Article 14.

Section 3
Conciliation Proceedings

Article 32

(1) The Commission shall be the judge of its own competence.

(2) Any objection by a party to the dispute that that dispute is not within the jurisdiction of the Centre, or for other reasons is not within the competence of the Commission, shall be considered by the Commission which shall determine whether to deal with it as a preliminary question or to join it to the merits of the dispute.

Article 33

Any conciliation proceeding shall be conducted in accordance with the provisions of this Section and, except as the parties otherwise agree, in accordance with the Conciliation Rules in effect on the date on which the parties consented to conciliation. If any question of procedure arises which is not covered by this Section or the Conciliation Rules or any rules agreed by the parties, the Commission shall decide the question.

Article 34

(1) It shall be the duty of the Commission to clarify the issues in dispute between the parties and to endeavour to bring about agreement between them upon mutually acceptable terms. To that end, the Commission may at any stage of the proceedings and from time to time recommend terms of settlement to the parties. The parties shall cooperate in good faith with the Commission in order

to enable the Commission to carry out its functions, and shall give their most serious consideration to its recommendations.

(2) If the parties reach agreement, the Commission shall draw up a report noting the issues in dispute and recording that the parties have reached agreement. If, at any stage of the proceedings, it appears to the Commission that there is no likelihood of agreement between the parties, it shall close the proceedings and shall draw up a report noting the submission of the dispute and recording the failure of the parties to reach agreement. If one party fails to appear or participate in the proceedings, the Commission shall close the proceedings and shall draw up a report noting that party's failure to appear or participate.

Article 35

Except as the parties to the dispute shall otherwise agree, neither party to a conciliation proceeding shall be entitled in any other proceeding, whether before arbitrators or in a court of law or otherwise, to invoke or rely on any views expressed or statements or admissions or offers of settlement made by the other party in the conciliation proceedings, or the report or any recommendations made by the Commission.

CHAPTER IV
Arbitration

Section I
Request for Arbitration

Article 36

(1) Any Contracting State or any national of a Contracting State wishing to institute arbitration proceedings shall address a request to that effect in writing to the Secretary-General who shall send a copy of the request to the other party.

(2) The request shall contain information concerning the issues in dispute, the identity of the parties and their consent to arbitration in accordance with the rules of procedure for the institution of conciliation and arbitration proceedings.

(3) The Secretary-General shall register the request unless he finds, on the basis of the information contained in the request, that the dispute is manifestly outside the jurisdiction of the Centre. He shall forthwith notify the parties of registration or refusal to register.

Section 2
Constitution of the Tribunal

Article 37

(1) The Arbitral Tribunal (hereinafter called the Tribunal) shall be constituted as soon as possible after registration of a request pursuant to Article 36.

(2)(a) The Tribunal shall consist of a sole arbitrator or any uneven number of arbitrators appointed as the parties shall agree.

(b) Where the parties do not agree upon the number of arbitrators and the method of their appointment, the Tribunal shall consist of three arbitrators, one arbitrator appointed by each party and the third, who shall be the president of the Tribunal, appointed by agreement of the parties.

Article 38

If the Tribunal shall not have been constituted within 90 days after notice of registration of the request has been dispatched by the Secretary-General in accordance with paragraph (3) of Article 36, or such other period as the parties may agree, the Chairman shall, at the request of either party and after consulting both parties as far as possible, appoint the arbitrator or arbitrators not yet appointed. Arbitrators appointed by the Chairman pursuant to this Article shall not be nationals of the Contracting State party to the dispute or of the Contracting State whose national is a party to the dispute.

Article 39

The majority of the arbitrators shall be nationals of States other than the Contracting State party to the dispute and the Contracting State whose national is a party to the dispute; provided, however, that the foregoing provisions of this Article shall not apply if the sole arbitrator or each individual member of the Tribunal has been appointed by agreement of the parties.

Article 40

(1) Arbitrators may be appointed from outside the Panel of Arbitrators, except in the case of appointments by the Chairman pursuant to Article 38.

(2) Arbitrators appointed from outside the Panel of Arbitrators shall possess the qualities stated in paragraph (1) of Article 14.

Section 3
Powers and Functions of the Tribunal

Article 41

(1) The Tribunal shall be the judge of its own competence.

(2) Any objection by a party to the dispute that that dispute is not within the jurisdiction of the Centre, or for other reasons is not within the competence of the Tribunal, shall be considered by the Tribunal which shall determine whether to deal with it as a preliminary question or to join it to the merits of the dispute.

Article 42

(1) The Tribunal shall decide a dispute in accordance with such rules of law as may be agreed by the parties. In the absence of such agreement, the Tribunal shall apply the law of the Contracting State party to the dispute (including its rules on the conflict of laws) and such rules of international law as may be applicable.

(2) The Tribunal may not bring in a finding of *non liquet* on the ground of silence or obscurity of the law.

(3) The provisions of paragraphs (1) and (2) shall not prejudice the power of the Tribunal to decide a dispute *ex aequo et bono* if the parties so agree.

Article 43

Except as the parties otherwise agree, the Tribunal may, if it deems it necessary at any stage of the proceedings,

 (a) call upon the parties to produce documents or other evidence, and

 (b) visit the scene connected with the dispute, and conduct such inquiries there as it may deem appropriate.

Article 44

Any arbitration proceeding shall be conducted in accordance with the provisions of this Section and, except as the parties otherwise agree, in accordance with the Arbitration Rules in effect on the date on which the parties consented to arbitration. If any question of procedure arises which is not covered by this Section or the Arbitration Rules or any rules agreed by the parties, the Tribunal shall decide the question.

Article 45

(1) Failure of a party to appear or to present his case shall not be deemed an admission of the other party's assertions.

(2) If a party fails to appear or to present his case at any stage of the proceedings the other party may request the Tribunal to deal with the questions submitted to it and to render an award. Before rendering an award, the Tribunal shall notify, and grant a period of grace to, the party failing to appear or to present its case, unless it is satisfied that that party does not intend to do so.

Article 46

Except as the parties otherwise agree, the Tribunal shall, if requested by a party, determine any incidental or additional claims or counterclaims arising directly out of the subject-matter of the dispute provided that they are within the scope of the consent of the parties and are otherwise within the jurisdiction of the Centre.

Article 47

Except as the parties otherwise agree, the Tribunal may, if it considers that the circumstances so require, recommend any provisional measures which should be taken to preserve the respective rights of either party.

Section 4
The Award

Article 48

(1) The Tribunal shall decide questions by a majority of the votes of all its members.

(2) The award of the Tribunal shall be in writing and shall be signed by the members of the Tribunal who voted for it.

(3) The award shall deal with every question submitted to the Tribunal, and shall state the reasons upon which it is based.

(4) Any member of the Tribunal may attach his individual opinion to the award, whether he dissents from the majority or not, or a statement of his dissent.

(5) The Centre shall not publish the award without the consent of the parties.

Article 49

(1) The Secretary-General shall promptly dispatch certified copies of the award to the parties. The award shall be deemed to have been rendered on the date on which the certified copies were dispatched.

(2) The Tribunal upon the request of a party made within 45 days after the date on which the award was rendered may after notice to the other party decide any question which it had omitted to decide in the award, and shall rectify any clerical, arithmetical or similar error in the award. Its decision shall become part of the

award and shall be notified to the parties in the same manner as the award. The periods of time provided for under paragraph (2) of Article 51 and paragraph (2) of Article 52 shall run from the date on which the decision was rendered.

Section 5
Interpretation, Revision and Annulment of the Award

Article 50

(1) If any dispute shall arise between the parties as to the meaning or scope of an award, either party may request interpretation of the award by an application in writing addressed to the Secretary-General.

(2) The request shall, if possible, be submitted to the Tribunal which rendered the award. If this shall not be possible, a new Tribunal shall be constituted in accordance with Section 2 of this Chapter. The Tribunal may, if it considers that the circumstances so require, stay enforcement of the award pending its decision.

Article 51

(1) Either party may request revision of the award by an application in writing addressed to the Secretary-General on the ground of discovery of some fact of such a nature as decisively to affect the award, provided that when the award was rendered that fact was unknown to the Tribunal and to the applicant and that the applicant's ignorance of that fact was not due to negligence.

(2) The application shall be made within 90 days after the discovery of such fact and in any event within three years after the date on which the award was rendered.

(3) The request shall, if possible, be submitted to the Tribunal which rendered the award. If this shall not be possible, a new Tribunal shall be constituted in accordance with Section 2 of this Chapter.

(4) The Tribunal may, if it considers that the circumstances so require, stay enforcement of the award pending its decision. If the applicant requests a stay of enforcement of the award in his application, enforcement shall be stayed provisionally until the Tribunal rules on such request.

Article 52

(1) Either party may request annulment of the award by an application in writing addressed to the Secretary-General on one or more of the following grounds:

   (a)   that the Tribunal was not properly constituted;

   (b)   that the Tribunal has manifestly exceeded its powers;

   (c)   that there was corruption on the part of a member of the Tribunal;

   (d)   that there has been a serious departure from a fundamental rule of procedure; or

   (e)   that the award has failed to state the reasons on which it is based.

(2) The application shall be made within 120 days after the date on which the award was rendered except that when annulment is requested on the ground of corruption such application shall be made within 120 days after discovery of the corruption and in any event within three years after the date on which the award was rendered.

(3) On receipt of the request the Chairman shall forthwith appoint from the Panel of Arbitrators an ad hoc Committee of three persons. None of the members of the Committee shall have been a member of the Tribunal which rendered the award, shall be of the same nationality as any such member, shall be a national of the State party to the dispute or of the State whose national is a party to the dispute, shall have been designated to the Panel of Arbitrators by either of those States, or shall have acted as a conciliator in the same dispute. The Committee shall have the authority to annul the award or any part thereof on any of the grounds set forth in paragraph (1).

(4) The provisions of Articles 41-45, 48, 49, 53 and 54, and of Chapters VI and VII shall apply mutatis mutandis to proceedings before the Committee.

(5) The Committee may, if it considers that the circumstances so require, stay enforcement of the award pending its decision. If the applicant requests a stay of enforcement of the award in his application, enforcement shall be stayed provisionally until the Committee rules on such request.

(6) If the award is annulled the dispute shall, at the request of either party, be submitted to a new Tribunal constituted in accordance with Section 2 of this Chapter.

Section 6
Recognition and Enforcement of the Award

Article 53

(1) The award shall be binding on the parties and shall not be subject to any appeal or to any other remedy except those provided for in this Convention. Each party shall abide by and comply with the terms of the award except to the extent that enforcement shall have been stayed pursuant to the relevant provisions of this Convention.

(2) For the purposes of this Section, "award" shall include any decision interpreting, revising or annulling such award pursuant to Articles 50, 51 or 52.

Article 54

(1) Each Contracting State shall recognize an award rendered pursuant to this Convention as binding and enforce the pecuniary obligations imposed by that award within its territories as if it were a final judgment of a court in that State. A Contracting State with a federal constitution may enforce such an award in or through its federal courts and may provide that such courts shall treat the award as if it were a final judgment of the courts of a constituent state.

(2) A party seeking recognition or enforcement in the territories of a Contracting State shall furnish to a competent court or other authority which such State shall have designated for this purpose a copy of the award certified by the Secretary-General. Each Contracting State shall notify the Secretary-General of the designation of the competent court or other authority for this purpose and of any subsequent change in such designation.

(3) Execution of the award shall be governed by the laws concerning the execution of judgments in force in the State in whose territories such execution is sought.

Article 55

Nothing in Article 54 shall be construed as derogating from the law in force in any Contracting State relating to immunity of that State or of any foreign State from execution.

CHAPTER V
Replacement and Disqualification of Conciliators and Arbitrators

Article 56

(1) After a Commission or a Tribunal has been constituted and proceedings have begun, its composition shall remain unchanged; provided, however, that if a conciliator or an arbitrator should die, become incapacitated, or resign, the resulting vacancy shall be filled in accordance with the provisions of Section 2 of Chapter III or Section 2 of Chapter IV.

(2) A member of a Commission or Tribunal shall continue to serve in that capacity notwithstanding that he shall have ceased to be a member of the Panel.

(3) If a conciliator or arbitrator appointed by a party shall have resigned without the consent of the Commission or Tribunal of which he was a member, the Chairman shall appoint a person from the appropriate Panel to fill the resulting vacancy.

Article 57

A party may propose to a Commission or Tribunal the disqualification of any of its members on account of any fact indicating a manifest lack of the qualities required by paragraph (1) of Article 14. A party to arbitration proceedings may, in addition, propose the disqualification of an arbitrator on the ground that he was ineligible for appointment to the Tribunal under Section 2 of Chapter IV.

Article 58

The decision on any proposal to disqualify a conciliator or arbitrator shall be taken by the other members of the Commission or Tribunal as the case may be, provided that where those members are equally divided, or in the case of a proposal to disqualify a sole conciliator or arbitrator, or a majority of the conciliators or arbitrators, the Chairman shall take that decision. If it is decided that the proposal is well-founded the conciliator or arbitrator to whom the decision relates shall be replaced in accordance with the provisions of Section 2 of Chapter III or Section 2 of Chapter IV.

CHAPTER VI
Cost of Proceedings

Article 59

The charges payable by the parties for the use of the facilities of the Centre shall be determined by the Secretary-General in accordance with the regulations adopted by the Administrative Council.

Article 60

(1) Each Commission and each Tribunal shall determine the fees and expenses of its members within limits established from time to time by the Administrative Council and after consultation with the Secretary-General.

(2) Nothing in paragraph (1) of this Article shall preclude the parties from agreeing in advance with the Commission or Tribunal concerned upon the fees and expenses of its members.

Article 61

(1) In the case of conciliation proceedings the fees and expenses of members of the Commission as well as the charges for the use of the facilities of the Centre, shall be borne equally by the parties. Each party shall bear any other expenses it incurs in connection with the proceedings.

(2) In the case of arbitration proceedings the Tribunal shall, except as the parties otherwise agree, assess the expenses incurred by the parties in connection with the proceedings, and shall decide how and by whom those expenses, the fees and expenses of the members of the Tribunal and the charges for the use of the facilities of the Centre shall be paid. Such decision shall form part of the award.

CHAPTER VII
Place of Proceedings

Article 62

Conciliation and arbitration proceedings shall be held at the seat of the Centre except as hereinafter provided.

Article 63

Conciliation and arbitration proceedings may be held, if the parties so agree,

(a)   at the seat of the Permanent Court of Arbitration or of any other appropriate institution, whether private or public, with which the Centre may make arrangements for that purpose; or

(b)   at any other place approved by the Commission or Tribunal after consultation with the Secretary-General.

CHAPTER VIII
Disputes Between Contracting States

Article 64

Any dispute arising between Contracting States concerning the interpretation or application of this Convention which is not settled by negotiation shall be referred to the International Court of Justice by the application of any party to such dispute, unless the States concerned agree to another method of settlement.

CHAPTER IX
Amendment

Article 65

Any Contracting State may propose amendment of this Convention. The text of a proposed amendment shall be communicated to the Secretary-General not less than 90 days prior to the meeting of the Administrative Council at which such amendment is to be considered and shall forthwith be transmitted by him to all the members of the Administrative Council.

Article 66

(1) If the Administrative Council shall so decide by a majority of two-thirds of its members, the proposed amendment shall be circulated to all Contracting States for ratification, acceptance or approval. Each amendment shall enter into force 30 days after dispatch by the depositary of this Convention of a notification to Contracting States that all Contracting States have ratified, accepted or approved the amendment.

(2) No amendment shall affect the rights and obligations under this Convention of any Contracting State or of any of its constituent subdivisions or agencies, or of any national of such State arising out of consent to the jurisdiction of the Centre given before the date of entry into force of the amendment.

CHAPTER X
Final Provisions

Article 67

This Convention shall be open for signature on behalf of States members of the Bank. It shall also be open for signature on behalf of any other State which is a party to the Statute of the International Court of Justice and which the Administrative Council, by a vote of two-thirds of its members, shall have invited to sign the Convention.

Article 68

(1) This Convention shall be subject to ratification, acceptance or approval by the signatory States in accordance with their respective constitutional procedures.

(2) This Convention shall enter into force 30 days after the date of deposit of the twentieth instrument of ratification, acceptance or approval. It shall enter into force for each State which subsequently deposits its instrument of ratification, acceptance or approval 30 days after the date of such deposit.

Article 69

Each Contracting State shall take such legislative or other measures as may be necessary for making the provisions of this Convention effective in its territories.

Article 70

This Convention shall apply to all territories for whose international relations a Contracting State is responsible, except those which are excluded by such State by written notice to the depositary of this Convention either at the time of ratification, acceptance or approval or subsequently.

Article 71

Any Contracting State may denounce this Convention by written notice to the depositary of this Convention. The denunciation shall take effect six months after receipt of such notice.

Article 72

Notice by a Contracting State pursuant to Articles 70 or 71 shall not affect the rights or obligations under this Convention of that State or of any of its constituent subdivisions or agencies or of any national of that State arising out of consent to the jurisdiction of the Centre given by one of them before such notice was received by the depositary.

Article 73

Instruments of ratification, acceptance or approval of this Convention and of amendments thereto shall be deposited with the Bank which shall act as the depositary of this Convention. The depositary shall transmit certified copies of this Convention to States members of the Bank and to any other State invited to sign the Convention.

Article 74

The depositary shall register this Convention with the Secretariat of the United Nations in accordance with Article 102 of the Charter of the United Nations and the Regulations thereunder adopted by the General Assembly.

Article 75

The depositary shall notify all signatory States of the following:

(a) signatures in accordance with Article 67;

(b) deposits of instruments of ratification, acceptance and approval in accordance with Article 73;

(c) the date on which this Convention enters into force in accordance with Article 68;

(d) exclusions from territorial application pursuant to Article 70;

(e) the date on which any amendment of this Convention enters into force in accordance with Article 66; and

(f) denunciations in accordance with Article 71.

DONE at Washington, in the English, French and Spanish languages, all three texts being equally authentic, in a single copy which shall remain deposited in the archives of the International Bank for Reconstruction and Development, which has indicated by its signature below its agreement to fulfil the functions with which it is charged under this Convention.

Annex 2

Rules of Procedure for the Institution of Conciliation and Arbitration Proceedings
(effective 10 April 2006)

Institution Rules

Rule 1
The Request

(1) Any Contracting State or any national of a Contracting State wishing to institute conciliation or arbitration proceedings under the Convention shall address a request to that effect in writing to the Secretary-General at the seat of the Centre. The request shall indicate whether it relates to a conciliation or an arbitration proceeding. It shall be drawn up in an official language of the Centre, shall be dated, and shall be signed by the requesting party or its duly authorized representative.

(2) The request may be made jointly by the parties to the dispute.

Rule 2
Contents of the Request

(1) The request shall:
 (a) designate precisely each party to the dispute and state the address of each;

(b) state, if one of the parties is a constituent subdivision or agency of a Contracting State, that it has been designated to the Centre by that State pursuant to Article 25(1) of the Convention;

(c) indicate the date of consent and the instruments in which it is recorded, including, if one party is a constituent subdivision or agency of a Contracting State, similar data on the approval of such consent by that State unless it had notified the Centre that no such approval is required;

(d) indicate with respect to the party that is a national of a Contracting State:

(i) its nationality on the date of consent; and

(ii) if the party is a natural person:

(A) his nationality on the date of the request; and

(B) that he did not have the nationality of the Contracting State party to the dispute either on the date of consent or on the date of the request; or

(iii) if the party is a juridical person which on the date of consent had the nationality of the Contracting State party to the dispute, the agreement of the parties that it should be treated as a national of another Contracting State for the purposes of the Convention;

(e) contain information concerning the issues in dispute indicating that there is, between the parties, a legal dispute arising directly out of an investment; and

(f) state, if the requesting party is a juridical person, that it has taken all necessary internal actions to authorize the request.

(2) The information required by subparagraphs (1)(c), (1)(d)(iii) and (1)(f) shall be supported by documentation.

(3) "Date of consent" means the date on which the parties to the dispute consented in writing to submit it to the Centre; if both parties did not act on the same day, it means the date on which the second party acted.

Rule 3
Optional Information in the Request

The request may in addition set forth any provisions agreed by the parties regarding the number of conciliators or arbitrators and the method of their appointment, as well as any other provisions agreed concerning the settlement of the dispute.

Rule 4
Copies of the Request

(1) The request shall be accompanied by five additional signed copies. The Secretary-General may require such further copies as he may deem necessary.

(2) Any documentation submitted with the request shall conform to the requirements of Administrative and Financial Regulation 30.

Rule 5
Acknowledgement of the Request

(1) On receiving a request the Secretary-General shall:

(a) send an acknowledgement to the requesting party;

(b) take no other action with respect to the request until he has received payment of the prescribed fee.

(2) As soon as he has received the fee for lodging the request, the Secretary-General shall transmit a copy of the request and of the accompanying documentation to the other party.

Rule 6
Registration of the Request

(1) The Secretary-General shall, subject to Rule 5(1)(b), as soon as possible, either:

(a) register the request in the Conciliation or the Arbitration Register and on the same day notify the parties of the registration; or

(b) if he finds, on the basis of the information contained in the request, that the dispute is manifestly outside the jurisdiction of the Centre, notify the parties of his refusal to register the request and of the reasons therefor.

(2) A proceeding under the Convention shall be deemed to have been instituted on the date of the registration of the request.

Rule 7
Notice of Registration

The notice of registration of a request shall:

(a) record that the request is registered and indicate the date of the registration and of the dispatch of that notice;

(b) notify each party that all communications and notices in connection with the proceeding will be sent to the address stated in the request, unless another address is indicated to the Centre;

(c) unless such information has already been provided, invite the parties to communicate to the Secretary-General any provisions agreed by them regarding the number and the method of appointment of the conciliators or arbitrators;

(d) invite the parties to proceed, as soon as possible, to constitute a Conciliation Commission in accordance with Articles 29 to 31 of the Convention, or an Arbitral Tribunal in accordance with Articles 37 to 40;

(e) remind the parties that the registration of the request is without prejudice to the powers and functions of the Conciliation Commission or Arbitral Tribunal in regard to jurisdiction, competence and the merits; and

(f) be accompanied by a list of the members of the Panel of Conciliators or of Arbitrators of the Centre.

Rule 8
Withdrawal of the Request

The requesting party may, by written notice to the Secretary-General, withdraw the request before it has been registered. The Secretary-General shall promptly notify the other party, unless, pursuant to Rule 5(1)(b), the request had not been transmitted to it.

Rule 9
Final Provisions

(1) The texts of these Rules in each official language of the Centre shall be equally authentic.

(2) These Rules may be cited as the "Institution Rules" of the Centre.

Rules of Procedure for Arbitration Proceedings
(effective 10 April 2006)

Arbitration Rules

Chapter I
Establishment of the Tribunal

Rule 1
General Obligations

(1) Upon notification of the registration of the request for arbitration, the parties shall, with all possible dispatch, proceed to constitute a Tribunal, with due regard to Section 2 of Chapter IV of the Convention.

(2) Unless such information is provided in the request, the parties shall communicate to the Secretary-General as soon as possible any provisions agreed by them regarding the number of arbitrators and the method of their appointment.

(3) The majority of the arbitrators shall be nationals of States other than the State party to the dispute and of the State whose national is a party to the dispute, unless the sole arbitrator or each individual member of the Tribunal is appointed by agreement of the parties. Where the Tribunal is to consist of three members, a national of either of these States may not be appointed as an arbitrator by a party without the agreement of the other party to the dispute. Where the Tribunal is to consist of five or more members, nationals of either

or these States may not be appointed as arbitrators by a party if appointment by the other party of the same number of arbitrators of either of these nationalities would result in a majority of arbitrators of these nationalities.

(4) No person who had previously acted as a conciliator or arbitrator in any proceeding for the settlement of the dispute may be appointed as a member of the Tribunal.

Rule 2
Method of Constituting the Tribunal in the Absence of Previous Agreement

(1) If the parties, at the time of the registration of the request for arbitration, have not agreed upon the number of arbitrators and the method of their appointment, they shall, unless they agree otherwise, follow the following procedure:

   (a)   the requesting party shall, within 10 days after the registration of the request, propose to the other party the appointment of a sole arbitrator or of a specified uneven number of arbitrators and specify the method proposed for their appointment;

   (b)   within 20 days after receipt of the proposals made by the requesting party, the other party shall:

      (i)   accept such proposals; or

      (ii)   make other proposals regarding the number of arbitrators and the method of their appointment;

   (c)   within 20 days after receipt of the reply containing any such other proposals, the requesting party shall notify the other party whether it accepts or rejects such proposals.

(2) The communications provided for in paragraph (1) shall be made or promptly confirmed in writing and shall either be transmitted through the Secretary-General or directly between the parties with a copy to the Secretary-General. The parties shall promptly notify the Secretary-General of the contents of any agreement reached.

(3) At any time 60 days after the registration of the request, if no agreement on another procedure is reached, either party may inform the Secretary-General that it chooses the formula provided for in Article 37(2)(b) of the Convention. The Secretary-General shall thereupon promptly inform the other party that the Tribunal is to be constituted in accordance with that Article.

Rule 3
Appointment of Arbitrators to a Tribunal Constituted in Accordance with Convention Article 37(2)(b)

(1) If the Tribunal is to be constituted in accordance with Article 37(2)(b) of the Convention:

   (a) either party shall in a communication to the other party:

      (i) name two persons, identifying one of them, who shall not have the same nationality as nor be a national of either party, as the arbitrator appointed by it, and the other as the arbitrator proposed to be the President of the Tribunal; and

      (ii) invite the other party to concur in the appointment of the arbitrator proposed to be the President of the Tribunal and to appoint another arbitrator;

   (b) promptly upon receipt of this communication the other party shall, in its reply:

      (i) name a person as the arbitrator appointed by it, who shall not have the same nationality as nor be a national of either party; and

      (ii) concur in the appointment of the arbitrator proposed to be the President of the Tribunal or name another person as the arbitrator proposed to be President;

   (c) promptly upon receipt of the reply containing such a proposal, the initiating party shall notify the other party whether it concurs in the appointment of the arbitrator proposed by that party to be the President of the Tribunal.

(2) The communications provided for in this Rule shall be made or promptly confirmed in writing and shall either be transmitted through the Secretary-General or directly between the parties with a copy to the Secretary-General.

Rule 4
Appointment of Arbitrators by the Chairman of the Administrative Council

(1) If the Tribunal is not constituted within 90 days after the dispatch by the Secretary-General of the notice of registration, or such other period as the parties may agree, either party may, through the Secretary-General, address to the Chairman of the Administrative Council a request in writing to appoint the arbitrator or arbitrators not yet appointed and to designate an arbitrator to be the President of the Tribunal.

(2) The provision of paragraph (1) shall apply *mutatis mutandis* in the event that the parties have agreed that the arbitrators shall elect the President of the Tribunal and they fail to do so.

(3) The Secretary-General shall forthwith send a copy of the request to the other party.

(4) The Chairman shall use his best efforts to comply with that request within 30 days after its receipt. Before he proceeds to make an appointment or designation, with due regard to Articles 38 and 40(1) of the Convention, he shall consult both parties as far as possible.

(5) The Secretary-General shall promptly notify the parties of any appointment or designation made by the Chairman.

Rule 5
Acceptance of Appointments

(1) The party or parties concerned shall notify the Secretary-General of the appointment of each arbitrator and indicate the method of his appointment.

(2) As soon as the Secretary-General has been informed by a party or the Chairman of the Administrative Council of the appointment of an arbitrator, he shall seek an acceptance from the appointee.

(3) If an arbitrator fails to accept his appointment within 15 days, the Secretary-General shall promptly notify the parties, and if appropriate the Chairman, and invite them to proceed to the appointment of another arbitrator in accordance with the method followed for the previous appointment.

Rule 6
Constitution of the Tribunal

(1) The Tribunal shall be deemed to be constituted and the proceeding to have begun on the date the Secretary-General notifies the parties that all the arbitrators have accepted their appointment.

(2) Before or at the first session of the Tribunal, each arbitrator shall sign a declaration in the following form:

"To the best of my knowledge there is no reason why I should not serve on the Arbitral Tribunal constituted by the International Centre for Settlement of Investment Disputes with respect to a dispute between _____ and _____.

I shall keep confidential all information coming to my knowledge as a result of my participation in this proceeding, as well as the contents of any award made by the Tribunal.

I shall judge fairly as between the parties, according to the applicable law, and shall not accept any instruction or compensation with regard to the proceeding from any source except as provided in the Convention on the Settlement of Investment Disputes between States and Nationals of Other States and in the Regulations and Rules made pursuant thereto.

Attached is a statement of (a) my past and present professional, business and other relationships (if any) with the parties and (b) any other circumstance that might cause my reliability for independent judgment to be questioned by a party. I acknowledge that by signing this declaration, I assume a continuing obligation promptly to notify the Secretary-General of the Centre of any such relationship or circumstance that subsequently arises during this proceeding."

Any arbitrator failing to sign a declaration by the end of the first session of the Tribunal shall be deemed to have resigned.

Rule 7
Replacement of Arbitrators

At any time before the Tribunal is constituted, each party may replace any arbitrator appointed by it and the parties may by common consent agree to replace any arbitrator. The procedure of such replacement shall be in accordance with Rules 1, 5 and 6.

Rule 8
Incapacity or Resignation of Arbitrators

(1) If an arbitrator becomes incapacitated or unable to perform the duties of his office, the procedure in respect of the disqualification of arbitrators set forth in Rule 9 shall apply.

(2) An arbitrator may resign by submitting his resignation to the other members of the Tribunal and the Secretary-General. If the arbitrator was appointed by one of the parties, the Tribunal shall promptly consider the reasons for his resignation and decide whether it consents thereto. The Tribunal shall promptly notify the Secretary-General of its decision.

Rule 9
Disqualification of Arbitrators

(1) A party proposing the disqualification of an arbitrator pursuant to Article 57 of the Convention shall promptly, and in any event before the proceeding is declared closed, file its proposal with the Secretary-General, stating its reasons therefor.

(2) The Secretary-General shall forthwith:

  (a) transmit the proposal to the members of the Tribunal and, if it relates to a sole arbitrator or to a majority of the members of the Tribunal, to the Chairman of the Administrative Council; and

(b) notify the other party of the proposal.

(3) The arbitrator to whom the proposal relates may, without delay, furnish explanations to the Tribunal or the Chairman, as the case may be.

(4) Unless the proposal relates to a majority of the members of the Tribunal, the other members shall promptly consider and vote on the proposal in the absence of the arbitrator concerned. If those members are equally divided, they shall, through the Secretary-General, promptly notify the Chairman of the proposal, of any explanation furnished by the arbitrator concerned and of their failure to reach a decision.

(5) Whenever the Chairman has to decide on a proposal to disqualify an arbitrator, he shall use his best efforts to take that decision within 30 days after he has received the proposal.

(6) The proceeding shall be suspended until a decision has been taken on the proposal.

Rule 10
Procedure during a Vacancy on the Tribunal

(1) The Secretary-General shall forthwith notify the parties and, if necessary, the Chairman of the Administrative Council of the disqualification, death, incapacity or resignation of an arbitrator and of the consent, if any, of the Tribunal to a resignation.

(2) Upon the notification by the Secretary-General of a vacancy on the Tribunal, the proceeding shall be or remain suspended until the vacancy has been filled.

Rule 11
Filling Vacancies on the Tribunal

(1) Except as provided in paragraph (2), a vacancy resulting from the disqualification, death, incapacity or resignation of an arbitrator shall be promptly filled by the same method by which his appointment had been made.

(2) In addition to filling vacancies relating to arbitrators appointed by him, the Chairman of the Administrative Council shall appoint a person from the Panel of Arbitrators:

   (a) to fill a vacancy caused by the resignation, without the consent of the Tribunal, of an arbitrator appointed by a party; or

   (b) at the request of either party, to fill any other vacancy, if no new appointment is made and accepted within 45 days of the notification of the vacancy by the Secretary-General.

(3) The procedure for filling a vacancy shall be in accordance with Rules 1, 4(4), 4(5), 5 and, *mutatis mutandis*, 6(2).

Rule 12
Resumption of Proceeding after Filling a Vacancy

As soon as a vacancy on the Tribunal has been filled, the proceeding shall continue from the point it had reached at the time the vacancy occurred. The newly appointed arbitrator may, however, require that the oral procedure be recommenced, if this had already been started.

Chapter II
Working of the Tribunal

Rule 13
Sessions of the Tribunal

(1) The Tribunal shall hold its first session within 60 days after its constitution or such other period as the parties may agree. The dates of that session shall be fixed by the President of the Tribunal after consultation with its members and the Secretary-General. If upon its constitution the Tribunal has no President because the parties have agreed that the President shall be elected by its members, the Secretary-General shall fix the dates of that session. In both cases, the parties shall be consulted as far as possible.

(2) The dates of subsequent sessions shall be determined by the Tribunal, after consultation with the Secretary-General and with the parties as far as possible.

(3) The Tribunal shall meet at the seat of the Centre or at such other place as may have been agreed by the parties in accordance with Article 63 of the Convention. If the parties agree that the proceeding shall be held at a place other than the Centre or an institution with which the Centre has made the necessary arrangements, they shall consult with the Secretary-General and request the approval of the Tribunal. Failing such approval, the Tribunal shall meet at the seat of the Centre.

(4) The Secretary-General shall notify the members of the Tribunal and the parties of the dates and place of the sessions of the Tribunal in good time.

Rule 14
Sittings of the Tribunal

(1) The President of the Tribunal shall conduct its hearings and preside at its deliberations.

(2) Except as the parties otherwise agree, the presence of a majority of the members of the Tribunal shall be required at its sittings.

(3) The President of the Tribunal shall fix the date and hour of its sittings.

Rule 15
Deliberations of the Tribunal

(1) The deliberations of the Tribunal shall take place in private and remain secret.

(2) Only members of the Tribunal shall take part in its deliberations. No other person shall be admitted unless the Tribunal decides otherwise.

Rule 16
Decisions of the Tribunal

(1) Decisions of the Tribunal shall be taken by a majority of the votes of all its members. Abstention shall count as a negative vote.

(2) Except as otherwise provided by these Rules or decided by the Tribunal, it may take any decision by correspondence among its members, provided that all of them are consulted. Decisions so taken shall be certified by the President of the Tribunal.

Rule 17
Incapacity of the President

If at any time the President of the Tribunal should be unable to act, his functions shall be performed by one of the other members of the Tribunal, acting in the order in which the Secretary-General had received the notice of their acceptance of their appointment to the Tribunal.

Rule 18
Representation of the Parties

(1) Each party may be represented or assisted by agents, counsel or advocates whose names and authority shall be notified by that party to the Secretary-General, who shall promptly inform the Tribunal and the other party.

(2) For the purposes of these Rules, the expression "party" includes, where the context so admits, an agent, counsel or advocate authorized to represent that party.

Chapter III
General Procedural Provisions

Rule 19
Procedural Orders

The Tribunal shall make the orders required for the conduct of the proceeding.

Rule 20
Preliminary Procedural Consultation

(1) As early as possible after the constitution of a Tribunal, its President shall endeavor to ascertain the views of the parties regarding questions of procedure.

For this purpose he may request the parties to meet him. He shall, in particular, seek their views on the following matters:

(a) the number of members of the Tribunal required to constitute a quorum at its sittings;

(b) the language or languages to be used in the proceeding;

(c) the number and sequence of the pleadings and the time limits within which they are to be filed;

(d) the number of copies desired by each party of instruments filed by the other;

(e) dispensing with the written or the oral procedure;

(f) the manner in which the cost of the proceeding is to be apportioned; and

(g) the manner in which the record of the hearings shall be kept.

(2) In the conduct of the proceeding the Tribunal shall apply any agreement between the parties on procedural matters, except as otherwise provided in the Convention or the Administrative and Financial Regulations.

Rule 21
Pre-Hearing Conference

(1) At the request of the Secretary-General or at the discretion of the President of the Tribunal, a pre-hearing conference between the Tribunal and the parties may be held to arrange for an exchange of information and the stipulation of uncontested facts in order to expedite the proceeding.

(2) At the request of the parties, a pre-hearing conference between the Tribunal and the parties, duly represented by their authorized representatives, may be held to consider the issues in dispute with a view to reaching an amicable settlement.

Rule 22
Procedural Languages

(1) The parties may agree on the use of one or two languages to be used in the proceeding, provided, that, if they agree on any language that is not an official

language of the Centre, the Tribunal, after consultation with the Secretary-General, gives its approval. If the parties do not agree on any such procedural language, each of them may select one of the official languages (i.e., English, French and Spanish) for this purpose.

(2) If two procedural languages are selected by the parties, any instrument may be filed in either language. Either language may be used at the hearings, subject, if the Tribunal so requires, to translation and interpretation. The orders and the award of the Tribunal shall be rendered and the record kept in both procedural languages, both versions being equally authentic.

Rule 23
Copies of Instruments

Except as otherwise provided by the Tribunal after consultation with the parties and the Secretary-General, every request, pleading, application, written observation, supporting documentation, if any, or other instrument shall be filed in the form of a signed original accompanied by the following number of additional copies:

(a) before the number of members of the Tribunal has been determined: five;

(b) after the number of members of the Tribunal has been determined: two more than the number of its members.

Rule 24
Supporting Documentation

Supporting documentation shall ordinarily be filed together with the instrument to which it relates, and in any case within the time limit fixed for the filing of such instrument.

Rule 25
Correction of Errors

An accidental error in any instrument or supporting document may, with the consent of the other party or by leave of the Tribunal, be corrected at any time before the award is rendered.

Rule 26
Time Limits

(1) Where required, time limits shall be fixed by the Tribunal by assigning dates for the completion of the various steps in the proceeding. The Tribunal may delegate this power to its President.

(2) The Tribunal may extend any time limit that it has fixed. If the Tribunal is not in session, this power shall be exercised by its President.

(3) Any step taken after expiration of the applicable time limit shall be disregarded unless the Tribunal, in special circumstances and after giving the other party an opportunity of stating its views, decides otherwise.

Rule 27
Waiver

A party which knows or should have known that a provision of the Administrative and Financial Regulations, of these Rules, of any other rules or agreement applicable to the proceeding, or of an order of the Tribunal has not been complied with and which fails to state promptly its objections thereto, shall be deemed – subject to Article 45 of the Convention – to have waived its right to object.

Rule 28
Cost of Proceeding

(1) Without prejudice to the final decision on the payment of the cost of the proceeding, the Tribunal may, unless otherwise agreed by the parties, decide:

(a) at any stage of the proceeding, the portion which each party shall pay, pursuant to Administrative and Financial Regulation 14, of the fees and expenses of the Tribunal and the charges for the use of the facilities of the Centre;

(b) with respect to any part of the proceeding, that the related costs (as determined by the Secretary-General) shall be borne entirely or in a particular share by one of the parties.

(2) Promptly after the closure of the proceeding, each party shall submit to the Tribunal a statement of costs reasonably incurred or borne by it in the proceeding and the Secretary-General shall submit to the Tribunal an account of all amounts paid by each party to the Centre and of all costs incurred by the Centre for the proceeding. The Tribunal may, before the award has been rendered, request the parties and the Secretary-General to provide additional information concerning the cost of the proceeding.

Chapter IV
Written and Oral Procedures

Rule 29
Normal Procedures

Except if the parties otherwise agree, the proceeding shall comprise two distinct phases: a written procedure followed by an oral one.

Rule 30
Transmission of the Request

As soon as the Tribunal is constituted, the Secretary-General shall transmit to each member a copy of the request by which the proceeding was initiated, of the supporting documentation, of the notice of registration and of any communication received from either party in response thereto.

Rule 31
The Written Procedure

(1) In addition to the request for arbitration, the written procedure shall consist of the following pleadings, filed within time limits set by the Tribunal:

(a) a memorial by the requesting party;

(b) a counter-memorial by the other party; and, if the parties so agree or the Tribunal deems it necessary:

(c) a reply by the requesting party; and

(d) a rejoinder by the other party.

(2) If the request was made jointly, each party shall, within the same time limit determined by the Tribunal, file its memorial and, if the parties so agree or the Tribunal deems it necessary, its reply; however, the parties may instead agree that one of them shall, for the purposes of paragraph (1), be considered as the requesting party.

(3) A memorial shall contain: a statement of the relevant facts; a statement of law; and the submissions. A counter-memorial, reply or rejoinder shall contain an admission or denial of the facts stated in the last previous pleading; any additional facts, if necessary; observations concerning the statement of law in the last previous pleading; a statement of law in answer thereto; and the submissions.

Rule 32
The Oral Procedure

(1) The oral procedure shall consist of the hearing by the Tribunal of the parties, their agents, counsel and advocates, and of witnesses and experts.

(2) Unless either party objects, the Tribunal, after consultation with the Secretary-General, may allow other persons, besides the parties, their agents, counsel and advocates, witnesses and experts during their testimony, and officers of the Tribunal, to attend or observe all or part of the hearings, subject to appropriate

logistical arrangements. The Tribunal shall for such cases establish procedures for the protection of proprietary or privileged information.

(3) The members of the Tribunal may, during the hearings, put questions to the parties, their agents, counsel and advocates, and ask them for explanations.

Rule 33
Marshalling of Evidence

Without prejudice to the rules concerning the production of documents, each party shall, within time limits fixed by the Tribunal, communicate to the Secretary-General, for transmission to the Tribunal and the other party, precise information regarding the evidence which it intends to produce and that which it intends to request the Tribunal to call for, together with an indication of the points to which such evidence will be directed.

Rule 34
Evidence: General Principles

(1) The Tribunal shall be the judge of the admissibility of any evidence adduced and of its probative value.

(2) The Tribunal may, if it deems it necessary at any stage of the proceeding:

(a) call upon the parties to produce documents, witnesses and experts; and

(b) visit any place connected with the dispute or conduct inquiries there.

(3) The parties shall cooperate with the Tribunal in the production of the evidence and in the other measures provided for in paragraph (2). The Tribunal shall take formal note of the failure of a party to comply with its obligations under this paragraph and of any reasons given for such failure.

(4) Expenses incurred in producing evidence and in taking other measures in accordance with paragraph (2) shall be deemed to constitute part of the expenses incurred by the parties within the meaning of Article 61(2) of the Convention.

Rule 35
Examination of Witnesses and Experts

(1) Witnesses and experts shall be examined before the Tribunal by the parties under the control of its President. Questions may also be put to them by any member of the Tribunal.

(2) Each witness shall make the following declaration before giving his evidence:

"I solemnly declare upon my honour and conscience that I shall speak the truth, the whole truth and nothing but the truth."

(3) Each expert shall make the following declaration before making his statement:

"I solemnly declare upon my honour and conscience that my statement will be in accordance with my sincere belief."

Rule 36
Witnesses and Experts: Special Rules

Notwithstanding Rule 35 the Tribunal may:

(a) admit evidence given by a witness or expert in a written deposition; and

(b) with the consent of both parties, arrange for the examination of a witness or expert otherwise than before the Tribunal itself. The Tribunal shall define the subject of the examination, the time limit, the procedure to be followed and other particulars. The parties may participate in the examination.

Rule 37
Visits and Inquiries; Submissions of Non-disputing Parties

(1) If the Tribunal considers it necessary to visit any place connected with the dispute or to conduct an inquiry there, it shall make an order to this effect. The order shall define the scope of the visit or the subject of the inquiry, the time limit, the procedure to be followed and other particulars. The parties may participate in any visit or inquiry.

(2) After consulting both parties, the Tribunal may allow a person or entity that is not a party to the dispute (in this Rule called the "non-disputing party") to file a written submission with the Tribunal regarding a matter within the scope of the dispute. In determining whether to allow such a filing, the Tribunal shall consider, among other things, the extent to which:

(a) the non-disputing party submission would assist the Tribunal in the determination of a factual or legal issue related to the proceeding by bringing a perspective, particular knowledge or insight that is different from that of the disputing parties;

(b) the non-disputing party submission would address a matter within the scope of the dispute;

(c) the non-disputing party has a significant interest in the proceeding.

The Tribunal shall ensure that the non-disputing party submission does not disrupt the proceeding or unduly burden or unfairly prejudice either party, and that both parties are given an opportunity to present their observations on the non-disputing party submission.

Rule 38
Closure of the Proceeding

(1) When the presentation of the case by the parties is completed, the proceeding shall be declared closed.

(2) Exceptionally, the Tribunal may, before the award has been rendered, reopen the proceeding on the ground that new evidence is forthcoming of such a nature as to constitute a decisive factor, or that there is a vital need for clarification on certain specific points.

Chapter V
Particular Procedures

Rule 39
Provisional Measures

(1) At any time after the institution of the proceeding, a party may request that provisional measures for the preservation of its rights be recommended by the Tribunal. The request shall specify the rights to be preserved, the measures the recommendation of which is requested, and the circumstances that require such measures.

(2) The Tribunal shall give priority to the consideration of a request made pursuant to paragraph (1).

(3) The Tribunal may also recommend provisional measures on its own initiative or recommend measures other than those specified in a request. It may at any time modify or revoke its recommendations.

(4) The Tribunal shall only recommend provisional measures, or modify or revoke its recommendations, after giving each party an opportunity of presenting its observations.

(5) If a party makes a request pursuant to paragraph (1) before the constitution of the Tribunal, the Secretary-General shall, on the application of either party, fix time limits for the parties to present observations on the request, so that the request and observations may be considered by the Tribunal promptly upon its constitution.

(6) Nothing in this Rule shall prevent the parties, provided that they have so stipulated in the agreement recording their consent, from requesting any judicial or other authority to order provisional measures, prior to or after the institution of the proceeding, for the preservation of their respective rights and interests.

Rule 40
Ancillary Claims

(1) Except as the parties otherwise agree, a party may present an incidental or additional claim or counter-claim arising directly out of the subject-matter of the dispute, provided that such ancillary claim is within the scope of the consent of the parties and is otherwise within the jurisdiction of the Centre.

(2) An incidental or additional claim shall be presented not later than in the reply and a counter-claim no later than in the counter-memorial, unless the Tribunal, upon justification by the party presenting the ancillary claim and upon considering any objection of the other party, authorizes the presentation of the claim at a later stage in the proceeding.

(3) The Tribunal shall fix a time limit within which the party against which an ancillary claim is presented may file its observations thereon.

Rule 41
Preliminary Objections

(1) Any objection that the dispute or any ancillary claim is not within the jurisdiction of the Centre or, for other reasons, is not within the competence of the Tribunal shall be made as early as possible. A party shall file the objection with the Secretary-General no later than the expiration of the time limit fixed for the filing of the counter-memorial, or, if the objection relates to an ancillary claim, for the filing of the rejoinder – unless the facts on which the objection is based are unknown to the party at that time.

(2) The Tribunal may on its own initiative consider, at any stage of the proceeding, whether the dispute or any ancillary claim before it is within the jurisdiction of the Centre and within its own competence.

(3) Upon the formal raising of an objection relating to the dispute, the Tribunal may decide to suspend the proceeding on the merits. The President of the Tribunal, after consultation with its other members, shall fix a time limit within which the parties may file observations on the objection.

(4) The Tribunal shall decide whether or not the further procedures relating to the objection made pursuant to paragraph (1) shall be oral. It may deal with the objection as a preliminary question or join it to the merits of the dispute. If the Tribunal overrules the objection or joins it to the merits, it shall once more fix time limits for the further procedures.

(5) Unless the parties have agreed to another expedited procedure for making preliminary objections, a party may, no later than 30 days after the constitution of the Tribunal, and in any event before the first session of the Tribunal, file an objection that a claim is manifestly without legal merit. The party shall specify as precisely as possible the basis for the objection. The Tribunal, after giving the parties the opportunity to present their observations on the objection, shall, at its first session or promptly thereafter, notify the parties of its decision on the objection. The decision of the Tribunal shall be without prejudice to the right of a party to file an objection pursuant to paragraph (1) or to object, in the course of the proceeding, that a claim lacks legal merit.

(6) If the Tribunal decides that the dispute is not within the jurisdiction of the Centre or not within its own competence, or that all claims are manifestly without legal merit, it shall render an award to that effect.

Rule 42
Default

(1) If a party (in this Rule called the "defaulting party") fails to appear or to present its case at any stage of the proceeding, the other party may, at any time prior to the discontinuance of the proceeding, request the Tribunal to deal with the questions submitted to it and to render an award.

(2) The Tribunal shall promptly notify the defaulting party of such a request. Unless it is satisfied that that party does not intend to appear or to present its case in the proceeding, it shall, at the same time, grant a period of grace and to this end:

   (a) if that party had failed to file a pleading or any other instrument within the time limit fixed therefor, fix a new time limit for its filing; or

(b) if that party had failed to appear or present its case at a hearing, fix a new date for the hearing.

The period of grace shall not, without the consent of the other party, exceed 60 days.

(3) After the expiration of the period of grace or when, in accordance with paragraph (2), no such period is granted, the Tribunal shall resume the consideration of the dispute. Failure of the defaulting party to appear or to present its case shall not be deemed an admission of the assertions made by the other party.

(4) The Tribunal shall examine the jurisdiction of the Centre and its own competence in the dispute and, if it is satisfied, decide whether the submissions made are well-founded in fact and in law. To this end, it may, at any stage of the proceeding, call on the party appearing to file observations, produce evidence or submit oral explanations.

Rule 43
Settlement and Discontinuance

(1) If, before the award is rendered, the parties agree on a settlement of the dispute or otherwise to discontinue the proceeding, the Tribunal, or the Secretary-General if the Tribunal has not yet been constituted, shall, at their written request, in an order take note of the discontinuance of the proceeding.

(2) If the parties file with the Secretary-General the full and signed text of their settlement and in writing request the Tribunal to embody such settlement in an award, the Tribunal may record the settlement in the form of its award.

Rule 44
Discontinuance at Request of a Party

If a party requests the discontinuance of the proceeding, the Tribunal, or the Secretary-General if the Tribunal has not yet been constituted, shall in an order fix a time limit within which the other party may state whether it opposes the discontinuance. If no objection is made in writing within the time limit, the other party shall be deemed to have acquiesced in the discontinuance and the Tribunal, or if appropriate the Secretary-General, shall in an order take note of the discontinuance of the proceeding. If objection is made, the proceeding shall continue.

Rule 45
Discontinuance for Failure of Parties to Act

If the parties fail to take any steps in the proceeding during six consecutive months or such period as they may agree with the approval of the Tribunal, or of the Secretary-General if the Tribunal has not yet been constituted, they shall be deemed to have discontinued the proceeding and the Tribunal, or if appropriate the Secretary-General, shall, after notice to the parties, in an order take note of the discontinuance.

Chapter VI
The Award

Rule 46
Preparation of the Award

The award (including any individual or dissenting opinion) shall be drawn up and signed within 120 days after closure of the proceeding. The Tribunal may, however, extend this period by a further 60 days if it would otherwise be unable to draw up the award.

Rule 47
The Award

(1) The award shall be in writing and shall contain:

  (a) a precise designation of each party;

  (b) a statement that the Tribunal was established under the Convention, and a description of the method of its constitution;

(c) the name of each member of the Tribunal, and an identification of the appointing authority of each;

(d) the names of the agents, counsel and advocates of the parties;

(e) the dates and place of the sittings of the Tribunal;

(f) a summary of the proceeding;

(g) a statement of the facts as found by the Tribunal;

(h) the submissions of the parties;

(i) the decision of the Tribunal on every question submitted to it, together with the reasons upon which the decision is based; and

(j) any decision of the Tribunal regarding the cost of the proceeding.

(2) The award shall be signed by the members of the Tribunal who voted for it; the date of each signature shall be indicated.

(3) Any member of the Tribunal may attach his individual opinion to the award, whether he dissents from the majority or not, or a statement of his dissent.

Rule 48
Rendering of the Award

(1) Upon signature by the last arbitrator to sign, the Secretary-General shall promptly:

(a) authenticate the original text of the award and deposit it in the archives of the Centre, together with any individual opinions and statements of dissent; and

(b) dispatch a certified copy of the award (including individual opinions and statements of dissent) to each party, indicating the date of dispatch on the original text and on all copies.

(2) The award shall be deemed to have been rendered on the date on which the certified copies were dispatched.

(3) The Secretary-General shall, upon request, make available to a party additional certified copies of the award.

(4) The Centre shall not publish the award without the consent of the parties. The Centre shall, however, promptly include in its publications excerpts of the legal reasoning of the Tribunal.

Rule 49
Supplementary Decisions and Rectification

(1) Within 45 days after the date on which the award was rendered, either party may request, pursuant to Article 49(2) of the Convention, a supplementary decision on, or the rectification of, the award. Such a request shall be addressed in writing to the Secretary-General. The request shall:

(a)   identify the award to which it relates;

(b)   indicate the date of the request;

(c)   state in detail:

  (i)   any question which, in the opinion of the requesting party, the Tribunal omitted to decide in the award; and

  (ii)   any error in the award which the requesting party seeks to have rectified; and

(d)   be accompanied by a fee for lodging the request.

(2) Upon receipt of the request and of the lodging fee, the Secretary-General shall forthwith:

(a)   register the request;

(b)   notify the parties of the registration;

(c)   transmit to the other party a copy of the request and of any accompanying documentation; and

(d) transmit to each member of the Tribunal a copy of the notice of registration, together with a copy of the request and of any accompanying documentation.

(3) The President of the Tribunal shall consult the members on whether it is necessary for the Tribunal to meet in order to consider the request. The Tribunal shall fix a time limit for the parties to file their observations on the request and shall determine the procedure for its consideration.

(4) Rules 46-48 shall apply, *mutatis mutandis*, to any decision of the Tribunal pursuant to this Rule.

(5) If a request is received by the Secretary-General more than 45 days after the award was rendered, he shall refuse to register the request and so inform forthwith the requesting party.

Chapter VII
Interpretation, Revision and Annulment of the Award

Rule 50
The Application

(1) An application for the interpretation, revision or annulment of an award shall be addressed in writing to the Secretary-General and shall:

(a) identify the award to which it relates;

(b) indicate the date of the application;

(c) state in detail:

(i) in an application for interpretation, the precise points in dispute;

(ii) in an application for revision, pursuant to Article 51(1) of the Convention, the change sought in the award, the discovery of some fact of such a nature as decisively to affect the award, and evidence that when the award was rendered that fact was unknown to the Tribunal and to the applicant, and that the applicant's ignorance of that fact was not due to negligence;

(iii) in an application for annulment, pursuant to Article 52(1) of the Convention, the grounds on which it is based. These grounds are limited to the following:

- that the Tribunal was not properly constituted;

- that the Tribunal has manifestly exceeded its powers;

- that there was corruption on the part of a member of the Tribunal;

- that there has been a serious departure from a fundamental rule of procedure;

- that the award has failed to state the reasons on which it is based;

(d) be accompanied by the payment of a fee for lodging the application.

(2) Without prejudice to the provisions of paragraph (3), upon receiving an application and the lodging fee, the Secretary-General shall forthwith:

(a) register the application;

(b) notify the parties of the registration; and

(c) transmit to the other party a copy of the application and of any accompanying documentation.

(3) The Secretary-General shall refuse to register an application for:

(a) revision, if, in accordance with Article 51(2) of the Convention, it is not made within 90 days after the discovery of the new fact and in any event within three years after the date on which the award was rendered (or any subsequent decision or correction);

(b) annulment, if, in accordance with Article 52(2) of the Convention, it is not made:

(i) within 120 days after the date on which the award was rendered (or any subsequent decision or correction) if the application is based on any of the following grounds:

- the Tribunal was not properly constituted;

> – the Tribunal has manifestly exceeded its powers;
>
> – there has been a serious departure from a fundamental rule of procedure;
>
> – the award has failed to state the reasons on which it is based;

(ii) in the case of corruption on the part of a member of the Tribunal, within 120 days after discovery thereof, and in any event within three years after the date on which the award was rendered (or any subsequent decision or correction).

(4) If the Secretary-General refuses to register an application for revision, or annulment, he shall forthwith notify the requesting party of his refusal.

Rule 51
Interpretation or Revision: Further Procedures

(1) Upon registration of an application for the interpretation or revision of an award, the Secretary-General shall forthwith:

(a) transmit to each member of the original Tribunal a copy of the notice of registration, together with a copy of the application and of any accompanying documentation; and

(b) request each member of the Tribunal to inform him within a specified time limit whether that member is willing to take part in the consideration of the application.

(2) If all members of the Tribunal express their willingness to take part in the consideration of the application, the Secretary-General shall so notify the members of the Tribunal and the parties. Upon dispatch of these notices the Tribunal shall be deemed to be reconstituted.

(3) If the Tribunal cannot be reconstituted in accordance with paragraph (2), the Secretary-General shall so notify the parties and invite them to proceed, as soon as possible, to constitute a new Tribunal, including the same number of arbitrators, and appointed by the same method, as the original one.

Rule 52
Annulment: Further Procedures

(1) Upon registration of an application for the annulment of an award, the Secretary-General shall forthwith request the Chairman of the Administrative Council to appoint an *ad hoc* Committee in accordance with Article 52(3) of the Convention.

(2) The Committee shall be deemed to be constituted on the date the Secretary-General notifies the parties that all members have accepted their appointment. Before or at the first session of the Committee, each member shall sign a declaration conforming to that set forth in Rule 6(2).

Rule 53
Rules of Procedure

The provisions of these Rules shall apply *mutatis mutandis* to any procedure relating to the interpretation, revision or annulment of an award and to the decision of the Tribunal or Committee.

Rule 54
Stay of Enforcement of the Award

(1) The party applying for the interpretation, revision or annulment of an award may in its application, and either party may at any time before the final disposition of the application, request a stay in the enforcement of part or all of the award to which the application relates. The Tribunal or Committee shall give priority to the consideration of such a request.

(2) If an application for the revision or annulment of an award contains a request for a stay of its enforcement, the Secretary-General shall, together with the notice of registration, inform both parties of the provisional stay of the award. As soon as the Tribunal or Committee is constituted it shall, if either party requests, rule within 30 days on whether such stay should be continued; unless it decides to continue the stay, it shall automatically be terminated.

(3) If a stay of enforcement has been granted pursuant to paragraph (1) or continued pursuant to paragraph (2), the Tribunal or Committee may at any time modify or terminate the stay at the request of either party. All stays shall automatically terminate on the date on which a final decision is rendered on the application, except that a Committee granting the partial annulment of an award may order the temporary stay of enforcement of the unannulled portion in order to give either party an opportunity to request any new Tribunal constituted pursuant to Article 52(6) of the Convention to grant a stay pursuant to Rule 55(3).

(4) A request pursuant to paragraph (1), (2) (second sentence) or (3) shall specify the circumstances that require the stay or its modification or termination. A request shall only be granted after the Tribunal or Committee has given each party an opportunity of presenting its observations.

(5) The Secretary-General shall promptly notify both parties of the stay of enforcement of any award and of the modification or termination of such a stay, which shall become effective on the date on which he dispatches such notification.

Rule 55
Resubmission of Dispute after an Annulment

(1) If a Committee annuls part or all of an award, either party may request the resubmission of the dispute to a new Tribunal. Such a request shall be addressed in writing to the Secretary-General and shall:

(a) identify the award to which it relates;

(b) indicate the date of the request;

(c) explain in detail what aspect of the dispute is to be submitted to the Tribunal; and

(d) be accompanied by a fee for lodging the request.

(2) Upon receipt of the request and of the lodging fee, the Secretary-General shall forthwith:

(a) register it in the Arbitration Register;

(b) notify both parties of the registration;

(c) transmit to the other party a copy of the request and of any accompanying documentation; and

(d) invite the parties to proceed, as soon as possible, to constitute a new Tribunal, including the same number of arbitrators, and appointed by the same method, as the original one.

(3) If the original award had only been annulled in part, the new Tribunal shall not reconsider any portion of the award not so annulled. It may, however, in accordance with the procedures set forth in Rule 54, stay or continue to stay the enforcement of the unannulled portion of the award until the date its own award is rendered.

(4) Except as otherwise provided in paragraphs (1)–(3), these Rules shall apply to a proceeding on a resubmitted dispute in the same manner as if such dispute had been submitted pursuant to the Institution Rules

Chapter VIII
General Provisions

Rule 56
Final Provisions

(1) The texts of these Rules in each official language of the Centre shall be equally authentic.

(2) These Rules may be cited as the "Arbitration Rules" of the Centre.

Annex 4

Rules Governing the Additional Facility for the Administration of Proceedings by the Secretariat of the International Centre for Settlement of Investment Disputes
(effective 10 April 2006)

Additional Facility Rules

Article 1
Definitions

(1) "Convention" means the Convention on the Settlement of Investment Disputes between States and Nationals of Other States, submitted to Governments by the Executive Directors of the International Bank for Reconstruction and Development on March 18, 1965, which entered into force on October 14, 1966.

(2) "Centre" means the International Centre for Settlement of Investment Disputes established pursuant to Article 1 of the Convention.

(3) "Secretariat" means the Secretariat of the Centre.

(4) "Contracting State" means a State for which the Convention has entered into force.

(5) "Secretary-General" means the Secretary-General of the Centre or his deputy.

(6) "National of another State" means a person who is not, or whom the parties to the proceeding in question have agreed not to treat as, a national of the State party to that proceeding.

Article 2
Additional Facility Rules

The Secretariat of the Centre is hereby authorized to administer, subject to and in accordance with these Rules, proceedings between a State (or a constituent subdivision or agency of a State) and a national of another State, falling within the following categories:

(a) conciliation and arbitration proceedings for the settlement of legal disputes arising directly out of an investment which are not within the jurisdiction of the Centre because either the State party to the dispute or the State whose national is a party to the dispute is not a Contracting State;

(b) conciliation and arbitration proceedings for the settlement of legal disputes which are not within the jurisdiction of the Centre because they do not arise directly out of an investment, provided that either the State party to the dispute or the State whose national is a party to the dispute is a Contracting State; and

(c) fact-finding proceedings.

The administration of proceedings authorized by these Rules is hereinafter referred to as the Additional Facility.

Article 3
Convention Not Applicable

Since the proceedings envisaged by Article 2 are outside the jurisdiction of the Centre, none of the provisions of the Convention shall be applicable to them or to recommendations, awards, or reports which may be rendered therein.

Article 4
Access to the Additional Facility in Respect of Conciliation and Arbitration
Proceedings Subject to Secretary-General's Approval

(1) Any agreement providing for conciliation or arbitration proceedings under the Additional Facility in respect of existing or future disputes requires the approval of the Secretary-General. The parties may apply for such approval at any time prior to the institution of proceedings by submitting to the Secretariat a copy of the agreement concluded or proposed to be concluded between them together with other relevant documentation and such additional information as the Secretariat may reasonably request.

(2) In the case of an application based on Article 2(a), the Secretary-General shall give his approval only if (a) he is satisfied that the requirements of that provision are fulfilled at the time, and (b) both parties give their consent to the jurisdiction of the Centre under Article 25 of the Convention (in lieu of the Additional Facility) in the event that the jurisdictional requirements *ratione personae* of that Article shall have been met at the time when proceedings are instituted.

(3) In the case of an application based on Article 2(b), the Secretary-General shall give his approval only if he is satisfied (a) that the requirements of that provision are fulfilled, and (b) that the underlying transaction has features which distinguish it from an ordinary commercial transaction.

(4) If in the case of an application based on Article 2(b) the jurisdictional requirements *ratione personae* of Article 25 of the Convention shall have been met and the Secretary-General is of the opinion that it is likely that a Conciliation Commission or Arbitral Tribunal, as the case may be, will hold that the dispute arises directly out of an investment, he may make his approval of the application conditional upon consent by both parties to submit any dispute in the first instance to the jurisdiction of the Centre.

(5) The Secretary-General shall as soon as possible notify the parties whether he approves or disapproves the agreement of the parties. He may hold discussions with the parties or invite the parties to a meeting with the officials of the

Secretariat either at the parties' request or at his own initiative. The Secretary-General shall, upon the request of the parties or any of them, keep confidential any or all information furnished to him by such parties or party in connection with the provisions of this Article.

(6) The Secretary-General shall record his approval of an agreement pursuant to this Article together with the names and addresses of the parties in a register to be maintained at the Secretariat for that purpose.

Article 5
Administrative and Financial Provisions

The responsibilities of the Secretariat in operating the Additional Facility and the financial provisions regarding its operation shall be as those established by the Administrative and Financial Regulations of the Centre for conciliation and arbitration proceedings under the Convention. Accordingly, Regulations 14 through 16, 22 through 30 and 34(1) of the Administrative and Financial Regulations of the Centre shall apply, *mutatis mutandis*, in respect of fact-finding, conciliation and arbitration proceedings under the Additional Facility.

Article 6
Schedules

Fact-finding, conciliation and arbitration proceedings under the Additional Facility shall be conducted in accordance with the respective Fact-finding (Additional Facility), Conciliation (Additional Facility) and Arbitration (Additional Facility) Rules set forth in Schedules A, B and C.

Schedule C. Arbitration (Additional Facility) Rules

Chapter I
Introduction

Article 1
Scope of Application

Where the parties to a dispute have agreed that it shall be referred to arbitration under the Arbitration (Additional Facility) Rules, the dispute shall be settled in accordance with these Rules, save that if any of these Rules is in conflict with a provision of the law applicable to the arbitration from which the parties cannot derogate, that provision shall prevail.

Chapter II
Institution of Proceedings

Article 2
The Request

(1) Any State or any national of a State wishing to institute arbitration proceedings shall send a request to that effect in writing to the Secretariat at the seat of the Centre. It shall be drawn up in an official language of the Centre, shall be dated and shall be signed by the requesting party or its duly authorized representative.

(2) The request may be made jointly by the parties to the dispute.

Article 3
Contents of the Request

(1) The request shall:
   (a) designate precisely each party to the dispute and state the address of each;
   (b) set forth the relevant provisions embodying the agreement of the parties to refer the dispute to arbitration;

(c) indicate the date of approval by the Secretary-General pursuant to Article 4 of the Additional Facility Rules of the agreement of the parties providing for access to the Additional Facility;

(d) contain information concerning the issues in dispute and an indication of the amount involved, if any; and

(e) state, if the requesting party is a juridical person, that it has taken all necessary internal actions to authorize the request.

(2) The request may in addition set forth any provisions agreed by the parties regarding the number of arbitrators and the method of their appointment, as well as any other provisions agreed concerning the settlement of the dispute.

(3) The request shall be accompanied by five additional signed copies and by the fee prescribed pursuant to Regulation 16 of the Administrative and Financial Regulation of the Centre.

Article 4
Registration of the Request

As soon as the Secretary-General shall have satisfied himself that the request conforms in form and substance to the provisions of Article 3 of these Rules, he shall register the request in the Arbitration (Additional Facility) Register and on the same day dispatch to the parties a notice of registration. He shall also transmit a copy of the request and of the accompanying documentation (if any) to the other party to the dispute.

Article 5
Notice of Registration

The notice of registration of a request shall:

(a) record that the request is registered and indicate the date of the registration and of the dispatch of the notice;

(b) notify each party that all communications in connection with the proceeding will be sent to the address stated in the request, unless another address is indicated to the Secretariat;

(c) unless such information has already been provided, invite the parties to communicate to the Secretary-General any provisions agreed by them regarding the number and the method of appointment of the arbitrators;

(d) remind the parties that the registration of the request is without prejudice to the powers and functions of the Arbitral Tribunal in regard to competence and the merits; and

(e) invite the parties to proceed, as soon as possible, to constitute an Arbitral Tribunal in accordance with Chapter III of these Rules.

Chapter III
The Tribunal

Article 6
General Provisions

(1) In the absence of agreement between the parties regarding the number of arbitrators and the method of their appointment, the Tribunal shall consist of three arbitrators, one arbitrator appointed by each party and the third, who shall be the President of the Tribunal, appointed by agreement of the parties, all in accordance with Article 9 of these Rules.

(2) Upon the dispatch of the notice of registration of the request for arbitration, the parties shall promptly proceed to constitute a Tribunal.

(3) The Tribunal shall consist of a sole arbitrator or any uneven number of arbitrators appointed as the parties shall agree.

(4) If the Tribunal shall not have been constituted within 90 days after the notice of registration of the request for arbitration has been dispatched by the Secretary-General, or such other period as the parties may agree, the Chairman of the Administrative Council (hereinafter called the "Chairman") shall, at the

request in writing of either party transmitted through the Secretary-General, appoint the arbitrator or arbitrators not yet appointed and, unless the President shall already have been designated or is to be designated later, designate an arbitrator to be President of the Tribunal.

(5) Except as the parties shall otherwise agree, no person who had previously acted as a conciliator or arbitrator in any proceeding for the settlement of the dispute or as a member of any fact-finding committee relating thereto may be appointed as a member of the Tribunal.

Article 7
Nationality of Arbitrators

(1) The majority of the arbitrators shall be nationals of States other than the State party to the dispute and of the State whose national is a party to the dispute, unless the sole arbitrator or each individual member of the Tribunal is appointed by agreement of the parties. Where the Tribunal is to consist of three members, a national of either of these States may not be appointed as an arbitrator by a party without the agreement of the other party to the dispute. Where the Tribunal is to consist of five or more members, nationals of either of these States may not be appointed as arbitrators by a party if appointment by the other party of the same number of arbitrators of either of these nationalities would result in a majority of arbitrators of these nationalities.

(2) Arbitrators appointed by the Chairman shall not be nationals of the State party to the dispute or of the State whose national is a party to the dispute.

Article 8
Qualifications of Arbitrators

Arbitrators shall be persons of high moral character and recognized competence in the fields of law, commerce, industry or finance, who may be relied upon to exercise independent judgment.

Article 9

Method of Constituting the Tribunal in the Absence of Agreement Between the Parties

(1) If the parties have not agreed upon the number of arbitrators and the method of their appointment within 60 days after the registration of the request, the Secretary-General shall, upon the request of either party promptly inform the parties that the Tribunal is to be constituted in accordance with the following procedure:

    (a) either party shall, in a communication to the other party:

        (i) name two persons, identifying one of them, who shall not have the same nationality as nor be a national of either party, as the arbitrator appointed by it, and the other as the arbitrator proposed to be the President of the Tribunal; and

        (ii) invite the other party to concur in the appointment of the arbitrator proposed to be the President of the Tribunal and to appoint another arbitrator;

    (b) promptly upon receipt of this communication the other party shall, in its reply:

        (i) name a person as the arbitrator appointed by it, who shall not have the same nationality as nor be a national of either party; and

        (ii) concur in the appointment of the arbitrator proposed to be the President of the Tribunal or name another person as the arbitrator proposed to be President; and

    (c) promptly upon receipt of the reply containing such a proposal, the initiating party shall notify the other party whether it concurs in the appointment of the arbitrator proposed by that party to be the President of the Tribunal.

(2) The communications provided for in paragraph (1) of this Article shall be made or promptly confirmed in writing and shall either be transmitted

through the Secretary-General or directly between the parties with a copy to the Secretary-General.

Article 10
Appointment of Arbitrators and Designation of President of Tribunal by the Chairman of the Administrative Council

(1) Promptly upon receipt of a request by a party to the Chairman to make an appointment or designation pursuant to Article 6(4) of these Rules, the Secretary-General shall send a copy thereof to the other party.

(2) The Chairman shall use his best efforts to comply with that request within 30 days after its receipt. Before he proceeds to make appointments or a designation, he shall consult both parties as far as possible.

(3) The Secretary-General shall promptly notify the parties of any appointment or designation made by the Chairman.

Article 11
Acceptance of Appointments

(1) The party or parties concerned shall notify the Secretary-General of the appointment of each arbitrator and indicate the method of his appointment.

(2) As soon as the Secretary-General has been informed by a party or the Chairman of the appointment of an arbitrator, he shall seek an acceptance from the appointee.

(3) If an arbitrator fails to accept his appointment within 15 days, the Secretary-General shall promptly notify the parties, and if appropriate the Chairman, and invite them to proceed to the appointment of another arbitrator in accordance with the method followed for the previous appointment.

Article 12
Replacement of Arbitrators prior to Constitution of the Tribunal

At any time before the Tribunal is constituted, each party may replace any arbitrator appointed by it and the parties may by common consent agree to replace any arbitrator.

Article 13
Constitution of the Tribunal

(1) The Tribunal shall be deemed to be constituted and the proceeding to have begun on the date the Secretary-General notifies the parties that all the arbitrators have accepted their appointment.

(2) Before or at the first session of the Tribunal, each arbitrator shall sign a declaration in the following form:

"To the best of my knowledge there is no reason why I should not serve on the Arbitral Tribunal constituted with respect to a dispute between _____ and _____ .

I shall keep confidential all information coming to my knowledge as a result of my participation in this proceeding, as well as the contents of any award made by the Tribunal.

I shall judge fairly as between the parties and shall not accept any instruction or compensation with regard to the proceeding from any source except as provided in the Administrative and Financial Regulations of the Centre.

Attached is a statement of (a) my past and present professional, business and other relationships (if any) with the parties and (b) any other circumstance that might cause my reliability for independent judgment to be questioned by a party. I acknowledge that by signing this declaration, I assume a continuing obligation promptly to notify the Secretary-General of the Centre of any such relationship or circumstance that subsequently arises during this proceeding."

Any arbitrator failing to sign such a declaration by the end of the first session of the Tribunal shall be deemed to have resigned.

Article 14
Replacement of Arbitrators after Constitution of the Tribunal

(1) After a Tribunal has been constituted and proceedings have begun, its composition shall remain unchanged; provided, however, that if an arbitrator should die, become incapacitated, resign or be disqualified, the resulting vacancy shall be filled as provided in this Article and Article 17 of these Rules.

(2) If an arbitrator becomes incapacitated or unable to perform the duties of his office, the procedure in respect of the disqualification of arbitrators set forth in Article 15 shall apply.

(3) An arbitrator may resign by submitting his resignation to the other members of the Tribunal and the Secretary-General. If the arbitrator was appointed by one of the parties, the Tribunal shall promptly consider the reasons for his resignation and decide whether it consents thereto. The Tribunal shall promptly notify the Secretary-General of its decision.

Article 15
Disqualification of Arbitrators

(1) A party may propose to a Tribunal the disqualification of any of its members on account of any fact indicating a manifest lack of the qualities required by Article 8 of these Rules, or on the ground that he was ineligible for appointment to the Tribunal under Article 7 of these Rules.

(2) A party proposing the disqualification of an arbitrator shall promptly, and in any event before the proceeding is declared closed, file its proposal with the Secretary-General, stating its reasons therefor.

(3) The Secretary-General shall forthwith:

(a) transmit the proposal to the members of the Tribunal and, if it relates to a sole arbitrator or to a majority of the members of the Tribunal, to the Chairman; and

(b) notify the other party of the proposal.

(4) The arbitrator to whom the proposal relates may, without delay, furnish explanations to the Tribunal or the Chairman, as the case may be.

(5) The decision on any proposal to disqualify an arbitrator shall be taken by the other members of the Tribunal except that where those members are equally divided, or in the case of a proposal to disqualify a sole arbitrator, or a majority of the arbitrators, the Chairman shall take that decision.

(6) Whenever the Chairman has to decide on a proposal to disqualify an arbitrator, he shall use his best efforts to take that decision within 30 days after he has received the proposal.

(7) The proceeding shall be suspended until a decision has been taken on the proposal.

Article 16
Procedure during a Vacancy on the Tribunal

(1) The Secretary-General shall forthwith notify the parties and, if necessary, the Chairman of the disqualification, death, incapacity or resignation of an arbitrator and of the consent, if any, of the Tribunal to a resignation.

(2) Upon the notification by the Secretary-General of a vacancy on the Tribunal, the proceeding shall be or remain suspended until the vacancy has been filled.

Article 17
Filling Vacancies on the Tribunal

(1) Except as provided in paragraph (2) of this Article, a vacancy resulting from the disqualification, death, incapacity or resignation of an arbitrator shall be promptly filled by the same method by which his appointment had been made.

(2) In addition to filling vacancies relating to arbitrators appointed by him, the Chairman shall:

(a) fill a vacancy caused by the resignation, without the consent of the Tribunal, of an arbitrator appointed by a party; or

(b) at the request of either party, fill any other vacancy, if no new appointment is made and accepted within 45 days of the notification of the vacancy by the Secretary-General.

(3) In filling a vacancy the party or the Chairman, as the case may be, shall observe the provisions of these Rules with respect to the appointment of arbitrators. Article 13(2) of these Rules shall apply *mutatis mutandis* to the newly appointed arbitrator.

Article 18
Resumption of Proceeding after Filling a Vacancy

As soon as a vacancy on the Tribunal has been filled, the proceeding shall continue from the point it had reached at the time the vacancy occurred. The newly appointed arbitrator may, however, require that the oral procedure be recommenced, if this had already been started

Chapter IV
Place of Arbitration

Article 19
Limitation on Choice of Forum

Arbitration proceedings shall be held only in States that are parties to the 1958 UN Convention on the Recognition and Enforcement of Foreign Arbitral Awards.

Article 20
Determination of Place of Arbitration

(1) Subject to Article 19 of these Rules the place of arbitration shall be determined by the Arbitral Tribunal after consultation with the parties and the Secretariat.

(2) The Arbitral Tribunal may meet at any place it deems appropriate for the inspection of goods, other property or documents. It may also visit any place connected with the dispute or conduct inquiries there. The parties shall be given sufficient notice to enable them to be present at such inspection or visit.

(3) The award shall be made at the place of arbitration.

Chapter V
Working of the Tribunal

Article 21
Sessions of the Tribunal

(1) The Tribunal shall meet for its first session within 60 days after its constitution or such other period as the parties may agree. The dates of that session shall be fixed by the President of the Tribunal after consultation with its members and the Secretariat, and with the parties as far as possible. If, upon its constitution, the Tribunal has no President, such dates shall be fixed by the Secretary-General after consultation with the members of the Tribunal, and with the parties as far as possible.

(2) Subsequent sessions shall be convened by the President within time limits determined by the Tribunal. The dates of such sessions shall be fixed by the President of the Tribunal after consultation with its members and the Secretariat, and with the parties as far as possible.

(3) The Secretary-General shall notify the members of the Tribunal and the parties of the dates and place of the sessions of the Tribunal in good time.

Article 22
Sittings of the Tribunal

(1) The President of the Tribunal shall conduct its hearings and preside at its deliberations.

(2) Except as the parties otherwise agree, the presence of a majority of the members of the Tribunal shall be required at its sittings.

(3) The President of the Tribunal shall fix the date and hour of its sittings.

Article 23
Deliberations of the Tribunal

(1) The deliberations of the Tribunal shall take place in private and remain secret.

(2) Only members of the Tribunal shall take part in its deliberations. No other person shall be admitted unless the Tribunal decides otherwise.

Article 24
Decisions of the Tribunal

(1) Any award or other decision of the Tribunal shall be made by a majority of the votes of all its members. Abstention by any member of the Tribunal shall count as a negative vote.

(2) Except as otherwise provided by these Rules or decided by the Tribunal, it may take any decisions by correspondence among its members, provided that all of them are consulted. Decisions so taken shall be certified by the President of the Tribunal.

Article 25
Incapacity of the President

If at any time the President of the Tribunal should be unable to act, his functions shall be performed by one of the other members of the Tribunal, acting in the order in which the Secretariat had received the notice of their acceptance of their appointment to the Tribunal.

Article 26
Representation of the Parties

(1) Each party may be represented or assisted by agents, counsel or advocates whose names and authority shall be notified by that party to the Secretariat, which shall promptly inform the Tribunal and the other party.

(2) For the purposes of these Rules, the expression "party" includes, where the context so admits, an agent, counsel or advocate authorized to represent that party.

Chapter VI
General Procedural Provisions

Article 27
Procedural Orders

The Tribunal shall make the orders required for the conduct of the proceeding.

Article 28
Preliminary Procedural Consultation

(1) As early as possible after the constitution of a Tribunal, its President shall endeavor to ascertain the views of the parties regarding questions of procedure. For this purpose he may request the parties to meet him. He shall, in particular, seek their views on the following matters:

(a) the number of members of the Tribunal required to constitute a quorum at its sittings;

(b) the language or languages to be used in the proceeding;

(c) the number and sequence of the pleadings and the time limits within which they are to be filed;

(d) the number of copies desired by each party of instruments filed by the other;

(e) dispensing with the written or oral procedure;

(f) the manner in which the cost of the proceeding is to be apportioned; and

(g) the manner in which the record of the hearings shall be kept.

(2) In the conduct of the proceeding the Tribunal shall apply any agreement between the parties on procedural matters, which is not inconsistent with any

provisions of the Additional Facility Rules and the Administrative and Financial Regulations of the Centre.

Article 29
Pre-Hearing Conference

(1) At the request of the Secretary-General or at the discretion of the President of the Tribunal, a pre-hearing conference between the Tribunal and the parties may be held to arrange for an exchange of information and the stipulation of uncontested facts in order to expedite the proceeding.

(2) At the request of the parties, a pre-hearing conference between the Tribunal and the parties, duly represented by their authorized representatives, may be held to consider the issues in dispute with a view to reaching an amicable settlement.

Article 30
Procedural Languages

(1) The parties may agree on the use of one or two languages to be used in the proceeding, provided that if they agree on any language that is not an official language of the Centre, the Tribunal, after consultation with the Secretary-General, gives its approval. If the parties do not agree on any such procedural language, each of them may select one of the official languages (i.e., English, French and Spanish) for this purpose. Notwithstanding the foregoing, one of the official languages of the Centre shall be used for all communications to and from the Secretariat.

(2) If two procedural languages are selected by the parties, any instrument may be filed in either language. Either language may be used at the hearing subject, if the Tribunal so requires, to translation and interpretation. The orders and the award of the Tribunal shall be rendered and the record kept in both procedural languages, both versions being equally authentic.

Article 31
Copies of Instruments

Except as otherwise provided by the Tribunal after consultation with the parties and the Secretariat, every request, pleading, application, written observation or other instrument shall be filed in the form of a signed original accompanied by the following number of additional copies:

(a) before the number of members of the Tribunal has been determined: five; and

(b) after the number of members of the Tribunal has been determined: two more than the number of its members.

Article 32
Supporting Documentation

Supporting documentation shall ordinarily be filed together with the instrument to which it relates, and in any case within the time limit fixed for the filing of such instrument.

Article 33
Time Limits

(1) Where required, time limits shall be fixed by the Tribunal by assigning dates for the completion of the various steps in the proceeding. The Tribunal may delegate this power to its President.

(2) The Tribunal may extend any time limit that it has fixed. If the Tribunal is not in session, this power shall be exercised by its President.

(3) Any step taken after expiration of the applicable time limit shall be disregarded unless the Tribunal, in special circumstances and after giving the other party an opportunity of stating its views, decides otherwise.

Article 34
Waiver

A party which knows or ought to have known that a provision of these Rules, of any other rules or agreement applicable to the proceeding, or of an order of the Tribunal has not been complied with and which fails to state promptly its objections thereto, shall be deemed to have waived the right to object.

Article 35
Filling of Gaps

If any question of procedure arises which is not covered by these Rules or any rules agreed by the parties, the Tribunal shall decide the question.

Chapter VII
Written and Oral Procedures

Article 36
Normal Procedures

Except if the parties otherwise agree, the proceeding shall comprise two distinct phases: a written procedure followed by an oral one.

Article 37
Transmission of the Request

As soon as the Tribunal is constituted, the Secretary-General shall transmit to each member of the Tribunal a copy of the request by which the proceeding was commenced, of the supporting documentation, of the notice of registration of the request and of any communication received from either party in response thereto.

Article 38
The Written Procedure

(1) In addition to the request for arbitration, the written procedure shall consist of the following pleadings, filed within time limits set by the Tribunal:

(a) a memorial by the requesting party;

(b) a counter-memorial by the other party;

and, if the parties so agree or the Tribunal deems it necessary:

(c) a reply by the requesting party; and

(d) a rejoinder by the other party.

(2) If the request was made jointly, each party shall, within the same time limit determined by the Tribunal, file its memorial. However, the parties may instead agree that one of them shall, for the purposes of paragraph (1) of this Article, be considered as the requesting party.

(3) A memorial shall contain: a statement of the relevant facts; a statement of law; and the submissions. A counter-memorial, reply or rejoinder shall contain an admission or denial of the facts stated in the last previous pleading; any additional facts, if necessary; observations concerning the statement of law in the last previous pleading; a statement of law in answer thereto; and the submissions.

Article 39
The Oral Procedure

(1) The oral procedure shall consist of the hearing by the Tribunal of the parties, their agents, counsel and advocates, and of witnesses and experts.

(2) Unless either party objects, the Tribunal, after consultation with the Secretary-General, may allow other persons, besides the parties, their agents, counsel and advocates, witnesses and experts during their testimony, and officers of the Tribunal, to attend or observe all or part of the hearings, subject to appropriate logistical arrangements. The Tribunal shall for such cases establish procedures for the protection of proprietary or privileged information.

(3) The members of the Tribunal may, during the hearings, put questions to the parties, their agents, counsel and advocates, and ask them for explanations.

Article 40
Marshalling of Evidence

Without prejudice to the rules concerning the production of documents, each party shall, within time limits fixed by the Tribunal, communicate to the Secretary-General, for transmission to the Tribunal and the other party, precise information regarding the evidence which it intends to produce and that which it intends to request the Tribunal to call for, together with an indication of the points to which such evidence will be directed.

Article 41
Evidence: General Principles

(1) The Tribunal shall be the judge of the admissibility of any evidence adduced and of its probative value.

(2) The Tribunal may, if it deems it necessary at any stage of the proceeding, call upon the parties to produce documents, witnesses and experts.

(3) After consulting both parties, the Tribunal may allow a person or entity that is not a party to the dispute (in this Article called the "non-disputing party") to file a written submission with the Tribunal regarding a matter within the scope of the dispute. In determining whether to allow such a filing, the Tribunal shall consider, among other things, the extent to which:

(a) the non-disputing party submission would assist the Tribunal in the determination of a factual or legal issue related to the proceeding by bringing a perspective, particular knowledge or insight that is different from that of the disputing parties;

(b) the non-disputing party submission would address a matter within the scope of the dispute;

(c) the non-disputing party has a significant interest in the proceeding.

The Tribunal shall ensure that the non-disputing party submission does not disrupt the proceeding or unduly burden or unfairly prejudice either party, and that both parties are given an opportunity to present their observations on the non-disputing party submission.

Article 42
Examination of Witnesses and Experts

Witnesses and experts shall be examined before the Tribunal by the parties under the control of its President. Questions may also be put to them by any member of the Tribunal.

Article 43
Witnesses and Experts: Special Rules

The Tribunal may:

(a) admit evidence given by a witness or expert in a written deposition;

(b) with the consent of both parties, arrange for the examination of a witness or expert otherwise than before the Tribunal itself. The Tribunal shall define the procedure to be followed. The parties may participate in the examination; and

(c) appoint one or more experts, define their terms of reference, examine their reports and hear from them in person.

Article 44
Closure of the Proceeding

(1) When the presentation of the case by the parties is completed, the proceeding shall be declared closed.

(2) Exceptionally, the Tribunal may, before the award has been rendered, reopen the proceeding on the ground that new evidence is forthcoming of such a nature as to constitute a decisive factor, or that there is a vital need for clarification on certain specific points.

Chapter VIII
Particular Procedures

Article 45
Preliminary Objections

(1) The Tribunal shall have the power to rule on its competence. For the purposes of this Article, an agreement providing for arbitration under the Additional Facility shall be separable from the other terms of the contract in which it may have been included.

(2) Any objection that the dispute is not within the competence of the Tribunal shall be filed with the Secretary-General as soon as possible after the constitution of the Tribunal and in any event no later than the expiration of the time limit fixed for the filing of the counter-memorial or, if the objection relates to an ancillary claim, for the filing of the rejoinder—unless the facts on which the objection is based are unknown to the party at that time.

(3) The Tribunal may on its own initiative consider, at any stage of the proceeding, whether the dispute before it is within its competence.

(4) Upon the formal raising of an objection relating to the dispute, the Tribunal may decide to suspend the proceeding on the merits. The President of the Tribunal, after consultation with its other members, shall fix a time limit within which the parties may file observations on the objection.

(5) The Tribunal shall decide whether or not the further procedures relating to the objection made pursuant to paragraph (2) shall be oral. It may deal with the objection as a preliminary question or join it to the merits of the dispute. If the Tribunal overrules the objection or joins it to the merits, it shall once more fix time limits for the further procedures.

(6) Unless the parties have agreed to another expedited procedure for making preliminary objections, a party may, no later than 30 days after the constitution of the Tribunal, and in any event before the first session of the Tribunal, file an objection that a claim is manifestly without legal merit. The party shall specify

as precisely as possible the basis for the objection. The Tribunal, after giving the parties the opportunity to present their observations on the objection, shall, at its first session or promptly thereafter, notify the parties of its decision on the objection. The decision of the Tribunal shall be without prejudice to the right of a party to file an objection pursuant to paragraph (2) or to object, in the course of the proceeding, that a claim lacks legal merit.

(7) If the Tribunal decides that the dispute is not within its competence or that all claims are manifestly without legal merit, it shall issue an award to that effect.

Article 46
Provisional Measures of Protection

(1) Unless the arbitration agreement otherwise provides, either party may at any time during the proceeding request that provisional measures for the preservation of its rights be ordered by the Tribunal. The Tribunal shall give priority to the consideration of such a request.

(2) The Tribunal may also recommend provisional measures on its own initiative or recommend measures other than those specified in a request. It may at any time modify or revoke its recommendations.

(3) The Tribunal shall order or recommend provisional measures, or any modification or revocation thereof, only after giving each party an opportunity of presenting its observations.

(4) The parties may apply to any competent judicial authority for interim or conservatory measures. By doing so they shall not be held to infringe the agreement to arbitrate or to affect the powers of the Tribunal.

Article 47
Ancillary Claims

(1) Except as the parties otherwise agree, a party may present an incidental or additional claim or counter-claim, provided that such ancillary claim is within the scope of the arbitration agreement of the parties.

(2) An incidental or additional claim shall be presented not later than in the reply and a counter-claim no later than in the counter-memorial, unless the Tribunal, upon justification by the party presenting the ancillary claim and upon considering any objection of the other party, authorizes the presentation of the claim at a later stage in the proceeding.

Article 48
Default

(1) If a party fails to appear or to present its case at any stage of the proceeding, the other party may request the Tribunal to deal with the questions submitted to it and to render an award.

(2) Whenever such a request is made by a party the Tribunal shall promptly notify the defaulting party thereof. Unless the Tribunal is satisfied that that party does not intend to appear or to present its case in the proceeding, it shall, at the same time, grant a period of grace and to this end:

(a) if that party had failed to file a pleading or any other instrument within the time limit fixed therefor, fix a new time limit for its filing; or

(b) if that party had failed to appear or present its case at a hearing, fix a new date for the hearing.

The period of grace shall not, without the consent of the other party, exceed 60 days.

(3) After the expiration of the period of grace or when, in accordance with paragraph (2) of this Article, no such period is granted, the Tribunal shall examine whether the dispute is within its jurisdiction and, if it is satisfied as to its jurisdiction, decide whether the submissions made are well-founded in fact and in law. To this end, it may, at any stage of the proceeding, call on the party appearing to file observations, produce evidence or submit oral explanations.

Article 49
Settlement and Discontinuance

(1) If, before the award is rendered, the parties agree on a settlement of the dispute or otherwise to discontinue the proceeding, the Tribunal, or the Secretary-General if the Tribunal has not yet been constituted, or has not yet met, shall, at their written request, in an order take note of the discontinuance of the proceeding.

(2) If requested by both parties and accepted by the Tribunal, the Tribunal shall record the settlement in the form of an award. The Tribunal shall not be obliged to give reasons for such an award. The parties will accompany their request with the full and signed text of their settlement.

Article 50
Discontinuance at Request of a Party

If a party requests the discontinuance of the proceeding, the Tribunal, or the Secretary-General if the Tribunal has not yet been constituted, shall in an order fix a time limit within which the other party may state whether it opposes the discontinuance. If no objection is made in writing within the time limit, the Tribunal, or if appropriate the Secretary-General, shall in an order take note of the discontinuance of the proceeding. If objection is made, the proceeding shall continue.

Article 51
Discontinuance for Failure of Parties to Act

If the parties fail to take any steps in the proceeding during six consecutive months or such period as they may agree with the approval of the Tribunal, or of the Secretary-General if the Tribunal has not yet been constituted, they shall be deemed to have discontinued the proceeding and the Tribunal, or if appropriate the Secretary-General, shall, after notice to the parties, in an order take note of the discontinuance.

Chapter IX
The Award

Article 52
The Award

(1) The award shall be made in writing and shall contain:

(a) a precise designation of each party;

(b) a statement that the Tribunal was established under these Rules, and a description of the method of its constitution;

(c) the name of each member of the Tribunal, and an identification of the appointing authority of each;

(d) the names of the agents, counsel and advocates of the parties;

(e) the dates and place of the sittings of the Tribunal;

(f) a summary of the proceeding;

(g) a statement of the facts as found by the Tribunal;

(h) the submissions of the parties;

(i) the decision of the Tribunal on every question submitted to it, together with the reasons upon which the decision is based; and

(j) any decision of the Tribunal regarding the cost of the proceeding.

(2) The award shall be signed by the members of the Tribunal who voted for it; the date of each signature shall be indicated. Any member of the Tribunal may attach his individual opinion to the award, whether he dissents from the majority or not, or a statement of his dissent.

(3) If the arbitration law of the country where the award is made requires that it be filed or registered by the Tribunal, the Tribunal shall comply with this requirement within the period of time required by law.

(4) The award shall be final and binding on the parties. The parties waive any time limits for the rendering of the award which may be provided for by the law of the country where the award is made.

Article 53
Authentication of the Award; Certified Copies; Date

(1) Upon signature by the last arbitrator to sign, the Secretary-General shall promptly:

  (a) authenticate the original text of the award and deposit it in the archives of the Secretariat, together with any individual opinions and statements of dissent; and

  (b) dispatch a certified copy of the award (including individual opinions and statements of dissent) to each party, indicating the date of dispatch on the original text and on all copies; provided, however, that if the original text of the award must be filed or registered as contemplated by Article 52(3) of these Rules the Secretary-General shall do so on behalf of the Tribunal or return the award to the Tribunal for this purpose.

(2) The award shall be deemed to have been rendered on the date on which the certified copies were dispatched.

(3) Except to the extent required for any registration or filing of the award by the Secretary-General under paragraph (1) of this Article, the Secretariat shall not publish the award without the consent of the parties. The Secretariat shall, however, promptly include in the publications of the Centre excerpts of the legal reasoning of the Tribunal.

Article 54
Applicable Law

(1) The Tribunal shall apply the rules of law designated by the parties as applicable to the substance of the dispute. Failing such designation by the parties, the Tribunal shall apply (a) the law determined by the conflict of laws rules which

it considers applicable and (b) such rules of international law as the Tribunal considers applicable.

(2) The Tribunal may decide *ex aequo et bono* if the parties have expressly authorized it to do so and if the law applicable to the arbitration so permits.

Article 55
Interpretation of the Award

(1) Within 45 days after the date of the award either party, with notice to the other party, may request that the Secretary-General obtain from the Tribunal an interpretation of the award.

(2) The Tribunal shall determine the procedure to be followed.

(3) The interpretation shall form part of the award, and the provisions of Articles 52 and 53 of these Rules shall apply.

Article 56
Correction of the Award

(1) Within 45 days after the date of the award either party, with notice to the other party, may request the Secretary-General to obtain from the Tribunal a correction in the award of any clerical, arithmetical or similar errors. The Tribunal may within the same period make such corrections on its own initiative.

(2) The provisions of Articles 52 and 53 of these Rules shall apply to such corrections.

Article 57
Supplementary Decisions

(1) Within 45 days after the date of the award either party, with notice to the other party may request the Tribunal, through the Secretary-General, to decide any question which it had omitted to decide in the award.

(2) The Tribunal shall determine the procedure to be followed.

(3) The decision of the Tribunal shall become part of the award and the provisions of Articles 52 and 53 of these Rules shall apply thereto.

Chapter X
Costs

Article 58
Cost of Proceeding

(1) Unless the parties otherwise agree, the Tribunal shall decide how and by whom the fees and expenses of the members of the Tribunal, the expenses and charges of the Secretariat and the expenses incurred by the parties in connection with the proceeding shall be borne. The Tribunal may, to that end, call on the Secretariat and the parties to provide it with the information it needs in order to formulate the division of the cost of the proceeding between the parties.

(2) The decision of the Tribunal pursuant to paragraph (1) of this Article shall form part of the award.

Chapter XI
General Provisions

Article 59
Final Provision

The text of these Rules in each official language of the Centre shall be equally authentic.

Model UK Bilateral Investment Treaty
(2005)

[DRAFT] AGREEMENT [_____]

BETWEEN THE GOVERNMENT OF THE UNITED KINGDOM

OF GREAT BRITAIN AND NORTHERN IRELAND

AND

THE GOVERNMENT OF [_____]

FOR THE PROMOTION AND PROTECTION OF INVESTMENTS

The Government of the United Kingdom of Great Britain and Northern Ireland and the Government of _____ ;

Desiring to create favourable conditions for greater investment by nationals and companies of one State in the territory of the other State;

Recognising that the encouragement and reciprocal protection under international agreement of such investments will be conducive to the stimulation of individual business initiative and will increase prosperity in both States;

Have agreed as follows:

Article 1
Definitions

For the purposes of this Agreement:

(a) "investment" means every kind of asset and in particular, though not exclusively, includes:

(i) movable and immovable property and any other property rights such as mortgages, liens or pledges;

(ii) shares in and stock and debentures of a company and any other form of participation in a company;

(iii) claims to money or to any performance under contract having a financial value;

(iv) intellectual property rights, goodwill, technical processes and know-how;

(v) business concessions conferred by law or under contract, including concessions to search for, cultivate, extract or exploit natural resources.

A change in the form in which assets are invested does not affect their character as investments and the term "investment" includes all investments, whether made before or after the date of entry into force of this Agreement;

(b) "returns" means the amounts yielded by an investment and in particular, though not exclusively, includes profit, interest, capital gains, dividends, royalties and fees;

(c) "nationals" means:

(i) in respect of the United Kingdom: physical persons deriving their status as United Kingdom nationals from the law in force in the United Kingdom;

(ii) in respect of _____ : _____ ;

(d) "companies" means:

(i) in respect of the United Kingdom: corporations, firms and associations incorporated or constituted under the law in force in any part of the United Kingdom or in any territory to which this Agreement is extended in accordance with the provisions of Article 12;

(ii) in respect of _____ : _____ ;

(e) "territory" means:

(i) in respect of the United Kingdom: Great Britain and Northern Ireland, including the territorial sea and maritime area situated beyond the territorial sea of the United Kingdom which has been or might in the future be designated under the national law of the United Kingdom in accordance with international law as an area within which the United Kingdom may exercise rights with regard to the sea-bed and subsoil and the natural resources and any territory to which this Agreement is extended in accordance with the provisions of Article 12;

(ii) in respect of _____ : _____ .

Article 2
Promotion and Protection of Investment

(1) Each Contracting Party shall encourage and create favourable conditions for nationals or companies of the other Contracting Party to invest capital in its territory, and, subject to its right to exercise powers conferred by its laws, shall admit such capital.

(2) Investments of nationals or companies of each Contracting Party shall at all times be accorded fair and equitable treatment and shall enjoy full protection and security in the territory of the other Contracting Party. Neither Contracting Party shall in any way impair by unreasonable or discriminatory measures the management, maintenance, use, enjoyment or disposal of investments in its territory of nationals or companies of the other Contracting Party. Each Contracting Party shall observe any obligation it may have entered into with regard to investments of nationals or companies of the other Contracting Party.

Article 3
National Treatment and Most-favoured-nation Provisions

(1) Neither Contracting Party shall in its territory subject investments or returns of nationals or companies of the other Contracting Party to treatment

less favourable than that which it accords to investments or returns of its own nationals or companies or to investments or returns of nationals or companies of any third State.

(2) Neither Contracting Party shall in its territory subject nationals or companies of the other Contracting Party, as regards their management, maintenance, use, enjoyment or disposal of their investments, to treatment less favourable that that which it accords to its own nationals or companies or to nationals or companies of any third State.

(3) For the avoidance of doubt it is confirmed that the treatment provided for in paragraphs (1) and (2) above shall apply to the provisions of Articles 1 to 11 of this Agreement.

Article 4
Compensation for Losses

(1) Nationals or companies of one Contracting Party whose investments in the territory of the other Contracting Party suffer losses owing to war or other armed conflict, revolution, a state of national emergency, revolt, insurrection or riot in the territory of the latter Contracting Party shall be accorded by the latter Contracting Party treatment, as regards restitution, indemnification, compensation or other settlement, no less favourable than that which the latter Contracting Party accords to its own nationals or companies or to nationals or companies of any third State. Resulting payments shall be freely transferable.

(2) Without prejudice to paragraph (1) of this Article, nationals or companies of one Contracting Party who in any of the situations referred to in that paragraph suffer losses in the territory of the other Contracting Party resulting from:

  (a) requisitioning of their property by its forces or authorities, or

  (b) destruction of their property by its forces or authorities, which was not caused in combat action or was not required by the necessity of the situation, shall be accorded restitution or adequate compensation. Resulting payments shall be freely transferable.

Article 5
Expropriation

(1) Investments of nationals or companies of either Contracting Party shall not be nationalised, expropriated or subjected to measures having effect equivalent to nationalisation or expropriation (hereinafter referred to as "expropriation") in the territory of the other Contracting Party except for a public purpose related to the internal needs of that Party on a non-discriminatory basis and against prompt, adequate and effective compensation. Such compensation shall amount to the genuine value of the investment expropriated immediately before the expropriation or before the impending expropriation became public knowledge, whichever is the earlier, shall include interest at a normal commercial rate until the date of payment, shall be made without delay, be effectively realizable and be freely transferable. The national or company affected shall have a right, under the law of the Contracting Party making the expropriation, to prompt review, by a judicial or other independent authority of that Party, of his or its case and of the valuation of his or its investment in accordance with the principles set out in this paragraph.

(2) Where a Contracting Party expropriates the assets of a company which is incorporated or constituted under the law in force in any part of its own territory, and in which nationals or companies of the other Contracting Party own shares, it shall ensure that the provisions of paragraph (1) of this Article are applied to the extent necessary to guarantee prompt, adequate and effective compensation in respect of their investment to such nationals or companies of the other Contracting Party who are owners of those shares.

Article 6
Repatriation of Investment and Returns

Each Contracting Party shall in respect of investments guarantee to nationals or companies of the other Contracting Party the unrestricted transfer of their investments and returns. Transfers shall be effected without delay in the convertible currency in which the capital was originally invested or in any other convertible currency agreed by the investor and the Contracting Party concerned. Unless otherwise agreed by the investor transfers shall be made at the rate of exchange applicable on the date of transfer pursuant to the exchange regulations in force.

Article 7
Exceptions

The provisions of this Agreement relative to the grant of treatment not less favourable than that accorded to the nationals or companies of either Contracting Party or of any third State shall not be construed so as to oblige one Contracting Party to extend to the nationals or companies of the other the benefit of any treatment, preference or privilege resulting from:

(a) any existing or future customs union or similar international agreement to which either of the Contracting Parties is or may become a party; or

(b) any international agreement or arrangement relating wholly or mainly to taxation or any domestic legislation relating wholly or mainly to taxation.

(c) any requirements of European Community law resulting from the United Kingdom's membership of the European Union prohibiting, restricting or limiting the movement of capital to or from any third country.

[Preferred]

Article 8
Reference to International Centre for Settlement of Investment Disputes

(1) Each Contracting Party hereby consents to submit to the International Centre for the Settlement of Investment Disputes (hereinafter referred to as "the Centre") for settlement by conciliation or arbitration under the Convention on the Settlement of Investment Disputes between States and Nationals of Other States opened for signature at Washington DC on 18 March 1965 any legal

dispute arising between that Contracting Party and a national or company of the other Contracting Party concerning an investment of the latter in the territory of the former.

(2) A company which is incorporated or constituted under the law in force in the territory of one Contracting Party and in which before such a dispute arises the majority of shares are owned by nationals or companies of the other Contracting Party shall in accordance with Article 25 (2) (b) of the Convention be treated for the purposes of the Convention as a company of the other Contracting Party.

(3) If any such dispute should arise and agreement cannot be reached within three months between the parties to this dispute through pursuit of local remedies or otherwise, then, if the national or company affected also consents in writing to submit the dispute to the Centre for settlement by conciliation or arbitration under the Convention, either party may institute proceedings by addressing a request to that effect to the Secretary-General of the Centre as provided in Articles 28 and 36 of the Convention. In the event of disagreement as to whether conciliation or arbitration is the more appropriate procedure the national or company affected shall have the right to choose. The Contracting Party which is a party to the dispute shall not raise as an objection at any stage of the proceedings or enforcement of an award the fact that the national or company which is the other party to the dispute has received in pursuance of an insurance contract an indemnity in respect of some or all of his or its losses.

(4) Neither Contracting Party shall pursue through the diplomatic channel any dispute referred to the Centre unless:

(a) the Secretary-General of the Centre, or a conciliation commission or an arbitral tribunal constituted by it, decides that the dispute is not within the jurisdiction of the Centre; or

(b) the other Contracting Party shall fail to abide by or to comply with any award rendered by an arbitral tribunal.

[Alternative]

Article 8
Settlement of Disputes between an Investor and a Host State

(1) Disputes between a national or company of one Contracting Party and the other Contracting Party concerning an obligation of the latter under this Agreement in relation to an investment of the former which have not been amicably settled shall, after a period of three months from written notification of a claim, be submitted to international arbitration if the national or company concerned so wishes.

(2) Where the dispute is referred to international arbitration, the national or company and the Contracting Party concerned in the dispute may agree to refer the dispute either to:

(a) the International Centre for the Settlement of Investment Disputes (having regard to the provisions, where applicable, of the Convention on the Settlement of Investment Disputes between States and Nationals of other States, opened for signature at Washington DC on 18 March 1965 and the Additional Facility for the Administration of Conciliation, Arbitration and Fact-Finding Proceedings); or

(b) the Court of Arbitration of the International Chamber of Commerce; or

(c) an international arbitrator or ad hoc arbitration tribunal to be appointed by a special agreement or established under the Arbitration Rules of the United Nations Commission on International Trade Law.

If after a period of three months from written notification of the claim there is no agreement to one of the above alternative procedures, the dispute shall at the request in writing of the national or company concerned be submitted to arbitration under the Arbitration Rules of the United Nations Commission on International Trade Law as then in force. The parties to the dispute may agree in writing to modify these Rules.

Article 9
Disputes between the Contracting Parties

(1) Disputes between the Contracting Parties concerning the interpretation or application of this Agreement should, if possible, be settled through the diplomatic channel.

(2) If a dispute between the Contracting Parties cannot thus be settled, it shall upon the request of either Contracting Party be submitted to an arbitral tribunal.

(3) Such an arbitral tribunal shall be constituted for each individual case in the following way. Within two months of the receipt of the request for arbitration, each Contracting Party shall appoint one member of the tribunal. Those two members shall then select a national of a third State who on approval by the two Contracting Parties shall be appointed Chairman of the tribunal. The Chairman shall be appointed within two months from the date of appointment of the other two members.

(4) If within the periods specified in paragraph (3) of this Article the necessary appointments have not been made, either Contracting Party may, in the absence of any other agreement, invite the President of the International Court of Justice to make any necessary appointments. If the President is a national of either Contracting Party or if he is otherwise prevented from discharging the said function, the Vice-President shall be invited to make the necessary appointments. If the Vice-President is a national of either Contracting Party or if he too is prevented from discharging the said function, the Member of the International Court of Justice next in seniority who is not a national of either Contracting Party shall be invited to make the necessary appointments.

(5) The arbitral tribunal shall reach its decision by a majority of votes. Such decision shall be binding on both Contracting Parties. Each Contracting Party shall bear the cost of its own member of the tribunal and of its representation in the arbitral proceedings; the cost of the Chairman and the remaining costs shall be borne in equal parts by the Contracting Parties. The tribunal may, however, in its decision direct that a higher proportion of costs shall be borne by one of the

two Contracting Parties, and this award shall be binding on both Contracting Parties. The tribunal shall determine its own procedure.

Article 10
Subrogation

(1) If one Contracting Party or its designated Agency ("the first Contracting Party") makes a payment under an indemnity given in respect of an investment in the territory of the other Contracting Party ("the second Contracting Party"), the second Contracting Party shall recognise:

    (a)   the assignment to the first Contracting Party by law or by legal transaction of all the rights and claims of the party indemnified; and

    (b)   that the first Contracting Party is entitled to exercise such rights and enforce such claims by virtue of subrogation, to the same extent as the party indemnified.

(2) The first Contracting Party shall be entitled in all circumstances to the same treatment in respect of:

    (a)   the rights and claims acquired by it by virtue of the assignment, and

    (b)   any payments received in pursuance of those rights and claims,

as the party indemnified was entitled to receive by virtue of this Agreement in respect of the investment concerned and its related returns.

(3) Any payments received in non-convertible currency by the first Contracting Party in pursuance of the rights and claims acquired shall be freely available to the first Contracting Party for the purpose of meeting any expenditure incurred in the territory of the second Contracting Party.

Article 11
Application of other Rules

If the provisions of law of either Contracting Party or obligations under international law existing at present or established hereafter between the Contracting

Parties in addition to the present Agreement contain rules, whether general or specific, entitling investments by nationals or companies of the other Contracting Party to a treatment more favourable than is provided for by the present Agreement, such rules shall to the extent that they are more favourable prevail over the present Agreement.

Article 12
Territorial Extension

At the time of [signature] [entry into force] [ratification] of this Agreement, or at any time thereafter, the provisions of this Agreement may be extended to such territories for whose international relations the Government of the United Kingdom are responsible as may be agreed between the Contracting Parties in an Exchange of Notes.

Article 13
Entry into Force

[This Agreement shall enter into force on the day of signature.]

or

[Each Contracting Party shall notify the other in writing of the completion of the constitutional formalities required in its territory for the entry into force of this Agreement. This Agreement shall enter into force on the date of the latter of the two notifications.]

or

[The Agreement shall be ratified and shall enter into force on the exchange of Instruments of Ratification.]

Article 14
Duration and Termination

This Agreement shall remain in force for a period of ten years. Thereafter it shall continue in force until the expiration of twelve months from the date on which either Contracting Party shall have given written notice of termination to the other. Provided that in respect of investments made whilst the Agreement is in force, its provisions shall continue in effect with respect to such investments for a period of twenty years after the date of termination and without prejudice to the application thereafter of the rules of general international law.

In witness whereof the undersigned, duly authorised thereto by their respective Governments, have signed this Agreement.

Done in duplicate at _____ this _____ day of _____ 20__ [in the English and _____ languages, both texts being equally authoritative].

For the Government of _____ :

For the Government of the United Kingdom of
Great Britain and Northern Ireland:

Treaty Between the United States of America and the Argentine Republic Concerning the Reciprocal Encouragement and Protection of Investment
(done in Washington, 14 November 1991)

Treaty Between the United States of America and the Argentine Republic Concerning the Reciprocal Encouragement and Protection of Investment

The United States of America and the Argentine Republic, hereinafter referred to as the Parties;

Desiring to promote greater economic cooperation between them, with respect to investment by nationals and companies of one Party in the territory of the other Party;

Recognizing that agreement upon the treatment to be accorded such investment will stimulate the flow of private capital and the economic development of the Parties;

Agreeing that fair and equitable treatment of investment is desirable in order to maintain a stable framework for investment and maximum effective use of economic resources;

Recognizing that the development of economic and business ties can contribute to the well-being of workers in both Parties and promote respect for internationally recognized worker rights; and

Having resolved to conclude a Treaty concerning the encouragement and reciprocal protection of investment;

Have agreed as follows:

Article I

1. For the purposes of this Treaty,

  a) "investment" means every kind of investment in the territory of one Party owned or controlled directly or indirectly by nationals or companies of the other Party, such as equity, debt, and service and investment contracts; and includes without limitation:

    (i) tangible and intangible property, including rights, such as mortgages, liens and pledges;

    (ii) a company or shares of stock or other interests in a company or interests in the assets thereof;

    (iii) a claim to money or a claim to performance having economic value and directly related to an investment;

    (iv) intellectual property which includes, inter alia, rights relating to: literary and artistic works, including sound recordings, inventions in all fields of human endeavor, industrial designs, semiconductor mask works, trade secrets, know-how, and confidential business information, and trademarks, service marks, and trade names; and

    (v) any right conferred by law or contract, and any licenses and permits pursuant to law;

  b) "company" of a Party means any kind of corporation, company, association, state enterprise, or other organization, legally constituted under the laws and regulations of a Party or a political subdivision thereof whether or not organized for pecuniary gain, and whether privately or governmentally owned;

  c) "national" of a Party means a natural person who is a national of a Party under its applicable law;

d) "return" means an amount derived from or associated with an investment, including profit; dividend; interest; capital gain; royalty payment; management, technical assistance or other fee; or returns in kind;

e) "associated activities" include the organization, control, operation, maintenance and disposition of companies, branches, agencies, offices, factories or other facilities for the conduct of business; the making, performance and enforcement of contracts; the acquisition, use, protection and disposition of property of all kinds including intellectual and industrial property rights; and the borrowing of funds, the purchase, issuance, and sale of equity shares and other securities, and the purchase of foreign exchange for imports.

f) "territory" means the territory of the United States or the Argentine Republic, including the territorial sea established in accordance with international law as reflected in the 1982 United Nations Convention on the Law of the Sea. This Treaty also applies in the seas and seabed adjacent to the territorial sea in which the United States or the Argentine Republic has sovereign rights or jurisdiction in accordance with international law as reflected in the 1982 United Nations Convention on the Law of the Sea.

2. Each Party reserves the right to deny to any company of the other Party the advantages of this Treaty if (a) nationals of any third country, or nationals of such Party, control such company and the company has no substantial business activities in the territory of the other Party, or (b) the company is controlled by nationals of a third country with which the denying Party does not maintain normal economic relations.

3. Any alteration of the form in which assets are invested or reinvested shall not affect their character as investment.

Article II

1. Each Party shall permit and treat investment, and activities associated therewith, on a basis no less favorable than that accorded in like situations to investment

or associated activities of its own nationals or companies, or of nationals or companies of any third country, whichever is the more favorable, subject to the right of each Party to make or maintain exceptions falling within one of the sectors or matters listed in the Protocol to this Treaty. Each Party agrees to notify the other Party before or on the date of entry into force of this Treaty of all such laws and regulations of which it is aware concerning the sectors or matters listed in the Protocol. Moreover, each Party agrees to notify the other of any future exception with respect to the sectors or matters listed in the Protocol, and to limit such exceptions to a minimum. Any future exception by either Party shall not apply to investment existing in that sector or matter at the time the exception becomes effective. The treatment accorded pursuant to any exceptions shall, unless specified otherwise in the Protocol, be not less favorable than that accorded in like situations to investments and associated activities of nationals or companies of any third country.

2. a) Investment shall at all times be accorded fair and equitable treatment, shall enjoy full protection and security and shall in no case be accorded treatment less than that required by international law.

  b) Neither Party shall in any way impair by arbitrary or discriminatory measures the management, operation, maintenance, use, enjoyment, acquisition, expansion, or disposal of investments. For the purposes of dispute resolution under Articles VII and VIII, a measure may be arbitrary or discriminatory notwithstanding the opportunity to review such measure in the courts or administrative tribunals of a Party.

  c) Each Party shall observe any obligation it may have entered into with regard to investments.

3. Subject to the laws relating to the entry and sojourn of aliens, nationals of either Party shall be permitted to enter and to remain in the territory of the other Party for the purpose of establishing, developing, administering or advising on the operation of an investment to which they, or a company of the first Party that employs them, have committed or are in the process of committing a substantial amount of capital or other resources.

4. Companies which are legally constituted under the applicable laws or regulations of one Party, and which are investments, shall be permitted to engage top managerial personnel of their choice, regardless of nationality.

5. Neither Party shall impose performance requirements as a condition of establishment, expansion or maintenance of investments, which require or enforce commitments to export goods produced, or which specify that goods or services must be purchased locally, or which impose any other similar requirements.

6. Each Party shall provide effective means of asserting claims and enforcing rights with respect to investments, investment agreements, and investment authorizations.

7. Each Party shall make public all laws, regulations, administrative practices and procedures, and adjudicatory decisions that pertain to or affect investments.

8. The treatment accorded by the United States of America to investments and associated activities of nationals and companies of the Argentine Republic under the provisions of this Article shall in any State, Territory or possession of the United States of America be no less favorable than the treatment accorded therein to investments and associated activities of nationals of the United States of America resident in, and companies legally constituted under the laws and regulations of, other States, Territories or possessions of the United States of America.

9. The most favored nation provisions of this Article shall not apply to advantages accorded by either Party to nationals or companies of any third country by virtue of that Party's binding obligations that derive from full membership in a regional customs union or free trade area, whether such an arrangement is designated as a customs union, free trade area, common market or otherwise.

Article III

This Treaty shall not preclude either Party from prescribing laws and regulations in connection with the admission of investments made in its territory by nationals or companies of the other Party or with the conduct of associated activities, provided, however, that such laws and regulations shall not impair the substance of any of the rights set forth in this Treaty.

Article IV

1. Investments shall not be expropriated or nationalized either directly or indirectly through measures tantamount to expropriation or nationalization ("expropriation") except for a public purpose; in a non-discriminatory manner; upon payment of prompt, adequate and effective compensation; and in accordance with due process of law and the general principles of treatment provided for in Article II (2) Compensation shall be equivalent to the fair market value of the expropriated investment immediately before the expropriatory action was taken or became known, whichever is earlier; be paid without delay; include interest at a commercially reasonable rate from the date of expropriation; be fully realizable; and be freely transferable at the prevailing market rate of exchange on the date of expropriation.

2. A national or company of either Party that asserts that all or part of its investment has been expropriated shall have a right to prompt review by the appropriate judicial or administrative authorities of the other Party to determine whether any such expropriation has occurred and, if so, whether such expropriation, and any compensation therefore, conforms to the provisions of this Treaty and the principles of international law.

3. Nationals or companies of either Party whose investments suffer losses in the territory of the other Party owing to war or other armed conflict, revolution, state of national emergency, insurrection, civil disturbance or other similar events shall be accorded treatment by such other Party no less favorable than that accorded to its own nationals or companies or to nationals or companies of any third country, whichever is the more favorable treatment, as regards any measures it adopts in relation to such losses.

Article V

1. Each Party shall permit all transfers related to an investment to be made freely and without delay into and out of its territory. Such transfers include: (a)

returns; (b) compensation pursuant to Article IV; (c) payments arising out of an investment dispute; (d) payments made under a contract, including amortization of principal and accrued interest payments made pursuant to a loan agreement directly related to an investment; (e) proceeds from the sale or liquidation of all or any part of an investment; and (f) additional contributions to capital for the maintenance or development of an investment.

2. Except as provided in Article IV paragraph 1, transfers shall be made in a freely usable currency at the prevailing market rate of exchange on the date of transfer with respect to spot transactions in the currency to be transferred. The free transfer shall take place in accordance with the procedures established by each Party; such procedures shall not impair the rights set forth in this Treaty.

3. Notwithstanding the provisions of paragraphs 1 and 2, either Party may maintain laws and regulations (a) requiring reports of currency transfer; and (b) imposing income taxes by such means as a withholding tax applicable to dividends or other transfers. Furthermore, either Party may protect the rights of creditors, or ensure the satisfaction of judgments in adjudicatory proceedings, through the equitable, nondiscriminatory and good faith application of its law.

Article VI

The Parties agree to consult promptly, on the request of either, to resolve any disputes in connection with the Treaty, or to discuss any matter relating to the interpretation or application of the Treaty.

Article VII

1. For purposes of this Article, an investment dispute is a dispute between a Party and a national or company of the other Party arising out of or relating to (a) an investment agreement between that Party and such national or company; (b) an investment authorization granted by that Party's foreign investment authority (if any such authorization exists) to such national or company; or (c) an alleged breach of any right conferred or created by this Treaty with respect to an investment.

2. In the event of an investment dispute, the parties to the dispute should initially seek a resolution through consultation and negotiation. If the dispute cannot be settled amicably, the national or company concerned may choose to submit the dispute for resolution:

(a) to the courts or administrative tribunals of the Party that is a party to the dispute; or

(b) in accordance with any applicable, previously agreed dispute-settlement procedures; or

(c) in accordance with the terms of paragraph 3.

3. (a) Provided that the national or company concerned has not submitted the dispute for resolution under paragraph 2 (a) or (b) and that six months have elapsed from the date on which the dispute arose, the national or company concerned may choose to consent in writing to the submission of the dispute for settlement by binding arbitration:

(i) to the International Centre for the Settlement of Investment Disputes ("Centre") established by the Convention on the Settlement of Investment Disputes between States and Nationals of other States, done at Washington, March 18, 1965 ("ICSID Convention"), provided that the Party is a party to such Convention: or

(ii) to the Additional Facility of the Centre, if the Centre is not available; or

(iii) in accordance with the Arbitration Rules of the United Nations Commission on International Trade Law (UNICTRAL); or

(iv) to any other arbitration institution, or in accordance with any other arbitration rules, as may be mutually agreed between the parties to the dispute.

(b) Once the national or company concerned has so consented, either party to the dispute may initiate arbitration in accordance with the choice so specified in the consent.

4. Each Party hereby consents to the submission of any investment dispute for settlement by binding arbitration in accordance with the choice specified in the written consent of the national or company under paragraph 3. Such consent, together with the written consent of the national or company when given under paragraph 3 shall satisfy the requirement for:

(a) written consent of the parties to the dispute for purposes of Chapter II of the ICSID Convention (Jurisdiction of the Centre) and for purposes of the Additional Facility Rules; and

(b) an "agreement in writing" for purposes of Article II of the United Nations Convention on the Recognition and Enforcement of Foreign Arbitral Awards, done at New York, June 10, 1958 ("New York Convention").

5. Any arbitration under paragraph 3(a)(ii), (iii) or (iv) of this Article shall be held in a state that is a party to the New York Convention.

6. Any arbitral award rendered pursuant to this Article shall be final and binding on the parties to the dispute. Each Party undertakes to carry out without delay the provisions of any such award and to provide in its territory for its enforcement.

7. In any proceeding involving an investment dispute, a Party shall not assert, as a defense, counterclaim, right of set-off or otherwise, that the national or company concerned has received or will receive, pursuant to an insurance or guarantee contract, indemnification or other compensation for all or part of its alleged damages.

8. For purposes of an arbitration held under paragraph 3 of this Article, any company legally constituted under the applicable laws and regulations of a Party or a political subdivision thereof but that, immediately before the occurrence of the event or events giving rise to the dispute, was an investment of nationals or companies of the other Party, shall be treated as a national or company of such other Party in accordance with Article 25(2)(b) of the ICSID Convention.

Article VIII

1. Any dispute between the Parties concerning the interpretation or application of the Treaty which is not resolved through consultations or other diplomatic channels, shall be submitted, upon the request of either Party, to an arbitral tribunal for binding decision in accordance with the applicable rules of international law. In the absence of an agreement by the Parties to the contrary, the arbitration rules of the United Nations Commission on International Trade Law (UNCITRAL), except to the extent modified by the Parties or by the arbitrators, shall govern.

2. Within two months of receipt of a request, each Party shall appoint an arbitrator. The two arbitrators shall select a third arbitrator as Chairman, who is a national of a third State. The UNCITRAL Rules for appointing members of three member panels shall apply mutatis mutandis to the appointment of the arbitral panel except that the appointing authority referenced in those rules shall be the Secretary General of the Permanent Court of Arbitration.

3. Unless otherwise agreed, all submissions shall be made and all hearings shall be completed within six months of the date of selection of the third arbitrator, and the Tribunal shall render its decisions within two months of the date of the final submissions or the date of the closing of the hearings, whichever is later.

4. Expenses incurred by the Chairman, the other arbitrators, and other costs of the proceedings shall be paid for equally by the Parties.

Article IX

The provisions of Article VII and VIII shall not apply to a dispute arising (a) under the export credit, guarantee or insurance programs of the Export-Import Bank of the United States or (b) under other official credit, guarantee or insurance arrangements pursuant to which the Parties have agreed to other means of settling disputes.

Article X

This Treaty shall not derogate from:

(a) laws and regulations, administrative practices or procedures, or administrative or adjudicatory decisions of either Party;

(b) international legal obligations; or

(c) obligations assumed by either Party, including those contained in an investment agreement or an investment authorization,

that entitle investments or associated activities to treatment more favorable than that accorded by this Treaty in like situations.

Article XI

This Treaty shall not preclude the application by either Party of measures necessary for the maintenance of public order, the fulfillment of its obligations with respect to the maintenance or restoration of international peace or security, or the Protection of its own essential security interests.

Article XII

1. With respect to its tax policies, each Party should strive to accord fairness and equity in the treatment of investment of nationals and companies of the other Party.

2. Nevertheless, the provisions of this Treaty, and in particular Article VII and VIII, shall apply to matters of taxation only with respect to the following:

(a) expropriation, pursuant to Article IV;

(b) transfers, pursuant to Article V; or

(c) the observance and enforcement of terms of an investment agreement or authorization as referred to in Article VII(1)(a) or (b),

to the extent they are not subject to the dispute settlement provisions of a Convention for the avoidance of double taxation between the two Parties, or have been raised under such settlement provisions and are not resolved within a reasonable period of time.

Article XIII

This Treaty shall apply to the political subdivisions of the Parties.

Article XIV

1. This Treaty shall enter into force thirty days after the date of exchange of instruments of ratification. It shall remain in force for a period of ten years and shall continue in force unless terminated in accordance with paragraph 2 of this Article. It shall apply to investments existing at the time of entry into force as well as to investments made or acquired thereafter.

2. Either Party may, by giving one year's written notice to the other Party, terminate this Treaty at the end of the initial ten year period or at any time thereafter.

3. With respect to investments made or acquired prior to the date of termination of this Treaty and to which this Treaty otherwise applies, the provisions of all of the other Articles of this Treaty shall thereafter continue to be effective for a further period of ten years from such date of termination.

4. The Protocol shall form an integral part of the Treaty.

IN WITNESS WHEREOF, the respective plenipotentiaries have signed this Treaty.

DONE in duplicate at Washington on the fourteenth day of November, 1991, in the English and Spanish languages, both texts being equally authentic.

For the United States of America:

For the Argentine Republic:

Protocol

1. During dispute settlement proceedings pursuant to Article VII, a party may be required to produce evidence of ownership or control consistent with Article I(1)(a).

2. With reference to Article II, paragraph 1, the United States reserves the right to make or maintain limited exceptions to national treatment in the following sectors: air transportation; ocean and coastal shipping; banking; insurance; energy and power production; custom house brokers; ownership and operation of broadcast or common carrier radio and television stations; ownership of real property; ownership of shares in the Communications Satellite Corporation; the provision of common carrier telephone and telegraph services; the provision of submarine cable services; use of land and natural resources

3. With reference to Article II, paragraph 1, the United States reserves the right to make or maintain limited exceptions to national treatment with respect to certain programs involving government grants, loans, and insurance.

4. With reference to Article II, paragraph 1, the United States reserves the right to make or maintain limited exceptions to national and most favored nation treatment in the following sectors, with respect to which treatment will be based on reciprocity: mining on the public domain; maritime services and maritime-related services; primary dealership in United States government securities.

5. With reference to Article II, paragraph 1, the Argentine Republic reserves the right to make or maintain limited exceptions to national treatment in the following sectors: real estate in the Border Areas; air transportation; shipbuilding; nuclear energy centers; uranium mining; insurance; mining; fishing.

6. The Parties understand that, with respect to rights reserved in Article XI of the Treaty, "obligations with respect to the maintenance or restoration of international peace or security" means obligations under the Charter of the United Nations.

7. The Parties acknowledge and agree that, to the extent of any conflict or inconsistency between the terms of this Treaty, and the terms of the Treaty of Friendship, Commerce, and Navigation between the Parties, entered into force December 20, 1854 (the "FCN Treaty"), the terms of this Treaty shall supersede the terms of the FCN Treaty, and shall control the resolution of such conflict.

8. The Parties confirm their mutual understanding that the provisions of this Treaty do not bind either Party in relation to any act or fact which took place

or any situation which ceased to exist before the date of the entry into force of this Treaty.

9. Notwithstanding Article II(5) and in accordance with the terms of this paragraph, the Government of the Argentine Republic may maintain, but not intensify, existing performance requirements in the automotive industry. The Government of the Argentine Republic shall exert best efforts to eliminate all such requirements within the shortest possible period, and shall ensure their elimination within eight years of the date of the entry into force of this Treaty. The Government of the Argentine Republic shall further ensure that such performance requirements are applied in a manner which does not place existing investments at a competitive disadvantage against new entrants in this industry. The Parties shall consult at the request of either on any matter concerning the implementation of these undertakings. For the purposes of this paragraph, "existing" means extant at the time of signature of this Treaty.

10. The Parties note that the Argentine Republic has had and may have in the future a debt-equity conversion program under which nationals or companies of the United States may choose to invest in the Argentine Republic through the purchase of debt at a discount.

The Parties agree that the rights provided in Article V, paragraph 1, with respect to the transfer of returns and of proceeds from the sale or liquidation of all or any part of an investment, remain or may be, as such rights would apply to that part of an investment financed through a debt-equity conversion, modified by the terms of any debt-equity conversion agreement between a national or company of the United States and the Government of the Argentine Republic, or any agency or instrumentality thereof.

The transfer of returns and of proceeds from the sale or liquidation of all or any part of an investment shall in no case be on terms less favorable than those accorded, in like circumstances, to nationals or companies of the Argentine Republic or any third country, whichever is more favorable.

11. The Parties note with satisfaction that the Argentine Republic is engaged in a process of privatization of various industries, including public utilities. They agree that they will undertake their best efforts, including through consultations,

to avoid any misinterpretation regarding the scope of Article II(5) that would adversely affect this privatization process.

Embassy of the United States of America
Buenos Aires, August 24, 1992
No. 453

Mr. Minister:

I have the honor to refer to the Treaty between the United States of America and the Argentine Republic concerning the reciprocal encouragement and protection of investment, with Protocol signed at Washington, November 14, 1991 ("The Treaty").

During the negotiation of the Treaty, the Government of the United States of America and the Government of the Argentine Republic discussed the inclusion in Section 5 of the Protocol to the Treaty of the Argentine Mining Sector. Based on those discussions and subsequent discussions regarding this matter, I wish to propose the deletion of the term "Mining" from the list of sectors in Section 5 of the Protocol.

If the foregoing is acceptable to your Government, I have the honor to propose that this note, together with your reply to that effect shall constitute an agreement between the two Governments amending the Treaty, which shall be subject to ratification.

Accept, Mr. Minister, the renewed assurances of my highest consideration.

Dr. Guido Di Tella,
Minister of Foreign Affairs and Worship,
Buenos Aires.

Department of State Office of Language Services, Translating Division

LS No. 140114   LM   SPA/ENG

Minister of Foreign Relations and Worship
Buenos Aires, November 6, 1992

Mr. Ambassador:

I have the honor to address you with regard to your note dated August 24, 1992, which reads as follows:

[The Spanish translation of Ambassador Todman's note of August 24, 1992, agrees in all substantive respects with the original English text.]

In that regard I wish to state that my Government agrees with the terms of the transcribed note and, therefore, I have the honor to inform you that the aforesaid note and this reply constitute an agreement between our two Governments that will enter into force open the exchange of instruments of ratification.

Accept, Sir, the assurances of my highest consideration.

[Signature]

His Excellency
Terence Todman,
Ambassador of the United States of America,
Buenos Aires, Argentina

North American Free Trade Agreement
(done in San Antonio, 17 December 1992)

PART FIVE
INVESTMENT, SERVICES AND RELATED MATTERS

Chapter Eleven: Investment

Section A – Investment

Article 1101: Scope and Coverage

1. This Chapter applies to measures adopted or maintained by a Party relating to:

  (a) investors of another Party;

  (b) investments of investors of another Party in the territory of the Party; and

  (c) with respect to Articles 1106 and 1114, all investments in the territory of the Party.

2. A Party has the right to perform exclusively the economic activities set out in Annex III and to refuse to permit the establishment of investment in such activities.

3. This Chapter does not apply to measures adopted or maintained by a Party to the extent that they are covered by Chapter Fourteen (Financial Services).

4. Nothing in this Chapter shall be construed to prevent a Party from providing a service or performing a function such as law enforcement, correctional services, income security or insurance, social security or insurance, social welfare, public education, public training, health, and child care, in a manner that is not inconsistent with this Chapter.

Article 1102: National Treatment

1. Each Party shall accord to investors of another Party treatment no less favorable than that it accords, in like circumstances, to its own investors with respect to the establishment, acquisition, expansion, management, conduct, operation, and sale or other disposition of investments.

2. Each Party shall accord to investments of investors of another Party treatment no less favorable than that it accords, in like circumstances, to investments of its own investors with respect to the establishment, acquisition, expansion, management, conduct, operation, and sale or other disposition of investments.

3. The treatment accorded by a Party under paragraphs 1 and 2 means, with respect to a state or province, treatment no less favorable than the most favorable treatment accorded, in like circumstances, by that state or province to investors, and to investments of investors, of the Party of which it forms a part.

4. For greater certainty, no Party may:

   (a) impose on an investor of another Party a requirement that a minimum level of equity in an enterprise in the territory of the Party be held by its nationals, other than nominal qualifying shares for directors or incorporators of corporations; or

   (b) require an investor of another Party, by reason of its nationality, to sell or otherwise dispose of an investment in the territory of the Party.

Article 1103: Most-Favored-Nation Treatment

1. Each Party shall accord to investors of another Party treatment no less favorable than that it accords, in like circumstances, to investors of any other Party or of a

non-Party with respect to the establishment, acquisition, expansion, management, conduct, operation, and sale or other disposition of investments.

2. Each Party shall accord to investments of investors of another Party treatment no less favorable than that it accords, in like circumstances, to investments of investors of any other Party or of a non-Party with respect to the establishment, acquisition, expansion, management, conduct, operation, and sale or other disposition of investments.

Article 1104: Standard of Treatment

Each Party shall accord to investors of another Party and to investments of investors of another Party the better of the treatment required by Articles 1102 and 1103.

Article 1105: Minimum Standard of Treatment

1. Each Party shall accord to investments of investors of another Party treatment in accordance with international law, including fair and equitable treatment and full protection and security.

2. Without prejudice to paragraph 1 and notwithstanding Article 1108(7) (b), each Party shall accord to investors of another Party, and to investments of investors of another Party, non-discriminatory treatment with respect to measures it adopts or maintains relating to losses suffered by investments in its territory owing to armed conflict or civil strife.

3. Paragraph 2 does not apply to existing measures relating to subsidies or grants that would be inconsistent with Article 1102 but for Article 1108(7)(b).

Article 1106: Performance Requirements

1. No Party may impose or enforce any of the following requirements, or enforce any commitment or undertaking, in connection with the establishment, acquisition, expansion, management, conduct or operation of an investment of an investor of a Party or of a non-Party in its territory:

(a) to export a given level or percentage of goods or services;

(b) to achieve a given level or percentage of domestic content;

(c) to purchase, use or accord a preference to goods produced or services provided in its territory, or to purchase goods or services from persons in its territory;

(d) to relate in any way the volume or value of imports to the volume or value of exports or to the amount of foreign exchange inflows associated with such investment;

(e) to restrict sales of goods or services in its territory that such investment produces or provides by relating such sales in any way to the volume or value of its exports or foreign exchange earnings;

(f) to transfer technology, a production process or other proprietary knowledge to a person in its territory, except when the requirement is imposed or the commitment or undertaking is enforced by a court, administrative tribunal or competition authority to remedy an alleged violation of competition laws or to act in a manner not inconsistent with other provisions of this Agreement; or

(g) to act as the exclusive supplier of the goods it produces or services it provides to a specific region or world market.

2. A measure that requires an investment to use a technology to meet generally applicable health, safety or environmental requirements shall not be construed to be inconsistent with paragraph 1(f). For greater certainty, Articles 1102 and 1103 apply to the measure.

3. No Party may condition the receipt or continued receipt of an advantage, in connection with an investment in its territory of an investor of a Party or of a non-Party, on compliance with any of the following requirements:

(a) to achieve a given level or percentage of domestic content;

(b) to purchase, use or accord a preference to goods produced in its territory, or to purchase goods from producers in its territory;

(c) to relate in any way the volume or value of imports to the volume or value of exports or to the amount of foreign exchange inflows associated with such investment; or

(d) to restrict sales of goods or services in its territory that such investment produces or provides by relating such sales in any way to the volume or value of its exports or foreign exchange earnings.

4. Nothing in paragraph 3 shall be construed to prevent a Party from conditioning the receipt or continued receipt of an advantage, in connection with an investment in its territory of an investor of a Party or of a non-Party, on compliance with a requirement to locate production, provide a service, train or employ workers, construct or expand particular facilities, or carry out research and development, in its territory.

5. Paragraphs 1 and 3 do not apply to any requirement other than the requirements set out in those paragraphs.

6. Provided that such measures are not applied in an arbitrary or unjustifiable manner, or do not constitute a disguised restriction on international trade or investment, nothing in paragraph 1(b) or (c) or 3(a) or (b) shall be construed to prevent any Party from adopting or maintaining measures, including environmental measures:

(a) necessary to secure compliance with laws and regulations that are not inconsistent with the provisions of this Agreement;

(b) necessary to protect human, animal or plant life or health; or

(c) necessary for the conservation of living or non-living exhaustible natural resources.

Article 1107: Senior Management and Boards of Directors

1. No Party may require that an enterprise of that Party that is an investment of an investor of another Party appoint to senior management positions individuals of any particular nationality.

2. A Party may require that a majority of the board of directors, or any committee thereof, of an enterprise of that Party that is an investment of an investor of another Party, be of a particular nationality, or resident in the territory of the Party, provided that the requirement does not materially impair the ability of the investor to exercise control over its investment.

Article 1108: Reservations and Exceptions

1. Articles 1102, 1103, 1106 and 1107 do not apply to:
   (a) any existing non-conforming measure that is maintained by
      (i) a Party at the federal level, as set out in its Schedule to Annex I or III,
      (ii) a state or province, for two years after the date of entry into force of this Agreement, and thereafter as set out by a Party in its Schedule to Annex I in accordance with paragraph 2, or
      (iii) a local government;
   (b) the continuation or prompt renewal of any non-conforming measure referred to in subparagraph (a); or
   (c) an amendment to any non-conforming measure referred to in subparagraph (a) to the extent that the amendment does not decrease the conformity of the measure, as it existed immediately before the amendment, with Articles 1102, 1103, 1106 and 1107.

2. Each Party may set out in its Schedule to Annex I, within two years of the date of entry into force of this Agreement, any existing nonconforming measure maintained by a state or province, not including a local government.

3. Articles 1102, 1103, 1106 and 1107 do not apply to any measure that a Party adopts or maintains with respect to sectors, subsectors or activities, as set out in its Schedule to Annex II.

4. No Party may, under any measure adopted after the date of entry into force of this Agreement and covered by its Schedule to Annex II, require an investor

of another Party, by reason of its nationality, to sell or otherwise dispose of an investment existing at the time the measure becomes effective.

5. Articles 1102 and 1103 do not apply to any measure that is an exception to, or derogation from, the obligations under Article 1703 (Intellectual Property National Treatment) as specifically provided for in that Article.

6. Article 1103 does not apply to treatment accorded by a Party pursuant to agreements, or with respect to sectors, set out in its Schedule to Annex IV.

7. Articles 1102, 1103 and 1107 do not apply to:

(a) procurement by a Party or a state enterprise; or

(b) subsidies or grants provided by a Party or a state enterprise, including government supported loans, guarantees and insurance.

8. The provisions of:

(a) Article 1106(1)(a), (b) and (c), and (3)(a) and (b) do not apply to qualification requirements for goods or services with respect to export promotion and foreign aid programs;

(b) Article 1106(1)(b), (c), (f) and (g), and (3)(a) and (b) do not apply to procurement by a Party or a state enterprise; and

(c) Article 1106(3)(a) and (b) do not apply to requirements imposed by an importing Party relating to the content of goods necessary to qualify for preferential tariffs or preferential quotas.

Article 1109: Transfers

1. Each Party shall permit all transfers relating to an investment of an investor of another Party in the territory of the Party to be made freely and without delay. Such transfers include:

(a) profits, dividends, interest, capital gains, royalty payments, management fees, technical assistance and other fees, returns in kind and other amounts derived from the investment;

(b) proceeds from the sale of all or any part of the investment or from the partial or complete liquidation of the investment;

(c) payments made under a contract entered into by the investor, or its investment, including payments made pursuant to a loan agreement;

(d) payments made pursuant to Article 1110; and

(e) payments arising under Section B.

2. Each Party shall permit transfers to be made in a freely usable currency at the market rate of exchange prevailing on the date of transfer with respect to spot transactions in the currency to be transferred.

3. No Party may require its investors to transfer, or penalize its investors that fail to transfer, the income, earnings, profits or other amounts derived from, or attributable to, investments in the territory of another Party.

4. Notwithstanding paragraphs 1 and 2, a Party may prevent a transfer through the equitable, non-discriminatory and good faith application of its laws relating to:

(a) bankruptcy, insolvency or the protection of the rights of creditors;

(b) issuing, trading or dealing in securities;

(c) criminal or penal offenses;

(d) reports of transfers of currency or other monetary instruments; or

(e) ensuring the satisfaction of judgments in adjudicatory proceedings.

5. Paragraph 3 shall not be construed to prevent a Party from imposing any measure through the equitable, non-discriminatory and good faith application of its laws relating to the matters set out in subparagraphs (a) through (e) of paragraph 4.

6. Notwithstanding paragraph 1, a Party may restrict transfers of returns in kind in circumstances where it could otherwise restrict such transfers under this Agreement, including as set out in paragraph 4.

Article 1110: Expropriation and Compensation

1. No Party may directly or indirectly nationalize or expropriate an investment of an investor of another Party in its territory or take a measure tantamount to nationalization or expropriation of such an investment ("expropriation"), except:

(a) for a public purpose;

(b) on a non-discriminatory basis;

(c) in accordance with due process of law and Article 1105(1); and

(d) on payment of compensation in accordance with paragraphs 2 through 6.

2. Compensation shall be equivalent to the fair market value of the expropriated investment immediately before the expropriation took place ("date of expropriation"), and shall not reflect any change in value occurring because the intended expropriation had become known earlier. Valuation criteria shall include going concern value, asset value including declared tax value of tangible property, and other criteria, as appropriate, to determine fair market value.

3. Compensation shall be paid without delay and be fully realizable.

4. If payment is made in a G7 currency, compensation shall include interest at a commercially reasonable rate for that currency from the date of expropriation until the date of actual payment.

5. If a Party elects to pay in a currency other than a G7 currency, the amount paid on the date of payment, if converted into a G7 currency at the market rate of exchange prevailing on that date, shall be no less than if the amount of compensation owed on the date of expropriation had been converted into that G7 currency at the market rate of exchange prevailing on that date, and interest had accrued at a commercially reasonable rate for that G7 currency from the date of expropriation until the date of payment.

6. On payment, compensation shall be freely transferable as provided in Article 1109.

7. This Article does not apply to the issuance of compulsory licenses granted in relation to intellectual property rights, or to the revocation, limitation or creation of intellectual property rights, to the extent that such issuance, revocation, limitation or creation is consistent with Chapter Seventeen (Intellectual Property).

8. For purposes of this Article and for greater certainty, a non-discriminatory measure of general application shall not be considered a measure tantamount to an expropriation of a debt security or loan covered by this Chapter solely on the ground that the measure imposes costs on the debtor that cause it to default on the debt.

Article 1111: Special Formalities and Information Requirements

1. Nothing in Article 1102 shall be construed to prevent a Party from adopting or maintaining a measure that prescribes special formalities in connection with the establishment of investments by investors of another Party, such as a requirement that investors be residents of the Party or that investments be legally constituted under the laws or regulations of the Party, provided that such formalities do not materially impair the protections afforded by a Party to investors of another Party and investments of investors of another Party pursuant to this Chapter.

2. Notwithstanding Articles 1102 or 1103, a Party may require an investor of another Party, or its investment in its territory, to provide routine information concerning that investment solely for informational or statistical purposes. The Party shall protect such business information that is confidential from any disclosure that would prejudice the competitive position of the investor or the investment. Nothing in this paragraph shall be construed to prevent a Party from otherwise obtaining or disclosing information in connection with the equitable and good faith application of its law.

Article 1112: Relation to Other Chapters

1. In the event of any inconsistency between this Chapter and another Chapter, the other Chapter shall prevail to the extent of the inconsistency.

2. A requirement by a Party that a service provider of another Party post a bond or other form of financial security as a condition of providing a service into its territory does not of itself make this Chapter applicable to the provision of that crossborder service. This Chapter applies to that Party's treatment of the posted bond or financial security.

Article 1113: Denial of Benefits

1. A Party may deny the benefits of this Chapter to an investor of another Party that is an enterprise of such Party and to investments of such investor if investors of a non-Party own or control the enterprise and the denying Party:

(a) does not maintain diplomatic relations with the non-Party; or

(b) adopts or maintains measures with respect to the non-Party that prohibit transactions with the enterprise or that would be violated or circumvented if the benefits of this Chapter were accorded to the enterprise or to its investments.

2. Subject to prior notification and consultation in accordance with Articles 1803 (Notification and Provision of Information) and 2006 (Consultations), a Party may deny the benefits of this Chapter to an investor of another Party that is an enterprise of such Party and to investments of such investors if investors of a non-Party own or control the enterprise and the enterprise has no substantial business activities in the territory of the Party under whose law it is constituted or organized.

Article 1114: Environmental Measures

1. Nothing in this Chapter shall be construed to prevent a Party from adopting, maintaining or enforcing any measure otherwise consistent with this Chapter that it considers appropriate to ensure that investment activity in its territory is undertaken in a manner sensitive to environmental concerns.

2. The Parties recognize that it is inappropriate to encourage investment by relaxing domestic health, safety or environmental measures. Accordingly, a Party should not waive or otherwise derogate from, or offer to waive or otherwise derogate

from, such measures as an encouragement for the establishment, acquisition, expansion or retention in its territory of an investment of an investor. If a Party considers that another Party has offered such an encouragement, it may request consultations with the other Party and the two Parties shall consult with a view to avoiding any such encouragement.

Section B – Settlement of Disputes between a Party and an Investor of Another Party

Article 1115: Purpose

Without prejudice to the rights and obligations of the Parties under Chapter Twenty (Institutional Arrangements and Dispute Settlement Procedures), this Section establishes a mechanism for the settlement of investment disputes that assures both equal treatment among investors of the Parties in accordance with the principle of international reciprocity and due process before an impartial tribunal.

Article 1116: Claim by an Investor of a Party on Its Own Behalf

1. An investor of a Party may submit to arbitration under this Section a claim that another Party has breached an obligation under:

   (a) Section A or Article 1503(2) (State Enterprises), or

   (b) Article 1502(3)(a) (Monopolies and State Enterprises) where the monopoly has acted in a manner inconsistent with the Party's obligations under Section A,

and that the investor has incurred loss or damage by reason of, or arising out of, that breach.

2. An investor may not make a claim if more than three years have elapsed from the date on which the investor first acquired, or should have first acquired, knowledge of the alleged breach and knowledge that the investor has incurred loss or damage.

Article 1117: Claim by an Investor of a Party on Behalf of an Enterprise

1. An investor of a Party, on behalf of an enterprise of another Party that is a juridical person that the investor owns or controls directly or indirectly, may submit to arbitration under this Section a claim that the other Party has breached an obligation under:

(a) Section A or Article 1503(2) (State Enterprises), or

(b) Article 1502(3)(a) (Monopolies and State Enterprises) where the monopoly has acted in a manner inconsistent with the Party's obligations under Section A, and that the enterprise has incurred loss or damage by reason of, or arising out of, that breach.

2. An investor may not make a claim on behalf of an enterprise described in paragraph 1 if more than three years have elapsed from the date on which the enterprise first acquired, or should have first acquired, knowledge of the alleged breach and knowledge that the enterprise has incurred loss or damage.

3. Where an investor makes a claim under this Article and the investor or a non-controlling investor in the enterprise makes a claim under Article 1116 arising out of the same events that gave rise to the claim under this Article, and two or more of the claims are submitted to arbitration under Article 1120, the claims should be heard together by a Tribunal established under Article 1126, unless the Tribunal finds that the interests of a disputing party would be prejudiced thereby.

4. An investment may not make a claim under this Section.

Article 1118: Settlement of a Claim through Consultation and Negotiation

The disputing parties should first attempt to settle a claim through consultation or negotiation.

Article 1119: Notice of Intent to Submit a Claim to Arbitration

The disputing investor shall deliver to the disputing Party written notice of its intention to submit a claim to arbitration at least 90 days before the claim is submitted, which notice shall specify:

(a) the name and address of the disputing investor and, where a claim is made under Article 1117, the name and address of the enterprise;

(b) the provisions of this Agreement alleged to have been breached and any other relevant provisions;

(c) the issues and the factual basis for the claim; and

(d) the relief sought and the approximate amount of damages claimed.

Article 1120: Submission of a Claim to Arbitration

1. Except as provided in Annex 1120.1, and provided that six months have elapsed since the events giving rise to a claim, a disputing investor may submit the claim to arbitration under:

(a) the ICSID Convention, provided that both the disputing Party and the Party of the investor are parties to the Convention;

(b) the Additional Facility Rules of ICSID, provided that either the disputing Party or the Party of the investor, but not both, is a party to the ICSID Convention; or

(c) the UNCITRAL Arbitration Rules.

2. The applicable arbitration rules shall govern the arbitration except to the extent modified by this Section.

Article 1121: Conditions Precedent to Submission of a Claim to Arbitration

1. A disputing investor may submit a claim under Article 1116 to arbitration only if:

(a) the investor consents to arbitration in accordance with the procedures set out in this Agreement; and

(b) the investor and, where the claim is for loss or damage to an interest in an enterprise of another Party that is a juridical person that the investor owns or controls directly or indirectly, the enterprise, waive their right to initiate or continue before any administrative tribunal or court under the law of any Party, or other dispute settlement procedures, any proceedings with respect to the measure of the disputing Party that is alleged to be a breach referred to in Article 1116, except for proceedings for injunctive, declaratory or other extraordinary relief, not involving the payment of damages, before an administrative tribunal or court under the law of the disputing Party.

2. A disputing investor may submit a claim under Article 1117 to arbitration only if both the investor and the enterprise:

(a) consent to arbitration in accordance with the procedures set out in this Agreement; and

(b) waive their right to initiate or continue before any administrative tribunal or court under the law of any Party, or other dispute settlement procedures, any proceedings with respect to the measure of the disputing Party that is alleged to be a breach referred to in Article 1117, except for proceedings for injunctive, declaratory or other extraordinary relief, not involving the payment of damages, before an administrative tribunal or court under the law of the disputing Party.

3. A consent and waiver required by this Article shall be in writing, shall be delivered to the disputing Party and shall be included in the submission of a claim to arbitration.

4. Only where a disputing Party has deprived a disputing investor of control of an enterprise:

(a) a waiver from the enterprise under paragraph 1(b) or 2(b) shall not be required; and

(b) Annex 1120.1(b) shall not apply.

Article 1122: Consent to Arbitration

1. Each Party consents to the submission of a claim to arbitration in accordance with the procedures set out in this Agreement.

2. The consent given by paragraph 1 and the submission by a disputing investor of a claim to arbitration shall satisfy the requirement of:

(a) Chapter II of the ICSID Convention (Jurisdiction of the Centre) and the Additional Facility Rules for written consent of the parties;

(b) Article II of the New York Convention for an agreement in writing; and

(c) Article I of the InterAmerican Convention for an agreement.

Article 1123: Number of Arbitrators and Method of Appointment

Except in respect of a Tribunal established under Article 1126, and unless the disputing parties otherwise agree, the Tribunal shall comprise three arbitrators, one arbitrator appointed by each of the disputing parties and the third, who shall be the presiding arbitrator, appointed by agreement of the disputing parties.

Article 1124: Constitution of a Tribunal When a Party Fails to Appoint an Arbitrator or the Disputing Parties Are Unable to Agree on a Presiding Arbitrator

1. The Secretary-General shall serve as appointing authority for an arbitration under this Section.

2. If a Tribunal, other than a Tribunal established under Article 1126, has not been constituted within 90 days from the date that a claim is submitted to arbitration, the Secretary-General, on the request of either disputing party, shall appoint, in his discretion, the arbitrator or arbitrators not yet appointed, except that the presiding arbitrator shall be appointed in accordance with paragraph 3.

3. The Secretary-General shall appoint the presiding arbitrator from the roster of presiding arbitrators referred to in paragraph 4, provided that the presiding arbitrator shall not be a national of the disputing Party or a national of the Party of the disputing investor. In the event that no such presiding arbitrator is available to serve, the Secretary-General shall appoint, from the ICSID Panel of Arbitrators, a presiding arbitrator who is not a national of any of the Parties.

4. On the date of entry into force of this Agreement, the Parties shall establish, and thereafter maintain, a roster of 45 presiding arbitrators meeting the qualifica-

tions of the Convention and rules referred to in Article 1120 and experienced in international law and investment matters. The roster members shall be appointed by consensus and without regard to nationality.

Article 1125: Agreement to Appointment of Arbitrators

For purposes of Article 39 of the ICSID Convention and Article 7 of Schedule C to the ICSID Additional Facility Rules, and without prejudice to an objection to an arbitrator based on Article 1124(3) or on a ground other than nationality:

   (a)   the disputing Party agrees to the appointment of each individual member of a Tribunal established under the ICSID Convention or the ICSID Additional Facility Rules;

   (b)   a disputing investor referred to in Article 1116 may submit a claim to arbitration, or continue a claim, under the ICSID Convention or the ICSID Additional Facility Rules, only on condition that the disputing investor agrees in writing to the appointment of each individual member of the Tribunal; and

   (c)   a disputing investor referred to in Article 1117(1) may submit a claim to arbitration, or continue a claim, under the ICSID Convention or the ICSID Additional Facility Rules, only on condition that the disputing investor and the enterprise agree in writing to the appointment of each individual member of the Tribunal.

Article 1126: Consolidation

1. A Tribunal established under this Article shall be established under the UNCITRAL Arbitration Rules and shall conduct its proceedings in accordance with those Rules, except as modified by this Section.

2. Where a Tribunal established under this Article is satisfied that claims have been submitted to arbitration under Article 1120 that have a question of law or fact in common, the Tribunal may, in the interests of fair and efficient resolution of the claims, and after hearing the disputing parties, by order:

(a) assume jurisdiction over, and hear and determine together, all or part of the claims; or

(b) assume jurisdiction over, and hear and determine one or more of the claims, the determination of which it believes would assist in the resolution of the others.

3. A disputing party that seeks an order under paragraph 2 shall request the Secretary-General to establish a Tribunal and shall specify in the request:

(a) the name of the disputing Party or disputing investors against which the order is sought;

(b) the nature of the order sought; and

(c) the grounds on which the order is sought.

4. The disputing party shall deliver to the disputing Party or disputing investors against which the order is sought a copy of the request.

5. Within 60 days of receipt of the request, the Secretary-General shall establish a Tribunal comprising three arbitrators. The Secretary-General shall appoint the presiding arbitrator from the roster referred to in Article 1124(4). In the event that no such presiding arbitrator is available to serve, the Secretary-General shall appoint, from the ICSID Panel of Arbitrators, a presiding arbitrator who is not a national of any of the Parties. The Secretary-General shall appoint the two other members from the roster referred to in Article 1124(4), and to the extent not available from that roster, from the ICSID Panel of Arbitrators, and to the extent not available from that Panel, in the discretion of the Secretary-General. One member shall be a national of the disputing Party and one member shall be a national of a Party of the disputing investors.

6. Where a Tribunal has been established under this Article, a disputing investor that has submitted a claim to arbitration under Article 1116 or 1117 and that has not been named in a request made under paragraph 3 may make a written request to the Tribunal that it be included in an order made under paragraph 2, and shall specify in the request:

(a) the name and address of the disputing investor;

(b) the nature of the order sought; and

(c) the grounds on which the order is sought.

7. A disputing investor referred to in paragraph 6 shall deliver a copy of its request to the disputing parties named in a request made under paragraph 3.

8. A Tribunal established under Article 1120 shall not have jurisdiction to decide a claim, or a part of a claim, over which a Tribunal established under this Article has assumed jurisdiction.

9. On application of a disputing party, a Tribunal established under this Article, pending its decision under paragraph 2, may order that the proceedings of a Tribunal established under Article 1120 be stayed, unless the latter Tribunal has already adjourned its proceedings.

10. A disputing Party shall deliver to the Secretariat, within 15 days of receipt by the disputing Party, a copy of:

(a) a request for arbitration made under paragraph (1) of Article 36 of the ICSID Convention;

(b) a notice of arbitration made under Article 2 of Schedule C of the ICSID Additional Facility Rules; or

(c) a notice of arbitration given under the UNCITRAL Arbitration Rules.

11. A disputing Party shall deliver to the Secretariat a copy of a request made under paragraph 3:

(a) within 15 days of receipt of the request, in the case of a request made by a disputing investor;

(b) within 15 days of making the request, in the case of a request made by the disputing Party.

12. A disputing Party shall deliver to the Secretariat a copy of a request made under paragraph 6 within 15 days of receipt of the request.

13. The Secretariat shall maintain a public register of the documents referred to in paragraphs 10, 11 and 12.

Article 1127: Notice

A disputing Party shall deliver to the other Parties:
  (a) written notice of a claim that has been submitted to arbitration no later than 30 days after the date that the claim is submitted; and
  (b) copies of all pleadings filed in the arbitration.

Article 1128: Participation by a Party

On written notice to the disputing parties, a Party may make submissions to a Tribunal on a question of interpretation of this Agreement.

Article 1129: Documents

1. A Party shall be entitled to receive from the disputing Party, at the cost of the requesting Party a copy of:
  (a) the evidence that has been tendered to the Tribunal; and
  (b) the written argument of the disputing parties.

2. A Party receiving information pursuant to paragraph 1 shall treat the information as if it were a disputing Party.

Article 1130: Place of Arbitration

Unless the disputing parties agree otherwise, a Tribunal shall hold an arbitration in the territory of a Party that is a party to the New York Convention, selected in accordance with:
  (a) the ICSID Additional Facility Rules if the arbitration is under those Rules or the ICSID Convention; or
  (b) the UNCITRAL Arbitration Rules if the arbitration is under those Rules.

Article 1131: Governing Law

1. A Tribunal established under this Section shall decide the issues in dispute in accordance with this Agreement and applicable rules of international law.

2. An interpretation by the Commission of a provision of this Agreement shall be binding on a Tribunal established under this Section.

Article 1132: Interpretation of Annexes

1. Where a disputing Party asserts as a defense that the measure alleged to be a breach is within the scope of a reservation or exception set out in Annex I, Annex II, Annex III or Annex IV, on request of the disputing Party, the Tribunal shall request the interpretation of the Commission on the issue. The Commission, within 60 days of delivery of the request, shall submit in writing its interpretation to the Tribunal.

2. Further to Article 1131(2), a Commission interpretation submitted under paragraph 1 shall be binding on the Tribunal. If the Commission fails to submit an interpretation within 60 days, the Tribunal shall decide the issue.

Article 1133: Expert Reports

Without prejudice to the appointment of other kinds of experts where authorized by the applicable arbitration rules, a Tribunal, at the request of a disputing party or, unless the disputing parties disapprove, on its own initiative, may appoint one or more experts to report to it in writing on any factual issue concerning environmental, health, safety or other scientific matters raised by a disputing party in a proceeding, subject to such terms and conditions as the disputing parties may agree.

Article 1134: Interim Measures of Protection

A Tribunal may order an interim measure of protection to preserve the rights of a disputing party, or to ensure that the Tribunal's jurisdiction is made fully effective, including an order to preserve evidence in the possession or control of a disputing party or to protect the Tribunal's jurisdiction. A Tribunal may not order attachment or enjoin the application of the measure alleged to constitute a breach referred to in Article 1116 or 1117. For purposes of this paragraph, an order includes a recommendation.

Article 1135: Final Award

1. Where a Tribunal makes a final award against a Party, the Tribunal may award, separately or in combination, only:

(a) monetary damages and any applicable interest;

(b) restitution of property, in which case the award shall provide that the disputing Party may pay monetary damages and any applicable interest in lieu of restitution.

A tribunal may also award costs in accordance with the applicable arbitration rules.

2. Subject to paragraph 1, where a claim is made under Article 1117(1):

(a) an award of restitution of property shall provide that restitution be made to the enterprise;

(b) an award of monetary damages and any applicable interest shall provide that the sum be paid to the enterprise; and

(c) the award shall provide that it is made without prejudice to any right that any person may have in the relief under applicable domestic law.

3. A Tribunal may not order a Party to pay punitive damages.

Article 1136: Finality and Enforcement of an Award

1. An award made by a Tribunal shall have no binding force except between the disputing parties and in respect of the particular case.

2. Subject to paragraph 3 and the applicable review procedure for an interim award, a disputing party shall abide by and comply with an award without delay.

3. A disputing party may not seek enforcement of a final award until:

(a) in the case of a final award made under the ICSID Convention

    (i)   120 days have elapsed from the date the award was rendered and no disputing party has requested revision or annulment of the award, or

    (ii) revision or annulment proceedings have been completed; and

  (b) in the case of a final award under the ICSID Additional Facility Rules or the UNCITRAL Arbitration Rules

    (i)   three months have elapsed from the date the award was rendered and no disputing party has commenced a proceeding to revise, set aside or annul the award, or

    (ii) a court has dismissed or allowed an application to revise, set aside or annul the award and there is no further appeal.

4. Each Party shall provide for the enforcement of an award in its territory.

5. If a disputing Party fails to abide by or comply with a final award, the Commission, on delivery of a request by a Party whose investor was a party to the arbitration, shall establish a panel under Article 2008 (Request for an Arbitral Panel). The requesting Party may seek in such proceedings:

  (a) a determination that the failure to abide by or comply with the final award is inconsistent with the obligations of this Agreement; and

  (b) a recommendation that the Party abide by or comply with the final award.

6. A disputing investor may seek enforcement of an arbitration award under the ICSID Convention, the New York Convention or the InterAmerican Convention regardless of whether proceedings have been taken under paragraph 5.

7. A claim that is submitted to arbitration under this Section shall be considered to arise out of a commercial relationship or transaction for purposes of Article I of the New York Convention and Article I of the InterAmerican Convention.

Article 1137: General

Time when a Claim is Submitted to Arbitration

1. A claim is submitted to arbitration under this Section when:

(a) the request for arbitration under paragraph (1) of Article 36 of the ICSID Convention has been received by the Secretary-General;

(b) the notice of arbitration under Article 2 of Schedule C of the ICSID Additional Facility Rules has been received by the Secretary-General; or

(c) the notice of arbitration given under the UNCITRAL Arbitration Rules is received by the disputing Party.

Service of Documents

2. Delivery of notice and other documents on a Party shall be made to the place named for that Party in Annex 1137.2.

Receipts under Insurance or Guarantee Contracts

3. In an arbitration under this Section, a Party shall not assert, as a defense, counterclaim, right of setoff or otherwise, that the disputing investor has received or will receive, pursuant to an insurance or guarantee contract, indemnification or other compensation for all or part of its alleged damages.

Publication of an Award

4. Annex 1137.4 applies to the Parties specified in that Annex with respect to publication of an award.

Article 1138: Exclusions

1. Without prejudice to the applicability or non-applicability of the dispute settlement provisions of this Section or of Chapter Twenty (Institutional Arrangements and Dispute Settlement Procedures) to other actions taken by a Party pursuant to Article 2102 (National Security), a decision by a Party to prohibit or restrict the acquisition of an investment in its territory by an investor

of another Party, or its investment, pursuant to that Article shall not be subject to such provisions.

2. The dispute settlement provisions of this Section and of Chapter Twenty shall not apply to the matters referred to in Annex 1138.2.

Section C – Definitions

Article 1139: Definitions

For purposes of this Chapter:

disputing investor means an investor that makes a claim under Section B;

disputing parties means the disputing investor and the disputing Party;

disputing party means the disputing investor or the disputing Party;

disputing Party means a Party against which a claim is made under Section B;

enterprise means an "enterprise" as defined in Article 201 (Definitions of General Application), and a branch of an enterprise;

enterprise of a Party means an enterprise constituted or organized under the law of a Party, and a branch located in the territory of a Party and carrying out business activities there.

equity or debt securities includes voting and non-voting shares, bonds, convertible debentures, stock options and warrants;

G7 Currency means the currency of Canada, France, Germany, Italy, Japan, the United Kingdom of Great Britain and Northern Ireland or the United States;

ICSID means the International Centre for Settlement of Investment Disputes;

ICSID Convention means the *Convention on the Settlement of Investment Disputes between States and Nationals of other States,* done at Washington, March 18, 1965;

InterAmerican Convention means the *InterAmerican Convention on International Commercial Arbitration,* done at Panama, January 30, 1975;

investment means:

(a) an enterprise;

(b) an equity security of an enterprise;

(c) a debt security of an enterprise

    (i) where the enterprise is an affiliate of the investor, or

    (ii) where the original maturity of the debt security is at least three years,

    but does not include a debt security, regardless of original maturity, of a state enterprise;

(d) a loan to an enterprise

    (i) where the enterprise is an affiliate of the investor, or

    (ii) where the original maturity of the loan is at least three years,

    but does not include a loan, regardless of original maturity, to a state enterprise;

(e) an interest in an enterprise that entitles the owner to share in income or profits of the enterprise;

(f) an interest in an enterprise that entitles the owner to share in the assets of that enterprise on dissolution, other than a debt security or a loan excluded from subparagraph (c) or (d);

(g) real estate or other property, tangible or intangible, acquired in the expectation or used for the purpose of economic benefit or other business purposes; and

(h) interests arising from the commitment of capital or other resources in the territory of a Party to economic activity in such territory, such as under

    (i) contracts involving the presence of an investor's property in the territory of the Party, including turnkey or construction contracts, or concessions, or

(ii) contracts where remuneration depends substantially on the production, revenues or profits of an enterprise;

but investment does not mean,

(i) claims to money that arise solely from

(i) commercial contracts for the sale of goods or services by a national or enterprise in the territory of a Party to an enterprise in the territory of another Party, or

(ii) the extension of credit in connection with a commercial transaction, such as trade financing, other than a loan covered by subparagraph (d); or

(j) any other claims to money,

that do not involve the kinds of interests set out in subparagraphs (a) through (h);

investment of an investor of a Party means an investment owned or controlled directly or indirectly by an investor of such Party;

investor of a Party means a Party or state enterprise thereof, or a national or an enterprise of such Party, that seeks to make, is making or has made an investment;

investor of a non-Party means an investor other than an investor of a Party, that seeks to make, is making or has made an investment;

New York Convention means the *United Nations Convention on the Recognition and Enforcement of Foreign Arbitral Awards*, done at New York, June 10, 1958;

Secretary-General means the Secretary-General of ICSID;

transfers means transfers and international payments;

Tribunal means an arbitration tribunal established under Article 1120 or 1126; and

UNCITRAL Arbitration Rules means the arbitration rules of the United Nations Commission on International Trade Law, approved by the United Nations General Assembly on December 15, 1976.

Annex 1120.1: Submission of a Claim to Arbitration

Mexico

With respect to the submission of a claim to arbitration:

(a) an investor of another Party may not allege that Mexico has breached an obligation under:

   (i) Section A or Article 1503(2) (State Enterprises), or

   (ii) Article 1502(3)(a) (Monopolies and State Enterprises) where the monopoly has acted in a manner inconsistent with the Party's obligations under Section A,

   both in an arbitration under this Section and in proceedings before a Mexican court or administrative tribunal; and

(b) where an enterprise of Mexico that is a juridical person that an investor of another Party owns or controls directly or indirectly alleges in proceedings before a Mexican court or administrative tribunal that Mexico has breached an obligation under:

   (i) Section A or Article 1503(2) (State Enterprises), or

   (ii) Article 1502(3)(a) (Monopolies and State Enterprises) where the monopoly has acted in a manner inconsistent with the Party's obligations under Section A,

   the investor may not allege the breach in an arbitration under this Section.

Annex 1137.2: Service of Documents on a Party Under Section B

Each Party shall set out in this Annex and publish in its official journal by January 1, 1994, the place for delivery of notice and other documents under this Section.

Annex 1137.4: Publication of an Award

Canada

Where Canada is the disputing Party, either Canada or a disputing investor that is a party to the arbitration may make an award public.

Mexico

Where Mexico is the disputing Party, the applicable arbitration rules apply to the publication of an award.

United States

Where the United States is the disputing Party, either the United States or a disputing investor that is a party to the arbitration may make an award public.

Annex 1138.2: Exclusions from Dispute Settlement

Canada

A decision by Canada following a review under the *Investment Canada Act*, with respect to whether or not to permit an acquisition that is subject to review, shall not be subject to the dispute settlement provisions of Section B or of Chapter Twenty (Institutional Arrangements and Dispute Settlement Procedures).

Mexico

A decision by the National Commission on Foreign Investment ("Comisión Nacional de Inversiones Extranjeras") following a review pursuant to Annex I, page IM4, with respect to whether or not to permit an acquisition that is subject to review, shall not be subject to the dispute settlement provisions of Section B or of Chapter Twenty (Institutional Arrangements and Dispute Settlement Procedures).

Annex 8

Energy Charter Treaty

(as opened for signature in Lisbon, 17 December 1994)

Part III. Investment Promotion and Protection

Article 10
Promotion, Protection and Treatment of Investments[1]

(1) Each Contracting Party shall, in accordance with the provisions of this Treaty, encourage and create stable, equitable, favourable and transparent conditions for Investors of other Contracting Parties to make Investments in its Area. Such conditions shall include a commitment to accord at all times to Investments of Investors of other Contracting Parties fair and equitable treatment. Such Investments shall also enjoy the most constant protection and security and no Contracting Party shall in any way impair by unreasonable or discriminatory measures their management, maintenance, use, enjoyment or disposal. In no case shall such Investments be accorded treatment less favourable than that required by international law, including treaty obligations.[2]

---

1 See Final Act of the European Energy Charter Conference, Understandings, n. 9. with respect to Articles 9, 10 and Part V, p. 27 and Declarations, n. 4. with respect to Article 10, p. 31.
2 See Final Act of the European Energy Charter Conference, Understandings, n. 17. with respect to Articles 26 and 27, p. 28 and Chairman's Statement at Adoption Session on 17 December 1994, p. 157.

Each Contracting Party shall observe any obligations it has entered into with an Investor or an Investment of an Investor of any other Contracting Party.[3]

(2) Each Contracting Party shall endeavour to accord to Investors of other Contracting Parties, as regards the Making of Investments in its Area, the Treatment described in paragraph (3).

(3) For the purposes of this Article, "Treatment" means treatment accorded by a Contracting Party which is no less favourable than that which it accords to its own Investors or to Investors of any other Contracting Party or any third state, whichever is the most favourable.

(4) A supplementary treaty shall, subject to conditions to be laid down therein, oblige each party thereto to accord to Investors of other parties, as regards the Making of Investments in its Area, the Treatment described in paragraph (3).

That treaty shall be open for signature by the states and Regional Economic Integration Organizations which have signed or acceded to this Treaty.

Negotiations towards the supplementary treaty shall commence not later than 1 January 1995, with a view to concluding it by 1 January 1998.[4]

(5)   Each Contracting Party shall, as regards the Making of Investments in its Area, endeavour to:

(a) limit to the minimum the exceptions to the Treatment described in paragraph (3);

(b) progressively remove existing restrictions affecting Investors of other Contracting Parties.

(6)(a) A Contracting Party may, as regards the Making of Investments in its Area, at any time declare voluntarily to the Charter Conference, through the

---

3   See Article 26(3)(c), p. 73; Article 27(2), p. 75 and Annex IA, p. 98.
4   See Final Act of the European Energy Charter Conference, Understandings, n. 10. with respect to Article 10(4), p. 27; n. 11 with respect to Articles 10(4) and 29(6), p. 28; Final Act of the European Energy Charter Conference, Declarations, n. 1. with respect to Article 1(6), p. 30 and Chairman's Statement at Adoption Session on 17 December 1994, p. 157.

Secretariat, its intention not to introduce new exceptions to the Treatment described in paragraph (3).

(b) A Contracting Party may, furthermore, at any time make a voluntary commitment to accord to Investors of other Contracting Parties, as regards the Making of Investments in some or all Economic Activities in the Energy Sector in its Area, the Treatment described in paragraph (3). Such commitments shall be notified to the Secretariat and listed in Annex VC and shall be binding under this Treaty.

(7) Each Contracting Party shall accord to Investments in its Area of Investors of other Contracting Parties, and their related activities including management, maintenance, use, enjoyment or disposal, treatment no less favourable than that which it accords to investments of its own Investors or of the Investors of any other Contracting Party or any third state and their related activities including management, maintenance, use, enjoyment or disposal, whichever is the most favourable.[5]

(8) The modalities of application of paragraph (7) in relation to programmes under which a Contracting Party provides grants or other financial assistance, or enters into contracts, for energy technology research and development, shall be reserved for the supplementary treaty described in paragraph (4). Each Contracting Party shall through the Secretariat keep the Charter Conference informed of the modalities it applies to the programmes described in this paragraph.

(9) Each state or Regional Economic Integration Organization which signs or accedes to this Treaty shall, on the date it signs the Treaty or deposits its instrument of accession, submit to the Secretariat a report summarizing all laws, regulations or other measures relevant to:

(a) exceptions to paragraph (2); or

(b) the programmes referred to in paragraph (8).

---

5   See Decisions with respect to the Energy Charter Treaty (Annex 2 to the Final Act of the European Energy Charter Conference), n. 2. with respect to Article 10(7), p. 135; Article 32(1), p. 79 and Annex T pp. 113 and 126.

A Contracting Party shall keep its report up to date by promptly submitting amendments to the Secretariat. The Charter Conference shall review these reports periodically.

In respect of subparagraph (a) the report may designate parts of the energy sector in which a Contracting Party accords to Investors of other Contracting Parties the Treatment described in paragraph (3).

In respect of subparagraph (b) the review by the Charter Conference may consider the effects of such programmes on competition and Investments.

(10) Notwithstanding any other provision of this Article, the treatment described in paragraphs (3) and (7) shall not apply to the protection of Intellectual Property; instead, the treatment shall be as specified in the corresponding provisions of the applicable international agreements for the protection of Intellectual Property rights to which the respective Contracting Parties are parties.

(11) For the purposes of Article 26, the application by a Contracting Party of a trade-related investment measure as described in Article 5(1) and (2) to an Investment of an Investor of another Contracting Party existing at the time of such application shall, subject to Article 5(3) and (4), be considered a breach of an obligation of the former Contracting Party under this Part.[6]

(12) Each Contracting Party shall ensure that its domestic law provides effective means for the assertion of claims and the enforcement of rights with respect to Investments, investment agreements, and investment authorizations.

Article 11
Key Personnel

(1) A Contracting Party shall, subject to its laws and regulations relating to the entry, stay and work of natural persons, examine in good faith requests by Investors of another Contracting Party, and key personnel who are employed by such Investors or by Investments of such Investors, to enter and remain temporarily in its Area to engage in activities connected with the making or the development,

---

6   See Final Act of the European Energy Charter Conference, Declarations, n. 2. with respect to Articles 5 and 10(11), p. 30.

management, maintenance, use, enjoyment or disposal of relevant Investments, including the provision of advice or key technical services.

(2) A Contracting Party shall permit Investors of another Contracting Party which have Investments in its Area, and Investments of such Investors, to employ any key person of the Investor's or the Investment's choice regardless of nationality and citizenship provided that such key person has been permitted to enter, stay and work in the Area of the former Contracting Party and that the employment concerned conforms to the terms, conditions and time limits of the permission granted to such key person.

Article 12
Compensation for Losses

(1) Except where Article 13 applies, an Investor of any Contracting Party which suffers a loss with respect to any Investment in the Area of another Contracting Party owing to war or other armed conflict, state of national emergency, civil disturbance, or other similar event in that Area, shall be accorded by the latter Contracting Party, as regards restitution, indemnification, compensation or other settlement, treatment which is the most favourable of that which that Contracting Party accords to any other Investor, whether its own Investor, the Investor of any other Contracting Party, or the Investor of any third state.

(2) Without prejudice to paragraph (1), an Investor of a Contracting Party which, in any of the situations referred to in that paragraph, suffers a loss in the Area of another Contracting Party resulting from

(a) requisitioning of its Investment or part thereof by the latter's forces or authorities; or

(b) destruction of its Investment or part thereof by the latter's forces or authorities, which was not required by the necessity of the situation, shall be accorded restitution or compensation which in either case shall be prompt, adequate and effective.

Article 13
Expropriation

(1) Investments of Investors of a Contracting Party in the Area of any other Contracting Party shall not be nationalized, expropriated or subjected to a measure or measures having effect equivalent to nationalization or expropriation (hereinafter referred to as "Expropriation") except where such Expropriation is:

(a) for a purpose which is in the public interest;

(b) not discriminatory;

(c) carried out under due process of law; and

(d) accompanied by the payment of prompt, adequate and effective compensation.

Such compensation shall amount to the fair market value of the Investment expropriated at the time immediately before the Expropriation or impending Expropriation became known in such a way as to affect the value of the Investment (hereinafter referred to as the "Valuation Date").

Such fair market value shall at the request of the Investor be expressed in a Freely Convertible Currency on the basis of the market rate of exchange existing for that currency on the Valuation Date. Compensation shall also include interest at a commercial rate established on a market basis from the date of Expropriation until the date of payment.

(2) The Investor affected shall have a right to prompt review, under the law of the Contracting Party making the Expropriation, by a judicial or other competent and independent authority of that Contracting Party, of its case, of the valuation of its Investment, and of the payment of compensation, in accordance with the principles set out in paragraph (1).

(3) For the avoidance of doubt, Expropriation shall include situations where a Contracting Party expropriates the assets of a company or enterprise in its Area in which an Investor of any other Contracting Party has an Investment, including through the ownership of shares.

Article 14
Transfers Related to Investments[7]

(1) Each Contracting Party shall with respect to Investments in its Area of Investors of any other Contracting Party guarantee the freedom of transfer into and out of its Area, including the transfer of:

  (a) the initial capital plus any additional capital for the maintenance and development of an Investment;

  (b) Returns;

  (c) payments under a contract, including amortization of principal and accrued interest payments pursuant to a loan agreement;

  (d) unspent earnings[8] and other remuneration of personnel engaged from abroad in connection with that Investment;

  (e) proceeds from the sale or liquidation of all or any part of an Investment;

  (f) payments arising out of the settlement of a dispute;

  (g) payments of compensation pursuant to Articles 12 and 13.

(2) Transfers under paragraph (1) shall be effected without delay and (except in case of a Return in kind) in a Freely Convertible Currency.[9]

(3) Transfers shall be made at the market rate of exchange existing on the date of transfer with respect to spot transactions in the currency to be transferred. In the absence of a market for foreign exchange, the rate to be used will be the most recent rate applied to inward investments or the most recent exchange rate for conversion of currencies into Special Drawing Rights, whichever is more favourable to the Investor.

---

7   See Decisions with respect to the Energy Charter Treaty (Annex 2 to the Final Act of the European Energy Charter Conference), n. 3. with respect to Article 14, p. 135.

8   See Article 32(1), p. 79 and Annex T, pp. 113 and 127.

9   See Decisions with respect to the Energy Charter Treaty (Annex 2 to the Final Act of the European Energy Charter Conference), n. 4. with respect to Article 14 (2), p. 136.

(4) Notwithstanding paragraphs (1) to (3), a Contracting Party may protect the rights of creditors, or ensure compliance with laws on the issuing, trading and dealing in securities and the satisfaction of judgements in civil, administrative and criminal adjudicatory proceedings, through the equitable, nondiscriminatory, and good faith application of its laws and regulations.

(5) Notwithstanding paragraph (2), Contracting Parties which are states that were constituent parts of the former Union of Soviet Socialist Republics may provide in agreements concluded between them that transfers of payments shall be made in the currencies of such Contracting Parties, provided that such agreements do not treat Investments in their Areas of Investors of other Contracting Parties less favourably than either Investments of Investors of the Contracting Parties which have entered into such agreements or Investments of Investors of any third state.[10]

(6) Notwithstanding subparagraph (1)(b), a Contracting Party may restrict the transfer of a Return in kind in circumstances where the Contracting Party is permitted under Article 29(2)(a) or the GATT and Related Instruments to restrict or prohibit the exportation or the sale for export of the product constituting the Return in kind; provided that a Contracting Party shall permit transfers of Returns in kind to be effected as authorized or specified in an investment agreement, investment authorization, or other written agreement between the Contracting Party and either an Investor of another Contracting Party or its Investment.

Article 15
Subrogation

(1) If a Contracting Party or its designated agency (hereinafter referred to as the "Indemnifying Party") makes a payment under an indemnity or guarantee given in respect of an Investment of an Investor (hereinafter referred to as the "Party Indemnified") in the Area of another Contracting Party (hereinafter referred to as the "Host Party"), the Host Party shall recognize:

---

10 See Final Act of the European Energy Charter Conference, Understandings, n. 12. with respect to Article 14(5), p. 28.

(a) the assignment to the Indemnifying Party of all the rights and claims in respect of such Investment; and

(b) the right of the Indemnifying Party to exercise all such rights and enforce such claims by virtue of subrogation.

(2) The Indemnifying Party shall be entitled in all circumstances to:

(a) the same treatment in respect of the rights and claims acquired by it by virtue of the assignment referred to in paragraph (1); and

(b) the same payments due pursuant to those rights and claims,

as the Party Indemnified was entitled to receive by virtue of this Treaty in respect of the Investment concerned.

(3) In any proceeding under Article 26, a Contracting Party shall not assert as a defence, counterclaim, right of set-off or for any other reason, that indemnification or other compensation for all or part of the alleged damages has been received or will be received pursuant to an insurance or guarantee contract.

Article 16
Relation to Other Agreements[11]

Where two or more Contracting Parties have entered into a prior international agreement, or enter into a subsequent international agreement, whose terms in either case concern the subject matter of Part III or V of this Treaty,

(1) nothing in Part III or V of this Treaty shall be construed to derogate from any provision of such terms of the other agreement or from any right to dispute resolution with respect thereto under that agreement; and

(2) nothing in such terms of the other agreement shall be construed to derogate from any provision of Part III or V of this Treaty or from any right to dispute resolution with respect thereto under this Treaty, where any such provision is more favourable to the Investor or Investment.

---

11 See Decisions with respect to the Energy Charter Treaty (Annex 2 to the Final Act of the European Energy Charter Conference), n. 1. with respect to the Treaty as a whole, p. 135 and n. 3. with respect to Article 14, p. 135.

Article 17
Non-Application of Part III in Certain Circumstances

Each Contracting Party reserves the right to deny the advantages of this Part to:

(1) a legal entity if citizens or nationals of a third state own or control such entity and if that entity has no substantial business activities in the Area of the Contracting Party in which it is organized; or

(2) an Investment, if the denying Contracting Party establishes that such Investment is an Investment of an Investor of a third state with or as to which the denying Contracting Party:

(a) does not maintain a diplomatic relationship; or

(b) adopts or maintains measures that:

(i) prohibit transactions with Investors of that state; or

(ii) would be violated or circumvented if the benefits of this Part were accorded to Investors of that state or to their Investments.

Part V. Dispute Settlement[12]

Article 26
Settlement of Disputes between an Investor and a Contracting Party[13]

(1) Disputes between a Contracting Party and an Investor of another Contracting Party relating to an Investment of the latter in the Area of the former, which concern an alleged breach of an obligation of the former under Part III shall, if possible, be settled amicably.

---

12   See Decisions with respect to the Energy Charter Treaty (Annex 2 to the Final Act of the European Energy Charter Conference), n. 1. with respect to the Treaty as a whole, p. 135 and Final Act of the European Energy Charter Conference, Understandings, n. 9. with respect to Articles 9, 10 and Part V, p. 27.

13   See Final Act of the European Energy Charter Conference, Understandings, n. 17. with respect to Articles 26 and 27, p. 28.

(2) If such disputes can not be settled according to the provisions of paragraph (1) within a period of three months from the date on which either party to the dispute requested amicable settlement, the Investor party to the dispute may choose to submit it for resolution:

(a) to the courts or administrative tribunals of the Contracting Party party to the dispute;[14]

(b) in accordance with any applicable, previously agreed dispute settlement procedure; or

(c) in accordance with the following paragraphs of this Article.

(3)(a) Subject only to subparagraphs (b) and (c), each Contracting Party hereby gives its unconditional consent to the submission of a dispute to international arbitration or conciliation in accordance with the provisions of this Article.

(b) (i) The Contracting Parties listed in Annex ID do not give such unconditional consent where the Investor has previously submitted the dispute under subparagraph (2)(a) or (b).

(ii) For the sake of transparency, each Contracting Party that is listed in Annex ID shall provide a written statement of its policies, practices and conditions in this regard to the Secretariat no later than the date of the deposit of its instrument of ratification, acceptance or approval in accordance with Article 39 or the deposit of its instrument of accession in accordance with Article 41.

(c) A Contracting Party listed in Annex IA does not give such unconditional consent with respect to a dispute arising under the last sentence of Article 10(1).

---

14 See Final Act of the European Energy Charter Conference, Understandings, n. 16. with respect to Article 26(2)(a), p. 28.

(4) In the event that an Investor chooses to submit the dispute for resolution under subparagraph (2)(c), the Investor shall further provide its consent in writing for the dispute to be submitted to:

(a) (i) The International Centre for Settlement of Investment Disputes, established pursuant to the Convention on the Settlement of Investment Disputes between States and Nationals of other States opened for signature at Washington, 18 March 1965 (hereinafter referred to as the "ICSID Convention"), if the Contracting Party of the Investor and the Contracting Party party to the dispute are both parties to the ICSID Convention; or

(ii) The International Centre for Settlement of Investment Disputes, established pursuant to the Convention referred to in subparagraph (a)(i), under the rules governing the Additional Facility for the Administration of Proceedings by the Secretariat of the Centre (hereinafter referred to as the "Additional Facility Rules"), if the Contracting Party of the Investor or the Contracting Party party to the dispute, but not both, is a party to the ICSID Convention;

(b) a sole arbitrator or ad hoc arbitration tribunal established under the Arbitration Rules of the United Nations Commission on International Trade Law (hereinafter referred to as "UNCITRAL"); or

(c) an arbitral proceeding under the Arbitration Institute of the Stockholm Chamber of Commerce.

(5)(a) The consent given in paragraph (3) together with the written consent of the Investor given pursuant to paragraph (4) shall be considered to satisfy the requirement for:

(i) written consent of the parties to a dispute for purposes of Chapter II of the ICSID Convention and for purposes of the Additional Facility Rules;

(ii) an "agreement in writing" for purposes of article II of the United Nations Convention on the Recognition and Enforcement of Foreign

Arbitral Awards, done at New York, 10 June 1958 (hereinafter referred to as the "New York Convention"); and

(iii) "the parties to a contract [to] have agreed in writing" for the purposes of article 1 of the UNCITRAL Arbitration Rules.

(b) Any arbitration under this Article shall at the request of any party to the dispute be held in a state that is a party to the New York Convention.

Claims submitted to arbitration hereunder shall be considered to arise out of a commercial relationship or transaction for the purposes of article I of that Convention.

(6) A tribunal established under paragraph (4) shall decide the issues in dispute in accordance with this Treaty and applicable rules and principles of international law.

(7) An Investor other than a natural person which has the nationality of a Contracting Party party to the dispute on the date of the consent in writing referred to in paragraph (4) and which, before a dispute between it and that Contracting Party arises, is controlled by Investors of another Contracting Party, shall for the purpose of article 25(2)(b) of the ICSID Convention be treated as a "national of another Contracting State" and shall for the purpose of article 1(6) of the Additional Facility Rules be treated as a "national of another State".

(8) The awards of arbitration, which may include an award of interest, shall be final and binding upon the parties to the dispute. An award of arbitration concerning a measure of a sub-national government or authority of the disputing Contracting Party shall provide that the Contracting Party may pay monetary damages in lieu of any other remedy granted. Each Contracting Party shall carry out without delay any such award and shall make provision for the effective enforcement in its Area of such awards.

Article 27
Settlement of Disputes between Contracting Parties[15]

(1) Contracting Parties shall endeavour to settle disputes concerning the application or interpretation of this Treaty through diplomatic channels.

(2) If a dispute has not been settled in accordance with paragraph (1) within a reasonable period of time, either party thereto may, except as otherwise provided in this Treaty or agreed in writing by the Contracting Parties, and except as concerns the application or interpretation of Article 6 or Article 19 or, for Contracting Parties listed in Annex IA, the last sentence of Article 10(1), upon written notice to the other party to the dispute submit the matter to an ad hoc tribunal under this Article.

(3) Such an ad hoc arbitral tribunal shall be constituted as follows:

(a) The Contracting Party instituting the proceedings shall appoint one member of the tribunal and inform the other Contracting Party to the dispute of its appointment within 30 days of receipt of the notice referred to in paragraph (2) by the other Contracting Party;

(b) Within 60 days of the receipt of the written notice referred to in paragraph (2), the other Contracting Party party to the dispute shall appoint one member. If the appointment is not made within the time limit prescribed, the Contracting Party having instituted the proceedings may, within 90 days of the receipt of the written notice referred to in paragraph (2), request that the appointment be made in accordance with subparagraph (d);

(c) A third member, who may not be a national or citizen of a Contracting Party party to the dispute, shall be appointed by the Contracting Parties parties to the dispute. That member shall be the President of the tribunal. If, within 150 days of the receipt of the notice referred to in paragraph (2), the Contracting Parties are unable to agree on the appointment of

---

15 See Final Act of the European Energy Charter Conference, Understandings, n. 17, with respect to Articles 26 and 27, p. 28 and Article 28, p. 76.

a third member, that appointment shall be made, in accordance with subparagraph (d), at the request of either Contracting Party submitted within 180 days of the receipt of that notice;

(d) Appointments requested to be made in accordance with this paragraph shall be made by the Secretary-General of the Permanent Court of International Arbitration within 30 days of the receipt of a request to do so. If the Secretary-General is prevented from discharging this task, the appointments shall be made by the First Secretary of the Bureau. If the latter, in turn, is prevented from discharging this task, the appointments shall be made by the most senior Deputy;

(e) Appointments made in accordance with subparagraphs (a) to (d) shall be made with regard to the qualifications and experience, particularly in matters covered by this Treaty, of the members to be appointed;

(f) In the absence of an agreement to the contrary between the Contracting Parties, the Arbitration Rules of UNCITRAL shall govern, except to the extent modified by the Contracting Parties parties to the dispute or by the arbitrators. The tribunal shall take its decisions by a majority vote of its members;

(g) The tribunal shall decide the dispute in accordance with this Treaty and applicable rules and principles of international law;

(h) The arbitral award shall be final and binding upon the Contracting Parties parties to the dispute;

(i) Where, in making an award, a tribunal finds that a measure of a regional or local government or authority within the Area of a Contracting Party listed in Part I of Annex P is not in conformity with this Treaty, either party to the dispute may invoke the provisions of Part II of Annex P;

(j) The expenses of the tribunal, including the remuneration of its members, shall be borne in equal shares by the Contracting Parties parties to the dispute. The tribunal may, however, at its discretion direct that a higher proportion of the costs be paid by one of the Contracting Parties parties to the dispute;

(k) Unless the Contracting Parties parties to the dispute agree otherwise, the tribunal shall sit in The Hague, and use the premises and facilities of the Permanent Court of Arbitration;

(l) A copy of the award shall be deposited with the Secretariat which shall make it generally available.

Article 28
Non-Application of Article 27 to Certain Disputes

A dispute between Contracting Parties with respect to the application or interpretation of Article 5 or 29 shall not be settled under Article 27 unless the Contracting Parties parties to the dispute so agree.

Annex 9

Selected bibliography

Books

Bishop, D., J. Crawford & M. Reisman. *Foreign Investment Disputes: Cases, Materials and Commentary.* The Netherlands: Kluwer Law International, 2005.

Blackaby, N., et al. *Redfern and Hunter on International Arbitration.* Oxford: Oxford University Press, 2009.

Cameron, P. *International Energy Investment Law: The Pursuit of Stability.* Oxford: Oxford University Press, 2010.

Dolzer, R. & M. Stevens. *Bilateral Investment Treaties.* Leiden: Martinus Nijhoff Publishers, 1995.

Dolzer, R. & C. Schreuer. *Principles of International Investment Law.* Oxford: Oxford University Press, 2008.

Douglas, Z. *The International Law of Investment Claims.* Oxford: Oxford University Press, 2009.

Hobér, K. *Investment Arbitration in Eastern Europe: In Search of a Definition of Expropriation.* New York: Juris Publishing, 2007.

Kinnear M., A. Bjorklund & J. Hannaford. *Investment Disputes Under NAFTA: An Annotated Guide to NAFTA Chapter 11.* The Netherlands: Kluwer Law International, 2006.

McLachlan, C., L. Shore & M. Weiniger. *International Investment Arbitration: Substantive Principles.* Oxford: Oxford University Press, 2007.

Newcombe, A. & L. Paradell. *Law and Practice of Investment Treaties: Standards of Treatment.* The Netherlands: Kluwer Law International, 2009.

Paulsson, J., N. Rawding & L. Reed. *The Freshfields Guide to Arbitration Clauses in International Contracts,* 3d. ed. The Netherlands: Kluwer Law International, 2010.

Rubins, N. & S. Kinsella. *International Investment, Political Risk and Dispute Resolution.* New York: Oxford University Press, 2005.

Schreuer, C., et al. *The ICSID Convention: A Commentary,* 2d ed. Cambridge: Cambridge University Press, 2009.

Vandevelde, K. *Bilateral Investment Treaties.* New York: Oxford University Press, 2010.

Waibel, M., et al. (eds). *The Backlash against Investment Arbitration: Perceptions and Reality.* The Netherlands: Kluwer Law International, 2010.

Articles

Antonietti, A. 'The 2006 Amendments of the ICSID Rules and Regulations and the Additional Facility Rules', *ICSID Review – FILJ* 21 (2006): 427.

Broches, A. 'The Convention on the Settlement of Investment Disputes between States and Nationals of Other States', *Recueil des Cours* 136 (1972-II): 331.

Craig, W.L. 'The Final Chapter in the Pyramids Case: Discounting an ICSID Award for Annulment Risk', *ICSID Review – FILJ* 8 (1993): 264.

Crawford, J. 'Treaty and Contract in Investment Arbitration', *Arbitration International* 24 (2008): 351.

Delaume, G. 'ICSID Arbitration: Practical Considerations', *Journal of International Arbitration* 1 (1984): 101.

Fortier, Y. & S. Drymer. 'Indirect Expropriation in the Law of International Investment: I Know it When I See It, or Caveat Investor', *ICSID Review – FILJ* 19 (2004): 293.

Friedland, P. 'Provisional Measures in ICSID Arbitration', *Arbitration International* 2 (1986): 335.

Hobér, K. 'Investment Arbitration and the Energy Charter Treaty', *Journal of International Dispute Settlement* 1 (2010): 153.

Kaufmann-Kohler, G., et al. 'Consolidation of Proceedings in Investment Arbitration: How Can Multiple Proceedings from the Same or Related Situations Be Handled Effectively?', *ICSID Review – FILJ* 21 (2006): 59.

Lalive, P. 'The First 'World Bank' Arbitration (*Holiday Inns v Morocco*) – Some Legal Problems', *British Year Book of International Law* 51 (1980): 123.

Legum, B. 'Defining Investment and Investor: Who is Entitled to Claim', *Arbitration International* 22 (2006): 521.

Mann, F.A. 'British Treaties for the Promotion and Protection of Investments', *British Yearbook of International Law* 52 (1981): 241.

Parra, A. 'The Role of the ICSID Secretariat in the Administration of Arbitration Proceedings Under the ICSID Convention', *ICSID Review – FILJ* 13 (1998): 85.

Paulsson, J. 'Arbitration Without Privity', *ICSID Review – FILJ* 10 (1995): 232.

Price, D. 'An Overview of the NAFTA Investment Chapter: Substantive Rules and Investor-State Dispute Settlement', *International Lawyer* 27 (1993): 727.

Reisman, W.M. 'The Breakdown of the Control Mechanism in ICSID Arbitration', *Duke Law Journal* 4 (1989): 739.

Shihata, I. 'Toward a Greater Depoliticization of Investment Disputes: The Roles of ICSID and MIGA', *ICSID Review – FILJ* 1 (1986): 4.

Szasz, P. 'A Practical Guide to the Convention on the Settlement of Investment Disputes', *Cornell International Law Journal* 1 (1968): 20.

van den Berg, A.J. 'Some Recent Problems in the Practice and Enforcement under the New York and ICSID Conventions', *ICSID Review – FILJ* 2 (1987): 439.

Vasciannie, S. 'The Fair and Equitable Treatment Standard in International Investment Law and Practice', *British Yearbook of International Law* 70 (1999): 99.

Verhoosel, G. 'Annulment and Enforcement Review of Treaty Awards: To ICSID Or Not To ICSID', *ICSID Review – FILJ* 23 (2008): 119.

Ziadé, N.G. 'ICSID Conciliation', *News from ICSID* 13-2 (1996): 3.

Websites

<icsid.worldbank.org>

<ita.law.uvic.ca/>

<www.unctad.org>

<www.kluwerarbitration.com>

<www.investmentclaims.com>

<www.iareporter.com>

<www.globalarbitrationreview.com>

<www.transnational-dispute-management.com>

Annex 10

Tables of ICSID awards and decisions on
substantive, procedural and other issues
(current through January 2010, unless otherwise stated)

I. Overview of Substantive Issues – Summary of Standards of Treatment in Decided ICSID Investment Treaty Cases

Case	Date of Award ("*" denotes annulment proceeding)	Standards of Protection ("√" – denotes breach found; "X" – denotes breach not found; "N" – denotes that claim was advanced but not considered; "W" – denotes that claim was advanced and withdrawn)						
		Fair and Equitable Treatment	Full Protection and Security	No Arbitrary or Discriminatory Measures Impairing the Investment	National/ MFN Treatment	Free Transfer of Funds Related to Investments	No Expropriation without Compensation	Observance of Specific Undertakings
Asian Agricultural Products Ltd. (AAPL) v. Democratic Socialist Republic of Sri Lanka, ICSID Case No. ARB/87/3	27 June 1990 (Award)		√		X (MFN)			
American Manufacturing & Trading Inc. v. Republic of Zaire, ICSID Case No. ARB/93/1	21 February 1997 (Award)		√					
Fedax N.V. v. Republic of Venezuela, ICSID Case No. ARB/96/3	9 March 1998 (Award)							√
Antoine Goetz and others v. Republic of Burundi; ICSID Case No. ARB/95/3	10 February 1999 (Award)						√ (settlement)	
Robert Azinian and others v. United Mexican States, ICSID Case No. ARB(AF)/97/2	1 November 1999 (Award)	X					X	
Metalclad Corporation v. United Mexican States. ICSID Case No. ARB(AF)/97/1	30 August 2000 (Award)	√					√	
Emilio Agustín Maffezini v. Kingdom of Spain, ICSID Case No. ARB/97/7	13 November 2000 (Award)	√	√					
Compañía de Aguas del Aconquija S.A. and Vivendi Universal S.A. v. Argentine Republic, ICSID Case No. ARB/97/3	21 November 2000 (Award)*	X	X				X	

Annex 10: Tables of ICSID awards and decisions on substantive, procedural and other issues

Standards of Protection ("√" – denotes breach found; "X" – denotes breach not found; "N" – denotes that claim was advanced but not considered; "W" – denotes that claim was advanced and withdrawn)

Case	Date of Award ("*" denotes annulment proceeding)	Fair and Equitable Treatment	Full Protection and Security	No Arbitrary or Discriminatory Measures Impairing the Investment	National/ MFN Treatment	Free Transfer of Funds Related to Investments	No Expropriation without Compensation	Observance of Specific Undertakings
Wena Hotels Ltd. v. Arab Republic of Egypt, ICSID Case No. ARB/98/4	8 December 2000 (Award)*	√	√				√	
Alex Genin and others v. Republic of Estonia, ICSID Case No. ARB/99/2	25 June 2001 (Award)	X	X	X		X	X	X
Eudoro A. Olguín v. Republic of Paraguay, ICSID Case No. ARB/98/5	26 July 2001 (Award)	X					X	
Middle East Cement Shipping and Handling Co. S.A. v. Arab Republic of Egypt, ICSID Case No. ARB/99/6	12 April 2002 (Award)	√	√				√	
Mondev International Ltd. v. United States of America, ICSID Case No. ARB(AF)/99/2	11 October 2002 (Award)	X	X		X (National Treatment)		X	
Marvin Roy Feldman Karpa v. United Mexican States, ICSID Case No. ARB(AF)/99/1	16 December 2002 (Award)	X	X		√ (National Treatment)		X	
ADF Group Inc. v. United States of America, ICSID Case No. ARB(AF)/00/1	9 January 2003 (Award)	X			X (National Treatment)			
Técnicas Medioambientales Tecmed, S.A. v. United Mexican States, ICSID Case No. ARB(AF)/00/2	29 May 2003 (Award)	√			X (MFN)		√	
Generation Ukraine Inc. v. Ukraine, ICSID Case No. ARB/00/9	16 September 2003 (Award)						X	

I. Overview of Substantive Issues – Summary of Standards of Treatment in Decided ICSID Investment Treaty Cases *(continued)*

Case	Date of Award ("*" denotes annulment proceeding)	Standards of Protection ("√" – denotes breach found; "X" – denotes breach not found; "N" – denotes that claim was advanced but not considered; "W" – denotes that claim was advanced and withdrawn)						
		Fair and Equitable Treatment	Full Protection and Security	No Arbitrary or Discriminatory Measures Impairing the Investment	National/ MFN Treatment	Free Transfer of Funds Related to Investments	No Expropriation without Compensation	Observance of Specific Undertakings
AIG Capital Partners, Inc. and CJSC Tema Real Estate Company v. Republic of Kazakhstan, ICSID Case No. ARB/01/6	7 October 2003 (Award)						√	
Consortium R.F.C.C. v. Kingdom of Morocco, ICSID Case No. ARB/00/6	22 December 2003 (Award)*	X			X (National Treatment)		X	
Patrick Mitchell v. Democratic Republic of the Congo, ICSID Case No. ARB/99/7	9 February 2004 (Award)*						√	
Waste Management, Inc. v. United Mexican States, ICSID Case No. ARB(AF)/00/3	30 April 2004 (Award)	X	X				X	
MTD Equity Sdn. Bhd. and MTD Chile S.A. v. Republic of Chile, ICSID Case No. ARB/01/7	25 May 2004 (Award)*	√		X	√ (MFN)		X	X
CMS Gas Transmission Company v. Argentine Republic, ICSID Case No. ARB/01/8	12 May 2005 (Award)*	√		X		W	X	√
Noble Ventures, Inc. v. Romania, ICSID Case No. ARB/01/11	12 October 2005 (Award)	X	X	X			X	X

Standards of Protection ("√" – denotes breach found; "X" – denotes breach not found; "N" – denotes that claim was advanced but not considered; "W" – denotes that claim was advanced and withdrawn)

Case	Date of Award ("*" denotes annulment proceeding)	Fair and Equitable Treatment	Full Protection and Security	No Arbitrary or Discriminatory Measures Impairing the Investment	National/ MFN Treatment	Free Transfer of Funds Related to Investments	No Expropriation without Compensation	Observance of Specific Undertakings
Azurix Corp. v. Argentine Republic, ICSID Case No. ARB/01/12	14 July 2006 (Award)*	√	√	√			X	X
Fireman's Fund Insurance Company v. United Mexican States, ICSID Case No. ARB(AF)/02/1	17 July 2006 (Award)						X	
ADC Affiliate Limited and ADC & ADMC Management Limited v. Republic of Hungary, ICSID Case No. ARB/03/16	2 October 2006 (Award)	√	√				√	
LG&E Energy Corp., LG&E Capital Corp. and LG&E International Inc. v. Argentine Republic, ICSID Case No. ARB/02/1	3 October 2006 (Decision on Liability)*	√		X (Arbitrary Measures) √ ((Discriminatory Measures)			X	√
Champion Trading Company and Ameritrade International, Inc. v. Arab Republic of Egypt, ICSID Case No. ARB/02/9	27 October 2006 (Award)	X	X		X (National Treatment)		N	
PSEG Global Inc. and Konya Ilgin Elektrik Üretim ve Ticaret Limited Sirketi v. Republic of Turkey, ICSID Case No. ARB/02/5	19 January 2007 (Award)	√	X	X			X	X
Siemens A.G. v. Argentine Republic, ICSID Case No. ARB/02/8	6 February 2007 (Award)*	√	√	√			√	X

I. Overview of Substantive Issues – Summary of Standards of Treatment in Decided ICSID Investment Treaty Cases (continued)

Case	Date of Award ("*" denotes annulment proceeding)	Standards of Protection ("√" – denotes breach found; "X" – denotes breach not found; "N" – denotes that claim was advanced but not considered; "W" – denotes that claim was advanced and withdrawn)						
		Fair and Equitable Treatment	Full Protection and Security	No Arbitrary or Discriminatory Measures Impairing the Investment	National/MFN Treatment	Free Transfer of Funds Related to Investments	No Expropriation without Compensation	Observance of Specific Undertakings
Enron Corporation and Ponderosa Assets, L.P. v. Argentine Republic, ICSID Case No. ARB/01/3	22 May 2007 (Award)*	√	X	X			X	√
Ahmonseto, Inc. and others v. Arab Republic of Egypt, ICSID Case No. ARB/02/15	18 June 2007 (Award)*	X	X		X (MFN)		X	
Tokios Tokelés v. Ukraine, ICSID Case No. ARB/02/18	26 July 2007 (Award)	X	X				X	
M.C.I. Power Group, L.C. and New Turbine, Inc. v. Republic of Ecuador, ICSID Case No. ARB/03/6	31 July 2007 (Award)*	X	X	X	X (MFN)		X	
Compañía de Aguas del Aconquija S.A. and Vivendi Universal S.A. v. Argentine Republic, ICSID Case No. ARB/97/3	20 August 2007 (Award)*	√	√				√	
Parkerings-Compagniet AS v. Republic of Lithuania, ICSID Case No. ARB/05/8	11 September 2007 (Award)	X	X		X (MFN)		X	
Sempra Energy International v. Argentine Republic, ICSID Case No. ARB/02/16	28 September 2007 (Award)*	√	X	X			X	√

Annex 10: Tables of ICSID awards and decisions on substantive, procedural and other issues

Standards of Protection ("√" – denotes breach was advanced but not considered; "X" – denotes breach found; "N" – denotes breach not found; "W" – denotes that claim was advanced and withdrawn)

Case	Date of Award ("*" denotes annulment proceeding)	Fair and Equitable Treatment	Full Protection and Security	No Arbitrary or Discriminatory Measures Impairing the Investment	National/ MFN Treatment	Free Transfer of Funds Related to Investments	No Expropriation without Compensation	Observance of Specific Undertakings
OKO Pankki Oyj and others v. Republic of Estonia, ICSID Case No. ARB/04/6	19 November 2007 (Award)	√	N				N	N
Archer Daniels Midland Company and Tate & Lyle Ingredients Americas, Inc. v. United Mexican States, ICSID Case No. ARB(AF)/04/5	21 November 2007 (Award)				√ (National Treatment)		X	
Corn Products International, Inc. v. United Mexican States, ICSID Case No. ARB(AF)/04/1	15 January 2008 (Decision on Responsibility)				√ (National Treatment)		X	
Desert Line Projects LLC v. Republic of Yemen, ICSID Case No. ARB/05/17	6 February 2008 (Award)	√	N	N			N	
Ares International S.r.l. and MetalGeo S.r.l. v. Georgia, ICSID Case No. ARB/05/23	28 February 2008 (Award)	√	X				X	
Victor Pey Casado and President Allende Foundation v. Republic of Chile, ICSID Case No. ARB/98/2	8 May 2008 (Award)*	√					X	
Metalpar S.A. and Buen Aire S.A. v. Argentine Republic, ICSID Case No. ARB/03/5	6 June 2008 (Award)	X		X		X	X	
Helnan International Hotels A/S v. Arab Republic of Egypt, ICSID Case No. ARB/05/19	3 July 2008 (Award)*	X	X	X			X	

I. Overview of Substantive Issues – Summary of Standards of Treatment in Decided ICSID Investment Treaty Cases (continued)

Standards of Protection ("√" – denotes breach found; "X" – denotes breach not found; "N" – denotes that claim was advanced but not considered; "W" – denotes that claim was advanced and withdrawn)

Case	Date of Award ("*" denotes annulment proceeding)	Fair and Equitable Treatment	Full Protection and Security	No Arbitrary or Discriminatory Measures Impairing the Investment	National/ MFN Treatment	Free Transfer of Funds Related to Investments	No Expropriation without Compensation	Observance of Specific Undertakings
Biwater Gauff (Tanzania) Limited v. United Republic of Tanzania, ICSID Case No. ARB/05/22	24 July 2008 (Award)	√	√	√		X	√	
Rumeli Telekom A.S. and Telsim Mobil Telekomunikasyon Hizmetleri A.S. v. Republic of Kazakhstan, ICSID Case No. ARB/05/16	29 July 2008 (Award)*	√	X	N	√ (MFN)		√	
Duke Energy Electroquil Partners and Electroquil S.A. v. Republic of Ecuador, ICSID Case No. ARB/04/19	18 August 2008 (Award)*	√	√	X				√
Plama Consortium Limited v. Republic of Bulgaria, ICSID Case No. ARB/03/24	27 August 2008 (Award)	X	X	X			X	X
Continental Casualty Company v. Argentine Republic, ICSID Case No. ARB/03/9	5 September 2008 (Award)*	√	X			X	X	X
Jan de Nul N.V. and Dredging International N.V. v. Arab Republic of Egypt, ICSID Case No. ARB/04/13	6 November 2008 (Award)	X	X					
LESI, S.p.A. and Astaldi, S.p.A. v. People's Democratic Republic of Algeria, ICSID Case No. ARB/05/3	12 November 2008 (Award)	X	X				X	

Standards of Protection ("√" – denotes breach found; "X" – denotes breach not found; "N" – denotes that claim was advanced but not considered; "W" – denotes that claim was advanced and withdrawn)

Case	Date of Award ("*" denotes annulment proceeding)	Fair and Equitable Treatment	Full Protection and Security	No Arbitrary or Discriminatory Measures Impairing the Investment	National/ MFN Treatment	Free Transfer of Funds Related to Investments	No Expropriation without Compensation	Observance of Specific Undertakings
Bernardus Henricus Funnekotter and others v. Republic of Zimbabwe, ICSID Case No. ARB/05/6	22 April 2009 (Award)	N					√	
Waguih Elie George Siag and Clorinda Vecchi v. Arab Republic of Egypt, ICSID Case No. ARB/05/15	1 June 2009 (Award)*	√	√	√	N		√	
Saipem S.p.A. v. People's Republic of Bangladesh, ICSID Case No. ARB/05/7	30 June 2009 (Award)						√	
Pantechniki S.A. Contractors & Engineers v. Republic of Albania, ICSID Case No. ARB/07/21	30 July 2009 (Award)	X	X					
Bayindir Insaat Turizm Ticaret Ve Sanayi A.Ş. v. Islamic Republic of Pakistan, ICSID Case No. ARB/03/29	27 August 2009 (Award)	X			X (National Treatment)		X	
Cargill, Inc. v. United Mexican States, ICSID Case No. ARB(AF)/05/2	18 September 2009 (Award)	√		√	√ (Nat'l Tr'mt) / X (MFN)		X	
EDF (Services) Ltd. v. Romania, ICSID Case No. ARB/05/13	8 October 2009 (Award)	X		X			X	X
Joseph C. Lemire v. Ukraine, ICSID Case No. ARB/06/18	21 January 2010 (Decision on Jurisdiction and Liability)	√	X	X			W	X

II. Substantive Issues by Topic – A. Fair and Equitable Treatment

Case	Date of Decision or Award	Tribunal (President denoted in bold)	Outcome
Robert Azinian and others v. United Mexican States, ICSID Case No. ARB(AF)/97/2	1 November 1999 (Award)	**Paulsson,** Civiletti, von Wobeser	No breach of NAFTA Article 1105 found
Metalclad Corporation v. United Mexican States, ICSID Case No. ARB(AF)/97/1	30 August 2000 (Award)	**Lauterpacht,** Civiletti, Luis Siqueiros	Breach of NAFTA Article 1105 found
Emilio Agustín Maffezini v. Kingdom of Spain, ICSID Case No. ARB/97/7	13 November 2000 (Award)	**Orrego Vicuña,** Buergenthal, Wolf	Breach of fair and equitable treatment standard found
Compañía de Aguas del Aconquija S.A. and Vivendi Universal S.A. v. Argentine Republic, ICSID Case No. ARB/97/3	21 November 2000 (Award)	**Rezek,** Buergenthal, Trooboff	No breach of fair and equitable treatment standard found
Wena Hotels Ltd. v. Arab Republic of Egypt, ICSID Case No. ARB/98/4	8 December 2000 (Award)	**Leigh,** Fadlallah, Wallace	Breach of fair and equitable treatment standard found
Alex Genin and others v. Republic of Estonia, ICSID Case No. ARB/99/2	25 June 2001 (Award)	**Fortier,** Heth, van den Berg	No breach of fair and equitable treatment standard found
Eudoro A. Olguín v. Republic of Paraguay, ICSID Case No. ARB/98/5	26 July 2001 (Final Award)	**Oreamuno,** Rezek, Mayora Alvarado	No breach of fair and equitable treatment standard found
Middle East Cement Shipping and Handling Co. S.A. v. Arab Republic of Egypt, ICSID Case No. ARB/99/6	12 April 2002 (Award)	**Böckstiegel,** Wallace, Bernardini	Breach of fair and equitable treatment standard found
Mondev International Ltd. v. United States of America, ICSID Case No. ARB(AF)/99/2	11 October 2002 (Award)	**Stephen,** Crawford, Schwebel	No breach of NAFTA Article 1105 found
Marvin Roy Feldman Karpa v. United Mexican States, ICSID Case No. ARB(AF)/99/1	16 December 2002 (Award)	**Kerameus,** Covarrubias Bravo, Gantz	No breach of NAFTA Article 1105 found
ADF Group Inc. v. United States of America, ICSID Case No. ARB(AF)/00/1	9 January 2003 (Award)	**Feliciano,** de Mestral, Lamm	No breach of NAFTA Article 1105 found
Técnicas Medioambientales Tecmed, S.A. v. United Mexican States, ICSID Case No. ARB(AF)/00/2	29 May 2003 (Award)	**Grigera Naón,** Bernal Verea, Fernández Rozas	Breach of fair and equitable treatment standard found

Case	Date of Decision or Award	Tribunal (President denoted in bold)	Outcome
Consortium R.F.C.C. v. Kingdom of Morocco, ICSID Case No. ARB/00/6	22 December 2003 (Award)	**Briner**, Cremades, Fadlallah	No breach of fair and equitable treatment standard found
Waste Management, Inc. v. United Mexican States, ICSID Case No. ARB(AF)/00/3	30 April 2004 (Award)	**Crawford**, Civiletti, Magallón Gómez	No breach of NAFTA Article 1105 found
MTD Equity Sdn. Bhd. and MTD Chile S.A. v. Republic of Chile, ICSID Case No. ARB/01/7	25 May 2004 (Award)	**Rigo Sureda**, Lalonde, Oreamuno	Breach of fair and equitable treatment standard found
CMS Gas Transmission Company v. Argentine Republic, ICSID Case No. ARB/01/8	12 May 2005 (Award)	**Orrego Vicuña**, Lalonde, Rezek	Breach of fair and equitable treatment standard found
Noble Ventures, Inc. v. Romania, ICSID Case No. ARB/01/11	12 October 2005 (Award)	**Böckstiegel**, Lever, Dupuy	No breach of fair and equitable treatment standard found
Azurix Corp. v. Argentine Republic, ICSID Case No. ARB/01/12	14 July 2006 (Award)	**Rigo Sureda**, Lalonde, Martins	Breach of fair and equitable treatment standard found
ADC Affiliate Limited and ADC & ADMC Management Limited v. Republic of Hungary, ICSID Case No. ARB/03/16	2 October 2006 (Award)	**Kaplan**, Brower, van den Berg	Breach of fair and equitable treatment standard found
LG&E Energy Corp., LG&E Capital Corp, and LG&E International Inc. v. Argentine Republic, ICSID Case No. ARB/02/1	3 October 2006 (Decision on Liability)	**de Maekelt**, Rezek, van den Berg	Breach of fair and equitable treatment standard found
Champion Trading Company and Ameritrade International, Inc. v. Arab Republic of Egypt, ICSID Case No. ARB/02/9	27 October 2006 (Award)	**Briner**, Fortier, Aynès	No breach of fair and equitable treatment standard found
PSEG Global Inc. and Konya Ilgin Elektrik Üretim ve Ticaret Limited Sirketi v. Republic of Turkey, ICSID Case No. ARB/02/5	19 January 2007 (Award)	**Orrego Vicuña**, Fortier, Kaufmann-Kohler	Breach of fair and equitable treatment standard found
Siemens A.G. v. Argentine Republic, ICSID Case No. ARB/02/8	6 February 2007 (Award)	**Rigo Sureda**, Brower, Bello Janeiro	Breach of fair and equitable treatment standard found
Enron Corporation and Ponderosa Assets, L.P. v. Argentine Republic, ICSID Case No. ARB/01/3	22 May 2007 (Award)	**Orrego Vicuña**, van den Berg, Tschanz	Breach of fair and equitable treatment standard found

II. Substantive Issues by Topic – A. Fair and Equitable Treatment (continued)

Case	Date of Decision or Award	Tribunal (President denoted in bold)	Outcome
Ahmonseto, Inc. and others v. Arab Republic of Egypt, ICSID Case No. ARB/02/15	18 June 2007 (Award)	**Tercier,** Fadlallah, Viandier	No breach of fair and equitable treatment standard found
Tokios Tokelės v. Ukraine, ICSID Case No. ARB/02/18	26 July 2007 (Award)	**Mustill,** Bernardini, Price	No breach of fair and equitable treatment standard found
M.C.I. Power Group, L.C. and New Turbine, Inc. v. Republic of Ecuador, ICSID Case No. ARB/03/6	31 July 2007 (Award)	**Vinuesa,** Greenberg, Irarrázabal	No breach of fair and equitable treatment standard found
Compañia de Aguas del Aconquija S.A. and Vivendi Universal S.A. v. Argentine Republic, ICSID Case No. ARB/97/3	20 August 2007 (Award)	**Rowley,** Kaufmann-Kohler, Bernal Verea	Breach of fair and equitable treatment standard found
Parkerings-Compagniet AS v. Republic of Lithuania, ICSID Case No. ARB/05/8	11 September 2007 (Award)	**Lew,** Lew, Lalonde	No breach of fair and equitable treatment standard found
Sempra Energy International v. Argentine Republic, ICSID Case No. ARB/02/16	28 September 2007 (Award)	**Orrego Vicuña,** Lalonde, Morelli Rico	Breach of fair and equitable treatment standard found
OKO Pankki Oyj and others v. Republic of Estonia, ICSID Case No. ARB/04/6	19 November 2007 (Award)	**de Witt Wijnen,** Veeder, Fortier	Breach of fair and equitable treatment standard found
Desert Line Projects LLC v. Republic of Yemen, ICSID Case No. ARB/05/17	6 February 2008 (Award)	**Tercier,** Paulsson, El-Kosheri	Breach of fair and equitable treatment standard found
Ares International S.r.l. and MetalGeo S.r.l. v. Georgia, ICSID Case No. ARB/05/23	28 February 2008 (Award)	**Rowley,** Beechey, Gaillard	Breach of fair and equitable treatment standard found
Victor Pey Casado and President Allende Foundation v. Republic of Chile, ICSID Case No. ARB/98/2	8 May 2008 (Award)	**Lalive,** Chemloul, Gaillard	Breach of fair and equitable treatment standard found
Metalpar S.A. and Buen Aire S.A. v. Argentine Republic, ICSID Case No. ARB/03/5	6 June 2008 (Award)	**Oreamuno,** Cameron, Chabaneix	No breach of fair and equitable treatment standard found
Helnan International Hotels A/S v. Arab Republic of Egypt, ICSID Case No. ARB/05/19	3 July 2008 (Award)	**Derains,** Dolzer, Lee	No breach of fair and equitable treatment standard found

Case	Date of Decision or Award	Tribunal (President denoted in bold)	Outcome
Biwater Gauff (Tanzania) Limited v. United Republic of Tanzania, ICSID Case No. ARB/05/22	24 July 2008 (Award)	**Hanotiau**, Born, Landau	Breach of fair and equitable treatment standard found
Rumeli Telekom A.S. and Telsim Mobil Telekomunikasyon Hizmetleri A.S. v. Republic of Kazakhstan, ICSID Case No. ARB/05/16	29 July 2008 (Award)	**Hanotiau**, Boyd, Lalonde	Breach of fair and equitable treatment standard found
Duke Energy Electroquil Partners and Electroquil S.A. v. Republic of Ecuador, ICSID Case No. ARB/04/19	18 August 2008 (Award)	**Kaufmann-Kohler**, Gómez-Pinzón, van den Berg	Breach of fair and equitable treatment standard found
Plama Consortium Limited v. Republic of Bulgaria, ICSID Case No. ARB/03/24	27 August 2008 (Award)	**Salans**, van den Berg, Veeder	No breach of fair and equitable treatment standard found
Continental Casualty Company v. Argentine Republic, ICSID Case No. ARB/03/9	5 September 2008 (Award)	**Sacerdoti**, Veeder, Nader	Breach of fair and equitable treatment standard found
Jan de Nul N.V. and Dredging International N.V. v. Arab Republic of Egypt, ICSID Case No. ARB/04/13	6 November 2008 (Award)	**Kaufmann-Kohler**, Mayer, Stern	No breach of fair and equitable treatment standard found
LESI, S.p.A. and Astaldi, S.p.A. v. People's Democratic Republic of Algeria, ICSID Case No. ARB/05/3	12 November 2008 (Award)	**Tercier**, Hanotiau, Gaillard	No breach of fair and equitable treatment standard found
Bernardus Henricus Funnekotter and others v. Republic of Zimbabwe, ICSID Case No. ARB/05/6	22 April 2009 (Award)	**Guillaume**, Cass, Wasi Zafar	Not considered
Waguih Elie George Siag and Clorinda Vecchi v. Arab Republic of Egypt, ICSID Case No. ARB/05/15	1 June 2009 (Award)	**Williams**, Pryles, Orrego Vicuña	Breach of fair and equitable treatment standard found
Pantechniki S.A. Contractors & Engineers v. Republic of Albania, ICSID Case No. ARB/07/21	30 July 2009 (Award)	**Paulsson**	No breach of fair and equitable treatment standard found
Bayindir Insaat Turizm Ticaret Ve Sanayi A.S. v. Islamic Republic of Pakistan, ICSID Case No. ARB/03/29	27 August 2009 (Award)	**Kaufmann-Kohler**, Berman, Böckstiegel	No breach of fair and equitable treatment standard found
Cargill, Inc. v. United Mexican States, ICSID Case No. ARB(AF)/05/2	18 September 2009 (Award)	**Pryles**, Caron, McRae	Breach of NAFTA Article 1105 found

II. Substantive Issues by Topic – A. Fair and Equitable Treatment *(continued)*

Case	Date of Decision or Award	Tribunal (President denoted in bold)	Outcome
EDF (Services) Ltd. v. Romania, ICSID Case No. ARB/05/13	8 October 2009 (Award)	**Bernardini**, Derains, Rovine	No breach of fair and equitable treatment standard found
Joseph C. Lemire v. Ukraine, ICSID Case No. ARB/06/18	21 January 2010 (Decision on Jurisdiction and Liability)	**Fernández-Armesto**, Paulsson, Voss	Breach of fair and equitable treatment standard found

II. Substantive Issues by Topic – B. Full Protection and Security

Case	Date of Decision or Award	Tribunal (President denoted in bold)	Outcome
Asian Agricultural Products Ltd. (AAPL) v. Democratic Socialist Republic of Sri Lanka, ICSID Case No. ARB/87/3	27 June 1990 (Award)	**El-Kosheri**, Goldman, Asante	Breach of full protection and security standard found
American Manufacturing & Trading, Inc. v. Republic of Zaire, ICSID Case No. ARB/93/1	21 February 1997 (Award)	**Sucharitkul**, Golsong, Mbaye	Breach of full protection and security standard found
Emilio Agustín Maffezini v. Kingdom of Spain, ICSID Case No. ARB/97/7	13 November 2000 (Award)	**Orrego Vicuña**, Buergenthal, Wolf	Breach of full protection and security standard found
Compañia de Aguas del Aconquija S.A. and Vivendi Universal S.A. v. Argentine Republic, ICSID Case No. ARB/97/3	21 November 2000 (Award)	**Rezek**, Buergenthal, Trooboff	No breach of full protection and security standard found
Wena Hotels Ltd. v. Arab Republic of Egypt, ICSID Case No. ARB/98/4	8 December 2000 (Award)	**Leigh**, Fadlallah, Wallace	Breach of full protection and security standard found
Alex Genin and others v. Republic of Estonia, ICSID Case No. ARB/99/2	25 June 2001 (Award)	**Fortier**, Heth, van den Berg	No breach of full protection and security standard found
Middle East Cement Shipping and Handling Co. S.A. v. Arab Republic of Egypt, ICSID Case No. ARB/99/6	12 April 2002 (Award)	**Böckstiegel**, Wallace, Bernardini	Breach of full protection and security standard found
Mondev International Ltd. v. United States of America, ICSID Case No. ARB(AF)/99/2	11 October 2002 (Award)	**Stephen**, Crawford, Schwebel	No breach of NAFTA Article 1105 found
Técnicas Medioambientales Tecmed, S.A. v. United Mexican States, ICSID Case No. ARB(AF)/00/2	29 May 2003 (Award)	**Grigera Naón**, Bernal Verea, Fernández Rozas	No breach of full protection and security standard found
Waste Management, Inc. v. United Mexican States, ICSID Case No. ARB(AF)/00/3	30 April 2004 (Award)	**Crawford**, Civiletti, Magallón Gómez	No breach of NAFTA Article 1105 found
Noble Ventures, Inc. v. Romania, ICSID Case No. ARB/01/11	12 October 2005 (Award)	**Böckstiegel**, Lever, Dupuy	No breach of full protection and security standard found
Azurix Corp. v. Argentine Republic, ICSID Case No. ARB/01/12	14 July 2006 (Award)	**Rigo Sureda**, Lalonde, Martins	Breach of full protection and security standard found

II. Substantive Issues by Topic – B. Full Protection and Security *(continued)*

Case	Date of Decision or Award	Tribunal (President denoted in bold)	Outcome
ADC Affiliate Limited and ADC & ADMC Management Limited v. Republic of Hungary, ICSID Case No. ARB/03/16	2 October 2006 (Award)	**Kaplan**, Brower, van den Berg	Breach of full protection and security standard found
Champion Trading Company and Ameritrade International, Inc. v. Arab Republic of Egypt, ICSID Case No. ARB/02/9	27 October 2006 (Award)	**Briner**, Fortier, Aynès	No breach of full protection and security standard found
PSEG Global Inc. and Konya Ilgin Elektrik Üretim ve Ticaret Limited Sirketi v. Republic of Turkey, ICSID Case No. ARB/02/5	19 January 2007 (Award)	**Orrego Vicuña**, Fortier, Kaufmann-Kohler	No breach of full protection and security standard found
Siemens A.G. v. Argentine Republic, ICSID Case No. ARB/02/8	6 February 2007 (Award)	**Rigo Sureda**, Brower, Bello Janeiro	Breach of full protection and security standard found
Enron Corporation and Ponderosa Assets, L.P. v. Argentine Republic, ICSID Case No. ARB/01/3	22 May 2007 (Award)	**Orrego Vicuña**, van den Berg, Tschanz	No breach of full protection and security standard found
Azmonseta, Inc. and others v. Arab Republic of Egypt, ICSID Case No. ARB/02/15	18 June 2007 (Award)	**Tercier**, Fadlallah, Viandier	No breach of full protection and security standard found
Tokios Tokelés v. Ukraine, ICSID Case No. ARB/02/18	26 July 2007 (Award)	**Mustill**, Bernardini, Price	No breach of full protection and security standard found
M.C.I. Power Group, L.C. and New Turbine, Inc. v. Republic of Ecuador, ICSID Case No. ARB/03/6	31 July 2007 (Award)	**Vinuesa**, Greenberg, Irarrázabal	No breach of full protection and security standard found
Compañía de Aguas del Aconquija S.A. and Vivendi Universal S.A. v. Argentine Republic, ICSID Case No. ARB/97/3	20 August 2007 (Award)	**Rowley**, Kaufmann-Kohler, Bernal Verea	Breach of full protection and security standard found
Parkerings-Compagniet AS v. Republic of Lithuania, ICSID Case No. ARB/05/8	11 September 2007 (Award)	**Lévy**, Lew, Lalonde	No breach of full protection and security standard found
Sempra Energy International v. Argentine Republic, ICSID Case No. ARB/02/16	28 September 2007 (Award)	**Orrego Vicuña**, Lalonde, Morelli Rico	No breach of full protection and security standard found
OKO Pankki Oyj and others v. Republic of Estonia, ICSID Case No. ARB/04/6	19 November 2007 (Award)	**de Witt Wijnen**, Veeder, Fortier	Not considered

Case	Date of Decision or Award	Tribunal (President denoted in bold)	Outcome
Desert Line Projects LLC v. Republic of Yemen, ICSID Case No. ARB/05/17	6 February 2008 (Award)	**Tercier**, Paulsson, El-Kosheri	Not considered
Ares International S.r.l. and MetalGeo S.r.l. v. Georgia, ICSID Case No. ARB/05/23	28 February 2008 (Award)	**Rowley**, Beechey, Gaillard	No breach of full protection and security standard found
Helnan International Hotels A/S v. Arab Republic of Egypt, ICSID Case No. ARB/05/19	3 July 2008 (Award)	**Derains**, Dolzer, Lee	No breach of full protection and security standard found
Biwater Gauff (Tanzania) Limited v. United Republic of Tanzania, ICSID Case No. ARB/05/22	24 July 2008 (Award)	**Hanotiau**, Born, Landau	Breach of full protection and security standard found
Rumeli Telekom A.S. and Telsim Mobil Telekomunikasyon Hizmetleri A.S. v. Republic of Kazakhstan, ICSID Case No. ARB/05/16	29 July 2008 (Award)	**Hanotiau**, Lalonde, Boyd	No breach of full protection and security standard found
Plama Consortium Limited v. Republic of Bulgaria, ICSID Case No. ARB/03/24	27 August 2008 (Award)	**Salans**, van den Berg, Veeder	No breach of full protection and security standard found
Continental Casualty Company v. Argentine Republic, ICSID Case No. ARB/03/9	5 September 2008 (Award)	**Sacerdoti**, Veeder, Nader	No breach of full protection and security standard found
Jan de Nul N.V. and Dredging International N.V. v. Arab Republic of Egypt, ICSID Case No. ARB/04/13	6 November 2008 (Award)	**Kaufmann-Kohler**, Mayer, Stern	No breach of full protection and security standard found
LESI, S.p.A. and Astaldi, S.p.A. v. People's Democratic Republic of Algeria, ICSID Case No. ARB/05/3	12 November 2008 (Award)	**Tercier**, Hanotiau, Gaillard	No breach of full protection and security standard found
Waguih Elie George Siag and Clorinda Vecchi v. Arab Republic of Egypt, ICSID Case No. ARB/05/15	1 June 2009 (Award)	**Williams**, Pryles, Orrego Vicuña	Breach of full protection and security standard found
Pantechniki S.A. Contractors & Engineers v. Republic of Albania, ICSID Case No. ARB/07/21	30 July 2009 (Award)	**Paulsson**	No breach of full protection and security standard found
Joseph C. Lemire v. Ukraine, ICSID Case No. ARB/06/18	21 January 2010 (Decision on Jurisdiction and Liability)	**Fernández-Armesto**, Paulsson, Voss	No breach of full protection and security standard found

II. Substantive Issues by Topic – C. No Arbitrary or Discriminatory Measures Impairing the Investment

Case	Date of Decision or Award	Tribunal (President denoted in bold)	Outcome
Alex Genin and others v. Republic of Estonia, ICSID Case No. ARB/99/2	25 June 2001 (Award)	**Fortier**, Heth, van den Berg	No breach of impairment standard found
MTD Equity Sdn. Bhd. and MTD Chile S.A. v. Republic of Chile, ICSID Case No. ARB/01/7	25 May 2004 (Award)	**Rigo Sureda**, Lalonde, Oreamuno	No breach of impairment standard found
CMS Gas Transmission Company v. Argentine Republic, ICSID Case No. ARB/01/8	12 May 2005 (Award)	**Orrego Vicuña**, Lalonde, Rezek	No breach of impairment standard found
Noble Ventures, Inc. v. Romania, ICSID Case No. ARB/01/11	12 October 2005 (Award)	**Böckstiegel**, Lever, Dupuy	No breach of impairment standard found
Azurix Corp. v. Argentine Republic, ICSID Case No. ARB/01/12	14 July 2006 (Award)	**Rigo Sureda**, Lalonde, Martins	Breach of impairment standard found
LG&E Energy Corp, LG&E Capital Corp. and LG&E International Inc. v. Argentine Republic, ICSID Case No. ARB/02/1	3 October 2006 (Decision on Liability)	**de Maekelt**, Rezek, van den Berg	Breach of discrimination standard found; no breach of arbitrariness standard found
PSEG Global Inc. and Konya Ilgin Elektrik Üretim ve Ticaret Limited Sirketi v. Republic of Turkey, ICSID Case No. ARB/02/5	19 January 2007 (Award)	**Orrego Vicuña**, Fortier, Kaufmann-Kohler	No breach of impairment standard found
Siemens A.G. v. Argentine Republic, ICSID Case No. ARB/02/8	6 February 2007 (Award)	**Rigo Sureda**, Brower, Bello Janeiro	Breach of arbitrariness standard found; no determination reached regarding breach of discrimination standard
Enron Corporation and Ponderosa Assets, L.P. v. Argentine Republic, ICSID Case No. ARB/01/3	22 May 2007 (Award)	**Orrego Vicuña**, van den Berg, Tschanz	No breach of impairment standard found
M.C.I. Power Group, L.C. and New Turbine, Inc. v. Republic of Ecuador, ICSID Case No. ARB/03/6	31 July 2007 (Award)	**Vinuesa**, Greenberg, Irarrázabal	No breach of impairment standard found
Sempra Energy International v. Argentine Republic, ICSID Case No. ARB/02/16	28 September 2007 (Award)	**Orrego Vicuña**, Lalonde, Morelli Rico	No breach of impairment standard found

Case	Date of Decision or Award	Tribunal (President denoted in bold)	Outcome
Desert Line Projects LLC v. Republic of Yemen, ICSID Case No. ARB/05/17	6 February 2008 (Award)	**Tercier**, Paulsson, El-Kosheri	Not considered
Metalpar S.A. and Buen Aire S.A. v. Argentine Republic, ICSID Case No. ARB/03/5	6 June 2008 (Award)	**Oreamuno**, Cameron, Chabaneix	No breach of impairment standard found
Helnan International Hotels A/S v. Arab Republic of Egypt, ICSID Case No. ARB/05/19	3 July 2008 (Award)	**Derains**, Dolzer, Lee	No breach of impairment standard found
Biwater Gauff (Tanzania) Limited v. United Republic of Tanzania, ICSID Case No. ARB/05/22	24 July 2008 (Award)	**Hanotiau**, Born, Landau	Breach of impairment standard found
Rumeli Telekom A.S. and Telsim Mobil Telekomunikasyon Hizmetleri A.S. v. Republic of Kazakhstan, ICSID Case No. ARB/05/16	29 July 2008 (Award)	**Hanotiau**, Boyd, Lalonde	Not considered
Duke Energy Electroquil Partners and Electroquil S.A. v. Republic of Ecuador, ICSID Case No. ARB/04/19	18 August 2008 (Award)	**Kaufmann-Kohler**, Gómez-Pinzón, van den Berg	No breach of impairment standard found
Plama Consortium Limited v. Republic of Bulgaria, ICSID Case No. ARB/03/24	27 August 2008 (Award)	**Salans**, van den Berg, Veeder	No breach of impairment standard found
Waguih Elie George Siag and Clorinda Vecchi v. Arab Republic of Egypt, ICSID Case No. ARB/05/15	1 June 2009 (Award)	**Williams**, Pryles, Orrego Vicuña	Breach of impairment standard found
EDF (Services) Ltd. v. Romania, ICSID Case No. ARB/05/13	8 October 2009 (Award)	**Bernardini**, Derains, Rovine	No breach of impairment standard found
Joseph C. Lemire v. Ukraine, ICSID Case No. ARB/06/18	21 January 2010 (Decision on Jurisdiction and Liability)	**Fernández-Armesto**, Paulsson, Voss	No breach of impairment standard found

II. Substantive Issues by Topic – D. National and "Most Favored Nation" Treatment

Case	Date of Decision or Award	Tribunal (President denoted in bold)	Outcome
i. National Treatment			
Mondev International Ltd. v. United States of America, ICSID Case No. ARB(AF)/99/2	11 October 2002 (Award)	**Stephen,** Crawford, Schwebel	No breach of NAFTA Article 1102 found
Marvin Roy Feldman Karpa v. United Mexican States, ICSID Case No. ARB(AF)/99/1	16 December 2002 (Award)	**Kerameus,** Covarrubias Bravo, Gantz	Breach of NAFTA Article 1102 found
ADF Group Inc. v. United States of America, ICSID Case No. ARB(AF)/00/1	9 January 2003 (Award)	**Feliciano,** de Mestral, Lamm	No breach of NAFTA Article 1102 found
Consortium R.F.C.C. v. Kingdom of Morocco, ICSID Case No. ARB/00/6	22 December 2003 (Award)	**Briner,** Cremades, Fadlallah	No breach of national treatment standard found
Champion Trading Company and Ameritrade International, Inc. v. Arab Republic of Egypt, ICSID Case No. ARB/02/9	27 October 2006 (Award)	**Briner,** Fortier, Aynès	No breach of national treatment standard found
Archer Daniels Midland Company and Tate & Lyle Ingredients Americas, Inc. v. United Mexican States, ICSID Case No. ARB(AF)/04/5	21 November 2007 (Award)	**Cremades,** Rovine, Siqueiros T.	Breach of NAFTA Article 1102 found
Corn Products International, Inc. v. United Mexican States, ICSID Case No. ARB(AF)/04/1	15 January 2008 (Decision on Responsibility)	**Greenwood,** Lowenfeld, Serrano de la Vega	Breach of NAFTA Article 1102 found
Waguih Elie George Siag and Clorinda Vecchi v. Arab Republic of Egypt, ICSID Case No. ARB/05/15	1 June 2009 (Award)	**Williams,** Pryles, Orrego Vicuña	Not considered
Bayindir Insaat Turizm Ticaret Ve Sanayi A.S. v. Islamic Republic of Pakistan, ICSID Case No. ARB/03/29	27 August 2009 (Award)	**Kaufmann-Kohler,** Berman, Böckstiegel	No breach of national treatment standard found
Cargill, Inc. v. United Mexican States, ICSID Case No. ARB(AF)/05/2	18 September 2009 (Award)	**Pryles,** Caron, McRae	Breach of NAFTA Article 1102 found

ii. "Most Favored Nation" Treatment

Case	Date of Decision or Award	Tribunal (President denoted in bold)	Outcome
Asian Agricultural Products Ltd. v. Democratic Socialist Republic of Sri Lanka, ICSID Case No. ARB/87/3	27 June 1990 (Award)	**El-Kosheri**, Goldman, Asante	MFN clause could not be justifiably invoked, as there was no established treatment (alleged absence of exemption from full protection and security standard) in other treaty more favorable than under the applicable BIT
Emilio Agustín Maffezini v. Kingdom of Spain, ICSID Case No. ARB/97/7	25 January 2000 (Decision on Jurisdiction)	**Orrego Vicuña**, Buergenthal, Wolf	MFN clause extended to dispute resolution provisions (requirement of 18-month submission of dispute to local courts)
ADF Group Inc. v. United States of America, ICSID Case No. ARB(AF)/00/1	9 January 2003 (Award)	**Feliciano**, de Mestral, Lamm	Claim under NAFTA Article 1103 dismissed as Claimant failed to prove that pertinent provisions of two other treaties provided for treatment more favorable than under NAFTA Article 1105(1)
Técnicas Medioambientales Tecmed, S.A. v. United Mexican States, ICSID Case No. ARB(AF)/00/2	29 May 2003 (Award)	**Grigera Naón**, Bernal Verea, Fernández Rozas	MFN clause could not be used to circumvent requirements that claims be based only on events after entry into force of the BIT and be filed within three years in ad hoc arbitration
MTD Equity Sdn. Bhd. and MTD Chile S.A. v. Republic of Chile, ICSID Case No. ARB/01/7	25 May 2004 (Award)	**Rigo Sureda**, Lalonde, Oreamuno	MFN clause extended to substantive provisions (observance of undertakings, unreasonable and discriminatory measures and failure to grant necessary permits), but no breach of such provisions found
Siemens A.G. v. Argentine Republic, ICSID Case No. ARB/02/8	3 August 2004 (Decision on Jurisdiction)	**Rigo Sureda**, Brower, Bello Janeiro	MFN clause extended to dispute resolution provisions (requirement of 18-month submission of dispute to local courts)
Salini Costruttori S.p.A. and Italstrade S.p.A. v. Hashemite Kingdom of Jordan, ICSID Case No. ARB/02/13	9 November 2004 (Decision on Jurisdiction)	**Guillaume**, Cremades, Sinclair	MFN clause did not extend to dispute resolution provisions (exclusion of contractual disputes from ICSID jurisdiction)

II. Substantive Issues by Topic – D. National and "Most Favored Nation" Treatment *(continued)*

Case	Date of Decision or Award	Tribunal (President denoted in bold)	Outcome
Plama Consortium Limited v. Republic of Bulgaria, ICSID Case No. ARB/03/24	8 February 2005 (Decision on Jurisdiction)	**Salans**, van den Berg, Veeder	MFN clause did not extend to dispute resolution provisions (requirement that only disputes involving amount of compensation for expropriation were covered in ad hoc arbitration)
Impregilo S.p.A. v. Islamic Republic of Pakistan, ICSID Case No. ARB/03/3	22 April 2005 (Decision on Jurisdiction)	**Guillaume**, Cremades, Landau	MFN clause did not extend to substantive provision (observance of undertakings)
Camuzzi International S.A. v. Argentine Republic, ICSID Case No. ARB/03/7	10 June 2005 (Decision on Objections to Jurisdiction)	**Gómez-Pinzón**, Alvarez, Gros Espiel	MFN clause extended to dispute resolution provisions (requirement of 18-month submission of dispute to local courts)
Gas Natural SDG, S.A. v. Argentine Republic, ICSID Case No. ARB/03/10	17 June 2005 (Decision of the Tribunal on Preliminary Questions of Jurisdiction)	**Lowenfeld**, Alvarez, Nikken	MFN clause extended to dispute resolution provisions (requirement of 18-month submission of dispute to local courts)
Bayindir Insaat Turizm Ticaret Ve Sanayi A.S. v. Islamic Republic of Pakistan, ICSID Case No. ARB/03/29	14 November 2005 (Decision on Jurisdiction)	**Kaufmann-Kohler**, Berman, Böckstiegel	MFN clause extended to substantive provision (fair and equitable treatment)
Suez, Sociedad General de Aguas de Barcelona S.A., and InterAguas Servicios Integrales del Agua S.A. v. Argentine Republic, ICSID Case No. ARB/03/17	16 May 2006 (Decision on Jurisdiction)	**Salacuse**, Kauffman-Kohler, Nikken	MFN clause extended to dispute resolution provisions (requirement of 18-month submission of dispute to local courts)
Suez, Sociedad General de Aguas de Barcelona S.A. and Vivendi Universal S.A. v. Argentine Republic, ICSID Case No. ARB/03/19	3 August 2006 (Decision on Jurisdiction)	**Salacuse**, Kaufmann-Kohler, Nikken	MFN clause extended to dispute resolution provisions (requirement of 18-month submission of dispute to local courts)
Telenor Mobile Communications AS v. Republic of Hungary, ICSID Case No. ARB/04/15	13 September 2006 (Decision on Jurisdiction)	**Goode**, Allard, Marriott	MFN clause did not extend to dispute resolution provisions (requirement that only disputes involving amount of compensation for expropriation were covered in ICSID arbitration)

Case	Date of Decision or Award	Tribunal (President denoted in bold)	Outcome
Atmonseto, Inc. and others v. Arab Republic of Egypt, ICSID Case No. ARB/02/15	18 June 2007 (Award)	**Tercier**, Fadlallah, Viandier	No breach of MFN clause found
M.C.I. Power Group, L.C. and New Turbine, Inc. v. Republic of Ecuador, ICSID Case No. ARB/03/6	31 July 2007 (Award)	**Vinuesa**, Greenberg, Irarrázabal	MFN clause could not be used to circumvent requirement that claims be based only on events after entry into force of the BIT
Parkerings-Compagniet AS v. Republic of Lithuania, ICSID Case No. ARB/05/8	11 September 2007 (Award)	**Lévy**, Lew, Lalonde	MFN clause applied, but no breach of MFN clause found as different treatment was held to be justified
Rumeli Telekom A.S. and Telsim Mobil Telekomunikasyon Hizmetleri A.S. v. Republic of Kazakhstan, ICSID Case No. ARB/05/16	29 July 2008 (Award)	**Hanotiau**, Boyd, Lalonde	MFN clause extended to substantive provisions (fair and equitable treatment, full protection and security, no arbitrary or discriminatory measures, Respondent did not object), breach of fair and equitable treatment standard found
Wintershall Aktiengesellschaft v. Argentine Republic, ICSID Case No. ARB/04/14	8 December 2008 (Award)	**Nariman**, Bernardini, Torres Bernardez	MFN clause did not extend to dispute resolution provisions (requirement of 18-month submission of dispute to local courts)
Tza Yap Shum v. Republic of Peru, ICSID Case No. ARB/07/6	19 June 2009 (Decision on Jurisdiction and Competence)	**Kessler**, Otero, Fernandez-Armesto	MFN clause did not extend to dispute resolution provisions (requirement that only disputes involving amount of compensation for expropriation were covered in ICSID arbitration)
Bayindir Insaat Turizm Ticaret Ve Sanayi A.S. v. Islamic Republic of Pakistan, ICSID Case No. ARB/03/29	27 August 2009 (Award)	**Kaufmann-Kohler**, Berman, Böckstiegel	MFN clause extended to fair and equitable treatment standard, but no breach of fair and equitable treatment standard found
Cargill, Inc. v. United Mexican States, ICSID Case No. ARB(AF)/05/2	18 September 2009 (Award)	**Pryles**, Caron, McRae	Claim under NAFTA Article 1103 dismissed because Claimant failed to show that it or its investment was in "like circumstances" with the investor/investment of another NAFTA Party or of a non-Party

II. Substantive Issues by Topic – E. Free Transfer of Funds Related to Investments

Case	Date of Decision or Award	Tribunal (President denoted in bold)	Outcome
Alex Genin and others v. Republic of Estonia, ICSID Case No. ARB/99/2	25 June 2001 (Award)	**Fortier**, Heth, van den Berg	No breach of free transfer of funds provision found
CMS Gas Transmission Company v. Argentine Republic, ICSID Case No. ARB/01/8	12 May 2005 (Award)	**Orrego Vicuña**, Lalonde, Rezek	Withdrawn
Metalpar S.A. and Buen Aire S.A. v. Argentine Republic, ICSID Case No. ARB/03/5	6 June 2008 (Award)	**Oreamuno**, Cameron, Chabaneix	No breach of free transfer of funds provision found
Biwater Gauff (Tanzania) Limited v. United Republic of Tanzania, ICSID Case No. ARB/05/22	24 July 2008 (Award)	**Hanotiau**, Born, Landau	No breach of free transfer of funds provision found
Continental Casualty Company v. Argentine Republic, ICSID Case No. ARB/03/9	5 September 2008 (Award)	**Sacerdoti**, Veeder, Nader	No breach of free transfer of funds provision found

II. Substantive Issues by Topic – F. No Expropriation Without Compensation

Case	Date of Decision or Award	Tribunal (President denoted in bold)	Outcome
Antoine Goetz and others v. Republic of Burundi, ICSID Case No. ARB/95/3	10 February 1999 (Award)	**Weil**, Bedjaoui, Bredin	Expropriation found (settlement)
Robert Azinian and others v. United Mexican States, ICSID Case No. ARB(AF)/97/2	1 November 1999 (Award)	**Paulsson**, Civiletti, von Wobeser	No breach of NAFTA Article 1110 found
Metalclad Corporation v. United Mexican States, ICSID Case No. ARB(AF)/97/1	30 August 2000 (Award)	**Lauterpacht**, Civiletti, Luis Siqueiros	Breach of NAFTA Article 1110 found
Compañía de Aguas del Aconquija S.A. and Vivendi Universal S.A. v. Argentine Republic, ICSID Case No. ARB/97/3	21 November 2000 (Award)	**Rezek**, Buergenthal, Trooboff	No expropriation found
Wena Hotels Ltd. v. Arab Republic of Egypt, ICSID Case No. ARB/98/4	8 December 2000 (Award)	**Leigh**, Fadlallah, Wallace	Expropriation found
Alex Genin and others v. Republic of Estonia, ICSID Case No. ARB/99/2	25 June 2001 (Award)	**Fortier**, Heth, van den Berg	No expropriation found
Eudoro A. Olguín v. Republic of Paraguay, ICSID Case No. ARB/98/5	26 July 2001 (Award)	**Oreamuno**, Rezek, Mayora Alvarado	No expropriation found
Middle East Cement Shipping and Handling Co. S.A. v. Arab Republic of Egypt, ICSID Case No. ARB/99/6	12 April 2002 (Award)	**Böckstiegel**, Wallace, Bernardini	Expropriation found
Mondev International Ltd. v. United States of America, ICSID Case No. ARB(AF)/99/2	11 October 2002 (Award)	**Stephen**, Crawford, Schwebel	No breach of NAFTA Article 1110 found
Marvin Roy Feldman Karpa v. United Mexican States, ICSID Case No. ARB(AF)/99/1	16 December 2002 (Award)	**Kerameus**, Covarrubias Bravo, Gantz	No breach of NAFTA Article 1110 found
Técnicas Medioambientales Tecmed, S.A. v. United Mexican States, ICSID Case No. ARB(AF)/00/2	29 May 2003 (Award)	**Grigera Naón**, Bernal Verea, Fernández Rozas	Expropriation found
Generation Ukraine Inc. v. Ukraine, ICSID Case No. ARB/00/9	16 September 2003 (Award)	**Paulsson**, Salpius, Voss	No expropriation found

II. Substantive Issues by Topic – F. No Expropriation Without Compensation *(continued)*

Case	Date of Decision or Award	Tribunal (President denoted in bold)	Outcome
AIG Capital Partners, Inc. and CJSC Tema Real Estate Company v. Republic of Kazakhstan, ICSID Case No. ARB/01/6	7 October 2003 (Award)	**Nariman**, Bernardini, Vukmir	Expropriation found
Consortium R.F.C.C. v. Kingdom of Morocco, ICSID Case No. ARB/00/6	22 December 2003 (Award)	**Briner**, Cremades, Fadlallah	No expropriation found
Patrick Mitchell v. Democratic Republic of the Congo, ICSID Case No. ARB/99/7	9 February 2004 (Award)	**Bucher**, Agboyibo, Lalonde	Expropriation found
Waste Management, Inc. v. United Mexican States, ICSID Case No. ARB(AF)/00/3	30 April 2004 (Award)	**Crawford**, Civiletti, Magallón Gómez	No breach of NAFTA Article 1110 found
MTD Equity Sdn. Bhd. and MTD Chile S.A. v. Republic of Chile, ICSID Case No. ARB/01/7	25 May 2004 (Award)	**Rigo Sureda**, Lalonde, Oreamuno	No expropriation found
CMS Gas Transmission Company v. Argentine Republic, ICSID Case No. ARB/01/8	12 May 2005 (Award)	**Orrego Vicuña**, Lalonde, Rezek	No expropriation found
Noble Ventures, Inc. v. Romania, ICSID Case No. ARB/01/11	12 October 2005 (Award)	**Böckstiegel**, Lever, Dupuy	No expropriation found
Azurix Corp. v. Argentine Republic, ICSID Case No. ARB/01/12	14 July 2006 (Award)	**Rigo Sureda**, Lalonde, Martins	No expropriation found
Fireman's Fund Insurance Company v. United Mexican States, ICSID Case No. ARB(AF)/02/1	17 July 2006 (Award)	**van den Berg**, Lowenfeld, Saavedra Olavarrieta	No breach of NAFTA Article 1110 found
ADC Affiliate Limited and ADC & ADMC Management Limited v. Republic of Hungary, ICSID Case No. ARB/03/16	2 October 2006 (Award)	**Kaplan**, Brower, van den Berg	Expropriation found
LG&E Energy Corp., LG&E Capital Corp. and LG&E International Inc. v. Argentine Republic, ICSID Case No. ARB/02/1	3 October 2006 (Decision on Liability)	**de Maekelt**, Rezek, van den Berg	No expropriation found
Champion Trading Company and Ameritrade International, Inc. v. Arab Republic of Egypt, ICSID Case No. ARB/02/9	27 October 2006 (Award)	**Briner**, Fortier, Aynès	Not considered

Case	Date of Decision or Award	Tribunal (President denoted in bold)	Outcome
PSEG Global Inc. and Konya Ilgin Elektrik Üretim ve Ticaret Limited Sirketi v. Republic of Turkey, ICSID Case No. ARB/02/5	19 January 2007 (Award)	**Orrego Vicuña,** Fortier, Kaufmann-Kohler	No expropriation found
Siemens A.G. v. Argentine Republic, ICSID Case No. ARB/02/8	7 February 2007 (Award)	**Rigo Sureda,** Brower, Bello Janeiro	Expropriation found
Enron Corporation and Ponderosa Assets, L.P. v. Argentine Republic, ICSID Case No. ARB/01/3	22 May 2007 (Award)	**Orrego Vicuña,** van den Berg, Tschanz	No expropriation found
Ahmonseto, Inc. and others v. Arab Republic of Egypt, ICSID Case No. ARB/02/15	18 June 2007 (Award)	**Tercier,** Fadlallah, Viandier	No expropriation found
Tokios Tokelés v. Ukraine, ICSID Case No. ARB/02/18	26 July 2007 (Award)	**Mustill,** Bernardini, Price	No expropriation found
M.C.I. Power Group, L.C. and New Turbine, Inc. v. Republic of Ecuador, ICSID Case No. ARB/03/6	31 July 2007 (Award)	**Vinuesa,** Greenberg, Irarrázabal	No expropriation found
Compañía de Aguas del Aconquija S.A. and Vivendi Universal S.A. v. Argentine Republic, ICSID Case No. ARB/97/3	20 August 2007 (Award)	**Rowley,** Kaufmann-Kohler, Bernal Verea	Expropriation found
Parkerings-Compagniet AS v. Republic of Lithuania, ICSID Case No. ARB/05/8	11 September 2007 (Award)	**Lévy,** Lew, Lalonde	No expropriation found
Sempra Energy International v. Argentine Republic, ICSID Case No. ARB/02/16	28 September 2007 (Award)	**Orrego Vicuña,** Lalonde, Morelli Rico	No expropriation found
OKO Pankki Oyj and others v. Republic of Estonia, ICSID Case No. ARB/04/6	19 November 2007 (Award)	**de Witt Wijnen,** Veeder, Fortier	Not considered
Archer Daniels Midland Company and Tate & Lyle Ingredients Americas, Inc. v. United Mexican States, ICSID Case No. ARB(AF)/04/5	21 November 2007 (Award)	**Cremades,** Rovine, Siqueiros T.	No breach of NAFTA Article 1110 found
Corn Products International, Inc. v. United Mexican States, ICSID Case No. ARB(AF)/04/1	15 January 2008 (Decision on Responsibility)	**Greenwood,** Lowenfeld, Serrano de la Vega	No breach of NAFTA Article 1110 found
Desert Line Projects LLC v. Republic of Yemen, ICSID Case No. ARB/05/17	6 February 2008 (Award)	**Tercier,** Paulsson, El-Kosheri	Not considered

II. Substantive Issues by Topic – F. No Expropriation Without Compensation (continued)

Case	Date of Decision or Award	Tribunal (President denoted in bold)	Outcome
Ares International S.r.l. and MetalGeo S.r.l. v. Georgia, ICSID Case No. ARB/05/23	28 February 2008 (Award)	**Rowley**, Beechey, Gaillard	No expropriation found
Victor Pey Casado and President Allende Foundation v. Republic of Chile, ICSID Case No. ARB/98/2	8 May 2008 (Award)	**Lalive**, Chemloul, Gaillard	No expropriation found
Metalpar S.A. and Buen Aire S.A. v. Argentine Republic, ICSID Case No. ARB/03/5	6 June 2008 (Award)	**Oreamuno**, Cameron, Chabaneix	No expropriation found
Helnan International Hotels A/S v. Arab Republic of Egypt, ICSID Case No. ARB/05/19	3 July 2008 (Award)	**Derains**, Dolzer, Lee	No expropriation found
Biwater Gauff (Tanzania) Limited v. United Republic of Tanzania, ICSID Case No. ARB/05/22	24 July 2008 (Award)	**Hanotiau**, Born, Landau	Expropriation found
Rumeli Telekom A.S. and Telsim Mobil Telekomunikasyon Hizmetleri A.S. v. Republic of Kazakhstan, ICSID Case No. ARB/05/16	29 July 2008 (Award)	**Hanotiau**, Boyd, Lalonde	Expropriation found
Plama Consortium Limited v. Republic of Bulgaria, ICSID Case No. ARB/03/24	27 August 2008 (Award)	**Salans**, van den Berg, Veeder	No expropriation found
Continental Casualty Company v. Argentine Republic, ICSID Case No. ARB/03/9	5 September 2008 (Award)	**Sacerdoti**, Veeder, Nader	No expropriation found
LESI, S.p.A. and Astaldi, S.p.A. v. People's Democratic Republic of Algeria, ICSID Case No. ARB/05/3	12 November 2008 (Award)	**Tercier**, Hanotiau, Gaillard	No expropriation found
Bernardus Henricus Funnekotter and others v. Republic of Zimbabwe, ICSID Case No. ARB/05/6	22 April 2009 (Award)	**Guillaume**, Cass, Wasi Zafar	Expropriation found
Waguih Elie George Siag and Clorinda Vecchi v. Arab Republic of Egypt, ICSID Case No. ARB/05/15	1 June 2009 (Award)	**Williams**, Pryles, Orrego Vicuña	Expropriation found

Case	Date of Decision or Award	Tribunal (President denoted in bold)	Outcome
Saipem S.p.A. v. People's Republic of Bangladesh, ICSID Case No. ARB/05/7	30 June 2009 (Award)	**Kaufmann-Kohler,** Schreuer, Otton	Expropriation found
Bayindir Insaat Turizm Ticaret Ve Sanayi A.Ş. v. Islamic Republic of Pakistan, ICSID Case No. ARB/03/29	27 August 2009 (Award)	**Kaufmann-Kohler,** Berman, Böckstiegel	No expropriation found
Cargill, Inc. v. United Mexican States, ICSID Case No. ARB(AF)/05/2	18 September 2009 (Award)	**Pryles,** Caron, McRae	No breach of NAFTA Article 1110 found
EDF (Services) Ltd. v. Romania, ICSID Case No. ARB/05/13	8 October 2009 (Award)	**Bernardini,** Derains, Rovine	No expropriation found
Joseph C. Lemire v. Ukraine, ICSID Case No. ARB/06/18	21 January 2010 (Decision on Jurisdiction and Liability)	**Fernández-Armesto,** Paulsson, Voss	Withdrawn

II. Substantive Issues by Topic – G. Observance of Specific Undertakings

Case	Date of Decision or Award	Tribunal (President denoted in bold)	Outcome
Fedax N.V. v. Republic of Venezuela, ICSID Case No. ARB/96/3	9 March 1998 (Award)	**Orrego Vicuña**, Heth, Owen	Breach found
Alex Genin and others v. Republic of Estonia, ICSID Case No. ARB/99/2	25 June 2001 (Award)	**Fortier**, Heth, van den Berg	No breach found
SGS Société Générale de Surveillance S.A. v. Islamic Republic of Pakistan, ICSID Case No. ARB/01/13	6 August 2003 (Decision on Jurisdiction)	**Feliciano**, Thomas, Faurés	Denial of jurisdiction on breach of contract claims on the basis that umbrella clauses held not to extend to such claims but for in exceptional circumstances
SGS Société Générale de Surveillance S.A. v. Republic of the Philippines, ICSID Case No. ARB/02/6	29 January 2004 (Decision on Jurisdiction)	**El-Kosheri**, Crawford, Crivellaro	Jurisdiction found on umbrella clause claim, but subject to forum selection clause in parties' contract
MTD Equity Sdn. Bhd. and MTD Chile S.A. v. Republic of Chile, ICSID Case No. ARB/01/7	25 May 2004 (Award)	**Rigo Sureda**, Lalonde, Oreamuno	No breach found
Joy Mining Machinery Ltd. v. Arab Republic of Egypt, ICSID Case No. ARB/03/11	6 August 2004 (Award on Jurisdiction)	**Orrego Vicuña**, Craig, Weeramantry	Denial of jurisdiction on umbrella clause claim
Salini Costruttori S.p.A. and Italstrade S.p.A. v. Hashemite Kingdom of Jordan, ICSID Case No. ARB/02/13	15 November 2004 (Decision on Jurisdiction	**Guillaume**, Cremades, Sinclair	Denial of jurisdiction on umbrella clause claim
Impregilo S.p.A. v. Islamic Republic of Pakistan, ICSID Case No. ARB/03/3	22 April 2005 (Decision on Jurisdiction)	**Guillaume**, Cremades, Landau	Denial of jurisdiction on umbrella clause claim
Sempra Energy International v. Argentine Republic, ICSID Case No. ARB/02/16	11 May 2005 (Decision on Objections to Jurisdiction)	**Orrego Vicuña**, Lalonde, Morelli Rico	Jurisdiction found on umbrella clause claim
CMS Gas Transmission Company v. Argentine Republic, ICSID Case No. ARB/01/18	12 May 2005 (Award)	**Orrego Vicuña**, Lalonde, Rezek	Breach found

Case	Date of Decision or Award	Tribunal (President denoted in bold)	Outcome
Noble Ventures, Inc. v. Romania, ICSID Case No. ARB/01/11	12 October 2005 (Award)	**Böckstiegel**, Lever, Dupuy	No breach found
El Paso Energy International Company v. Argentine Republic, ICSID Case No. ARB/03/15	27 April 2006 (Decision on Jurisdiction)	**Caflisch**, Stern, Bernardini	Jurisdiction found on umbrella clause claim
Azurix Corp. v. Argentine Republic, ICSID Case No. ARB/01/12	14 July 2006 (Award)	**Rigo Sureda**, Lalonde, Martins	No breach found
Pan American Energy LLC and BP Argentina Exploration Company v. Argentine Republic, ICSID Case No. ARB/03/13; BP America Production Co. and Others v. Argentine Republic, ICSID Case No. ARB/04/8	27 July 2006 (Decision on Preliminary Objections)	**Caflisch**, Stern, van den Berg	Jurisdiction found on umbrella clause claim
LG&E Energy Corp., LG&E Capital Corp. and LG&E International Inc. v. Argentine Republic, ICSID Case No. ARB/02/1	3 October 2006 (Award)	**de Maekelt**, Rezek, van den Berg	Breach found
PSEG Global Inc. and Konya Ilgin Elektrik Üretim ve Ticaret Limited Sirketi v. Republic of Turkey, ICSID Case No. ARB/02/5	19 January 2007 (Award)	**Orrego Vicuña**, Fortier, Kaufmann-Kohler	No breach found
Siemens A.G. v. Argentine Republic, ICSID Case No. ARB/02/8	6 February 2007 (Award)	**Rigo Sureda**, Brower, Bello Janeiro	No breach found
Enron Corporation and Ponderosa Assets, L.P. v. Argentine Republic, ICSID Case No. ARB/01/3	22 May 2007 (Award)	**Orrego Vicuña**, van den Berg, Tschanz	Breach found
CMS Gas Transmission Company v. Argentine Republic, ICSID Case No. ARB/01/8	25 September 2007 (Annulment Decision)	**Guillaume**, Elaraby, Crawford	Tribunal's finding of umbrella clause breach annulled
Sempra Energy International v. Argentine Republic, ICSID Case No. ARB/02/16	28 September 2007 (Award)	**Orrego Vicuña**, Lalonde, Morelli Rico	Breach found
OKO Pankki Oyj and others v. Republic of Estonia, ICSID Case No. ARB/04/6	19 November 2007 (Award)	**de Witt Wijnen**, Veeder, Fortier	Not considered
Duke Energy Electroquil Partners & Electroquil S.A. v. Republic of Ecuador, ICSID Case No. ARB/04/19	18 August 2008 (Award)	**Kaufmann-Kohler**, Gómez-Pinzón, van den Berg	Breach found

II. Substantive Issues by Topic – G. Observance of Specific Undertakings *(continued)*

Case	Date of Decision or Award	Tribunal (President denoted in bold)	Outcome
Plama Consortium Limited v. Republic of Bulgaria, ICSID Case No. ARB/03/24	27 August 2008 (Award)	**Salans**, van den Berg, Veeder	No breach found
Continental Casualty Company v. Argentine Republic, ICSID Case No. ARB/03/9	5 September 2008 (Award)	**Sacerdoti**, Veeder, Nader	No breach found
Bureau Veritas, Inspection, Valuation, Assessment and Control, BIVAC B.V. v. Republic of Paraguay, ICSID Case No. ARB/07/9	29 May 2009 (Decision of the Tribunal on Objections to Jurisdiction)	**Knieper**, Fortier, Sands	Jurisdiction found on umbrella clause claim, but claim held to be inadmissible
Toto Costruzioni Generali S.p.A. v. Republic of Lebanon, ICSID Case No. ARB/07/12	11 September 2009 (Decision on Jurisdiction)	**van Houtte**, Feliciano, Moghaizel	Denial of jurisdiction on umbrella clause claim
EDF (Services) Limited v. Romania, ICSID Case No. ARB/05/13	8 October 2009 (Award)	**Bernardini**, Derains, Rovine	No breach found
Joseph C. Lemire v. Ukraine, ICSID Case No. ARB/06/18	21 January 2010 (Decision on Jurisdiction and Liability)	**Fernández-Armesto**, Paulsson, Voss	No breach found

III. Procedural and Other Issues – A. Participation of Non-Disputing Parties

Case	Date of Decision	Tribunal (President denoted in bold)	Outcome
Aguas del Tunari S.A. v. Republic of Bolivia, ICSID Case No. ARB/02/3	29 January 2003 (Letter from the President of Tribunal)	**Caron**, Alberro-Semerena, Álvarez	Denied
Suez, Sociedad General de Aguas de Barcelona S.A. and Vivendi Universal S.A. v. Argentine Republic, ICSID Case No. ARB/03/19	19 May 2005 (Order in Response to a Petition for Transparency and Participation as Amicus Curiae)	**Salacuse**, Kaufmann-Kohler, Nikken	Permitted in principle
Suez, Sociedad General de Aguas de Barcelona S.A. and Interaguas Servicios Integrales de Agua S.A. v. Argentine Republic, ICSID Case No. ARB/03/17	17 March 2006 (Order in Response to a Petition for Participation as Amicus Curiae)	**Salacuse**, Kaufmann-Kohler, Nikken	Permitted in principle; no petition from non-disputing party filed thereafter
Biwater Gauff (Tanzania) Ltd. v. United Republic of Tanzania, ICSID Case No. ARB/05/22	2 February 2007 (Procedural Order No. 5)	**Hanotiau**, Born, Landau	Permitted; non-disputing parties filed observations
Suez, Sociedad General de Aguas de Barcelona S.A. and Vivendi Universal S.A. v. Argentine Republic, ICSID Case No. ARB/03/19	12 February 2007 (Order in Response to a Petition by Five Non-Governmental Organizations for Permission to Make an Amicus Curiae Submission)	**Salacuse**, Kaufmann-Kohler, Nikken	Permitted; non-disputing parties filed observations
AES Summit Generation Ltd. and AES-Tisza Erőmű Kft. v. Republic of Hungary, ICSID Case No. ARB/07/22	26 November 2008 (unpublished)	**von Wobeser**, Rowley, Stern	Permitted; non-disputing party filed observations
Electrabel S.A. v. Republic of Hungary, ICSID Case No. ARB/07/19	28 April 2009 (unpublished)	**Veeder**, Kaufmann-Kohler, Stern	Permitted; non-disputing party filed observations

III. Procedural and Other Issues – A. Participation of Non-Disputing Parties (*continued*)

Case	Date of Decision	Tribunal (President denoted in bold)	Outcome
Ioan Micula, Viorel Micula and others v. Romania, ICSID Case No. ARB/05/20	15 May 2009 (unpublished)	**Lévy**, Alexandrov, Ehlermann	Permitted; non-disputing party filed observations
Piero Foresti, Laura de Carli and others v. Republic of South Africa, ICSID Case No. ARB(AF)/07/1	5 October 2009 (Letter communicating Tribunal's decision on Non-Disputing Parties)	**Lowe**, Brower, Matthews	Permitted; applications filed by non-disputing parties but no observations filed

III. Procedural and Other Issues – B. Annulment Proceedings

Case (Party requesting annulment denoted in bold)	Date of Decision	Ad Hoc Committee (President denoted in bold)	Article 52(1) Annulment Grounds Invoked	Outcome
Klöckner Industrie-Anlagen GmbH and others v. United Republic of Cameroon and Société Camerounaise des Engrais, ICSID Case No. ARB/81/2	3 May 1985 (Decision on Annulment)	**Lalive,** El-Kosheri, Seidl-Hohenveldern	Manifest excess of powers; Departure from a fundamental rule of procedure; Failure to state reasons	Application for annulment granted (Manifest excess of powers; Failure to state reasons)
Amco Asia Corporation and others v. **Republic of Indonesia,** ICSID Case No. ARB/81/1	16 May 1986 (Decision on the Application for Annulment)	**Seidl-Hohenveldern,** Feliciano, Giardina	Manifest excess of powers; Departure from a fundamental rule of procedure; Failure to state reasons	Application for annulment granted (Manifest excess of powers; Failure to state reasons)
Maritime International Nominees Establishment v. **Republic of Guinea,** ICSID Case No. ARB/84/4	22 December 1989 (Decision on Annulment)	**Sucharitkul,** Broches, Mbaye	Manifest excess of powers; Departure from a fundamental rule of procedure; Failure to state reasons	Application for annulment granted (Failure to state reasons)
Klöckner Industrie-Anlagen GmbH and others v. United Republic of Cameroon and Société Camerounaise des Engrais, ICSID Case No. ARB/81/2	17 May 1990 (Decision on Annulment) (Resubmitted Case)	**Sucharitkul,** Giardina, Mbaye	Manifest excess of powers; Departure from a fundamental rule of procedure; Failure to state reasons	Applications for annulment rejected
Amco Asia Corporation and others v. **Republic of Indonesia,** ICSID Case No. ARB/81/1	3 December 1992 (Decision on Annulment of Award of 5 June 1990 and Supplemental Award of 17 October 1990) (Resubmitted Case)	**Sucharitkul,** Fatouros, Schindler	Manifest excess of powers; Departure from a fundamental rule of procedure; Failure to state reasons	Applications for annulment rejected with respect to Award of 5 June 1990 Application for annulment granted with respect to Supplemental Award of 17 October 1990 (Departure from a fundamental rule of procedure)

III. Procedural and Other Issues – B. Annulment Proceedings *(continued)*

Case (Party requesting annulment denoted in bold)	Date of Decision	Ad Hoc Committee (President denoted in bold)	Article 52(1) Annulment Grounds Invoked	Outcome
Southern Pacific Properties (Middle East) Ltd. v. **Arab Republic of Egypt**, ICSID Case No. ARB/84/3	9 March 1993 (Date of Order taking note of discontinuance, settlement agreed by the parties)	**Reymond**, Fatouros, Mbaye	Proceedings discontinued by agreement of the parties	
Wena Hotels Ltd. v. **Arab Republic of Egypt**, ICSID Case No. ARB/98/4	5 February 2002 (Decision on the Application for Annulment)	**Kerameus**, Bucher, Orrego Vicuña	Manifest excess of powers; Departure from a fundamental rule of procedure; Failure to state reasons	Application for annulment rejected
Philippe Gruslin v. Malaysia, ICSID Case No. ARB/99/3	2 April 2002 (Date of Order taking note of discontinuance, lack of payment of advances)	**Buergenthal**, Hossein, Kaufmann-Kohler	Proceedings discontinued for nonpayment of fees	
Compañía de Aguas del Aconquija S.A. and Vivendi Universal S.A. v. Argentine Republic, ICSID Case No. ARB/97/3	3 July 2002 (Decision on Annulment)	**Fortier**, Crawford, Fernández Rozas	Manifest excess of powers; Departure from a fundamental rule of procedure; Failure to state reasons	Application for annulment granted in part (Manifest excess of powers)
CDC Group P.L.C. v. **Republic of Seychelles**, ICSID Case No. ARB/02/14	29 June 2005 (Decision of the Ad Hoc Committee on the Application for Annulment of the Republic of Seychelles)	**Brower**, Hwang, Williams	Manifest excess of powers; Departure from a fundamental rule of procedure; Failure to state reasons	Application for annulment rejected

Case (Party requesting annulment denoted in bold)	Date of Decision	Ad Hoc Committee (President denoted in bold)	Article 52(1) Annulment Grounds Invoked	Outcome
Joy Mining Machinery Ltd. *v Arab Republic of Egypt,* ICSID Case No. ARB/03/11	16 December 2005 (Date of Order taking note of discontinuance, settlement agreed by the parties)	**Dimolitsa,** Hwang, Shaw	Proceedings discontinued by agreement of the parties	
Consortium R.F.C.C. *v. Kingdom of Morocco,* ICSID Case No. ARB/00/6	18 January 2006 (Decision on Annulment)	**Hanotiau,** Fatouros, Berman		Unpublished
Patrick Mitchell v. **Democratic Republic of Congo,** ICSID Case No. ARB/99/7	1 November 2006 (Decision on the Application for Annulment of the Award)	**Dimolitsa,** Dossou, Giardina	Manifest excess of powers; Failure to state reasons	Application for annulment granted (Manifest excess of powers; Failure to state reasons)
Repsol YPF Ecuador S.A. v. **Empresa Estatal Petroleos del Ecuador (Petroecuador),** ICSID Case No. ARB/01/10	8 January 2007 (Decision on the Application for Annulment)	**Kessler,** Bernardini, Biggs	Manifest excess of powers; Departure from a fundamental rule of procedure	Application for annulment rejected
MTD Equity Sdn. Bhd. and MTD Chile S.A. v. **Republic of Chile,** ICSID Case No. ARB/01/7	21 March 2007 (Decision on the Application for Annulment)	**Guillaume,** Crawford, Ordoñez Noriega	Manifest excess of powers; Departure from a fundamental rule of procedure; Failure to state reasons	Application for annulment rejected
Hussein Nuaman Soufraki *v. United Arab Emirates,* ICSID Case No. ARB/02/7	5 June 2007 (Decision of the Ad Hoc Committee on the Application for Annulment of Mr. Soufraki)	**Feliciano,** Nabulsi (dissenting opinion), Stern	Manifest excess of powers; Failure to state reasons	Application for annulment rejected

III. Procedural and Other Issues – B. Annulment Proceedings (continued)

Case (Party requesting annulment denoted in bold)	Date of Decision	Ad Hoc Committee (President denoted in bold)	Article 52(1) Annulment Grounds Invoked	Outcome
Industria Nacional de Alimentos, S.A. and Indalsa Perú, S.A. (formerly Empresas Lucchetti, S.A. and Lucchetti Perú, S.A.) v. Republic of Peru, ICSID Case No. ARB/03/4	5 September 2007 (Decision on Annulment)	**Dandius**, Giardina, Berman (dissenting opinion)	Manifest excess of powers; Departure from a fundamental rule of procedure; Failure to state reasons	Application for annulment rejected
CMS Gas Transmission Company v. **Argentine Republic**, ICSID Case No. ARB/01/8	25 September 2007 (Decision of the Ad Hoc Committee on the Application for Annulment of the Argentine Republic)	**Guillaume**, Elaraby, Crawford	Manifest excess of powers; Failure to state reasons	Application for annulment granted in part (Failure to state reasons)
Malaysian Historical Salvors Sdn., Bhd. v. The Government of Malaysia, ICSID Case No. ARB/05/10	16 April 2009 (Decision on the Application for Annulment)	**Schwebel**, Shahabuddeen (dissenting opinion), Tomka	Manifest excess of powers	Application for annulment granted (Manifest excess of powers)
Azurix Corp. v. **Argentine Republic**, ICSID Case No. ARB/01/12	1 September 2009 (Decision on the Application for Annulment of the Argentine Republic)	**Griffith**, Ajibola, Hwang	Improper constitution of the tribunal; Manifest excess of powers; Departure from a fundamental rule of procedure; Failure to state reasons	Application for annulment rejected
Siemens A.G. v. **Argentine Republic**, ICSID Case No. ARB/02/8	28 September 2009 (Date of Order taking note of discontinuance)	**Guillaume**, Shahabuddeen, Feliciano	Proceedings discontinued by agreement of the parties	
M.C.I. Power Group L.C. and New Turbine, Inc. v. Republic of Ecuador, ICSID Case No. ARB/03/6	19 October 2009 (Decision on Annulment)	**Hascher**, Danelius, Tomka	Manifest excess of powers; Failure to state reasons	Application for annulment rejected

Case (Party requesting annulment denoted in bold)	Date of Decision	Ad Hoc Committee (President denoted in bold)	Article 52(1) Annulment Grounds Invoked	Outcome
*Rumeli Telekom A.S. and Telsim Mobil Telekomünikasyon Hizmetleri A.S. v. **Republic of Kazakhstan**,* ICSID Case No. ARB/05/16	25 March 2010 (Decision of the Ad Hoc Committee)	**Schwebel**, McLachlan, Silva Romero	Manifest excess of powers; Departure from a fundamental rule of procedure; Failure to state reasons	Application for annulment rejected
Helnan International Hotels A/S v. Arab Republic of Egypt, ICSID Case No. ARB/05/19	14 June 2010 (Decision of the Ad Hoc Committee)	**Schwebel**, Ajibola, McLachlan	Manifest excess of powers; Departure from a fundamental rule of procedure; Failure to state reasons	Application for annulment granted in part (Manifest excess of powers)
*Sempra Energy International v. **Argentine Republic**,* ICSID Case No. ARB/02/16	29 June 2010 (Decision on the Argentine Republic's Application for Annulment of the Award)	**Söderlund**, Edward, Jacovides	Improper constitution of the tribunal; Manifest excess of powers; Departure from a fundamental rule of procedure; Failure to state reasons	Application for annulment granted (Manifest excess of powers)
*Enron Creditors Recovery Corp. (formerly Enron Corp.) and Ponderosa Assets, L.P. v. **Argentine Republic**,* ICSID Case No. ARB/01/3	30 July 2010 (Decision on the Application for Annulment of the Argentine Republic)	**Griffith**, Robinson, Tresselt	Manifest excess of powers; Departure from a fundamental rule of procedure; Failure to state reasons	Application for annulment granted (Manifest excess of powers; Failure to state reasons)
*Compañía de Aguas del Aconquija S.A. and Vivendi Universal S.A. v. **Argentine Republic**,* ICSID Case No. ARB/97/3	10 August 2010 (Decision on the Argentine Republic's Request for Annulment of the Award rendered on 20 August 2007) (Resubmitted Case)	**El-Kosheri**, Dalhuisen (additional opinion), Jacovides	Improper constitution of the tribunal; Manifest excess of powers; Departure from a fundamental rule of procedure; Failure to state reasons; Corruption on the part of a member of the tribunal (withdrawn)	Application for annulment rejected

405

III. Procedural and Other Issues – C. Challenges to Arbitrators

Case	Date of Decision	Arbitrator Challenged	Decision-Maker on Challenge	Outcome
Amco Asia Corporation and others v. Republic of Indonesia, ICSID Case No. ARB/81/1	24 June 1982 (summarized in 20 November 1984 Award)	Rubin	Goldman, Foighel	Rejected
Eudoro A. Olguín v. Republic of Paraguay, ICSID Case No. ARB/98/5	16 March 1999 (date of challenge, no decision rendered) (summarized in 8 August 2000 Decision on Jurisdiction)	Furnish	n/a	Resignation
World Duty Free Company Ltd. v. Republic of Kenya, ICSID Case No. ARB/00/7	15 January 2001 (date of challenge, no decision rendered) (summarized in 4 October 2006 Award)	Crawford	n/a	Resignation
Zhinvali Development Ltd. v. Republic of Georgia, ICSID Case No. ARB/00/1	19 January 2001 (summarized in 24 January 2003 Award)	Jacovides	Robinson, Rubin	Rejected
Generation Ukraine Inc. v. Ukraine, ICSID Case No. ARB/00/9	5 July 2001 (summarized in 16 September 2003 Award)	Voss	Paulsson, Salpius (no agreement) / ICSID Administrative Council Chairman (requested Secretary-General of the Permanent Court of Arbitration to decide challenge) / Secretary-General of the Permanent Court of Arbitration	Rejected
Compañiá de Aguas del Aconquija S.A. and Vivendi Universal v. Argentine Republic, ICSID Case No. ARB/97/3	3 October 2001 (Decision on the Challenge to the President of the Committee)	Fortier	Fernández Rozas, Crawford	Rejected
SGS Société Générale de Surveillance S.A. v. Islamic Republic of Pakistan, ICSID Case No. ARB/01/13	19 December 2002 (Decision on Claimant's Proposal to Disqualify Arbitrator)	Thomas	Feliciano, Faurès	Rejected
Salini Costruttori S.p.A. and Italstrade S.p.A. v. Hashemite Kingdom of Jordan, ICSID Case No. ARB/02/13	8 April 2003 (date of challenge, no decision rendered) (summarized in 29 November 2004 Decision on Jurisdiction)	Schwartz	n/a	Resignation

Case	Date of Decision	Arbitrator Challenged	Decision-Maker on Challenge	Outcome
Azurix Corp. v. Argentine Republic, ICSID Case No. ARB/01/12	25 February 2005 (summarized in 1 September 2009 Decision on the Application for Annulment of the Argentine Republic)	Rigo Sureda	Lalonde, Martins	Rejected
Siemens A.G. v. Argentine Republic, ICSID Case No. ARB/02/8	15 April 2005 (summarized in 6 February 2007 Award)	Rigo Sureda	Bello Janeiro, Brower (no agreement) / ICSID Administrative Council Chairman (requested Secretary-General of the Permanent Court of Arbitration to decide challenge) / Secretary-General of the Permanent Court of Arbitration	Rejected
Saipem S.p.A. v. People's Republic of Bangladesh, ICSID Case No. ARB/05/7	11 October 2005 (summarized in 30 June 2009 Award)	Schreuer	Otton, Kaufmann-Kohler	Rejected
Victor Pey Casado and President Allende Foundation v. Republic of Chile, ICSID Case No. ARB/98/2	21 February 2006 (summarized in 8 May 2008 Award)	Leoro Franco, Lalive, Bedjaoui	ICSID Administrative Council Chairman (requested Secretary-General of the Permanent Court of Arbitration to decide challenge) / Secretary-General of the Permanent Court of Arbitration	Resignation, Rejected, Affirmed
African Holding Company of America, Inc. and Société Africaine de Construction au Congo S.A.R.L. v. Democratic Republic of the Congo, ICSID Case No. ARB/05/21	11 May 2006 (date of challenge, no decision rendered) (summarized in 29 July 2008 Sentence sur les déclinatoires de compétence et la recevabilité)	Giovannini	n/a	Resignation
Rail World LLC and others v. Republic of Estonia, ICSID Case No. ARB/06/6	31 July 2006 (summarized in 5 February 2007 Order of the Tribunal Taking Note of the Discontinuance of the Proceeding)	Raeside	n/a	Resignation
Asset Recovery Trust S.A. v. Argentine Republic, ICSID Case No. ARB/05/11	27 November 2006	Irarrázabal Covarrubias	Canales Santos, Cançado Trindade	Rejected

III. Procedural and Other Issues – C. Challenges to Arbitrators (continued)

Case	Date of Decision	Arbitrator Challenged	Decision-Maker on Challenge	Outcome
Sempra Energy International v. Argentine Republic, ICSID Case No. ARB/02/16	5 June 2007 (summarized in 28 September 2007 Award)	Orrego Vicuña, Lalonde, Morelli Rico	ICSID Administrative Council Chairman	Rejected
Suez, Sociedad General de Aguas de Barcelona S.A. and InterAgua Servicios Integrales de Agua S.A. v. Argentine Republic, ICSID Case No. ARB/03/17; *Suez, Sociedad General de Aguas de Barcelona S.A. and Vivendi Universal S.A. v. Argentine Republic*, ICSID Case No. ARB/03/19	22 October 2007 (Decision on the Proposal for the Disqualification of a Member of the Arbitral Tribunal)	Kaufmann-Kohler	Salacuse, Nikken	Rejected
Electrabel S.A. v. Republic of Hungary, ICSID Case No. ARB/07/19	25 February 2008 (unpublished)	Stern	Veeder, Kaufmann-Kohler	Rejected
Saba Fakes v. Republic of Turkey, ICSID Case No. ARB/07/20	28 April 2008 (summarized in 14 July 2010 Award)	Lévy	Gaillard, van Houtte	Rejected
Suez, Sociedad General de Aguas de Barcelona S.A. and InterAgua Servicios Integrales de Agua S.A. v. Argentine Republic, ICSID Case No. ARB/03/17; *Suez, Sociedad General de Aguas de Barcelona S.A. and Vivendi Universal S.A. v. Argentine Republic*, ICSID Case No. ARB/03/19	12 May 2008 (Decision on a Second Proposal for the Disqualification of a Member of the Arbitral Tribunal)	Kaufmann-Kohler	Salacuse, Nikken	Rejected
EDF International S.A., SAUR International S.A. and León Participaciones Argentinas S.A. v. Argentine Republic, ICSID Case No. ARB/03/23	25 June 2008 (Challenge Decision Regarding Professor Gabrielle Kaufmann-Kohler)	Kaufmann-Kohler	Park, Remón	Rejected
Joseph C. Lemire v. Ukraine, ICSID Case No. ARB/06/18	23 September 2008 (summarized in 14 January 2010 Decision on Liability and Jurisdiction)	Paulsson	Voss, Fernández-Armesto	Rejected

Case	Date of Decision	Arbitrator Challenged	Decision-Maker on Challenge	Outcome
S&T Oil Equipment & Machinery Ltd. v. Romania, ICSID Case No. ARB/07/13	9 April 2009 (date of challenge, no decision rendered) (unpublished)	Savage	n/a	Resignation
CEMEX Caracas Investments B. V. and CEMEX Caracas II Investments B.V. v. Bolivarian Republic of Venezuela, ICSID Case No. ARB/08/15	6 November 2009 (Decision on the Respondent's Proposal to Disqualify a Member of the Tribunal)	von Mehren	Guillaume, Abi-Saab	Rejected
Participaciones Inversiones Portuarias SARL v. Gabonese Republic, ICSID Case No. ARB/08/17	12 November 2009 (Decision on the Proposal to Disqualify an Arbitrator)	Fadlallah	Paulsson, Stern (no agreement) / ICSID Administrative Council Chairman	Rejected
Perenco Ecuador Ltd. v. Republic of Ecuador and Empresa Estatal Petróleos del Ecuador (Petroecuador)', ICSID Case No. ARB/08/6	8 December 2009 (Decision on Challenge to Arbitrator)	Brower	Permanent Court of Arbitration (party agreement in advance that challenges to be heard by the Permanent Court of Arbitration)	Affirmed (Resignation)

III. Procedural and Other Issues – D. Costs

Case	Date of Decision or Award	Tribunal / Ad Hoc Committee (President denoted in bold)	Outcome ("ICSID costs" denotes costs of arbitration proceeding, including fees and expenses of arbitrators and costs of ICSID Secretariat)
Waste Management, Inc. v. United Mexican States, ICSID Case No. ARB(AF)/00/3	30 April 2004 (Award)	**Crawford**, Civiletti, Magallón Gómez	Each party bears its own legal costs and equal division of ICSID costs
MTD Equity Sdn. Bhd. and MTD Chile S.A. v. Republic of Chile, ICSID Case No. ARB/01/7	25 May 2004 (Award)	**Rigo Sureda**, Lalonde, Oreamuno	Each party bears its own legal costs and equal division of ICSID costs
Joy Mining Machinery Ltd. v. Arab Republic of Egypt, ICSID Case No. ARB/03/11	6 August 2004 (Award on Jurisdiction)	**Orrego Vicuña**, Craig, Weeramantry	Each party bears its own legal costs and equal division of ICSID costs
Československá Obchodní Banka, A.S. v. Slovak Republic, ICSID Case No. ARB/97/4	29 December 2004 (Award)	**van Houtte**, Bernardini, Bucher	Respondent to pay approximately 61% of Claimant's legal costs and ICSID costs
Consortium Groupement L.E.S.I.- DIPENTA v. People's Democratic Republic of Algeria, ICSID Case No. ARB/03/08	10 January 2005 (Award)	**Tercier**, Faurès, Gaillard	Each party bears its own legal costs and equal division of ICSID costs
Empresas Lucchetti S.A. and Lucchetti Peru S.A. v. Republic of Peru, ICSID Case No. ARB/03/4	7 February 2005 (Award)	**Buergenthal**, Cremades, Paulsson	Each party bears its own legal costs and equal division of ICSID costs
CMS Gas Transmission Company v. Argentine Republic, ICSID Case No. ARB/01/8	12 May 2005 (Award)	**Orrego Vicuña**, Lalonde, Rezek	Each party bears its own legal costs and equal division of ICSID costs
CDC Group P.L.C. v. Republic of Seychelles, ICSID Case No. ARB/02/14	29 June 2005 (Decision of the Ad Hoc Committee on the Application for Annulment of the Republic of the Seychelles)	**Brower**, Hwang, Williams	Respondent to pay 100% of Claimant's legal costs and ICSID costs of annulment proceeding
Noble Ventures, Inc. v. Romania, ICSID Case No. ARB/01/11	12 October 2005 (Award)	**Böckstiegel**, Lever, Dupuy	Each party bears its own legal costs and equal division of ICSID costs

Case	Date of Decision or Award	Tribunal / Ad Hoc Committee (President denoted in bold)	Outcome ("ICSID costs" denotes costs of arbitration proceeding including fees and expenses of arbitrators and costs of ICSID Secretariat)
Salini Costruttori S.p.A. and Italstrade S.p.A. v. Hashemite Kingdom of Jordan, ICSID Case No. ARB/02/13	31 January 2006 (Award)	**Guillaume**, Cremades, Sinclair (dissent on costs)	Each party bears its own legal costs and equal division of ICSID costs
F-W Oil Interests, Inc. v. Republic of Trinidad and Tobago, ICSID Case No. ARB/01/14	3 March 2006 (Award)	**Nariman**, Berman, Mustill	Each party bears its own legal costs and equal division of ICSID costs
Azurix Corp. v. Argentine Republic, ICSID Case No. ARB/01/12	14 July 2006 (Award)	**Rigo Sureda**, Lalonde, Martins	Each party bears its own legal costs and Respondent to pay ICSID costs (but for portion of ICSID costs borne by Claimant related to provisional measures and procedural incident)
Fireman's Fund Insurance Company v. United Mexican States, ICSID Case No. ARB(AF)/02/1	17 July 2006 (Award)	**van den Berg**, Lowenfeld, Saavedra Olavarrieta	Each party bears its own legal costs and equal division of ICSID costs
Inceysa Vallisoletana S.L. v. Republic of El Salvador, ICSID Case No. ARB/03/26	2 August 2006 (Award)	**Oreamuno**, Landy, von Wobeser	Each party bears its own legal costs and Claimant to pay 100% of ICSID costs
Telenor Mobile Communications A.S. v. Republic of Hungary, ICSID Case No. ARB/04/15	13 September 2006 (Award)	**Goode**, Allard, Marriott	Claimant to pay 100% of Respondent's legal costs and ICSID costs
ADC Affiliate Ltd. and ADC & ADMC Management Ltd. v. Republic of Hungary, ICSID Case No. ARB/03/16	2 October 2006 (Award)	**Kaplan**, Brower, van den Berg	Respondent to pay 100% of Claimants' legal costs and ICSID costs
World Duty Free Company Ltd. v. Republic of Kenya, ICSID Case No. ARB/00/7	4 October 2006 (Award)	**Guillaume**, Rogers, Veeder	Each party bears its own legal costs and equal division of ICSID costs
Champion Trading Company and Ameritrade International, Inc. v. Arab Republic of Egypt, ICSID Case No. ARB/02/9	27 October 2006 (Award)	**Briner**, Fortier, Aynès	Claimants to pay 50% of Respondent's legal costs and 100% of ICSID costs
Patrick Mitchell v. Democratic Republic of Congo, ICSID Case No. ARB/99/7	1 November 2006 (Decision on the Application for Annulment of the Award)	**Dimolitsa**, Dossou, Giardina	Each party bears its own legal costs and equal division of ICSID costs of annulment proceeding

411

III. Procedural and Other Issues – D. Costs *(continued)*

Case	Date of Decision or Award	Tribunal / Ad Hoc Committee (President denoted in bold)	Outcome ("ICSID costs" denotes costs of arbitration proceeding, including fees and expenses of arbitrators and costs of ICSID Secretariat)
Repsol YPF Ecuador S.A. v. Empresa Estatal Petroleos del Ecuador (Petroecuador), ICSID Case No. ARB/01/10	8 January 2007 (Decision on the Application for Annulment)	**Kessler**, Bernardini, Biggs	Respondent to pay 50% of Claimant's legal costs and 100% of ICSID costs of annulment proceeding
PSEG Global Inc. and Konya Ilgin Elektrik Üretim ve Ticaret Limited Sirketi v. Republic of Turkey, ICSID Case No. ARB/02/5	19 January 2007 (Award)	**Orrego Vicuña**, Fortier, Kaufmann-Kohler	Respondent to pay 65% of total legal and ICSID costs and Claimants to pay 35% of total legal and ICSID costs
Siemens A.G. v. Argentine Republic, ICSID Case No. ARB/02/08	6 February 2007 (Award)	**Rigo Sureda**, Brower, Bello Janeiro (dissent on costs)	Each party bears its own legal costs and 75% (Respondent) / 25% (Claimant) division of ICSID costs
MTD Equity Sdn. Bhd. and MTD Chile S.A. v. Republic of Chile, ICSID Case No. ARB/01/7	21 March 2007 (Decision on Annulment)	**Guillaume**, Crawford, Ordóñez Noriega	Each party bears its own legal costs and equal division of ICSID costs of annulment proceeding
Enron Corporation and Ponderosa Assets, L.P. v. Argentine Republic, ICSID Case No. ARB/01/3	22 May 2007 (Award)	**Orrego Vicuña**, van den Berg, Tschanz	Each party bears its own legal costs and equal division of ICSID costs
Hussein Nuaman Soufraki v. United Arab Emirates, ICSID Case No. ARB/02/7	5 June 2007 (Decision of the Ad Hoc Committee on the Application for Annulment of Mr. Soufraki)	**Feliciano**, Nabulsi, Stern	Each party bears its own legal costs and equal division of ICSID costs of annulment proceeding
Almonsesta, Inc. and others v. Arab Republic of Egypt, ICSID Case No. ARB/02/15	18 June 2007 (Award)	**Tercier**, Fadlallah, Viandier	Each party bears its own legal costs and equal division of ICSID costs of annulment proceeding
Bayview Irrigation District et al. v. United Mexican States, ICSID Case No. ARB(AF)/05/1	19 June 2007 (Award)	**Lowe**, Gómez-Palacio, Meese III	Each party bears its own legal costs and equal division of ICSID costs
LG&E Energy Corp. and others v. Argentine Republic, ICSID Case No. ARB/02/1	25 July 2007 (Award)	**de Maekelt**, van den Berg, Rezek	Each party bears its own legal costs and equal division of ICSID costs

Case	Date of Decision or Award	Tribunal / Ad Hoc Committee (President denoted in bold)	Outcome ("ICSID costs" denotes costs of arbitration proceeding, including fees and expenses of arbitrators and costs of ICSID Secretariat)
Tokios Tokelés v. Ukraine, ICSID Case No. ARB/02/18	26 July 2007 (Award)	**Mustill**, Bernardini, Price	Each party bears its own legal costs and equal division of ICSID costs
M.C.I. Power Group L.C. and New Turbine, Inc. v. Republic of Ecuador, ICSID Case No. ARB/03/6	31 July 2007 (Award)	**Vinuesa**, Greenberg, Irarrázabal	Each party bears its own legal costs and equal division of ICSID costs
Fraport AG Frankfurt Airport Services Worldwide v. Republic of the Philippines, ICSID Case No. ARB/03/25	16 August 2007 (Award)	**Fortier**, Cremades, Reisman	Each party bears its own legal costs and equal division of ICSID costs
Compañía de Aguas del Aconquija S.A. and Vivendi Universal S.A. v. Argentine Republic, ICSID Case No. ARB/97/3	20 August 2007 (Award)	**Rowley**, Kaufmann-Kohler, Bernal Verea	Respondent to pay 100% of Claimants' legal costs for jurisdictional phase, equal division of legal costs for merits phase, and equal division of ICSID costs
Sociedad Anónima Eduardo Vieira v. Republic of Chile, ICSID Case No. ARB/04/7	21 August 2007 (Award)	**von Wobeser**, Reisman, Czar de Zalduendo	Each party bears its own legal costs and equal division of ICSID costs
Industria Nacional de Alimentos, S.A. and Indalsa Perú, S.A. (formerly Empresas Lucchetti, S.A. and Lucchetti Perú, S.A.) v. Republic of Peru, ICSID Case No. ARB/03/4	5 September 2007 (Decision on Annulment)	**Danelius**, Berman, Giardina	Each party bears its own legal costs and equal division of ICSID costs of annulment proceeding
Parkerings-Compagniet AS v. Republic of Lithuania, ICSID Case No. ARB/05/8	11 September 2007 (Award)	**Lévy**, Lew, Lalonde	Each party bears its own legal costs and equal division of ICSID costs
CMS Gas Transmission Company v. Argentine Republic, ICSID Case No. ARB/01/8	25 September 2007 (Decision of the Ad Hoc Committee on the Application for Annulment of the Argentine Republic)	**Guillaume**, Crawford, Elaraby	Each party bears its own legal costs and equal division of ICSID costs of annulment proceeding
Sempra Energy International v. Argentine Republic, ICSID Case No. ARB/02/16	28 September 2007 (Award)	**Orrego Vicuña**, Lalonde, Morelli Rico	Each party bears its own legal costs and equal division of ICSID costs

III. Procedural and Other Issues – D. Costs (continued)

Case	Date of Decision or Award	Tribunal / Ad Hoc Committee (President denoted in bold)	Outcome ("ICSID costs" denotes costs of arbitration proceeding, including fees and expenses of arbitrators and costs of ICSID Secretariat)
Enron Corporation and Ponderosa Assets, L.P. v. Argentine Republic, ICSID Case No. ARB/01/3	25 October 2007 (Decision on Claimants' Request for Rectification and/or Supplementary Decision of the Award)	**Orrego Vicuña**, van den Berg, Tschanz	Each party bears its own legal costs and Claimants to pay 100% of ICSID costs of rectification proceeding
OKO Pankki Oyj and others v. Republic of Estonia, ICSID Case No. ARB/04/6	19 November 2007 (Award)	**de Witt Wijnen**, Veeder, Fortier	Respondent to pay a portion of Claimant's legal costs and 100% of ICSID costs
Archer Daniels Midland Company and Tate & Lyle Ingredients Americas, Inc. v. United Mexican States, ICSID Case No. ARB(AF)/04/5	21 November 2007 (Award)	**Cremades**, Rovine, Siqueiros T.	Each party bears its own legal costs and equal division of ICSID costs
Desert Line Projects LLC v. Republic of Yemen, ICSID Case No. ARB/05/17	6 February 2008 (Award)	**Tercier**, Paulsson, El-Kosheri	Respondent to pay approximately 40% of Claimant's legal costs, and 70% (Respondent) / 30% (Claimant) division of ICSID costs
Ares International S.r.l. and MetalGeo S.r.l. v. Georgia, ICSID Case No. ARB/05/23	28 February 2008 (Award)	**Rowley**, Beechey, Gaillard	Each party bears its own legal costs and equal division of ICSID costs (but for transcription and translation services related to one witness to be borne by Respondent)
Victor Pey Casado and President Allende Foundation v. Republic of Chile, ICSID Case No. ARB/98/2	8 May 2008 (Award)	**Lalive**, Chemloul, Gaillard	Respondent to pay 14% of Claimants' legal costs and 75% (Respondent) / 25% (Claimant) division of ICSID costs
Metalpar S.A. and Buen Aire S.A. v. Argentine Republic, ICSID Case No. ARB/03/5	6 June 2008 (Award)	**Oreamuno**, Cameron, Chabaneix	Each party bears its own legal costs and equal division of ICSID costs
Heinan International Hotels A/S v. Arab Republic of Egypt, ICSID Case No. ARB/05/19	3 July 2008 (Award)	**Derains**, Dolzer, Lee	Each party bears its own legal costs and equal division of ICSID costs

Case	Date of Decision or Award	Tribunal / Ad Hoc Committee (President denoted in bold)	Outcome ("ICSID costs" denotes costs of arbitration proceeding, including fees and expenses of arbitrators and costs of ICSID Secretariat)
Biwater Gauff (Tanzania) Ltd. v. United Republic of Tanzania, ICSID Case No. ARB/05/22	24 July 2008 (Award)	**Hanotiau**, Born (dissent on costs), Landau	Each party bears its own legal costs and equal division of ICSID costs
Rumeli Telekom A.S. and Telsim Mobil Telekomikasyon Hizmetleri A.S. v. Republic of Kazakhstan, ICSID Case No. ARB/05/16	29 July 2008 (Award)	**Hanotiau**, Boyd, Lalonde	Respondent to pay 50% of Claimants' legal costs and equal division of ICSID costs
African Holding Company of America, Inc. and Société Africaine de Construction au Congo S.A.R.L. v. Democratic Republic of the Congo, ICSID Case No. ARB/05/21	29 July 2008 (Sentence sur les déclinatoires de compétence et la recevabilité)	**Orrego Vicuña**, de Witt Wijnen, Grisay	Each party bears its own legal costs and equal division of ICSID costs
Duke Energy Electroquil Partners and Electroquil S.A. v. Republic of Ecuador, ICSID Case No. ARB/04/19	18 August 2008 (Award)	**Kaufmann-Kohler**, Gómez Pinzón, van den Berg	Each party bears its own legal costs and equal division of ICSID costs
Plama Consortium Ltd. v. Republic of Bulgaria, ICSID Case No. ARB/03/24	27 August 2008 (Award)	**Salans**, van den Berg, Veeder	Claimant to pay approximately 53% of Respondent's legal costs and 100% of ICSID costs
Continental Casualty Company v. Argentine Republic, ICSID Case No. ARB/03/9	5 September 2008 (Award)	**Sacerdoti**, Veeder, Nader	Each party bears its own legal costs and equal division of ICSID costs
Jan de Nul N.V. and Dredging International N.V. v. Arab Republic of Egypt, ICSID Case No. ARB/04/13	6 November 2008 (Award)	**Kaufmann-Kohler**, Mayer, Stern	Each party bears its own legal costs and equal division of ICSID costs
L.E.S.I. S.p.A. and ASTALDI S.p.A. v. People's Democratic Republic of Algeria, ICSID Case No. ARB/05/3	12 November 2008 (Award)	**Tercier**, Hanotiau, Gaillard	Each party bears its own legal costs and equal division of ICSID costs
Wintershall Aktiengesellschaft v. Argentine Republic, ICSID Case No. ARB/04/14	8 December 2008 (Award)	**Nariman**, Torres Bernárdez, Bernardini	Each party bears its own legal costs and equal division of ICSID costs
Aguaytia Energy LLC v. Republic of Peru, ICSID Case No. ARB/06/13	11 December 2008 (Award)	**Briner**, Rowley, von Wobeser	Each party bears its own legal costs and equal division of ICSID costs
TSA Spectrum de Argentina S.A. v. Argentine Republic, ICSID Case No. ARB/05/5	19 December 2008 (Award)	**Danelius**, Abi-Saab, Aldonas	Each party bears its own legal costs and equal division of ICSID costs

III. Procedural and Other Issues – D. Costs *(continued)*

Case	Date of Decision or Award	Tribunal / Ad Hoc Committee (President denoted in bold)	Outcome ("ICSID costs" denotes costs of arbitration proceeding, including fees and expenses of arbitrators and costs of ICSID Secretariat)
RSM Production Corporation v. Grenada, ICSID Case No. ARB/05/14	13 March 2009 (Award)	**Veeder**, Audit, Berry	Each party bears its own legal costs and equal division of ICSID costs
Phoenix Action, Ltd. v. Czech Republic, ICSID Case No. ARB/06/5	15 April 2009 (Award)	**Stern**, Bucher, Fernández-Armesto	Claimant to pay 100% of Respondent's legal costs and 100% of ICSID costs
Malaysian Historical Salvors Sdn. Bhd. v. Government of Malaysia, Case No. ARB/05/10	16 April 2009 (Decision on the Application for Annulment)	**Schwebel**, Shahabuddeen, Tomka	Each party bears its own legal costs and Respondent to pay 100% of ICSID costs of annulment proceeding
Bernardus Henricus Funnekotter and others v. Republic of Zimbabwe, ICSID Case No. ARB/05/6	22 April 2009 (Award)	**Guillaume**, Cass, Wasi Zafar	Each party bears its own legal costs and Respondent to pay 100% of ICSID costs
Waguih Elie George Siag and Clorinda Vecchi v. Arab Republic of Egypt, ICSID Case No. ARB/05/15	1 June 2009 (Award)	**Williams**, Pryles, Orrego Vicuña (dissent on costs)	Respondent to pay approximately 75% of Claimant's legal costs and equal division of ICSID costs
Empresa Eléctrica del Ecuador, Inc. v. Republic of Ecuador, ICSID Case No. ARB/05/9	2 June 2009 (Award)	**Sepúlveda**, Rooney, Reisman	Each party bears its own legal costs and equal division of ICSID costs
Saipem S.p.A. v. People's Republic of Bangladesh, ICSID Case No. ARB/05/7	30 June 2009 (Award)	**Kaufmann-Kohler**, Schreuer, Otton	Each party bears its own legal costs and equal division of ICSID costs
Pantechniki S.A. Contractors & Engineers (Greece) v. Republic of Albania, ICSID Case No. ARB/07/21	30 July 2009 (Award)	**Paulsson**	Each party bears its own legal costs and equal division of ICSID costs
Europe Cement Investment & Trade S.A. v. Republic of Turkey, ICSID Case No. ARB(AF)/07/2	13 August 2009 (Award)	**McRae**, Lévy, Lew	Claimant to pay 100% of Respondent's legal costs and ICSID costs
Bayindir Insaat Turizm Ticaret Ve Sanayi A.Ş. v. Islamic Republic of Pakistan, ICSID Case No. ARB/03/29	27 August 2009 (Award)	**Kaufmann-Kohler**, Berman, Böckstiegel	Each party bears its own legal costs and equal division of ICSID costs

Case	Date of Decision or Award	Tribunal / Ad Hoc Committee (President denoted in bold)	Outcome ("ICSID costs" denotes costs of arbitration proceeding, including fees and expenses of arbitrators and costs of ICSID Secretariat)
Azurix Corp. v. Argentine Republic, ICSID Case No. ARB/01/12	1 September 2009 (Decision on the Application for Annulment of the Argentine Republic)	**Griffith,** Ajibola, Hwang	Each party bears its own legal costs and Respondent to pay 100% of ICSID costs of annulment proceeding
Azpetrol International Holdings B.V. and others v. Republic of Azerbaijan, ICSID Case No. ARB/06/15	8 September 2009 (Award)	**Feliciano,** Brower, Greenwood	Each party bears its own legal costs and equal division of ICSID costs
Cementownia "Nowa Huta" S.A. v. Republic of Turkey, ICSID Case No. ARB(AF)/06/2	17 September 2009 (Award)	**Tercier,** Lalonde, Thomas	Claimant to pay 100% of Respondent's legal costs and ICSID costs
Cargill, Inc. v. United Mexican States, ICSID Case No. ARB(AF)/05/2	18 September 2009 (Award)	**Pryles,** Caron, McRae	Respondent to pay 50% of Claimant's legal costs and 100% of ICSID costs
EDF (Services) Limited v. Romania, ICSID Case No. ARB/05/13	8 October 2009 (Award)	**Bernardini,** Derains, Rovine (dissent on costs)	Claimant to pay approximately 32% of Respondent's legal costs and equal division of ICSID costs
M.C.I. Power Group L.C. and New Turbine, Inc. v. Republic of Ecuador, ICSID Case No. ARB/03/6	19 October 2009 (Decision on Annulment)	**Hascher,** Danelius, Tomka	Each party bears its own legal costs and Claimant to pay 100% of ICSID costs of annulment proceeding

III. Procedural and Other Issues – E. Provisional Measures

Case	Date of Decision	Tribunal (President denoted in bold)	Measures Requested	Outcome
Holiday Inns S.A. and others v. Morocco, ICSID Case No. ARB/72/1	2 July 1972 (as summarized in Pierre Lalive's article "The First 'World Bank' Arbitration (*Holiday Inns v. Morocco*) – Some Legal Problems", ICSID Reports 1 (1993): 653-659).	**Petrén**, Reuter, Foster	Claimant requested that the Tribunal recommend that Respondent cease its actions before domestic courts and otherwise in relation to Claimant's investment	Granted in part: 1. the Tribunal invited the parties "to abstain from any measure incompatible with the upholding of the Contract and to make sure that the action already taken should not result in any consequences in the future which would go against such upholding"; 2. the Tribunal issued a recommendation concerning the exchange of information by the parties regarding the management of the completed hotels and the completion of those hotels still to be constructed; and 3. the Tribunal recommended consultations "in order to maintain in the hotels the character of the enterprise which is part of the international chain of Holiday Inns Hotels"
AGIP S.p.A. v. People's Republic of the Congo, ICSID Case No. ARB/77/1	18 January 1979 (Letter decision issued by the Tribunal, summarized in 30 November 1979 Award)	**Trolle**, Dupuy, Rouhani	Claimant requested that the Tribunal recommend that Respondent: 1. collect all books, cards, registers and accounting documents held at Claimant's registered office; 2. notify the Tribunal and Claimant of the complete list of books, registers and documents collected; and 3. preserve such documents for the arbitration	Granted
Amco Asia Corporation and others v. Republic of Indonesia, ICSID Case No. ARB/81/1	9 December 1983 (Decision on Provisional Measures)	**Goldman**, Foighel, Rubin	Respondent requested that the Tribunal recommend that Claimants take no action to aggravate or extend the dispute and abstain from promoting, stimulating, or instigating the publication of propaganda	Denied

Case	Date of Decision	Tribunal (President denoted in bold)	Measures Requested	Outcome
Atlantic Triton Company Limited v. People's Revolutionary Republic of Guinea, ICSID Case No. ARB/84/1	18 December 1984	**Sanders**, Prat, van den Berg	Respondent requested that the Tribunal: 1. recommend that Claimant lift a domestic court attachment it had secured; 2. grant damages, or a guarantee to cover Respondent's losses arising from the attachment; and 3. an order that both parties desist from actions before other jurisdictions Claimant requested that Respondent post security for costs	Denied
Maritime International Nominees Establishment v. Republic of Guinea, ICSID Case No. ARB/84/4	4 December 1985 (summarized in 6 January 1988 Award)	**Zubrod**, Berg, Sharpe	Respondent requested that the Tribunal recommend that Claimant dissolve all pending attachments of Respondent's assets	Granted
Vacuum Salt Products Ltd. v. Republic of Ghana, ICSID Case No. ARB/92/1	3 December 1992 (Decision No. 1, summarized in Decision No. 3)	**Jennings**, Brower, Hossain	Claimant requested that the Tribunal make certain recommendations in relation to the preservation of Claimant's corporate records and the requirement for submission of disputes related to Claimant's investment to domestic courts	Held unnecessary: Tribunal took note of undertakings made by Respondent in relation to negotiations with Claimant and preservation of Claimant's corporate records, which were accepted by Claimant
Vacuum Salt Products Ltd. v. Republic of Ghana, ICSID Case No. ARB/92/1	14 June 1993 (Decision No. 3)	**Jennings**, Brower, Hossain	Claimant reinstated and renewed its original request for provisional measures given Respondent's conduct	Denied
Metalclad Corporation v. United Mexican States, ICSID Case No. ARB(AF)/97/1	27 October 1997 (Decision on a Request by the Respondent for an Order Prohibiting the Claimant from Revealing Information Regarding ICSID Case No. ARB(AF)/97/1)	**Lauterpacht**, Civiletti, Siqueiros	Respondent requested that the Tribunal to issue a formal order declaring that the proceedings are confidential and that breach of such order would permit Respondent to enforce sanctions	Denied, but the Tribunal held that the Parties should limit public discussion of the case to a minimum, subject to any obligations of disclosure

III. Procedural and Other Issues – E. Provisional Measures *(continued)*

Case	Date of Decision	Tribunal (President denoted in bold)	Measures Requested	Outcome
Československá Obchodní Banka, A.S. v. Slovak Republic, ICSID Case No. ARB/97/4	9 September 1998 (Procedural Order No. 2)	**Buergenthal,** Bernardini, Bucher	Claimant requested that the Tribunal recommend the suspension of pending domestic bankruptcy proceedings	Denied Claimant's request for emergency interim restraining measures and reserved decision on provisional measures until it was able to consider the parties' observations
Československá Obchodní Banka, A.S. v. Slovak Republic, ICSID Case No. ARB/97/4	5 November 1998 (Procedural Order No. 3)	**Buergenthal,** Bernardini, Bucher	Claimant requested that the Tribunal recommend the suspension of pending domestic bankruptcy proceedings and that Respondent take no action of any kind that might aggravate or further undermine the dispute submitted to this Tribunal	Denied resubmitted request for emergency measures and request that Respondent take no action that might aggravate or further undermine the dispute before Tribunal, but deferred decision on provisional measures regarding bankruptcy proceedings pending outcome of Claimant's application there
Československá Obchodní Banka, A.S. v. Slovak Republic, ICSID Case No. ARB/97/4	11 January 1999 (Procedural Order No. 4)	**Buergenthal,** Bernardini, Bucher	Claimant requested that the Tribunal recommend the suspension of pending domestic bankruptcy proceedings	Granted
Compañía del Desarrollo de Santa Elena S.A. v. Republic of Costa Rica, ICSID Case No. ARB/96/1	10 May 1999 (Oral Hearing, summarized in 17 February 2000 Final Award)	**Fortier,** Lauterpacht, Weil	Respondent requested that the Tribunal order Claimant not to engage in various activities on the property at issue in the arbitration, including any earth-moving activity for the purpose of constructing new roads, removal of any vegetation, and ignition or failure to extinguish any fire	Denied
Barro American Resources, Inc. and Société Aurifère du Kivu et du Maniema S.A.R.L. v. Democratic Republic of the Congo, ICSID Case No. ARB/98/7	23 July 1999	**Weil,** Diagne, Geach		Unpublished

Case	Date of Decision	Tribunal (President denoted in bold)	Measures Requested	Outcome
Emilio Agustín Maffezini v. Kingdom of Spain, ICSID Case No. ARB/97/7	28 October 1999 (Procedural Order No. 2)	**Orrego Vicuña**, Buergenthal, Wolf	Respondent requested that the Tribunal require Claimant to post security for costs	Denied
Tanzania Electric Supply Company Ltd. v. Independent Power Tanzania Ltd, ICSID Case No. ARB/98/8	20 December 1999 (Decision on the Respondent's Request for Provisional Measures)	**Rokison**, Brower, Rogers	Respondent requested that the Tribunal recommend that Claimant permit commercial operation of the facility at issue in the arbitration, make accumulated capacity payments to Respondent, and continue to pay capacity payments until the arbitration is completed	Denied
Československá Obchodní Banka, A.S. v. Slovak Republic, ICSID Case No. ARB/97/4	1 March 2000 (Procedural Order No. 5)	**Buergenthal**, Bernardini, Bucher	Claimant requested that the Tribunal reaffirm Procedural Order No. 4 regarding the suspension of pending domestic bankruptcy proceedings	Granted
Marvin Roy Feldman Karpa v. United Mexican States, ICSID Case No. ARB(AF)/99/1	3 May 2000 (Procedural Order No. 2 Concerning a Request for Provisional Measures and the Schedule of the Proceeding)	**Kerameus**, Covarrubias Bravo, Gantz	Claimant requested that the Tribunal recommend preservation of the status quo between the Parties during the proceedings and order Respondent to cease and desist from any interference with Claimant or his property	Denied
World Duty Free Company Ltd. v. Republic of Kenya, ICSID Case No. ARB/00/7	25 April 2001 (summarized in 4 October 2006 Award)	**Guillaume**, Veeder, Rogers	Respondent requested that the Tribunal issue an order on confidentiality	Granted in part: The Tribunal directed the Parties to avoid any action that would aggravate or exacerbate the dispute, and to ensure that any public discussion of the case should be accurate
Victor Pey Casado and President Allende Foundation v. Republic of Chile, ICSID Case No. ARB/98/2	25 September 2001 (Decision on the Adoption of Provisional Measures Requested by the Parties)	**Lalive**, Leoro Franco, Bedjaoui	Claimants requested that the Tribunal recommend that Respondent suspend execution of a particular ministerial decision Respondent requested that the Tribunal order Claimants to post security for costs	Denied

III. Procedural and Other Issues – E. Provisional Measures (continued)

Case	Date of Decision	Tribunal (President denoted in bold)	Measures Requested	Outcome
Zhinvali Development Ltd. v. Republic of Georgia, ICSID Case No. ARB/00/1	24 January 2002 (summarized in 24 January 2003 Award)	**Robinson,** Jacovides, Rubin	Claimant requested that the Tribunal recommend domestic proceedings related to Claimant's interest in its Agreement with Respondent be suspended	Granted
SGS Société Générale de Surveillance S.A. v. Islamic Republic of Pakistan, ICSID Case No. ARB/01/13	16 October 2002 (Procedural Order No. 2)	**Feliciano,** Faurés, Thomas	Claimant requested that the Tribunal recommend: 1. that Respondent immediately withdraw and discontinue domestic court proceedings relating in any way to the ICSID arbitration; 2. that the pending contractual arbitration between the Parties be stayed; and 3. that Respondent take no action that might aggravate or further extend the dispute	Granted in part: 1. the Tribunal recommended that Respondent not take any step to initiate a complaint for contempt, and if any such proceedings are initiated, that such proceedings are not acted upon; and 2. the Tribunal recommended that the pending contractual arbitration be stayed
Tokios Tokelés v. Ukraine, ICSID Case No. ARB/02/18	1 July 2003 (Order No. 1, Claimant's Request for Provisional Measures)	**Weil,** Price, Bernardini	Claimant requested that the Tribunal recommend that Respondent discontinue domestic proceedings involving Claimant or its investment	Granted: The Tribunal found that both parties should refrain from, suspend and discontinue any domestic proceedings, judicial or other, concerning Claimant or its investment which might prejudice an award or aggravate the dispute
Azurix Corp. v. Argentine Republic, ICSID Case No. ARB/01/12	6 August 2003 (Decision on Provisional Measures) (summarized in 8 December 2003 Decision on Jurisdiction)	**Rigo Sureda,** Lauterpacht, Martins	Claimant requested that the Tribunal recommend that Respondent refrain from any action or omission capable of aggravating or extending the dispute	Denied, but the Tribunal invited the Parties to abstain from measures which could aggravate or extend the dispute
Ahmonseto, Inc. and others v. Arab Republic of Egypt, ICSID Case No. ARB/02/15	10 October 2003	**Tercier,** Fadlallah, Viandier	Unpublished	

Case	Date of Decision	Tribunal (President denoted in bold)	Measures Requested	Outcome
Bayindir Insaat Turizm Ticaret Ve Sanayi A.Ş. v. Islamic Republic of Pakistan, ICSID Case No. ARB/03/29	29 November 2004 (summarized in 14 November 2005 Decision on Jurisdiction)	**Kaufmann-Kohler**, Berman, Böckstiegel	Claimant requested that the Tribunal order Respondent to stay all proceedings pending before the Courts of Pakistan and Turkey Respondent requested that Claimant provide security for costs	Granted in part: 1. The Tribunal recommended that Respondent take whatever steps may be necessary to ensure that any final judgment obtained from the Turkish courts with regard to the Mobilisation Advance Guarantees is not enforced; and 2. the Tribunal dismissed Respondent's request that Claimant should provide security for costs
Tokios Tokelés v. Ukraine, ICSID Case No. ARB/02/18	18 January 2005 (Order No. 3)	**Mustill**, Price, Bernardini	Claimant requested that the Tribunal reaffirm its previously ordered provisional measures (Order No. 1 of 1 July 2003) and to "issue a procedural Order" that would call on Respondent to "refrain from, suspend, and discontinue": (a) the criminal proceedings against Claimant's subsidiaries in Ukraine; (b) the arrest of the general director of assets of Claimant's subsidiaries; and (c) tax investigations of Claimant's subsidiaries	Denied
Fraport AG Frankfurt Airport Services Worldwide v. Republic of the Philippines, ICSID Case No. ARB/03/25	27 January 2005 (date request for provisional measures withdrawn, summarized in 16 August 2007 Award)	**Fortier**, Cremades, Reisman	Unpublished	Withdrawn
Duke Energy International Peru Investments No. 1, Ltd. v. Republic of Peru, ICSID Case No. ARB/03/28	24 February 2005 (date request for provisional measures withdrawn, summarized in 1 February 2006 Decision on Jurisdiction)	**Fortier**, Tawil, Nikken	Respondent requested that the Tribunal recommend that Claimant withdraw its petition before the U.S. Trade Representative to revoke or suspend Peru's beneficiary status under the Andean Trade Preference Act, that Claimant seek no new remedy in non-ICSID proceedings, and that the Tribunal suspend its proceeding until Claimant complies	Withdrawn

III. Procedural and Other Issues – E. Provisional Measures (*continued*)

Case	Date of Decision	Tribunal (President denoted in bold)	Measures Requested	Outcome
Plama Consortium Ltd. v. Republic of Bulgaria, ICSID Case No. ARB/03/24	6 September 2005 (Order)	**Salans**, van den Berg, Veeder	Claimant requested that the Tribunal order: 1. that Respondent immediately discontinue and/or cause to be discontinued all pending proceedings, and refrain from bringing or participating in any future proceedings relating in any way to this arbitration; 2. that Respondent takes no action of any kind that might aggravate or further extend the dispute submitted to the Tribunal; 3. that the Tribunal grant any further relief that it deems appropriate to preserve Claimant's rights; and 4. that Respondent pay the full costs of this application, including the fees and expenses of Claimant's legal counsel	Denied
Sempra Energy International v. Argentine Republic, ICSID Case No. ARB/02/16	16 January 2006 (Letter from the Secretary on behalf of the Tribunal, summarized in 28 September 2007 Award)	**Orrego Vicuña**, Lalonde, Morelli Rico	Claimant requested that the Tribunal make recommendations regarding the evidence of a witness put forward by Claimant in light of an injunction issued by a domestic court	Granted
Biwater Gauff (Tanzania) Ltd. v. United Republic of Tanzania, ICSID Case No. ARB/05/22	31 March 2006 (Procedural Order No. 1)	**Hanotiau**, Born, Landau	Claimant requested that the Tribunal order Respondent: 1. to preserve certain categories of documents; 2. to compile an inventory of documents; 3. to produce certain categories of documents; and 4. to compile a statement of account	Granted in part: 1. the Tribunal held that Respondent should preserve certain categories of documents; 2. the Tribunal held that Respondent should take all necessary steps to have an inventory of documents compiled; 3. the Tribunal denied the request for the production of documents (but Respondent was ordered to take all necessary steps to ensure that certain bank statements were delivered); and 4. the Tribunal denied the request for a statement of account

Case	Date of Decision	Tribunal (President denoted in bold)	Measures Requested	Outcome
Helnan International Hotels A/S v. Arab Republic of Egypt, ICSID Case No. ARB/05/19	17 May 2006 (summarized in 17 October 2006 Decision of the Tribunal on Objection to Jurisdiction)	**Derains**, Lee, Dolzer	Claimant requested that the Tribunal order Respondent to refrain from: 1. taking any action to evict Claimant from the Shepheard Hotel; and 2. proceeding with any procedures to sell the Shepheard Hotel to any third party until the issuance of the award in the arbitration	Denied
Inceysa Vallisoletana S.L. v. Republic of El Salvador, ICSID Case No. ARB/03/26	2 August 2006 (Award)	**Oreamuno**, Landy, von Wobeser	Respondent requested that the Tribunal order Claimant to take certain measures with respect to the fees and expenses of the proceeding	Declined to rule: The Tribunal held that a decision on the application was unnecessary in light of dismissal and order that Claimant must pay all ICSID fees and expenses
Biwater Gauff (Tanzania) Ltd. v. United Republic of Tanzania, ICSID Case No. ARB/05/22	29 September 2006 (Procedural Order No. 3)	**Hanotiau**, Born, Landau	Claimant requested that the Tribunal order that the parties: 1. undertake to discuss the publication of all decisions other than the Award; 2. refrain from disclosing pleadings to third parties; 3. refrain from disclosing documents to third parties; and 4. refrain from disclosing any correspondence between the parties and/or the Tribunal to third parties	Granted: 1. the Tribunal ordered that any disclosure of decisions, orders or directions of the Tribunal to third parties was subject to prior permission by the Tribunal absent agreement between the Parties; 2. the Tribunal ordered all parties to refrain from disclosing pleadings to third parties; 3. the Tribunal ordered all parties to refrain from disclosing documents to third parties; and 4. the Tribunal ordered all parties to refrain from disclosing any correspondence between the Parties and/or the Tribunal to third parties
Enron Corporation and Ponderosa Assets L.P. v. Argentine Republic, ICSID Case No. ARB/01/3	13 December 2006 (summarized in 22 May 2007 Award)	**Orrego Vicuña**, van den Berg, Tschanz	Claimants requested that the Tribunal order Respondent: 1. to cease its actions with respect to Claimants' investment and ensure the resumption of Claimants' right to consummate certain financial transactions; and 2. to refrain from taking any action to aggravate the dispute	Denied

III. Procedural and Other Issues – E. Provisional Measures (continued)

Case	Date of Decision	Tribunal (President denoted in bold)	Measures Requested	Outcome
RSM Production Corporation v. Grenada, ICSID Case No. ARB/05/14	Between 21 December 2006 and 22 February 2007	**Veeder**, Audit, Berry	Unpublished	
Saipem S.p.A. v. People's Republic of Bangladesh, ICSID Case No. ARB/05/7	21 March 2007 (Decision on Jurisdiction and Recommendation on Provisional Measures)	**Kaufmann-Kohler**, Schreuer, Otton	Claimant requested that the Tribunal recommend that Respondent: 1. return warranty bond to Claimant for cancellation, and the termination or suspension of pending litigation in Bangladesh; and 2. return certain retention monies or place retention monies in an escrow account	Granted in part: 1. the Tribunal held that Respondent should take the necessary steps to ensure that Petrobangla does not proceed to encash the warranty bond; and 2. the Tribunal dismissed Claimant's second request
Phoenix Action Ltd. v. Czech Republic, ICSID Case No. ARB/06/5	6 April 2007 (Decision on Provisional Measures)	**Stern**, Bucher, Fernández-Armesto	Claimant requested that the Tribunal order: 1. an injunction regarding certain plots of land and buildings; 2. the release of certain frozen monies from bank accounts; and 3. the opening of classified governmental secret service archives	Denied
Togo Electricité and GDF-Suez Energie Services v. Republic of Togo, ICSID Case No. ARB/06/7	13 April 2007	**El-Kosheri**, Grüninger, Lalonde	Unpublished	
Chevron Bangladesh Block Twelve, Ltd. and Chevron Bangladesh Blocks Thirteen and Fourteen, Ltd. v. People's Republic of Bangladesh, ICSID Case No. ARB/06/10	14 April 2007	**Buergenthal**, Beechey, Nariman	Unpublished	

Case	Date of Decision	Tribunal (President denoted in bold)	Measures Requested	Outcome
RSM Production Corporation v. Grenada, ICSID Case No. ARB/05/14	Between 9 May 2007 and 14 May 2007	**Veeder,** Audit, Berry		Unpublished
Occidental Petroleum Corporation and Occidental Exploration and Production Company v. Republic of Ecuador, ICSID Case No. ARB/06/11	17 August 2007 (Decision on Provisional Measures)	**Fortier,** Stern, Williams	Claimant requested that the Tribunal order Respondent: 1. to immediately cease its occupation of the concession area and Claimants' facilities; 2. to immediately take all necessary measures to enable Claimant to resume its operations in the concession area; 3. to refrain from taking Claimant's share in the production from the concession area; and 4. to refrain from entering into a contract with another party to carry out exploration and exploitation activities in the concession area	Denied
Barmek Holding A.S. v. Republic of Azerbaijan, ICSID Case No. ARB/06/16	29 August 2007	**Lowe,** Galbraith, Stern		Unpublished
Fondel Metal Participations B.V. v. Republic of Azerbaijan, ICSID Case No. ARB/07/1	11 October 2007 (parties reached agreement on Claimant's request for provisional measures)	**Williams,** Rowley, Schwebel		Unpublished
Togo Electricité and GDF-Suez Energie Services v. Republic of Togo, ICSID Case No. ARB/06/7	26 October 2007	**El-Kosheri,** Grüninger, Lalonde		Unpublished

427

III. Procedural and Other Issues – E. Provisional Measures *(continued)*

Case	Date of Decision	Tribunal (President denoted in bold)	Measures Requested	Outcome
City Oriente Ltd. v. Ecuador and Empresa Estatal Petróleos del Ecuador (Petroecuador), ICSID Case No. ARB/06/21	19 November 2007 (Decision on Provisional Measures)	**Fernández-Armesto**, Thomas, Grigera Naón	Claimant requested that the Tribunal order Respondent: 1. to refrain from prosecuting the enforced collection of any present or future amounts disputed in this arbitration; 2. to refrain from initiating a proceeding for the administrative declaration of termination of the concession on account of non-payment of monies pending the final award; and 3. to refrain from any other conduct that may directly or indirectly affect or alter the legal situation agreed upon under the contract at issue in the arbitration	Granted
Europe Cement Investment & Trade S.A. v. Republic of Turkey, ICSID Case No. ARB(AF)/07/2	22 January 2008 (Procedural Order No. 1, summarized in 13 August 2009 Award)	**McRae**, Lew, Lévy	Respondent requested that the Tribunal order Claimant to post security for the costs of the arbitration Claimant requested that the Tribunal order certain documents allegedly seized from the premises of the companies in which Claimant alleged to have an ownership interest be preserved and protected	Denied: 1. postponed decision on security for costs; and 2. denied request relating to the protection of documents, noting Respondent's policy with respect to such documents
Cementownia "Nowa Huta" S.A. v. Republic of Turkey, ICSID Case No. ARB(AF)/06/2	25 January 2008 (Procedural Order No. 1, summarized in 17 September 2009 Award)	**Tercier**, Lalonde, Thomas	Respondent requested that the Tribunal order Claimant to post security for the costs of the arbitration Claimant requested that the Tribunal order certain documents be preserved and protected	Denied: 1. denied the request for security for costs; and 2. denied request relating to the protection of documents, noting Respondent's policy with respect to such documents

Case	Date of Decision	Tribunal (President denoted in bold)	Measures Requested	Outcome
Cementownia "Nowa Huta" S.A. v. Republic of Turkey, ICSID Case No. ARB(AF)/06/2	14 March 2008 (Procedural Order No. 2, summarized in 17 September 2009 Award)	**Tercier**, Lalonde, Thomas	Claimant requested that the Tribunal make various recommendations relating to surveillance	Granted: 1. the Tribunal ordered Respondent to reply to Claimant's request for provisional measures in relation to surveillance; 2. the Tribunal ordered Respondent to immediately discontinue all forms of surveillance directed at Claimant and its legal counsel; and 3. the Tribunal ordered Respondent to conserve all emails or other electronic messages and recordings of telephone calls related to the arbitration
Libananco Holdings Co. Ltd. v. Republic of Turkey, ICSID Case No. ARB/06/8	1 May 2008 (Letter to the Parties, summarized in 23 June 2008 Decision on Preliminary Issues)	**Hwang**, Álvarez, Berman	Claimant requested that the Tribunal make various recommendations relating to surveillance	Granted in part: 1. ordered Respondent not to intercept or record communications between Claimant and its counsel; 2. ordered Respondent to grant Claimant access to any person in Turkey for purposes of preparing its case; 3. ordered Respondent to obtain within 30 days a statement from the Public Prosecutor of Sisli that all intercepted emails and communications that relate in any way to this arbitration have been or will be destroyed within 30 days; and 4. made orders regarding confidentiality of certain documents and communications, and excluded certain evidence to be received in this arbitration
City Oriente Ltd. v. Ecuador and Empresa Estatal Petróleos del Ecuador (Petroecuador), ICSID Case No. ARB/06/21	13 May 2008 (Decision on Revocation of Provisional Measures and Other Procedural Matters)	**Fernández-Armesto**, Thomas, Grigera Naón	Respondent requested that the provisional measures previously ordered by the Tribunal be overturned	Denied

III. Procedural and Other Issues – E. Provisional Measures *(continued)*

Case	Date of Decision	Tribunal (President denoted in bold)	Measures Requested	Outcome
EDF (Services) Ltd. v. Romania, ICSID Case No. ARB/05/13	30 May 2008 (Procedural Order No. 2)	**Bernardini,** Rovine, Derains	Respondent requested that the Tribunal order Claimant to refrain from: 1. disclosing to the public any pleadings, evidence, decisions, transcripts or correspondence; 2. disclosing information and providing commentary to the public or the press; and 3. taking any steps that might undermine the procedural integrity or orderly working of the arbitration and/or might aggravate or exacerbate the dispute	Granted in part: 1. the Tribunal ordered that both parties refrain from taking any steps which might undermine the integrity of the arbitral process or its orderly working and/or that more generally might aggravate or exacerbate the dispute; and 2. the Tribunal held that disclosure of documents produced by the opposing party or originated during the proceedings fall within the recommended measure, but that general discussion of the case in public is not restricted if not used to antagonize, exacerbate the dispute or render resolution potentially more difficult
Europe Cement Investment & Trade S.A. v. Republic of Turkey, ICSID Case No. ARB(AF)/07/2	4 June 2008 (Procedural Order No. 4, summarized in 13 August 2009 Award)	**McRae,** Lew, Lévy	Claimant requested that the Tribunal make various recommendations relating to surveillance	Held unnecessary in light of Respondent's assurances
Libananco Holdings Co. Ltd. v. Republic of Turkey, ICSID Case No. ARB/06/8	23 June 2008 (Decision on Preliminary Issues)	**Hwang,** Álvarez, Berman	Respondent requested that the Tribunal order Claimant to post security for costs in the form of an irrevocable letter of credit or bank guarantee	Denied
Spyridon Roussalis v. Romania, ICSID Case No. ARB/06/1	22 July 2008	**Briner,** Giardina, Reisman		Unpublished
ABCI Investments N.V. v. Republic of Tunisia, ICSID Case No. ARB/04/12	29 August 2008	**Orrego Vicuña,** Bernardini, Stern		Unpublished

Case	Date of Decision	Tribunal (President denoted in bold)	Measures Requested	Outcome
ABCI Investments N.V. v. Republic of Tunisia, ICSID Case No. ARB/04/12	30 September 2008	**Orrego Vicuña,** Bernardini, Stern		Unpublished
Azpetrol International Holdings B.V. and others v. Republic of Azerbaijan, ICSID Case No. ARB/06/15	6 October 2008	**Feliciano,** Brower, Greenwood		Unpublished
Saba Fakes v. Republic of Turkey, ICSID Case No. ARB/07/20	6 October 2008	**Gaillard,** van Houtte, Lévy		Unpublished
Railroad Development Corporation v. Republic of Guatemala, ICSID Case No. ARB/07/23	15 October 2008 (Decision on Provisional Measures)	**Rigo Sureda,** Eizenstat, Crawford	Claimant requested that the Tribunal order Respondent to preserve four categories of documents while the ICSID arbitration proceedings remain pending	Denied
Joseph Charles Lemire v. Ukraine, ICSID Case No. ARB/06/18	22 October 2008 (date request for provisional measures withdrawn, summarized in 21 January 2010 Decision on Jurisdiction and Liability)	**Fernández-Armesto,** Paulsson, Voss	Claimant requested that the Tribunal require certain measures concerning Respondent's decision to charge a certain fee for the renewal of a broadcasting license	Withdrawn
Alasdair Ross Anderson and others v. Republic of Costa Rica, ICSID Case No. ARB(AF)/07/3	5 November 2008 (summarized in 19 May 2010 Award)	**Morelli Rico,** Salacuse, Vinuesa	Respondent requested that the Tribunal order: 1. Claimants to post a bank guarantee (or an escrow account deposit administered by ICSID); and 2. Claimants to represent that they agree to be held jointly and severally liable for any award of costs	Denied

III. Procedural and Other Issues – E. Provisional Measures *(continued)*

Case	Date of Decision	Tribunal (President denoted in bold)	Measures Requested	Outcome
Murphy Exploration and Production Company International v. Republic of Ecuador, ICSID Case No. ARB/08/4	13 March 2009 (date request for provisional measures withdrawn)	**Oreamuno**, Grigera Naón, Vinuesa	Unpublished	Withdrawn
Perenco Ecuador Ltd. v. Republic of Ecuador and Empresa Estatal Petróleos del Ecuador (Petroecuador), ICSID Case No. ARB/08/6	8 May 2009 (Decision on Provisional Measures)	**Bingham**, Brower, Thomas	Claimant requested that the Tribunal enjoin Respondents from: 1. demanding that Claimant pay any amounts allegedly due pursuant to Ecuadorian law; 2. instituting or pursuing any action to collect any payments Respondent claim are owed by Claimant pursuant to Ecuadorian law; 3. instituting or pursuing any action against Claimant or any of its officers or employees in relation to the contracts at issue in the arbitration; and 4. unilaterally amending, rescinding, terminating, repudiating or engaging in any other conduct which may alter the legal situation under the contracts at issue in the arbitration	Granted
Repsol YPF Ecuador, S.A. and others v. Republic of Ecuador and Empresa Estatal Petróleos del Ecuador (PetroEcuador), ICSID Case No. ARB/08/10	17 June 2009 (Procedural Order No. 1 Concerning Provisional Measures)	**Oreamuno**, Grigera Naón, Vinuesa	Unpublished	

Case	Date of Decision	Tribunal (President denoted in bold)	Measures Requested	Outcome
Gustav F W Hamester GmbH & Co KG v. Republic of Ghana, ICSID Case No. ARB/07/24	24 June 2009	**Stern,** Cremades, Landau	Unpublished	
Burlington Resources, Inc., and others v. Republic of Ecuador and Empresa Estatal Petróleos del Ecuador (Petroecuador), ICSID Case No. ARB/08/5	29 June 2009 (Procedural Order No. 1 on Burlington Oriente's Request for Provisional Measures)	**Kaufmann-Kohler,** Stern, Orrego Vicuña	Claimant requested that the Tribunal order Respondent to refrain from: 1. demanding that Claimant pay any amounts allegedly due pursuant to Ecuadorian law and instituting or pursuing any action to collect any payments Respondent claim are owed by Claimant pursuant to Ecuadorian law; 2. making or implementing any measure, decision or resolution that affects the legal situation of or is intended to terminate the contracts at issue in the arbitration; and 3. engaging in any other conduct that aggravates the dispute and/or alters the status quo between the parties	Granted in part: 1. the Tribunal ordered that the Parties confer and make best efforts to agree on opening of escrow account for Claimant to deposit allegedly due payments under Ecuadorian law; 2. the Tribunal ordered Respondent to discontinue the proceedings pending against Claimant and not initiate any new actions; and 3. the Tribunal ordered both parties to refrain from conduct that may lead to an aggravation of the dispute until issuance of the Award or reconsideration of the order
Caratube International Oil Company LLP v. Republic of Kazakhstan, ICSID Case No. ARB/08/12	31 July 2009	**Böckstiegel,** Griffith, Hossain	Unpublished	
EVN AG v. Macedonia, former Yugoslav Republic of, ICSID Case No. ARB/09/10	9 September 2009 (date request for provisional measures withdrawn)	**Bernardini,** Lowe, Orrego Vicuña	Unpublished	Withdrawn
Millicom International Operations B.V. and Sentel GSM S.A. v. Republic of Senegal, ICSID Case No. ARB/08/20	9 December 2009	**Tercier,** Abraham, Hobér	Unpublished	

III. Procedural and Other Issues – E. Provisional Measures *(continued)*

Case	Date of Decision	Tribunal (President denoted in bold)	Measures Requested	Outcome
Karner Marble Tourism Construction Industry and Commerce Limited Liability Company v. Georgia, ICSID Case No. ARB/08/19	25 January 2010	**Lalonde**, Orrego Vicuña, Schwartz	Unpublished	

III. Procedural and Other Issues – F. Stay of Enforcement of the Award

Case	Date of Decision	Ad Hoc Committee (President denoted in bold)	Outcome
Amco Asia Corporation and others v. Republic of Indonesia, ICSID Case No. ARB/81/1	17 May 1985 (Order staying enforcement of the award (unpublished), summarized in 16 May 1986 Decision on Annulment)	**Seidl-Hohenveldern,** Feliciano, Giardina	Stay of enforcement continued; Respondent required to provide irrevocable and unconditional bank guarantee in the amount of the award plus interest as condition of security
Maritime International Nominees Establishment v. Republic of Guinea, ICSID Case No. ARB/84/4	12 August 1988 (Interim Order No. 1 on Guinea's Application for Stay of Enforcement of the Award)	**Sucharitkul,** Broches, Mbaye	Stay of enforcement continued; no condition of security
Amco Asia Corporation and others v. Republic of Indonesia, ICSID Case No. ARB/81/1	2 March 1991 (Interim Order No. 1, annexed to 3 December 1992 Decision on Annulment)	**Sucharitkul,** Fatouros, Schindler	Stay of enforcement continued; Respondent required to provide irrevocable and unconditional bank guarantee in the amount of the award plus interest as condition of security
Southern Pacific Properties (Middle East) Ltd. v. Arab Republic of Egypt, ICSID Case No. ARB/84/3	9 March 1993 (Date of Order taking note of discontinuance, settlement agreed by the parties)	**Reymond,** Fatouros, Mbaye	Stay of enforcement continued by party agreement; Respondent agreed to post a bank guarantee
Wena Hotels Ltd. v. Arab Republic of Egypt, ICSID Case No. ARB/98/4	5 April 2001 (Procedural Order No. 1 of the ad hoc Committee Concerning the Continuation of the Stay of Enforcement of the Award)	**Kerameus,** Bucher, Orrego Vicuña	Stay of enforcement continued; Respondent required to provide irrevocable and unconditional bank guarantee in the amount of the award plus interest as condition of security
CDC Group P.L.C. v. Republic of the Seychelles, ICSID Case No. ARB/02/14	14 July 2004 (Decision on Whether or Not to Continue Stay and Order)	**Brower,** Hwang, Williams	Stay of enforcement continued; Respondent required to provide irrevocable and unconditional bank guarantee in the amount of the award plus interest as condition of security
Patrick Mitchell v. Democratic Republic of the Congo, ICSID Case No. ARB/99/7	30 November 2004 (Decision on the Stay of Enforcement of the Award)	**Dimolitsa,** Dossou, Giardina	Stay of enforcement continued; no condition of security

III. Procedural and Other Issues – F. Stay of Enforcement of the Award (*continued*)

Case	Date of Decision	Ad Hoc Committee (*President denoted in bold*)	Outcome
MTD Equity Sdn. Bhd. and MTD Chile S.A. v. Republic of Chile, ICSID Case No. ARB/01/7	1 June 2005 (Decision on the Respondent's Request for a Continued Stay of Execution (Rule 54 of the ICSID Arbitration Rules))	**Guillaume**, Crawford, Ordóñez Noriega	Stay of enforcement continued; no condition of security
Repsol YPF Ecuador S.A. v. Empresa Estatal Petróleos del Ecuador (Petroecuador), ICSID Case No. ARB/01/10	22 December 2005 (Procedural Order No. 1)	**Kessler**, Bernardini, Biggs	Stay of enforcement continued; Respondent required to provide irrevocable and unconditional bank guarantee in the amount of the award plus interest as condition of security
Repsol YPF Ecuador S.A. v. Empresa Estatal Petróleos del Ecuador (Petroecuador), ICSID Case No. ARB/01/10	22 February 2006 (Procedural Order No. 4)	**Kessler**, Bernardini, Biggs	Stay of enforcement terminated because Respondent failed to post required security with period ordered by the ad hoc committee
CMS Gas Transmission Company v. Argentine Republic, ICSID Case No. ARB/01/8	1 September 2006 (Decision on the Argentine Republic's Request for a Continued Stay of Enforcement of the Award (Rule 54 of the ICSID Arbitration Rules))	**Guillaume**, Elaraby, Crawford	Stay of enforcement continued; no condition of security
Azurix Corp. v. Argentine Republic, ICSID Case No. ARB/01/12	28 December 2007 (Decision on the Argentine Republic's Request for a Continued Stay of Enforcement of the Award (Rule 54 of the ICSID Arbitration Rules))	**Griffith**, Ajibola, Hwang	Stay of enforcement continued; no condition of security
Enron Corporation and Ponderosa Assets, L.P. v. Argentine Republic, ICSID Case No. ARB/01/3	7 October 2008 (Decision on the Argentine Republic's Request for a Continued Stay of Enforcement of the Award (Rule 54 of the ICSID Arbitration Rules))	**Griffith**, Robinson, Tresselt	Stay of enforcement continued; no condition of security

Case	Date of Decision	Ad Hoc Committee (President denoted in bold)	Outcome
Compañía de Aguas del Aconquija S.A. and Vivendi Universal S.A. v. Argentine Republic, ICSID Case No. ARB/97/3	4 November 2008 (Decision on the Argentine Republic's Request for a Continued Stay of Enforcement of the Award rendered on 20 August 2007 (Rule 54 of the ICSID Arbitration Rules))	**El-Kosheri**, Dalhuisen, Jacovides	Stay of enforcement continued; Respondent required to provide commitment letter, failing which Respondent required to provide irrevocable and unconditional bank guarantee
Sempra Energy International v. Argentine Republic, ICSID Case No. ARB/02/16	5 March 2009 (Decision on the Argentine Republic's Request for a Continued Stay of Enforcement of the Award (Rule 54 of the ICSID Arbitration Rules))	**Söderlund**, Edward, Jacovides	Stay of enforcement continued; Respondent required to place funds (approximately 58% of the amount of the award) in escrow account as condition of security
Rumeli Telekom A.S. and Telsim Mobil Telekomunikasyon Hizmetleri A.S. v. Republic of Kazakhstan, ICSID Case No. ARB/05/16	19 March 2009 (Decision on Stay of Enforcement of the Award, summarized in 25 March 2010 annulment decision)	**Schwebel**, McLachlan, Silva Romero	Stay of enforcement continued; Respondent required to provide written assurance of full payment of award within fixed period of time, failing which Respondent would be required to deposit 50% of the principal amount of the award in escrow in order to maintain stay
Enron Creditors Recovery Corp. (formerly Enron Corp.) and Ponderosa Assets, L.P. v. Argentine Republic, ICSID Case No. ARB/01/3	20 May 2009 (Decision the Claimants' Second Request to Lift Provisional Stay of Enforcement of the Award)	**Griffith**, Robinson, Tresselt	Stay of enforcement continued; no condition of security
Sempra Energy International v. Argentine Republic, ICSID Case No. ARB/02/16	7 August 2009 (Decision on Sempra Energy International's Request for the Termination of the Stay of Enforcement of the Award (Rule 54 of the ICSID Arbitration Rules))	**Söderlund**, Edward, Jacovides	Stay of enforcement terminated because Respondent failed to post required security
Continental Casualty Company v. Argentine Republic, ICSID Case No. ARB/03/9	23 October 2009 (Decision on Argentina's Application for a Stay of Enforcement of the Award)	**Griffith**, Ajibola, Söderlund	Stay of enforcement continued; no condition of security

Table of cases

ADC Affiliate Limited and ADC & ADMC Management Limited v. Republic of Hungary, ICSID Case No. ARB/03/16, Award (2 October 2006), pp. 91, 156

ADF Group Inc. v. United States of America, ICSID Case No. ARB(AF)/00/1, p. 107

AES Summit Generation Limited and AES-Tisza Erömü Kft. v. Republic of Hungary, ICSID Case No. ARB/07/22, pp. 15, 120, 141

AES Summit Generation Limited v. Republic of Hungary, ICSID Case No. ARB/01/4, p. 119

AGIP S.p.A. v. The Government of the People's Republic of the Congo, ICSID Case No. ARB/77/1, Award (30 November 1979), *ICSID Reports* 1 (1993), pp. 143, 146

Aguas del Tunari S.A. v. Republic of Bolivia, ICSID Case No. ARB/02/3, Decision on Respondent's Objections to Jurisdiction (21 October 2005), p. 65

Ahmonseto, Inc. and others v. Arab Republic of Egypt, ICSID Case No. ARB/02/15, p. 163

AIG Capital Partners, Inc. and CJSC Tema Real Estate Company v. Republic of Kazakhstan, ICSID Case No. ARB/01/6, Decision of the High Court, Queens Bench Division (Commercial Court) (20 October 2005), *ICSID Reports* 11 (2007), pp. 188-189

Alapli Elektrik B.V. v. Republic of Turkey, ICSID Case No. ARB/08/13, p. 120

Alcoa Minerals of Jamaica, Inc. v. Jamaica, ICSID Case No. ARB/74/2, Decision on Jurisdiction and Competence (6 July 1975) in ed. P. Sanders, *Yearbook Commercial Arbitration*, vol. IV (The Hague: Kluwer Law International, 1979), p. 38

Alstom Power Italia SpA and Alstom SpA v. Republic of Mongolia, ICSID Case No. ARB/04/10, p. 119

Amco Asia Corporation and others v. Republic of Indonesia, ICSID Case No. ARB/81/1, Decision on the proposal to disqualify an arbitrator (24 June 1982) in M. Reisman et al., *International Commercial Arbitration* (New York: The Foundation Press, Inc., 1997), 624-631, p. 134

Amco Asia Corporation and others v. Republic of Indonesia, ICSID Case No. ARB/81/1, Decision on Jurisdiction (25 September 1983), *ICSID Reports* 1 (1993), pp. 28, 41, 42

Amco Asia Corporation and others v. Indonesia, ICSID Case No. ARB/81/1, Award (20 November 1984), *ICSID Reports* 1 (1993), p. 167

Amco Asia Corporation and others v. Indonesia, ICSID Case No. ARB/81/1, Decision on the Application for Annulment (16 May 1986), *ICSID Reports* 1 (1993), pp. 167-169, 173, 176

Amco Asia Corporation and others v. Republic of Indonesia, ICSID Case No. ARB/81/1, Award in Resubmitted Case (31 May 1990), *ICSID Reports* 1 (1993), p. 47

Amco v. Indonesia, Resubmitted Case: Decision on Annulment (3 December 1992) (*Amco Asia II*), *ICSID Reports* 9 (2006), pp. 168, 170

American Manufacturing & Trading, Inc. v. Republic of Zaire, ICSID Case No. ARB/93/1, Award (21 February 1997), pp. 72, 79, 128, 161

Antoine Goetz and others v. Republic of Burundi, ICSID Case No. ARB/95/3, Award (10 February 1999), pp. 81, 98

Archer Daniels Midland Company and Tate & Lyle Ingredients Americas, Inc. v. United Mexican States, ICSID Case No. ARB(AF)/04/5, Award (21 November 2007), pp. 83, 108, 115, 116

Archer Daniels Midland Company and Tate & Lyle Ingredients Americas, Inc. v. United Mexican States, ICSID Case No. ARB(AF)/04/5, Decision on the Requests for

Benvenuti & Bonfant Srl. v. Government People's Republic of the Congo, ICSID Case No. ARB 77/2, Decision of Cour d'Appel, Paris (26 June 1981), *ICSID Reports* 1 (1993), pp. 187

Bernardus Henricus Funnekotter and others v. Republic of Zimbabwe, ICSID Case No. ARB/05/6, Award (22 April 2009), p. 91

Berschader v. Russian Federation, SCC Case No. 080/2004, Award (21 April 2006), p. 86

BG Group plc v. Republic of Argentina, UNCITRAL, Final Award (24 December 2007), pp. 75, 80, 90

Biwater Gauff (Tanzania) Ltd. v. United Republic of Tanzania, ICSID Case No. ARB/05/22, Procedural Order No. 1 (31 March 2006), p. 146

Biwater Gauff (Tanzania) Ltd. v. United Republic of Tanzania, ICSID Case No. ARB/05/22, Procedural Order No. 3 (29 September 2006), p. 147

Biwater Gauff (Tanzania) Ltd. v. United Republic of Tanzania, ICSID Case No. ARB/05/22, Award (24 July 2008), pp. 69, 78, 80, 81, 88, 98

Brandes Investment Partners, LP v. Bolivarian Republic of Venezuela, ICSID Case No. ARB/08/3, Decision on the Respondent's Objection Under Rule 41(5) of the ICSID Arbitration Rules (2 February 2009), p. 145

Bureau Veritas, Inspection, Valuation, Assessment and Control, BIVAC B.V. v. Republic of Paraguay, ICSID Case No. ARB/07/9, Decision of the Tribunal on Objections to Jurisdiction (29 May 2009), pp. 96, 104

Burlington Resources, Inc. and others v. Republic of Ecuador and Empresa Estatal Petróleos del Ecuador (Petroecuador), ICSID Case No. ARB/08/5, Procedural Order No. 1 on Burlington Oriente's Request for Provisional Measures (29 June 2009), p. 147

Cable Television of Nevis, Ltd. and Cable Television of Nevis Holdings, Ltd. v. Federation of St. Kitts and Nevis, ICSID Case No. ARB/95/2, Award (13 January 1997), *ICSID Reports* 5 (2002), pp. 32, 33

CMS Gas Transmission Company v. Republic of Argentina, ICSID Case No. ARB/01/8, Decision of the Tribunal on Objections to Jurisdiction (17 July 2003), *ICSID Reports* 7 (2005), pp. 62-64, 101

CMS Gas Transmission Company v. Argentine Republic, ICSID Case No. ARB/01/18, Award (12 May 2005), pp. 73, 95, 171

CMS Gas Transmission Company v. Argentine Republic, ICSID Case No. ARB/01/8, Decision of the *ad hoc* Committee on the Application for Annulment of the Argentine Republic (25 September 2007), pp. 95, 96, 164, 170-172

Compañía de Aguas del Aconquija S.A. and Compagnie Générale des Eaux v. Argentine Republic, ICSID Case No. ARB/97/3, Award (21 November 2000) (***Vivendi I (Award)***), pp. 72, 101-103, 170

Compañía de Aguas del Aconquija S.A. & Vivendi Universal v. Argentine Republic, ICSID Case No. ARB/97/3, Decision on the Challenge to the President of the Committee (3 October 2001) (***Vivendi I (Decision on the Challenge to the President of the Committee)***), *ICSID Review—FILJ* 17 (2002), p. 134

Compañía de Aguas del Aconquija S.A. and Compagnie Générale des Eaux v. Argentine Republic, ICSID Case No. ARB/97/3, Decision on Annulment (3 July 2002) (***Vivendi I (Decision on Annulment)***), pp. 72, 101-104, 165, 169, 170

Compañía de Aguas del Aconquija S.A. and Vivendi Universal S.A. v. Argentine Republic, ICSID Case No. ARB/97/3, Decision of the ad hoc Committee on the Request for Supplementation and Rectification of its Decision Concerning Annulment of the Award (28 May 2003), p. 153

Compañía de Aguas del Aconquija S.A. and Vivendi Universal v. Argentine Republic, ICSID Case No. ARB/97/3, Award (20 August 2007) (***Vivendi II (Award)***), pp. 80, 102, 156, 170

Compañía de Aguas del Aconquija S.A. and Vivendi Universal S.A. v. Argentine Republic, ICSID Case No. ARB/97/3, Decision on the Argentine Republic's Request for a Continued Stay of Enforcement of the Award rendered on 20

Eastern Sugar B.V. v. Czech Republic, SCC Case No. 088/2004, Partial Award (27 March 2007), pp. 75, 80, 90

EDF International S.A., SAUR International S.A. and León Participaciones Argentinas S.A. v. Argentine Republic, ICSID Case No. ARB/03/23, Challenge Decision Regarding Professor Gabrielle Kaufmann-Kohler (25 June 2008), p. 134

El Paso Energy International Company v. Argentine Republic, ICSID Case No. ARB/03/15, Decision on Jurisdiction (27 April 2006), pp. 64, 96

Electrabel S.A. v. Republic of Hungary, ICSID Case No. ARB/07/19, Decision on the Proposal for the Disqualification of an Arbitrator (25 February 2008) (unpublished), pp. 15, 120, 135, 141

Emilio Agustín Maffezini v. Kingdom of Spain, ICSID Case No. ARB/97/7, Decision of the Tribunal on Objections to Jurisdiction (25 January 2000), pp. 72, 85, 100

Emilio Agustín Maffezini v. Kingdom of Spain, ICSID Case No. ARB/97/7, Procedural Order No. 2 (28 October 1999), *ICSID Review–FILJ* 16 (2001), p. 146

EnCana Corporation v. Republic of Ecuador, LCIA Case No. UN3481, UNCITRAL, Award (3 February 2006), p. 90

Enron Corporation and Ponderosa Assets, L.P. v. Argentine Republic, ICSID Case No. ARB/01/3, Decision on Jurisdiction (14 January 2004), pp. 64, 98, 101

Enron Corporation and Ponderosa Assets, L.P. v. Argentine Republic, ICSID Case No. ARB/01/3, Award (22 May 2007), p. 95

Enron Corporation and Ponderosa Assets, L.P. v. Argentine Republic, ICSID Case No. ARB/01/3, Decision on the Argentine Republic's Request for a Continued Stay of Enforcement of the Award (Rule 54 of the ICSID Arbitration Rules) (7 October 2008), p. 184

Enron Creditors Recovery Corp. (formerly Enron Corp.) and Ponderosa Assets, L.P. v. Argentine Republic, ICSID Case No. ARB/01/3, Decision on the Claimants' Second Request to Lift Provisional Stay of Enforcement of the Award (Rule 54 of the ICSID Arbitration Rules) (20 May 2009), p. 184

Glamis Gold, Ltd. v. United States of America, UNCITRAL, Award (8 June 2009), pp. 76, 90

Grand River Enterprises Six Nations, Ltd., et al. v. United States of America, UNCITRAL, Decision on the Challenge to Arbitrator (28 November 2007), p. 20

Helnan International Hotels A/S v. Arab Republic of Egypt, ICSID Case No. ARB/05/19, Decision of the Tribunal on Objection to Jurisdiction (17 October 2006), pp. 70

Helnan International Hotels A/S v. Arab Republic of Egypt, ICISD Case No. ARB/05/19, Decision of the *ad hoc* Committee (14 June 2010), pp. 171, 173

Holiday Inns S.A. and others v. Morocco, ICSID Case No. ARB/72/1 (unpublished), pp. 40, 42

Hrvatska Elektroprivreda d.d. v. Republic of Slovenia, ICSID Case No. ARB/05/24, p. 119

Hussein Nuaman Soufraki v. United Arab Emirates, ICSID Case No. ARB/02/7, pp. 170-171

Impregilo S.p.A v. Islamic Republic of Pakistan, ICSID Case No. ARB/03/3, Decision on Jurisdiction (22 April 2005), p. 104

Inceysa Vallisoletana S.L. v. Republic of El Salvador, ICSID Case No. ARB/03/26, Award (2 August 2006), p. 67

Indústria Nacional de Alimentos, S.A. and Indalsa Perú, S.A. (formerly Empresas Lucchetti, S.A. and Lucchetti Perú, S.A.) v. Republic of Peru, ICSID Case No. ARB/03/4, p. 171

International Thunderbird Gaming Corporation v. United Mexican States, UNCITRAL, Arbitral Award (26 January 2006), pp. 76, 90, 116

Ioan Micula, Viorel Micula and others v. Romania, ICSID Case No. ARB/05/20, pp. 16, 141

Liberian Eastern Timber Corporation (LETCO) v. Republic of Liberia, ICSID Case No. ARB/83/2, Award (31 March 1986), *ICSID Reports* 2 (1994), p. 29, 30, 148

Liberian Eastern Timber Corporation (LETCO) v. Republic of Liberia, ICSID Case No. ARB/83/2, Decision on Rectification (14 May 1986), *ICSID Reports* 2 (1994), p. 188

Liberian Eastern Timber Corporation (LETCO) v. Republic of Liberia, ICSID Case No. ARB/83/2, Decision of United States District Court, Southern District of New York (5 September 1986), *ICSID Reports* 2 (1994), p. 188

Liberian Eastern Timber Corporation (LETCO) v. Republic of Liberia, ICSID Case No. ARB/83/2, Decision of United States District Court, Southern District of New York (12 December 1986), *ICSID Reports* 2 (1994), 650 F.Supp. 73 (S.D.N.Y. 1986), p. 188

Liberian Eastern Timber Corporation (LETCO) v. Republic of Liberia, ICSID Case No. ARB/83/2, Decision of United States District Court, District of Columbia (16 April 1987), *ICSID Reports* 2 (1994): 390, 659 F.Supp. 606 (D.D.C. 1987), p. 188

Liman Caspian Oil BV and NCL Dutch Investment BV v. Republic of Kazakhstan, ICSID Case No. ARB/07/14, p. 119

Limited Liability Company Amto (Latvia) v. Ukraine, SCC Case No. 080/2005 (Award rendered on 26 March 2008), p. 119

LG&E Energy Corp., LG&E Capital Corp. and LG&E International Inc. v. Argentine Republic, ICSID Case No. ARB/02/1, p. 163

LG&E Energy Corp. and others v. Argentine Republic, ICSID Case No. ARB/02/1, Decision of the Arbitral Tribunal on Objections to Jurisdiction (30 April 2004), pp. 64, 101-102

LG&E Energy Corp. and others v. Argentine Republic, ICSID Case No. ARB/02/1, Decision on Liability (3 October 2006), pp. 78, 81, 95

Middle East Cement Shipping and Handling Co. S.A. v. Arab Republic of Egypt, ICSID Case No. ARB/99/6, Award (12 April 2002), p. 101

Mihaly International Corporation v. Democratic Socialist Republic of Sri Lanka, ICSID Case No. ARB/00/2, Award (15 March 2002), p. 70

Mobil Investments Canada Inc. and Murphy Oil Corporation v. Canada, ICSID Case No. ARB(AF)/07/4, p. 107

Mondev International Ltd. v. United States of America, ICSID Case No. ARB(AF)/99/2, pp. 107, 116

MTD Equity Sdn. Bhd. and MTD Chile S.A. v. Republic of Chile, ICSID Case No. ARB/01/7, Award (25 May 2004), p. 84

MTD Equity Sdn. Bhd. and MTD Chile S.A. v. Republic of Chile, ICSID Case No. ARB/01/7, Decision on Annulment (21 March 2007), pp. 73, 170, 173

National Grid plc v. Argentine Republic, UNCITRAL, Decision on Jurisdiction (20 June 2006), p. 86

National Grid plc v. Argentine Republic, UNCITRAL, Award (3 November 2008), pp. 75, 80, 90

Noble Energy Inc. and MachalaPower Cía. Ltda. v. Republic of Ecuador and Consejo Nacional de Electricidad, ICSID Case No. ARB/05/12, Decision on Jurisdiction (5 March 2008), pp. 33, 42

Noble Ventures, Inc. v. Romania, ICSID Case No. ARB/01/11, Award (12 October 2005), p. 96

Nykomb Synergetics Technology Holding AB (Sweden) v. Latvia, SCC Case No. 118/2001 (Award rendered on 16 December 2003), p. 119

Occidental Exploration and Production Company v. Republic of Ecuador, LCIA Case No. UN3467, Final Award (1 July 2004), p. 75

Phoenix Action, Ltd. v. Czech Republic, ICSID Case No. ARB/06/5, Award (15 April 2009), pp. 67, 70, 156

Plama Consortium Limited v. Bulgaria, ICSID Case No. ARB/03/24, Decision on Jurisdiction (8 February 2005), p. 86

Plama Consortium Limited v. Bulgaria, ICSID Case No. ARB/03/24, Award (27 August 2008), pp. 67, 119, 120, 156

Pope & Talbot Inc. v. Government of Canada, UNCITRAL, Award on the Merits of Phase 2 (10 April 2001), pp. 75, 108, 114, 115

PSEG Global Inc. and Konya Ilgin Elektrik Üretim ve Ticaret Limited Sirketi v. Republic of Turkey, ICSID Case No. ARB/02/5, Award (19 January 2007), pp. 78, 80

Renta 4 S.V.S.A et al. v. Russian Federation, SCC No. 24/2007, Award on Preliminary Objections (20 March 2009), p. 86

Repsol YPF Ecuador S.A. v. Empresa Estatal Petróleos del Ecuador (Petroecuador), ICSID Case No. ARB/01/10, p. 33

Repsol YPF Ecuador, S.A. v. Empresa Estatal Petróleos del Ecuador (Petroecuador), ICSID Case No. ARB/01/10, Decision on the Application for Annulment (8 January 2007), pp. 157, 170

Reynolds Jamaica Mines Limited and Reynolds Metals Company v. Jamaica, ICSID Case No. ARB/74/4 (unpublished), p. 38

Robert Azinian and others v. United Mexican States, ICSID Case No. ARB(AF)/97/2, pp. 107, 115

Ron Fuchs v. Georgia, ICSID Case No. ARB/07/15, p. 163

Ronald S. Lauder v. Czech Republic, UNCITRAL, Final Award (3 September 2001), pp. 76, 78, 90

RosInvestCo UK Ltd. v. Russian Federation, SCC Case No. Arb. V079/2005, Award on Jurisdiction (October 2007), p. 86

Sempra Energy International v. Argentine Republic, ICSID Case No. ARB/02/16, Decision on the Argentine Republic's Request for a Continued Stay of Enforcement of the Award (Rule 54 of the ICSID Arbitration Rules) (5 March 2009), p. 185

Sempra Energy International v. Argentine Republic, ICSID Case No. ARB/02/16, Decision on the Argentine Republic's Application for Annulment of the Award (29 June 2010), pp. 95, 171, 173, 174, 184

SGS Société Générale de Surveillance S.A. v. Islamic Republic of Pakistan, ICSID Case No. ARB/01/13, Decision on Claimant's Proposal to Disqualify Arbitrator (19 December 2002), *ICSID Reports* 8 (2005), p. 135

SGS Société Générale de Surveillance S.A. v. Islamic Republic of Pakistan, ICSID Case No. ARB/01/13, Decision of the Tribunal on Objections to Jurisdiction (6 August 2003), pp. 93-95, 98, 104

SGS Société Générale de Surveillance SA v. Republic of the Philippines, ICSID Case No. ARB/02/6, Decision of the Tribunal on Objections to Jurisdiction (29 January 2004), pp. 94, 95

Shareholders of SESAM v. Central African Republic, ICSID Case No. CONC/07/1, p. 22

Siemens A.G. v. Argentine Republic, ICSID Case No. ARB/02/8, Decision on Jurisdiction (3 August 2004), pp. 64, 85, 100

Siemens A.G. v. Argentine Republic, ICSID Case No. ARB/02/8, Award (6 February 2007), pp. 80, 81, 136

Sociedad Anónima Eduardo Vieira v. Republic of Chile, ICSID Case No. ARB/04/7, p. 163

Société Ouest Africaine de Bétons Industriels (SOABI) v. State of Senegal, ICSID Case No. ARB/82/1, Decision on Jurisdiction (1 August 1984), *ICSID Reports* 2 (1994), p. 29

Société Ouest Africaine de Bétons Industriels (SOABI) v. State of Senegal, ICSID Case No. ARB/82/1, Award (25 February 1988), *ICSID Reports* 2 (1994), pp. 29, 187

Wena Hotels Ltd. v. Arab Republic of Egypt, ICSID Case No. ARB/98/4, Decision on the Application by the Arab Republic of Egypt for the Annulment of the Arbitral Award dated December 8, 2000 (5 February 2002), pp. 72, 165, 169

Wena Hotels Ltd. v. Arab Republic of Egypt, ICSID Case No. ARB/98/4, Decision on the Application by Wena Hotels Ltd. for Interpretation of the Arbitral Award dated December 8, 2000 in the above matter (31 October 2005), p. 160

Western NIS Enterprise Fund v. Ukraine, ICSID Case No. ARB/04/2, Order (16 March 2006), pp. 98-99

Wintershall Aktiengesellschaft v. Argentine Republic, ICSID Case No. ARB/04/14, Award (8 December 2008), pp. 86, 100

World Duty Free Company Ltd. v. Republic of Kenya, ICSID Case No. ARB/00/7, Award (4 October 2006), p. 147

Zhinvali Development Ltd. v. Republic of Georgia, ICSID Case No. ARB/00/1, Award (24 January 2003), *ICSID Reports* 10 (2006), p. 70

Index by subject